Living the Principle:
My Progenitors and Polygamy

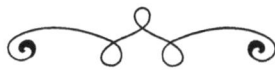

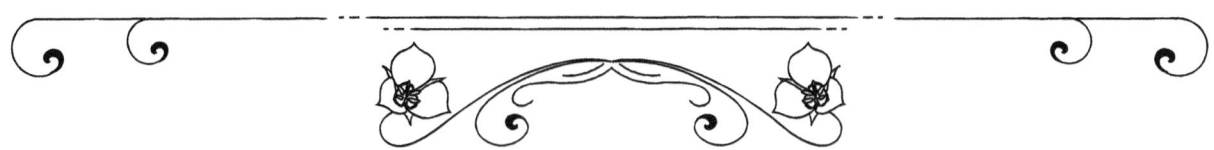

Living the Principle: My Progenitors and Polygamy

By Charlotte Cannon Johnston

with *Mary B. Johnston*

© Copyright 2016
ISBN: 978-0-692-81476-5
Printed by CreateSpace, An Amazon.com Company

Edited by Mary B. Johnston of Wordworks
www.marywordworks.com

Cover and Book design by Laura Pierce Design
as well as extensive photo restoration on images and maps
www.laurapiercedesign.com

*Dedicated to my parents,
Alan M. Cannon and Mary Parkinson Cannon,
who gave me a love and appreciation for
my polygamous pioneer heritage*

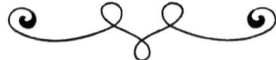

Table of Contents

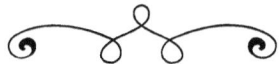

Foreword ix
Author's Preface xi
Editor's Preface xvii
Acknowledgements xix
Introduction 1
Timeline 18

Chapters

1. The Birth of Polygamy
    The Travails of Leonora Cannon Taylor 32

2. Hierarchy in Polygamy
    The Preeminent Position of Elizabeth Hoagland, a First Wife 70

3. Men's and Women's Places in Polygamy's Patriarchal Order
    Each Gender's Unique Power 92

4. Sisterhood
    Networking among Sister Wives 112

5. The Underground
    Polygamy Goes Under Cover. 126

6. Life After Polygamy
    Strains of the Post-Manifesto Period 148

7. Polygamy in Contemporary Mormon Culture and Doctrine
    Our Past Is in Our Present 190

8. A Personal Retrospective
    Thoughts of a Contemporary Mormon Great-grandmother 208

Appendices 223
    A. Book Review of A Mormon Mother 224
    B. Life Sketch of Ann Amanda Mousley Cannon 226
    C. Life Sketch of Charlotte Smart Parkinson 228
    D. A Granddaughter's Memories of Charlotte Smart Parkinson 232
    E. Life Sketch of Mary Lloyd Maughan 234
    F. Letter from Leonora Cannon Taylor to John Taylor 237
    G. Letter from Leonora Cannon Taylor to Governor Ford 240
    H. Letter from Mary Alice Cannon to Her Adopted Sister, Rosa . . . 242
    I. Letters from Mary Alice (Mamie) and Lewis Cannon to Eugene Cannon . . . 244
    J. Life on the Cannon Farm 249
    K. Chart of Polygamous Families Discussed in the Book 260
    L. The 1890 Manifesto 265
    M. Excerpts from Three Addresses Regarding the Manifesto 267
    N. The 1904 Manifesto 269
    O. The Family: A Proclamation to the World 270

Illustration Credits 273
Bibliography 277
Index 281

Foreword

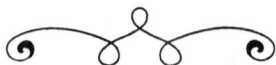

Living the Principle: My Progenitors and Polygamy, Charlotte Johnston's exploration of the rigors, practices, and rewards of polygamy is a very personal book that deals with the experiences of her ancestors. The book is edited by her daughter, Mary Johnston, and many relatives are credited with helping the project along. The author comes from a family built on the practice of polygamy, a family still strong in the Mormon faith. She is engaged in justifying, as well as describing and attempting to understand, the strange marital practices of nineteenth-century Mormons. Her family has honored the polygamous ancestors of the past and has described the households as wholesome and happy. Her discovery of the autobiography of Annie Cannon Tanner, which presents a different picture, and which she reviewed some forty years ago, inspired her to collect and explicate her own family materials to learn more.

This resulting book, an historical account of polygamy—along with family materials collected, explicated and interpreted—is the best kind of personal family history: a collection of materials from the past as well as personal insights and commentary that put the whole story into historical context. There is no replacing the original documents; they must be preserved and honored to the end of time. But they must be interpreted for later audiences.

Early Mormon converts generally accepted the principle of plural marriage. Joseph Smith introduced the idea gradually and secretly to his most devoted followers, initiating them into a higher caste, promising blessings here and in the hereafter. Brigham Young popularized and democratized the practice, domesticating polygamy by recognizing and living with his wives, and requiring the practice of his fellow church leaders as a sign of loyalty. While polygamy operated against the ideas of exclusive attachment and romantic love, it served practical purposes of not only absorbing many of the single female converts who came to Zion but also providing leading men with more extensive progeny as well as building them castles in the hereafter.

That others in the nation found the practice abhorrent distanced the Mormons from their neighbors, who forced them ever west to settle anew. The practice also made Mormons the subject of intense scrutiny from afar. Some imagined that beautiful young girls must have been kidnapped and held captive to satisfy the lusts of randy old goats. One man visiting Salt Lake City in 1870 was shocked, as Mark Twain had been, to find the women were worn and dowdy country women without much beauty or fashionable clothing. He described them as "a harem of hags," finding renewed reason to admire the Mormon men who put up with them. He said that these were men of substance who could have succeeded anywhere. That they chose their demanding religion, the desert wastes, and their homely, if multiple wives was a sign of their strength and commitment.

Charlotte Johnston has ancestors in all stages of the practice of polygamy from 1840 to its official discontinuance in the 1890s. Hers were notable and important leaders, those in the high end of the number of wives with sufficient resources and high mindedness to adjust to this marital pattern with dignity and grace.

But Johnston includes multiple examples of a wider sampling of polygamous experiences and describes it all against the background of political and religious developments, making it clear that polygamous marriages were as varied and personal as we know that monogamous marriages are. Her very close and intimate vision of her family relationships during all stages of the practice of polygamy provides a gift to her readers. She gives us their actions, feelings and voices—a rich selection of attitudes. While many reactions were unvoiced, suppressed, or just unrecorded, we will not likely get much closer to the practice of polygamy than this.

Johnston's review of this practice from its inception to its official discontinuance and beyond shows the many variations, ambiguities, tensions, contradictions, injustices, pains, good deeds, and triumphs that attended Mormon polygamy. She rightly goes on to show that many of the same disjunctions still characterize marital practices in the contemporary LDS Church. Such tensions have a long way to go before they can reach resolution. The question continually asked is what is possible and what is allowed in marital and non-marital relationships.

Johnston tells us that her ancestors practiced polygamy, as she describes it, "with dignity and grace." They certainly made valiant efforts and seem to have succeeded, at least most of the time. Once again, Living the Principle is the best kind of personal history. The author tells us what happened, how she fits in, and then makes a real effort to tell us what it all means.

Claudia L. Bushman
Author of *Contemporary Mormonism*

Author's Preface

Charlotte Cannon Johnston

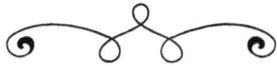

IN MY MID-SEVENTIES I began working on my life story. As I wrote, I realized that for my story to make sense, I first needed to tell the stories of my ancestors, narratives that are inextricably linked to the history of Mormon polygamy. I offer this volume not as a thorough history of polygamy, or The Principle, as adherents often called it. I am not a historian and multiple books about the history of polygamy have already been written. The purpose of my book, *Living The Principle: My Progenitors and Polygamy*, is to offer a window into the lives of the early Saints, the people from whom I descend. I have always been interested in polygamy, probably because my father and all four of my grandparents grew up in polygamous families.

My mother had an avid interest in and loyalty to her pioneer forbears. A fierce advocate of her Parkinson and Maughan heritage, Mother attended and hosted family reunions, wrote accounts of parents' and grandparents' lives, and produced a Cecille B. DeMille-esque program honoring her mother for a Parkinson family reunion.[1] Her children's lives were enriched by her family stories. Our forbears became very known and immediate to me, a closeness for which I am grateful. Polygamy was a given in the family stories, but I don't recall my mother talking about the dynamics of it, such as what the living arrangements were or what her parents' feelings were as children in polygamist homes. Nor were there any personal stories of what her grandparents experienced practicing polygamy. Only one of my grandparents, my mother's father, J. S. Parkinson, was living when I was a child. I never heard him or my mother refer to his experiences as a child in a polygamous family.

My father, also from polygamous roots, was very proud of his Cannon ancestry. His stories focused on the noteworthy accomplishments of his ancestors and the challenges they faced. Many of his stories centered on his pride in his grandfather, George Q. Cannon, and the tales that he had heard of George Q.'s life on the Cannon Farm with his five wives. Every story and detail reinforced my understanding that polygamous ancestors were happy and successful. That one man had more than one wife did not seem extraordinary or troubling to me; it was just the

---

1 My parents had a running contest as to whose pioneer ancestry was more illustrious. Sometime after Mother's death at age eighty-six my father quipped, "Now I can get in two words about the Cannons." Mother often joked, "The Cannons marry each other because they think no one else is good enough for them."

way it was. Not until I was an adult did I learn of the complexities that accompanied polygamy, such as the pain my father experienced growing up in a post-Manifesto polygamous family. His father married a second wife, Lillian, in the late 1890s about the time my father was born.

I first revisited my simplistic, two-dimensional view of polygamy when my husband Peter and I and our four children lived in Boston in 1970. We spent a year there for Peter to further his training in a community mental health program at Harvard. While in Boston, I joined a group of Mormon women interested in talking about Mormon women's relationship to the Women's Movement. That year the group was publishing an edition of *Dialogue* devoted to women's issues; it was dubbed the *Pink Dialogue*.[2] I wrote a review of Annie Clark Tanner's *A Mormon Mother* for the publication. In her autobiography Tanner contrasts the happy, settled life she experienced growing up as a child in the 1860s and 1870s in a polygamous home to the trauma she experienced as a plural wife in the 1880s and later.[3] The book was unsettling not only because of what she had to say but also because her account was so different from the stories I had grown up hearing. She wrote about the pain and trauma of being the second wife to Joseph Marion Tanner, a prominent educator. They were married December 27, 1883. In her 1941 handwritten account, the seventy-eight-year-old author detailed ordeals such as being alone much of the time (even on her wedding night), not living openly as a married woman during the Underground, raising her ten children essentially alone with little financial help, and coping with her husband's marrying additional wives both before and after the Manifesto. At her husband's request, the marriage ended in 1912. He gave no explanation and told her she would need to turn to her brothers for financial help and that he would not be back. Reading about her painful experiences was jarring and writing the review was a challenge.[4]

Reading *A Mormon Mother* and exploring the implications of the national Women's Movement with other Mormon women regenerated my interest in polygamy—this time with a curiosity about how it had felt to the wives. When I returned to Chicago from Boston, I was determined to pursue a broader vision of what I could do with my life. I earned a master's degree at the University of Chicago and became a reading specialist. At about the same time I served as the stake Relief Society president in the newly formed Chicago Heights Stake, where I initiated programs inspired by my own and others' burgeoning interest in women's issues. In 1976 I presented a paper in an Institute class taught by Vicky Burgess Olsen at the University of Chicago.[5] My paper was about five Cannon women, three of whom—Leonora Cannon Taylor,

---

2 *Dialogue* is a Mormon publication, not sponsored by the Church, that furnishes a forum for discussing issues related to Mormonism. It began in 1966.

3 Annie's father, Ezra T. Clark, married his first wife, Mary, twenty-four years before he married Susan, his second wife. He met Susan, Annie's mother, when he was on a mission to England in 1856 and married her in Salt Lake in 1861 as a plural wife. The two families lived across the street from each other and were very compatible. See Charlotte Cannon Johnston, "A Mormon Mother," review of *A Mormon Mother: An Autobiography*, by Annie Clark Tanner, *Dialogue: A Journal of Mormon Thought* 6, no. 2 (Summer 1971): 127–128.

4 My review of *A Mormon Mother* is included in Appendix A.

5 Olsen obtained her Ph.D. at Northwestern in Psychology. Her dissertation was about noteworthy Mormon pioneer women. In 1978 she edited *Sister Saints*, a compilation of biographies of Mormon pioneer women.

Elizabeth Hoagland Cannon, and Mary Alice Cannon—were first wives who faced the challenge of entering plural marriage.[6] In this book I explore their lives as well as the lives of my other polygamous forbears.[7]

Now, decades after I wrote that paper, I still wonder how to view polygamy. I wonder what practicing plural marriage meant to these women. Were any of their experiences akin to the wrenching experiences of Annie Clark Tanner? In my review I wrote that her story was a minority report. Is that an accurate claim? Over the past few years I have devoted myself to learning more of how polygamous marriage was for my ancestors—not just to answer my own questions but also to tell their stories to help ensure that their lives are not forgotten.

It is a tremendous advantage to have Annie Clark Tanner's own words about her experiences with and feelings about plural marriage. While we have an abundance of information written by men, including their journals, newspaper articles, religious books, and Church-sanctioned declarations, most of this material explains the doctrine of polygamy without offering insight into their personal experiences with the practice. We also have some written material by women, mostly letters and journals. Although even these personal documents lack introspection, they have helped me understand my relatives' experiences. Family histories written by family members in all four of my great-grandparents' families have also provided invaluable information.

My father's cousin, Trix Painter, gave me a journal that I treasure. It belonged to Elizabeth Hoagland, my great-grandmother. In this journal she wrote of her experiences during the six-week tour of Europe that she and her husband, George Q. Cannon, took in 1862 when he was serving as president of the European Mission. The only other writings I had seen by a female relative were isolated quotations from Leonora Cannon Taylor's *First Diary* in which she summarized her early life.[8] Fortuitously, in early 2012, while visiting the new Church History Library in Salt Lake City, I found a copy of the diary Leonora Cannon Taylor wrote in 1846 and 1847.[9] In it she described her journey from Nauvoo to the Salt Lake Valley with her husband, John Taylor, their children, and three sister wives.[10] Its pages reveal the sacrifices and tensions that accompanied the complex dynamics of polygamy. Although I don't have other first-person accounts written by other female relatives about what it was like to be a polygamous wife, I do have information about their lives and their marriages and I have learned how polygamy functioned in the Territory of Utah as well as how it was seen by the larger American society.

In this book, I start with an introduction explaining the first phase of polygamy in the Church and the course the practice took. My goal is to furnish an understanding of the practice and give a context for the commitment my relatives had to plural marriage. In Chapter One I illustrate the early days of polygamy with the life of Leonora Cannon, my great-great-

---

6   Mary Alice was often affectionately called Mamie. I use both of her names in this book.

7   For a chart of the polygamous families discussed in this book, see Appendix K

8   Taylor, Leonora Cannon. *First Diary, Summary of Her Early Life*. Located in the Church History Library in Salt Lake City, UT.

9   Taylor, Leonora Cannon. *Trail Diary, February 1846-October 1847*. Located in the Church History Library in Salt Lake City, UT.

10 Leonora captures vivid word pictures of the trek. I will stray from the polygamy topic to include some of her portrayal of the countryside and the native people they meet.

grandfather's sister. Leonora married John Taylor before they joined the Church and before polygamy was introduced; she was later joined by six sister wives. Chapter Two explores the life of my father's maternal grandmother, Elizabeth Hoagland, the childhood sweetheart and first wife of George Q. Cannon. Their story epitomizes polygamy in its heyday in the 1860s and early 1870s. In Chapter Three, using the life of my father's paternal grandmother, Amanda Mousley, and her marriage to Angus M. Cannon as a springboard, I examine how men's attitudes and behaviors influenced the dynamics of their families. Chapter Four looks at the strength of sisterly bonds among wives as illustrated in the life of Charlotte Smart, my mother's paternal grandmother. Chapter Five explores the unsettled days of the Underground with the story of William H. Maughan and Mary Lloyd, his fourth wife and my mother's maternal grandmother, as illustrative of the tumultuous times.

In Chapter Six I write about the life of my father's mother and father, Mary Alice Cannon and Lewis Cannon. I also look at other post-Manifesto marriages in my extended family and seek to unveil the problems polygamous families encountered in the post-Manifesto period. In Chapter Seven I discuss the evolution from polygamy to monogamy and the costs associated with that change. In Chapter Eight I express personal insights I have gained through researching and writing this book.

The appendices include short biographies of my great-grandmothers and other materials that furnish a fuller picture of polygamy. I have preserved the original spelling and grammar of historical sources. I have used footnotes to give context and further information. The bibliography contains a list of reference books I consulted. In several instances, accounts vary as to where and when events such as births and marriages took place. I have noted discrepancies when it seemed important.

My focus in this book is on the stories of my relatives' experiences with polygamy. So, you find here neither exhaustive biographies of them nor a comprehensive history of polygamy. I have relied on their lives to show major currents of how polygamy operated, how it affected individual members, and how they were part of a social experiment. They devoutly believed in it. They lived plural marriage with grace and dignity.

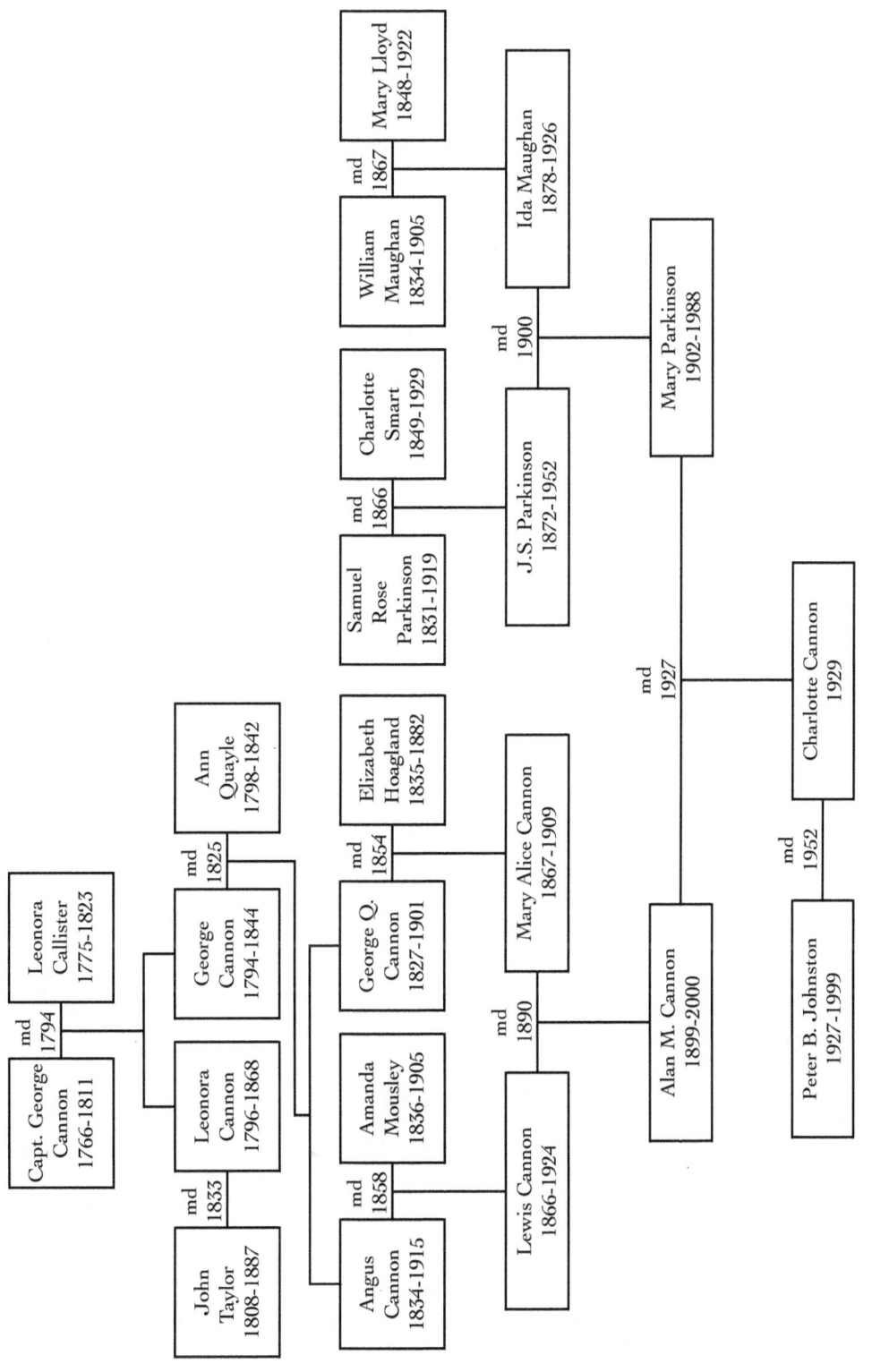

Chart illustrating the author's relationship to the people discussed in the book

Editor's Preface

Mary B. Johnston

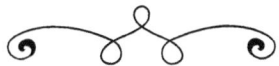

W E HAVE FOLLOWED *The Chicago Manual of Style, 16th Edition* regarding style conventions. Researching and writing this book has involved using primary documents from the 1800s and early 1900s, when writing conventions were different than they are today. In addition, much of the writing we have included from this time period has spelling and punctuation variations that today we would call errors. Unless the author's meaning is unclear, we have chosen to retain an author's idiosyncratic spelling and punctuation to retain the authenticity of the document, the voice of the writer, and the feel for the era from which the documents come. For example, when "north" or "temple" is capitalized, we have kept the author's original punctuation. There are two exceptions to retaining the original punctuation. If the writer of the primary document did not include a period at the end of a sentence, we have added four spaces in order to clarify where one sentence ends and the next begins. Also, when letters included in the appendices have especially long paragraphs, we have taken the liberty of dividing those paragraphs.

If a writer makes a reference that requires an explanation, we have either inserted bracketed information, when only a few words are required, or included a footnote, when more detail is necessary. When handwritten materials—letters and journals—are cited, the text is italicized in an effort to simulate cursive.

Most of the footnoted material comes from published books that are easy to locate and cite. Unpublished sources such as family letters, life sketches, conversations, personal writings, and journals are difficult to cite completely when the author is unknown, the original location of the document is unknown, or the date of the conversation was not recorded. In such cases, we have included all the information we have. In some instances the paucity of details about a source required us to devise our own way of citing a reference.

When my mother first introduces a relative, she refers to them by their full name. If she grew up calling that person aunt or uncle or hearing other relatives refer to them with such a title, her subsequent references often use aunt and uncle. In the case of her father's mother, Mary Alice Cannon, who was known in the family as Mamie, my mother usually refers to her as Mamie. Given that this is a family history, my mother feels strongly that referring to her ancestors by the names they went by in her family acknowledges her relationships to them and better honors their memory.

Acknowledgements

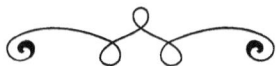

IN WRITING THIS BOOK about my family and polygamy, I have benefited from many written records. The Angus and George Q. Cannon families as well as the Parkinson and Maughan families have compiled significant family histories that have been very helpful. Besides other books listed in the bibliography, I have also benefited from reading articles written more recently by B. Carmon Hardy, Stephen C. Taysom, as well as O. Kendall and Daryl White, all of which I recommend for a current understanding of polygamy. *A Mormon Mother* by Annie Clark Tanner continues to be a seminal reference. All of these articles and books are included in the bibliography. I am grateful to Annie Clark Tanner for telling her story; it kindled my desire to learn more about the polygamous women in my family.

Writing the book became a family project. The entire process of collecting and interpreting writings about our forbears and plural marriage was a collaborative effort with my daughter, Mary B. Johnston. We have worked well together, emailing edited manuscripts back and forth between Chicago and Charleston. Halfway through the project, Mary came to Chicago for several days to work on an overall organization and I spent an extended Christmas visit in Charleston in 2011 to flesh out Chapters Five and Six. I attribute any poetic imagery to her as well as many helpful edits. It has strengthened the bond between us as we grappled with thorny issues of what turned out to be a difficult topic. She supervised the publishing of the book.

My other children were also a tremendous help. I thank Jim for helping with the footnotes and proofreading the final draft, Jeff for helping me find the Leonora Cannon Taylor diaries in the Church libraries, and David 's help in synthesizing concepts and helping me keep things in perspective. My granddaughter Annie scanned and organized the photos in a PDF file. She also took photos with me in Franklin, Idaho, and Wellsville, Utah, and helped with the index and citations, and final edits. My granddaughter Carla researched articles on the effects of polygamy on contemporary Mormon culture and lifestyle and sent both the articles and her analysis of them to Mary and me. Jim's wife, Mary, researched dates of family groups on FamilySearch and both Jim and Mary went with me to Franklin, Wellsville and Cannon homes on the west side of Salt Lake. My brother Joe Cannon drove with me to Wellsville to meet a surviving Maughan cousin from our mother's generation and to establish in which house Mary Lloyd had raised her family. My sister-in-law Arlene Cannon designed the chart detailing Cannon family relationships including Lewis Cannon's marriages and proofread the final draft. My grandson Matt Johnston created the map showing the relationship of Rexburg, Idaho, to northern Utah. My niece's husband, David DeBry, furnished digital images of family pictures, and my nephew's wife, Jennifer Cannon, helped with her computer skills.

I also wish to thank extended family members: Ken Cannon for sharing his knowledge of Abram H. Cannon's diaries and other Cannon lore; Clarke, Kenny, and Dale Maughan, Mother's cousins, who helped me understand Wellsville family history; Margaret Clayton, John Pingree, Mary Alice Collins, Irene Cannon Salahor, and Sue Gillmore for their insight into Cannon family history; Joanne Austin Linford for our candid conversations and her insight on the post-Manifesto period and Ray Linford, Joanne's husband, for editing help. In 2013 in a treasured visit with Winnifred C. Jardine, she said she would be honored to have her essay "Life on the Cannon Farm" included in my book. Winnifred passed away in 2015. All of these interactions strengthened not only the content of the book but also family bonds. I could not have brought this project to fruition without the help of my family and all the others who have helped me.

Sarah Deppermann deserves special mention for her work on the footnotes. I also want to thank Katherine Shumway, Jessica Hammond, Erin Fillmore, Chelsea Hall, Tara Parker, and Jenny Gannaway for their help with understanding the intricacies and mysteries of the computer and for their help with the manuscript itself. Thanks also to Mary Fullmer for her help with FamilySearch, the sister missionary from FamilySearch who helped me on the phone research family records, and LuAnn Bates, who gave me vital information from the deed she found she had kept in her basement of the sale of the Wellsville family home belonging to Mary Lloyd. Elizabeth Miles, the intellectual properties coordinator at the Church History Library, helped me navigate the process of getting permission to use images from The Church History Library. I would also like to thank Laura Allred Hurtado at the Church History Museum for her help in obtaining important images for the book.

I want to thank historian Claudia Bushman for her insightful preface. I extend a thank you to historians Susan Sessions Rugh and Marvin Hill and his wife, Lila Hill, for their insight and general encouragement of the project; Kathryn Daynes for her support; Lavina Fielding Anderson for her helpful suggestions; the personnel at the Family History Museum and new Church History Museum for their help in accessing documents about John Taylor's wives and Leonora Cannon Taylor's diaries; Laurel Thatcher Ulrich for pointing me to the originals of Leonora's diaries; and Erin Fillmore for transcribing Leonora's trail diary. I am grateful to Darla Barnett for her careful work creating the book's index and am indebted to Laura Pierce for her creative book design that captures the era that *Living the Principle* explores and for her willingness to add "just one more change." Finally, I thank my mother for her indefatigable efforts to collect and tell stories of her ancestors and both my parents for the love they had of their heritage.

Introduction

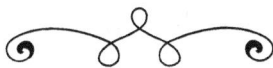

MY ANCESTORS and other Saints accepted the practice of polygamy because they saw it in the larger context of the restoration of Christ's original church, the Church of Jesus Christ of Latter-day Saints. Integral to the teachings of the restored gospel was that the original church of Christ's time had been restored by God through Joseph Smith, a prophet in modern times. Central to that restoration was reaping the blessings of the covenant God made with Abraham that his posterity would be as numerous as the sands of the sea. Joseph Smith saw polygamy as ensuring this posterity in present times. This restoration also included reestablishing the structure of the original church, including a prophet who had priesthood authority to act in God's name and the capacity to receive revelation from God. Joseph's early revelations directed the Saints to build a new Zion, or Kingdom of God, on Earth. These revelations indicated that spreading the gospel and performing essential ordinances, which came to include plural marriage, were urgent because the Second Coming was imminent. Believing that the end of the Earth was close at hand heightened the importance of celestial polygamous marriage ordinances and likely lessened anxiety about difficult living arrangements that Joseph and his fellow Saints believed would be short-lived.

Extensive missionary efforts drew converts from the eastern United States and Europe. Among those joining the Church from the British Isles were my ancestors. These converts were willing to forgo satisfying personal needs and desires for the larger cause of building a new Zion. They had great faith in the Prophet and the stream of revelations he received about how to build the Kingdom of God on earth. These revelations included references to sacred temple ceremonies including the endowment and eternal marriage.

The endowment is a sacred contract between God and an individual. In it a person receives knowledge necessary to return to God and receive special blessings.[11] The endowment is referred to in the Doctrine and Covenants in Kirtland in 1833, in Missouri in 1834, and at the dedication of the Kirtland Temple in 1836. Nine men received the basic endowment in Nauvoo in an upper room of the red brick store on May 4, 1842.[12] A year later, the first woman, Emma Smith, Joseph's wife, received hers. The complete endowment, which includes eternal marriage, was revealed to Joseph in Nauvoo and was introduced in Doctrine and Covenants Section 131 in May 1843 and expanded in Section 132 in July 1843.[13]

---

11 Kathryn M. Daynes, *More Wives than One: Transformation of the Mormon Marriage System 1840–1910* (Chicago: University of Illinois Press, 2001): 25.

12 Such ordinances could be performed in designated places outside the temple until the first temple was completed.

13 For an insightful discussion of the beginnings of polygamy in Nauvoo, see Daynes, 17–35.

The complete endowment, usually referred to as simply the *endowment,* rests on a distinctly Mormon doctrine of family perpetuation through the eternities; the endowment not only sanctifies family relationships but also shows that eternal marriage is part of exaltation to godhood. According to this doctrine, people who remain single or are married only for time have no possibility of being "exalted," which in Mormon theology means receiving the highest glory in the next life.[14]

Designed to prepare Latter-day Saints to become exalted in the afterlife, the endowment ceremony includes reenacting both the creation and the fall of Adam and Eve as well as making a series of promises to God. This ceremony prepares participants to meet God upon their death and to have powers and capacities similar to their Creator. Though people receive their endowments individually, the highest exaltation in the afterlife is reserved for men and women who are individually endowed and then married or sealed to one another, i.e., bound to each other. Joseph called this relationship the "new and everlasting covenant" and "eternal marriage."[15] In the early days of the Church, these terms were interchangeable with the term polygamy.

Old Testament prophets had more than one wife. This gave strong support to the early Saints' view that plural marriage was a valid commandment. Joseph Smith frequently referred to the prophets, temples, and polygamy present in the Old Testament; they were sources for his sense of prophetic mission and for the doctrine of polygamy.[16] God's oft-repeated promise to Abraham that his posterity would be as numerous as the sands of the sea shows what a premium the Lord put on having a large posterity.[17] God also promised Sarah that she would be a mother of nations.[18] When Sarah had not yet borne children, Abraham, following Sarah's lead, turned to Hagar, Sarah's maid,[19] to bear children for him to fulfill those promises. Because Abraham and other ancient prophets had taken more than one wife, the Lord's commandment that it be

---

14 Daynes, 5. For a rich discussion of the meaning and blessings of the endowment and of men and women needing each other to realize the full blessings of the endowment, see Jill Mulvay Derr, Janath Russell Cannon, and Maureen Ursenbach Beecher, *Women of Covenant: The Story of Relief Society* (Salt Lake City, UT: Deseret Book, 1992): 53–58.

15 Doctrine & Covenants 132. In this book I have used the current and standard version of this body of scripture used by the Church of Jesus Christ of Latter-day Saints. Hereafter, all footnote citiations will refer to it as D&C rather than Doctrine & Covenants.

16 Todd Compton, *In Sacred Loneliness: The Plural Wives of Joseph Smith* (Salt Lake City, UT: Signature Books, 1997): 11.

17 Gen. 13:16, 15:5, 17:4–7. For the purposes of this book, I have used the King James version printed by the Church of Jesus Christ of Latter-day Saints.

18 Gen. 17:16, 22:17.

19 Hagar and other women in her position are referred to in a variety of ways, including concubine, slave girl, maid, maidservant, and mistress, depending on the translation and the story. Like sister wives, they had a lower status than first wives.

practiced in the restored Church felt right and valid.[20] Plural marriage identified the Saints as a peculiar people who chose to live separately from the mainstream American culture and irrevocably linked the practice to Mormonism.[21]

The early leaders interpreted Joseph's revelation on polygamy to mean that if a man married a second wife or additional wives, all of his wives and children received the highest exaltation in the afterlife. Joseph taught that the second wife opened the door of salvation in the celestial kingdom not only for herself but also for her husband and his first wife as well as all of their children.[22] A man's foothold in heaven increases with the number of his wives and children. His family becomes an ever-expanding network, the power of which is increased with each member. Because many early Mormons were children of parents who were not Church members, many of them were "adopted to" prominent men in the Church. Sometimes women were sealed to prominent priesthood leaders to assure that in the next life they would be attached to families that held the priesthood. These adoptions were also made vicariously for people who had died. In these cases, the focus was on creating extensive family networks, not on having children.[23] These family ties carried with them all the moral obligations associated with a family and strengthened the bonds of loyalty among the leading families.[24] Expansive networks of eternal families were created by laterally sealing families together. In addition, women were sealed to prominent Church leaders. Many of these marriages were never consummated.[25] By 1893 about thirteen thousand such adoptions for those living and on behalf of people who had died had occurred. In 1894 President Wilford Woodruff proclaimed that only sealings to direct ancestors would be valid—a significant change in how eternal families would be formed, a change that led to widespread researching of direct lines of ancestors.[26]

---

20 D&C 132:1, 132:30–32, 132:37–39.

21 Klaus J. Hansen, "Changing Perspectives on Sexuality and Marriage," in *Multiply and Replenish the Earth: Mormon Essays on Sex and Family*, ed. Brent Corcoran (Salt Lake City, UT: Signature Books, 1994): 27.

22 Annie Clark Tanner, *A Mormon Mother: An Autobiography*. (Salt Lake City, UT: University of Utah Press, 1969): 56.

23 James B. Allen and Glen M. Leonard, *The Story of the Latter-day Saints* (Salt Lake City, UT: Deseret Book, 1976): 424. For a thoroughly researched well documented treatment of Joseph Smith and his wives, see Compton, *In Sacred Loneliness*.

24 "For example, Joseph Smith became the son-in-law of Apostle Heber C. Kimball by marrying his daughter, and the Prophet became the brother-in-law of Apostle Brigham Young by marrying Young's sister. Marriage among other Mormons expanded these relationships, such as when Isaac Morley's daughter Theressa became a plural wife of Heber C. Kimball. Morley thus became the brother-in-law of the father-in-law of Joseph Smith." Daynes, *More Wives than One*, 26.

25 Daynes, 76–77.

26 Allen and Leonard, 424.

Because plural marriage allowed a man's posterity to extend beyond the biological limitations of one woman, the practice had doctrinal appeal. "Eternal marriage has a dual purpose: first, on this earth, to prepare bodies to receive spirits waiting in the pre-existent state and to train them properly so that they will choose righteous ways; second, in heaven, to continue the procreation of spirits for new worlds, thus increasing the dominions and glory of God himself."[27]

The fervor around people receiving their own endowments as well as sitting in proxy for those who had died was intense. Even after Joseph's death in June 1844, the Saints felt strongly enough about these ordinances that, at great sacrifice and peril from Illinoisans opposed to their being there, they completed crucial parts of the temple that allowed them to do ordinance work. From December 1845 through February 1846, when they were forced to leave Nauvoo, the endowment ceremony was performed twenty-four hours a day for Saints eager to receive their endowments and be sealed to loved ones. Thirty-six women participated as ordinance workers in this marathon effort during this short time period.[28] Altogether five thousand endowments were performed for the living and the dead.[29] My great-great-aunt Leonora and her husband John Taylor as well as my great-great-grandfather Peter Maughan and his wife Mary Ann Weston were among those who received their endowments.[30]

Scholars have divided polygamous marriages into four types: assistance, dynastic, friendship, and proximity.[31] There are several instances in my family of a marriage occurring to assist a woman. For example, during the last year of her life when she was very ill, Elizabeth Hoagland Cannon encouraged her husband, George Q., to marry Emily, her recently divorced sister, not only for her sister's welfare but also so Emily could help with Elizabeth's children.[32] Mary Lloyd, my mother's maternal grandmother, was orphaned as a girl in Wales and came to the

---

27 Daynes, 71.

28 Leonora Cannon Taylor may well have been among these women.

29 Carol Cornwall Madsen, "Mormon Women and the Temple: Toward a New Understanding," in *Sisters in Spirit: Mormon Women in Historical and Cultural Perspective*, ed. Maureen Ursenbach Beecher and Lavina Fielding Anderson (Urbana: University of Illinois Press, 1987): 87.

30 Peter Maughan's first wife, Ruth Harrison, my great-great-grandmother, died in England before Peter emigrated to the United States with their five children.

31 Craig L. Foster, "The Plural Wives of the Prophets: From Brigham Young to Heber J. Grant" (Paper presented Mormon History Association conference, Calgary, Alberta, Canada, June 28 – July 1, 2012).

32 Emily was not woven into the family structure. For instance there is no mention of her in Beatrice Cannon Evans and Janath Russell Cannon, eds., *Cannon Family Historical Treasury*, (Salt Lake City, UT: George Cannon Family Association, 1967), and she was never included in family stories of his wives. Even so, George Q. remembered her in his will.

Mormon settlement of Wellsville, Utah on September 8, 1861, with Church members William Fayle and Catherine Hughes Fayle, her adoptive parents.[33] Mary Lloyd is an example of a woman who found a safe haven in her polygamous marriage to William Maughan.

Dynastic marriages, those that occurred among relatives, were very common among my ancestors.[34] For instance, Ann Amanda and Sarah Maria Mousley's younger sister Wilhelmina was a plural wife of David M. Cannon, who was the younger brother of their husband Angus Cannon. Mary Alice Cannon's brother Abram was married to another Wilhelmina Cannon, the older sister to her husband Lewis, and Lewis was her cousin! In the Parkinson family Sam Monson, a grandson of Maria Smart Parkinson (my great-grandmother Charlotte's sister and sister-wife) has written an engaging essay about having over five hundred cousins and the multiple ways family members were related to each other.[35]

Friendship probably influenced my great-grandfather Samuel Rose Parkinson's choice to marry Charlotte and Maria Smart, daughters of Thomas Smart. Samuel Rose and Thomas settled Franklin, Idaho, together and were good friends. The proximity category refers to plural wives' country of origin being the same as that of the husband, a frequent occurrence. Six of John Taylor's seven wives hailed from the British Isles, as did he.[36]

Though polygamy figures prominently in the early history of the Church, only a minority of members practiced it. Figures vary widely about how many people practiced polygamy. James Allen, a retired BYU history professor and one of the founders of the Mormon History Association, estimates that between ten and fifteen percent of the families in pioneer Utah participated.[37] An essay on the Church's website about plural marriage indicates that "half of those living in Utah Territory in 1857 experienced life in a polygamous family as a husband, wife, or child at some time during their lives."[38] A dozen years later, the percentage of people living in polygamous households dropped to twenty-five percent and continued to decrease over the next twenty years.[39]

---

33 Janice Uhl Maughan, ed., *William Harrison Maughan Family History* (Providence, UT: Keith W. Watkins and Sons, Inc., 1986): 4a.

34 Gen. 20:12. As it does for polygamy, the Old Testament furnishes a precedent for dynastic marriages. Abraham and Sarah were each other's half-brother and half-sister.

35 Samuel C. Monson, ". . . And His Sister, and His Cousins, and His Aunts, a privately published article the author, Sam Monson gave to Charlotte Johnston.

36 Foster, "The Plural Wives of the Prophets."

37 Allen and Leonard, 278.

38 "Plural Marriage and Families in Early Utah," https://www.lds.org/topics/plural-marriage-and-families-in-early-utah?lang=eng#21.

39 Ibid.

Another study using a sample of more than six thousand Mormon families found that between fifteen and twenty percent were polygamous. Using a subset of 1,784 polygamous men, the study found that a large majority, sixty-six percent, married only the one extra wife considered necessary for the highest exaltation in the celestial kingdom. Another twenty-one percent married three wives, and seven percent took four wives. The remaining group of less than six percent married five or more women.[40]

Leaders, who tended to be economically well situated, were strongly encouraged to practice polygamy. This included the general authorities as well as stake presidents and bishops.[41] That my forbears all took more than two wives paralleled their high social and economic status in their communities as well as their commitment to the practice. Among the general authorities appointed from 1845 to 1888 only fourteen (thirty-two percent) were monogamous.

Permission from Church leaders to marry more than one woman depended upon a man's spiritual worthiness as well as his economic status. Customarily, a man also had to receive the permission from his first wife and often conferred with her regarding the choice of the second wife.[42] In many cases, the second wife was a sister or close friend. In some instances, a first wife encouraged her husband to take a second wife to ensure their celestial blessings.

Accepting plural marriage was difficult for many of the Saints. It ran counter to their monogamous moral values. However, men such as Brigham Young and John Taylor, who initially had significant hesitation and reluctance to enter plural marriage, ultimately became strong advocates of the practice.[43] Emma, Joseph's wife, was not among those who became comfortable with polygamy. Also, she vacillated between admitting and denying that her husband took other wives. Faithful to Joseph through the persecutions of New York, Ohio, and Missouri; supportive of him in his administrative duties; homemaker and wife to him; hostess to his guests and mother to his children; she willingly followed him everywhere—except into polygamy. Her ultimate rejection of the doctrine was one reason she and others including members of her immediate family did not follow the Saints west.

Secrecy surrounded the practice of polygamy from the beginning. We will see in Chapter One that Leonora Cannon, my great-great-grandfather's sister, and her husband John Taylor, practiced plural marriage secretly starting in 1843.[44] After much speculation from outsiders that

---

40 Janice Maughan, 112.

41 Daynes, 72.

42 In subsequent chapters I will tell the stories of relatives for whom this was the case.

43 Janice Maughan, 14; Francis M. Gibbons, *John Taylor: Mormon Philosopher, Prophet of God* (Salt Lake City, UT: Deseret Book, 1985): 51.

44 The introduction to Section 132 of the Doctrine and Covenants indicates Joseph Smith received a revelation as early as 1831.

plural marriage was being practiced among the Mormons, the doctrine was announced publicly August 29, 1852, at General Conference in Salt Lake City.[45] Orson Pratt, an apostle, stated the following from the pulpit:

> The constitution gives the privilege to all the inhabitants of this country of the free exercise of their religious notions, and the freedom of their faith, and the practice of it. Then, if it can be proven to a demonstration, that the Latter-day Saints have actually embraced, as a part and portion of their religion, the doctrine of a plurality of wives, it is constitutional. And should there ever be laws enacted by the government to restrict them from the free exercise of this part of their religion, such laws must be unconstitutional.[46]

This pronouncement, underscoring the constitutionality of the practice, clearly indicates the Saints foresaw that the federal government could contest their right to practice plural marriage.

In the 1850s, the federal government was concerned with what they saw as two barbarisms: slavery and polygamy. After the Civil War settled the question of slavery, they turned their attention to eradicating polygamy. In her book, *Faithful Transgressions in the American West: Six Twentieth-Century Mormon Women's Autobiographical Acts*, Laura Bush wrote:

> In the preface to Stenhouse's exposé autobiography . . . Harriet Beecher Stowe declares, "Shall we not then hope that the hour is come to loose the bonds of a cruel slavery whose chains have cut into the hearts of thousands of our sisters—a slavery which debases and degrades womanhood, motherhood, and the family?" The connection that Stowe makes between slavery and Mormon polygamy was a common one in the late 1800s.[47]

The federal government was also concerned about the firm control Church leaders had on the local government in the Territory of Utah and felt that this as well as polygamy should bar it from becoming a state. The Church, however, very much wanted the Territory to become a state. The motivation to become a state may have been that territories did not have the same rights states had to determine marital laws. In 1862 Brigham Young, with the backing of the general assembly of the territory, appointed William H. Hooper and my great-grandfather George Q.

---

45 Because most states had laws against bigamy Brigham Young delayed public announcement of polygamy until he had established a quasi-independent political kingdom in the Rocky Mountains. Hansen, "Changing Perspectives on Sexuality and Marriage," 27.

46 *Millennial Star,* Supplement, (1853), quoted in *Church History in the Fulness of Times: The History of The Church of Jesus Christ of Latter-day Saints* (Salt Lake City, UT: The Church of Jesus Christ of Latter-day Saints, 1993): 424.

47 Laura Bush, *Faithful Transgressions in the American West: Six Twentieth-Century Mormon Women's Autogbiographical Acts* (Logan, UT: Utah State University Press, 2004): 64.

Cannon to serve in Congress. Their mandate was to gain statehood for the Territory.[48] Instead, Congress passed the Morrill Anti-Bigamy Act, which outlawed bigamy, annulled the territorial legislature's incorporation of the Church, and prohibited any religious organization in the territories from owning real estate valued at more than fifty thousand dollars. This bill was signed into law July 8, 1862, by Abraham Lincoln, who chose not to enforce the law.[49] Lincoln's leniency postponed active antagonism between the Church and the government for some time. Geographical isolation was another protection from scrutiny.

When the Saints arrived in Utah in 1847, they, as well as previous settlers, felt they were "a thousand miles from anywhere."[50] Brigham Young saw the isolation as an asset because it helped them create their own society. For better or worse, their seclusion was short-lived. In 1869 the Central Pacific from the west and the Union Pacific from the east joined at Promontory Point, thirty-two miles west of current-day Brigham City, in Utah Territory. This increased the Saints' exposure to the rest of the country and focused renewed attention on the Mormons and their practice of polygamy.

The federal government and most citizens saw Mormon women as victims of a repressive patriarchy. In response, some members of Congress proposed a law that would give the women of the Territory the right to vote, anticipating that Mormon women would vote down plural marriage at the ballot box. However, the women gave such enthusiastic support to polygamy that the sponsors dropped the bill.[51] Soon thereafter, on February 12, 1870, the Territory successfully passed its own measure, giving women residents the right to vote. To the nation's surprise, Mormon women used that right and the power of assembly to *support* rather than object to polygamy. Elizabeth Hoagland Cannon, my great-grandmother, whose story I tell in Chapter Two, was among a group of women who wrote a letter to the legislature thanking them for passing the bill to enfranchise women.[52] At this same time, the Cullom Bill of 1870 passed the House of Representatives. It required that all cases involving plural marriage be heard exclusively by federal judges and that juries be selected by federally appointed marshals and attorneys. Before it came to a vote in the Senate, three thousand Latter-day Saint women held a massive protest meeting in the Salt Lake Tabernacle.[53]

In response to a reporter's question about the effect Gentiles were having on Church membership and whether or not the polygamy controversy would cause Church members to abandon their religion, George Q. Cannon, a territorial representative to Congress during this tumultuous time, replied with deep conviction of the rightness of their position:

---

48 Davis Bitton, *George Q. Cannon: A Biography* (Salt Lake City, UT: Deseret Book, 1999): 17.

49 Allen and Leonard, 312–313.

50 Commonly attributed to Jim Bridger.

51 Allen and Leonard, 345.

52 Bitton, 163.

53 Allen and Leonard, 344.

> Yes, sir, and, viewing from a natural, non-Mormon standpoint, the influences now surrounding the Church must ultimately destroy it. With a hostile press constantly attacking the Church, with the railroads, the telegraphs, the various proselyting efforts of all the different denominations through their free schools and other agencies, working against it, nothing but the interposition of Divine power can prevent the ultimate downfall of the system. This will, as anyone can see, be the natural result, but as a Mormon, firmly believing in the faith, I have no doubt of Divine succor, and, in common with my fellow religionists, I look for the promised protection from above.[54]

Attacks on polygamy came from every direction. A group of non-Mormon women known as the Anti-Polygamists held a meeting in the Congregational Church in Salt Lake City on November 7, 1878. Included on their agenda was a proposal to repeal Utah women's right to vote, eliminate polygamy, and rescue the public schools from Mormon control.[55] About two hundred people, mostly women, attended. Mrs. Sarah A. Cooke, who had once been a Mormon, presided. They sent a document addressed to Mrs. Rutherford B. Hayes, the wife of the president, stating that the women of the United States felt the practice of polygamy was a "great crime" and was "barbaric." The document went on to say

> that it should be practiced in the name of and under the cloak of religion and that an Apostle, a polygamist with four acknowledged wives, is permitted to sit in Congress, only adds to the enormity of the crime, and makes it more revolting to our common Christian principles. . . . [T]he Christian women of the United States and every minister of the Gospel . . . join in urging Congress to empower its courts to arrest the further progress of this evil, and to delay the admission of Utah into Statehood until this is accomplished.[56]

Despite the many forces working against them, Church leaders felt that the Morrill Anti-Bigamy Act, which had passed in 1862, would be overturned when it reached the Supreme Court. It did come before the Court in 1879 when George Reynolds, a Mormon who had more than one wife, was charged with bigamy. In the Reynolds case, the Church appealed to the Supreme Court to overturn the guilty verdict of the Territory's highest court. The Saints believed that the Morrill Anti-Bigamy Act would be found unconstitutional because polygamy was not intrinsically evil; rather it was an integral part of their social and religious life and as such should be left alone. To their disappointment, the Court ruled "that polygamy constituted

---

54 *Deseret News*, February 6, 1878, quoted in Bitton, 216.

55 Allen and Leonard, 392.

56 Orson F. Whitney, *Popular History of Utah* (Salt Lake City, UT: The Deseret News, 1916): 332. George Q. Cannon is the apostle referred to as having four wives. Later he married his fifth and sixth wives, Caroline Young Croxall and Emily Hoagland Little.

an offense against society" and was illegal.⁵⁷ The ruling stated that while the government "cannot interfere with mere religious belief and opinions, they may with practices."⁵⁸ On January 6, 1879, the Morrill Anti-Bigamy Act of 1862 was affirmed as the constitutional law of the land.⁵⁹

Church members faced a difficult dilemma: should they continue to practice what they believed was a divine law, or should they conform to the law of the land? Bishop Francis Brown's poignant and poetic defense of his stand on polygamy eloquently sums up the predicament. In his testimony, Bishop Brown shared that he was descended from Puritan stock, had been taught from childhood to love his country and to render strict obedience to its laws, and for over forty years had been a member of The Church of Jesus Christ of Latter-day Saints and had been called to practice plural marriage:

> I now ask your Honor what I am to do. Shall I break the most sacred obligations that man can enter into? Shall I abandon my wives and children and cast them off upon the charities of a cold world? I know not of what metal your Honor is composed, but for myself, before I will prove recreant to my wives and children and betray my trust, I will suffer my head to be severed from my body.... I stand here innocent of any crime. I have a conscience devoid of offense.... I have made up my mind that while water runs, or grass grows, or a drop of blood flows through my veins, I shall obey the supreme laws of my God in preference to the changeable and imperfect laws of man.⁶⁰

Bishop Brown was convicted to serve in the penitentiary despite his heartfelt testimony. No witnesses were called to testify.⁶¹

John Taylor, the prophet at the time, had two choices: to ask the Saints to break the law of the land or to stop living a divinely inspired practice and abandon their families. After the Reynolds decision, John Taylor said the following in an interview with O. J. Hollister, a correspondent for the *New York Tribune* and a tax collector for Utah:

> I know that God has given this [plural marriage] to us for our guidance. You may not know, but I know that this is a revelation from God and a command to his people, and therefore, it is my religion. I do not believe that the Supreme Court of the United States or the

---

57 Allen and Leonard, 358.

58 Janice Maughan, 15.

59 Allen and Leonard, 358.

60 Whitney, 402–403.

61 Ibid., 403.

Congress of the United States has any right to interfere with my religious views, and in doing it, they are violating their most sacred obligations.[62]

In 1882 Congress passed the Edmunds Act, which made it illegal to even support and care for more than one woman. If a man did, he could be arrested. The law also disenfranchised polygamists and prohibited them from holding public office. In fact, just believing in plural marriage disqualified men from jury service, a requirement that flew in the face of the distinction the Reynolds case had made about belief and practice. All local election officers were dismissed and a board of commissioners was appointed by the president of the United States to govern the Utah Territory. Both the Mormons and appointed officials, many of whom were reluctant to be sent to the Territory, were displeased with the situation.[63]

Defending the right to practice polygamy took on a life of its own. The Saints were not just defending a religious belief; they were defending what they thought was a constitutional right, much like the Confederates did prior to and during the Civil War. Polygamous men and some women practicing polygamy went into hiding, commonly called the "Underground" (the name indicating an identification with the Abolitionist movement), to evade the federal prosecutors. After the Edmunds Act passed, to be on the safe side of the law, polygamist husbands gave their families separate houses and for the most part stopped living with them. They continued to provide for their children, which was not against the law. For instance, President John Taylor lived in the Gardo House with his widowed sister, Mrs. Agnes Taylor Schwartz; his five living wives and their children lived in their homes at a distance.[64] His first wife, Leonora Cannon, had died years earlier in 1868.

President John Taylor went underground early in 1885 and conducted all business from various locations. While in hiding, he began to realize that because of the strictures imposed by the government, the Church could not survive without modifying its stance on plural marriage. Despite his deeply held belief that it was the Church's right to practice polygamy and that God wanted them to do so, President Taylor supported John T. Caine in his proposal that the state constitution include a prohibition of the practice of polygamy in Utah, but not in areas outside of the United States.[65] The document didn't address the issue of belief. Congress failed to act on the proposed petition for statehood, postponing again the question of polygamy and statehood.

President Taylor's health deteriorated sharply after supporting the proposal that opposed the religious doctrine he had defended for so long.[66] He died at his hiding place in Kaysville, Utah, on July 25, 1887. President Taylor's death occurred during the tense interplay between the Saints who were defending their right to practice polygamy and the government that was

---

62 Janice Maughan, 142.

63 *Fulness of Times*, 427.

64 Whitney, 394.

65 Francis M. Gibbons, *John Taylor: Mormon Philosopher, Prophet of God* (Salt Lake City, UT: Deseret Book, 1985): 268.

66 For a fuller picture of John Taylor's part in the transition of giving up polygamy, see Chapter Six.

contesting that right. The government even took measures to suppress Mormon emigration from other countries. Perhaps the most revealing evidence of the continuing animosity in the country against the Mormons' practice of polygamy was the fact that every president of the United States in this period crusaded against polygamy and identified Mormons as a political threat because they voted as a block.[67]

Despite the explicit laws that now prohibited polygamy, Mormons continued to marry more than one wife. In fact, the prohibitions seemed to increase their allegiance to plural marriage. Not surprisingly, the government became concerned that decisions made by individual Mormons were unduly influenced by allegiance to their prophet and were outside the jurisdiction of the government. A string of federal officials were sent to the Utah Territory to govern and run the court system, but of course the Mormons wanted to rule themselves and practice their religion without government interference. Plural marriage served as the lightning rod for all the grievances the government had toward the Saints; for Mormons it became a point of honor to serve time in the penitentiary. Nearly one thousand people, mostly men, were imprisoned.[68] My four great-grandfathers all served time in the penitentiary.

The 1887 Edmunds-Tucker Act, which was more specific and harsher than the Edmunds Act enacted five years earlier, officially dissolved the Church as a legal entity, required it to forfeit all property in excess of fifty thousand dollars (which included the temples) to the United States, and abolished women's suffrage. In fact, no one could vote, serve on a jury, or hold public office without pledging support to the anti-polygamy laws. In addition, polygamous wives were required to attend polygamy trials and testify against their husbands. Because the ordinance work was performed in temples, the government's threat to confiscate the temples was extremely disconcerting to the Saints and their leaders.[69] Judge Zane, one of the federal judges, recognized this and declared, "This law will go on to grind you and your institutions to powder."[70] Clearly, the Edmunds-Tucker Act would be a death knell to the Church unless Church leadership changed its doctrine and practice.

Finally, the Church changed its course. At the direction of the First Presidency, no public mention was made of polygamy after 1887. In 1889 the Endowment House, where many polygamous marriages had taken place and therefore had become a symbol of plural marriage, was torn down.[71] These changes culminated in Wilford Woodruff's 1890 Manifesto, an official declaration that the Church had halted the teaching of plural marriage and was not allowing anyone to enter into the practice.[72] After the Manifesto was read by Apostle Orson F. Whitney at October General Conference in 1890, George Q. Cannon delivered a powerful message that supported the end of the practice. For scriptural backing, he referred to the 1841 revelation

---

67 Allen and Leonard, 393.

68 Whitney, 407.

69 Allen and Leonard, 406–7.

70 Whitney, 406.

71 Allen and Leonard, 406.

72 D&C OD 1. The 1890 Manifesto, three letters associated with it, and the 1904 Manifesto are included in Appendices L, M, and N.

Joseph Smith received when persecution from Missourians made it impossible for the Saints to build a temple in Independence, Missouri. At that point, the Prophet had said that given the persecution from their enemies, the Saints were released from the commandment to build a temple in Missouri at that time.[73] And now they were released from the commandment to practice plural marriage. Wilford Woodruff closed the meeting, strongly and eloquently defending his action and reaffirming that the practice of plural marriage should cease:

> I want to say to all Israel that the step which I have taken in issuing this manifesto has not been done without earnest prayer before the Lord. I am about to go into the spirit world, like other men of my age. I expect to meet the face of my Heavenly Father—the Father of my spirit; I expect to meet the face of Joseph Smith, of Brigham Young, of John Taylor, and of the apostles, and for me to have taken a stand in anything which is not pleasing in the sight of God, or before the heavens, I would rather have gone out and been shot. . . . I am not ignorant of the feelings that have been engendered through the course I have pursued. But I have done my duty, and the nation of which we form a part must be responsible for that which has been done in relation to this principle.[74]

President Woodruff was feeling the weight of the course he had taken. Then and later many Saints struggled with accepting the Manifesto and with how to interpret it. Many of the later problems associated with giving up polygamy began with the vagueness of the 1890 Manifesto, which did not address the issue of what the future living arrangement would be of a husband to women he married before 1890, nor whether the Manifesto applied outside the United States and its territories. Soon after issuing it, President Woodruff said, "The manifesto only refers to future marriages and does not affect past conditions. I did not, could not and would not promise that you would desert your wives and children. This you cannot do in honor."[75]

However, the following year, when pressed on the issue of the legal status of properties belonging to plural wives, President Woodruff said the Manifesto should be understood as applicable to both future and existing polygamous marriages and that neither new marriages nor living with wives of earlier marriages would be permitted in the future.[76] He later explained to the Quorum of the Twelve Apostles that he could not have answered otherwise given the position in which he was placed.[77]

---

73 D&C 124:49.

74 *Millennial Star*, November 24, 1890, quoted in *Fulness of Times*, 441–42.

75 Victor W. Jorgensen and B. Carmon Hardy, "The Taylor-Cowley Affair and the Watershed of Mormon History," *Utah Historical Quarterly*, Winter 1980, Volume 48/Number 1, 7 as cited in *Abraham Hoagland Cannon Journal*, Vol. 13, 133.

76 Joregenson and Hardy, 7.

77 Ibid., 8.

At a stake conference in Logan, Utah, he laid the problem before the Saints and told them that they must decide for themselves whether to accept the directive to abandon plural marriage but stressed that he had acted on a revelation from God:

> The Lord showed me by vision and revelation exactly what would take place if we did not stop this practice. . . . You would have had no use for . . . any of the men in this temple at Logan; for all ordinances would have been stopped throughout the land of Zion. Confusion would reign throughout Israel. . . . This trouble would have come upon the whole Church, and we should have been compelled to stop the practice. Now, the question is, whether it should be stopped in this manner, or in the way the Lord has manifested to us, and leave our Prophets and Apostles and fathers free men, and the temples in the hands of the people, so that the dead may be redeemed. . . . This is the question that I lay before the Latter-day Saints. You have to judge for yourselves. I want you to answer it for yourselves. I shall not answer it; but I say to you that that is exactly the condition we as a people would have been in had we not taken the course we have. . . .
>
> I have had this spirit upon me for a long time. But I want to say this: I should have let all the temples go out of our hands; I should have gone to prison myself, and let every other man go there, had not the God of heaven commanded me to do what I did do; and when the hour came that I was commanded to do that, it was all clear to me. I went before the Lord, and I wrote what the Lord told me to write.[78]

Here Wilford Woodruff presented in plain language the importance of the Manifesto and how dire circumstances would have been had the Saints not given up polygamy. An unanswered question is what course the Church would have taken had the federal government not forced our hand, a topic I explore in Chapter Eight.

---

78 D&C OD 1, 2.

The year 1890 is seen as a watershed year in Mormon history. The Saints had successfully battled harsh physical conditions and created a viable society. They had achieved enough strength, cohesiveness, and numbers that they were ready to move from being an insular, defensive society to becoming part of mainstream American life. Giving up plural marriage was an important catalyst of that change.[79]

The Salt Lake Temple, the construction of which began in 1853 and ended in 1893, symbolized a new beginning for the Church. Temples now performed only monogamous marriages. In 1894 Wilford Woodruff initiated another important policy changes with the revelation that members would be sealed only to ancestors and descendants rather than being adopted into other families.[80]

The federal government responded favorably to the 1890 Manifesto. On January 4, 1893, two months before he left office, President Benjamin Harrison offered amnesty to all Saints who had been in compliance with the law since 1890.[81] On September 25, 1894, President Grover Cleveland issued a more general amnesty and returned Church property.[82]

Once the Church withdrew support from the practice of plural marriage, there remained the other obstacle to gaining statehood: the monolithic way the Church exercised political power. Church leaders quelled the federal government's fear of Mormons voting as a block by creating a two-party system to replace the Church's single political party. The proposed state constitution ensured the complete separation of church and state and prohibited plural marriage. As a result of these guarantees, more than forty years after Brigham Young and the legislative body of the Territory had appointed George Q. Cannon, my great-grandfather, to serve in Congress to work toward statehood, Utah finally became a state on January 4, 1896.[83]

When the 1890 Manifesto was issued, many members were relieved that polygamy was ending and most accepted the authority of their prophet, Wilford Woodruff, believing that he had received divine revelation. Although most stopped initiating plural marriage, it would be easy to underestimate how painful and complicated it was for the Saints to abandon what had

---

79 The Saints' participation in the Exposition was an expression of their branching out into the larger world. The Mormon Tabernacle Choir sang and Mormon women joined Susan B. Anthony and other progressive women at the Women's Building.

80 Allen and Leonard, 424. A month later the Genealogical Society of Utah (now known as FamilySearch) was formed; tracing ancestry and doing their temple work has become a focus of the Church. People of other faiths make wide use of our extensive family records.

81 Benjamin Harrison, "Proclamation 346—Granting Amnesty and Pardon for the Offense of Engaging in Polygamous or Plural Marriage to Members of the Church of Latter-Day Saints, January 4, 1893," The American Presidency Project, http://www.presidency.ucsb.edu/ws/?pid=71164.

82 Grover Cleveland, "Proclamation 369—Granting Amnesty and Pardon for the Offenses of Polygamy, Bigamy, Adultery, or Unlawful Cohabitation to Members of the Church of Latter-day Saints, September 25, 1894," The American Presidency Project, http://www.presidency.ucsb.edu/ws/?pid=70911.

83 Allen and Leonard, 418.

become the defining symbol of who they were. In fact, it was probably even more difficult for the Saints to let go of polygamy than it had been for those of an earlier generation to accept it. As Bishop Brown so eloquently stated, they had created families to whom they were emotionally and spiritually attached and committed. Belief in plural marriage was an integral part of their beings and couldn't be switched off like a light.

That the Manifesto required the Saints to let go of the *practice* of plural marriage, not belief in it, gave room for the Saints to have a variety of responses to the Manifesto. Despite the Church's expressed support for stopping the practice of polygamy, for a time after the Manifesto some polygamous marriages were performed. (This included one involving my Cannon grandparents, Lewis and Mary Alice Cannon, and Lillian Hamlin, whose story I tell in Chapter Six.) Because the literal reading of the Manifesto did not preclude polygamous marriages in Mexico and Canada, most post-Manifesto marriages took place there.[84]

Continuing hostility toward Mormons, engendered by the practice of plural marriage and perceived intrusion of the Church into politics, was evident when B. H. Roberts ran for a seat in the U.S. House of Representatives in 1898.[85] Seven million people signed a petition opposing his being seated and succeeded in their efforts.[86] Four years later Reed Smoot, also a member of the Twelve but a monogamist, was elected to the U.S. Senate. Feelings ran high to remove him from office. Beginning in January 1904, the thirty-month hearings to unseat him again drew national attention to the Mormons. He retained his sea and went on to serve a distinguished thirty-year career in the Senate.[87]

In response to the unfavorable publicity directed at the Church during the Smoot hearings, several changes in Church policy were made. In December 1903 Joseph F. Smith, who had become president of the Church upon the death of Lorenzo Snow in 1901, issued a statement clarifying that the term "Kingdom of God" did not mean that the Church saw itself as constituting a political kingdom. He and other leaders declared they did not attempt to control state elections and cited a Church census of 1902 showing 897 polygamous families as compared to 2,451 polygamous families in 1890 as evidence that the practice was dying out.[88]

Another consequence of the Smoot hearings was President Joseph F. Smith's issuing a new "Official Statement" in 1904 in which he denied that any marriages violating the law of the land had taken place "with the sanction, consent or knowledge of the Church" and declared that any known transgressor would be excommunicated. This statement did not accurately represent what some Church authorities had done between 1890 and 1904, but did represent the authorities' actions thereafter. This "Second Manifesto" was a clear public signal that plural

---

84 During this period many polygamists fled to Mexico to live on land that John Taylor had purchased in 1885. During the post-Manifesto period some continued to live there with their families and also in Canada. On the rationale that the Manifesto didn't apply to areas outside the United States, some polygamous marriages were performed in Mexico and Canada.

85 Roberts was a member of The First Council of the Seventy who became a polygamist before the Manifesto.

86 Allen and Leonard, 439.

87 Ibid., 443.

88 Ibid., 441.

marriage even outside the United States would end.[89] The Church honored this commitment. The Manifesto of 1890 was added to the Doctrine and Covenants in 1906, making it official doctrine.[90]

In 1907 the First Presidency published "An Address: The Church of Jesus Christ of Latter-day Saints to the World," a sixteen-page document that replied to the polygamy charges made during the Smoot hearings. Written in a conciliatory spirit, the address restates the basic religious beliefs of the Church and affirms that it was loyal to the federal government, had no intention of politically dominating the state, and had abandoned plural marriage. It was adopted unanimously at the April 1907 General Conference and was an important step in Mormons becoming understood by other Americans and part of mainstream society.[91]

Some Church members chose a literal interpretation of both the 1890 and 1904 Manifestos saying that adherence applied only to the United States; they could not support the decision that the practice of plural marriage must be stopped outside of the United States.[92] To this day various fundamental groups base their doctrine on Joseph Smith's original teachings and continue practicing polygamy. I discuss the development of their thinking in Chapter Six.

A century later, plural marriage is not a part of the current Mormon identity. Rather, it is now a piece of the Church's history that does not resemble current practices. However, it should be remembered that courageous men and women, including many in my family, lived what to them was a central doctrine with steadfastness and courage. They also had the strength to follow the directive to move away from plural marriage and yet found ways to stay close to the families to whom they had made a commitment. This book documents not only my extended family's experiences with polygamy but also examines the effects this doctrine and practice had, and still have, on Mormon culture and belief.

---

89   Ibid., 443.

90   Ibid., 444.

91   Ibid., 445.

92   Ibid., 443. John W. Taylor and Matthias Cowley, whom we learn more about in Chapter Six, were apostles who supported this position.

Timeline

Year	National	Church and Utah	Author's great-great-great aunt and that aunt's family	Author's great-grandmothers and their families					Author's grandmother
			Leonora Cannon	Elizabeth Hoagland	Amanda Mousley	Charlotte Smart	Mary Jane Lloyd	Mary Alice (Mamie) Cannon
1796 TO 1806		Brigham Young is born in Whitingham, Vermont, in 1801. Joseph Smith is born in Sharon, Vermont, in 1805.	Leonora Cannon is born on the Isle of Man in 1796.[1]					
1807 TO 1823		Wilford Woodruff is born in Farmington, Connecticut, in 1807.	John Taylor is born in Milnthorpe, England, in 1808.					
1824						Samuel Rose Parkinson's first wife, Arabella Chandler, is born in Cheltenham, England.		
1827				George Q. Cannon, Leonora's nephew and Angus M.'s brother, is born on the Isle of Man.	Sarah Maria Mousley, Amanda's sister, is born in Centreville, Delaware.[2]			
1829	Andrew Jackson becomes U.S. president.							
1830		The Church of Jesus Christ of Latter-day Saints is founded with Joseph Smith as president.[3]						
1831						Samuel Rose Parkinson is born in Barrowford, England.		

TIMELINE

Year	National	Church and Utah	Leonora Cannon	Elizabeth Hoagland	Amanda Mousley	Charlotte Smart	Mary Jane Lloyd	Mary Alice (Mamie) Cannon
1832			John and Leonora, independently of each other, move from England to Toronto.					
1833			John (age 24) and Leonora (age 36) marry.					
1834					Angus M. Cannon, Leonora's nephew and brother to George Q., is born on the Isle of Man.		William Harrison Maughan is born in Alston, England.	
1835				Elizabeth Hoagland is born in Royal Oaks, Michigan.				
1836		Kirtland, Ohio Temple is dedicated.	John and Leonora join the Church.		Amanda Mousley is born in Centreville, Delaware.			
1837	Martin Van Buren becomes U.S. president.							
1838			John and Leonora move from Toronto to Far West, Missouri, with their three children. in Missouri. John is ordained an apostle.					
1839			John leaves on a mission to England, where he introduces the gospel to Leonora's brother George and his wife Ann Quayle. The couple and their children join the Church.					

Year	National	Church and Utah	Leonora Cannon	Elizabeth Hoagland	Amanda Mousley	Charlotte Smart	Mary Jane Lloyd	Mary Alice (Mamie) Cannon
1840					Amanda's mother, Ann McMenemy Mousley, and some of her older children join the Church.			
1841	William Henry Harrison is U.S. president for one month; John Tyler follows.							
1842		Relief Society of the Church is established.	George and Ann Quayle Cannon and their six children emigrate to join the Saints. Ann dies on the voyage.					
1843		Joseph Smith shares with apostles his revelation regarding polygamy, later codified as Section 132 in the Doctrine and Covenants. Polygamy is announced at the Nauvoo, Illinois High Council.	John marries Elizabeth Kaighin (age 32).					
1844		Joseph and Hyrum Smith are killed by a mob while in Carthage, Illinois Jail. John Taylor and Willard Richards are with them; John suffers serious injuries. Brigham Young leads the Church as president of the Quorum of the Twelve Apostles.	John marries Jane Ballantyne (age 31). Leonora writes a letter to Governor Ford pleading for justice to come to the mobsters who attacked Carthage Jail. Leonora takes her brother George's children under her wing after his death in St. Louis.					
1845	James Polk becomes U.S. president.							

TIMELINE

Year	National	Church and Utah	Leonora Cannon	Elizabeth Hoagland	Amanda Mousley	Charlotte Smart	Mary Jane Lloyd	Mary Alice (Mamie) Cannon
1846		Saints in Nauvoo begin their trek west.	John marries Mary Ann Oakley (age 19).					
		Mormon Battalion is mustered.	John and his family leave Nauvoo in February and arrive in Council Bluffs in June.					
		Winter Quarters in Nebraska is established.	Leonora keeps a trail diary of the family's journey across the plains.					
			John Taylor, Parley P. Pratt, and Orson Hyde leave for England to address the Church's financial problems in Great Britain.					
1847		Brigham Young becomes president of the Church.	John returns from England.				Mary Jane Lloyd is born in Montgomery, North Wales. Both of her parents die within the year. She is adopted by Thomas and Catherine Hughes, stalwart Church members.	
			John marries Sophia Whitaker (age 21).					
		Brigham Young and party arrive in the Salt Lake Valley.	The Taylors' company leaves Winter Quarters in June.					
			In September Leonora gives the "feast in the wilderness" to Brigham Young's group, which is travelling east to Winter Quarters.	George Q. Cannon and his sister Ann meet Elizabeth and her family while traveling west with the Taylor family.				
		Brigham Young and apostles leave Salt Lake to return to Winter Quarters.	John and his family arrive in Salt Lake in October.					
			John marries Sophia's sister, Harriet Whitaker (age 30).					

Year	National	Church and Utah	Leonora Cannon	Elizabeth Hoagland	Amanda Mousley	Charlotte Smart	Mary Jane Lloyd	Mary Alice (Mamie) Cannon
1849	Zachary Taylor becomes U.S. president.		John serves a four-year mission to France and Germany.			Charlotte Smart is born in St. Louis, Missouri.		
1850	Millard Fillmore becomes U.S. president.			George Q. begins a three-year mission in Hawaii.				
1852		The practice of polygamy is publicly announced in Salt Lake.						
1853	Franklin Pierce becomes U.S. president.					Samuel Rose marries Arabella Chandler (age 27).	William marries Barbara Morgan (age 19).	
1854			John is called to the Eastern States Mission to publish The Mormon, a newspaper defending the Church. He continues to publish the newspaper until 1857.	George Q. marries Elizabeth (age 19).	Angus meets the Mousley family in Centreville, Delaware, while on his four-year mission. Amanda joins the Church.			
1856		Congress rejects Utah Territory's proposal for statehood.	John marries Margaret Young (age 19).					
1857	James Buchanan becomes U.S. president.	Mountain Meadows Massacre takes place. Johnston's Army approaches Salt Lake. Parley P. Pratt is killed in Arkansas. Women of Salt Lake 14th Ward make Album Quilt.	Leonora makes quilt block, In God Is Our Trust, for Salt Lake 14th Ward Album Quilt.					

Year	National	Church and Utah	Leonora Cannon	Elizabeth Hoagland	Amanda Mousley	Charlotte Smart	Mary Jane Lloyd	Mary Alice (Mamie) Cannon
1858				George Q. marries Sarah Jane Jenne (age 18). George Q.'s family moves to Fillmore, Utah, where he publishes The Deseret News.	Angus marries Sarah (age 29) and Amanda (age 22).			
1860				George Q. is ordained an apostle. George Q. and Elizabeth move to England, where he serves as mission president for three years.			William marries Elizabeth Brice Hill (age 22)	
1861	Abraham Lincoln becomes U.S. president. Civil War begins.							
1862	Morrill Anti-Bigamy Act prohibits plural marriage in territories of the United States. President Lincoln chooses not to enforce it.			Elizabeth keeps a journal during their tour of the European mission.				
1863							William marries Margaret Ward Nibley (age 20).	

TIMELINE

Year	National	Church and Utah	Leonora Cannon	Elizabeth Hoagland	Amanda Mousley	Charlotte Smart	Mary Jane Lloyd	Mary Alice (Mamie) Cannon
1865	Andrew Johnson becomes U.S. president. Civil War ends. After freeing of slaves, the federal government turns its effort to eliminate the country's second barbarism—polygamy.[4]			George Q. marries Eliza Tenney (age 21).				
1866					Amanda's son Lewis Mousley Cannon is born.	Samuel Rose marries Charlotte Smart (age 17).		Lewis Mousley Cannon is born in St. George, Utah.
1867				Elizabeth and George's daughter Mary Alice (Mamie) Cannon is born.			William marries Mary Jane Lloyd (age 19).	Mary Alice (Mamie) Cannon is born in Salt Lake City.
1868			Leonora dies.	George Q. marries Martha Telle (age 21).		Samuel Rise marries Maria Smart (age 16).		
1869	Ulysses S. Grant becomes U.S. president.	Central Pacific and Union Pacific tracks meet at Promontory, Utah, decreasing Utah's isolation.						
1870	Collum Bill fails to pass. It would have allowed federal judges to try polygamists.	Utah legislature gives women the right to vote.						
1871							William marries Rachel Barnes Woodward (age 19)	

TIMELINE

Year	National	Church and Utah	Leonora Cannon	Elizabeth Hoagland	Amanda Mousley	Charlotte Smart	Mary Jane Lloyd	Mary Alice (Mamie) Cannon
1872		George Q. Cannon is territorial delegate to Congress from 1872 to 1882. The newspaper Woman's Exponent is published from 1872 to 1914.						
1874	The Poland Act gives the federal government authority to prosecute polygamists.							
1875					Angus marries Clarissa Cordelia Moses Mason (age 36).			
1877	Rutherford Hayes becomes U.S. president.	Brigham Young dies. John Taylor leads the Church as president of the Quorum of the Twelve Apostles.	John leads the Church as the president of the Quorum of the Twelve Apostles.					
1878	A group of anti-polygamists, headed by the President Hayes' wife, calls polygamy a "great crime."			George Q. and his family establish the Cannon Farm. George Q., Elizabeth, and three of their children travel to Washington, DC, to defend the Church's right to practice polygamy.				
1879	Supreme Court's unanimous decision upholds Reynolds' bigamy conviction.			George Q. and his family again travel to Washington, DC.				

Year	National	Church and Utah	Leonora Cannon	Elizabeth Hoagland	Amanda Mousley	Charlotte Smart	Mary Jane Lloyd	Mary Alice (Mamie) Cannon
1880		John Taylor becomes president of the Church.	John becomes president of the Church.				William marries Euphemia Nibley (age 25).	
1881	James Garfield is U.S. president for five months; Chester Arthur follows.			George Q. marries Elizabeth's sister Emily (age 43).				
1882		Edmunds Anti-Polygamy Act is enacted. It is harsher than the 1862 Morrill Act.		Elizabeth dies.				
1884				George Q. marries Caroline (Carlie) Young Croxall (age 33).	Angus marries Martha Maria Hughes (age 27).			
1885	Grover Cleveland becomes U.S. president.	First groups of polygamists move to Mexico and Canada, where anti-polygamy laws were not enforced.	John takes an extensive trip in the western states and Mexico to learn about Saints' experiences practicing polygamy.		Angus is imprisoned six months for practicing polygamy.			
1886					Angus marries Maria Bennion (age 28).	Samuel Rose is imprisoned six months for practicing polygamy.		
1887		Edmunds-Tucker Act, which disincorporates the Church, is signed. John Taylor dies while in hiding. Wilford Woodruff leads the Church as president of the Quorum of the Twelve.	John dies while in hiding.					
1889	Benjamin Harrison becomes U.S. president.	Wilford Woodruff becomes president of the Church.		George Q. is imprisoned for six months for practicing polygamy.			William is imprisoned for nine months for practicing polygamy.	

Year	National	Church and Utah	Leonora Cannon	Elizabeth Hoagland	Amanda Mousley	Charlotte Smart	Mary Jane Lloyd	Mary Alice (Mamie) Cannon
1890		Wilford Woodruff announces First Manifesto in September; it is accepted in the October General Conference. Edmunds-Tucker Act is upheld by the Supreme Court.						Mary Alice and Lewis marry in Logan Temple.
1892								David Cannon, Mary Alice's brother and Lillian Hamlin's fiancé, dies while on a Church mission in Germany.
1893	Grover Cleveland becomes U.S. president.	Salt Lake Temple is dedicated. Church members participate in and attend the Columbian Exposition in Chicago.						Mary Alice and Lewis attend the Columbian Exposition in Chicago.
1894		Sealings in Church temples are no longer lateral; now they are only to direct ancestors.						
1896		Utah becomes a state.						Abram Cannon, David and Mary Alice's brother, marries David's betrothed, Lillian (age 26) for time. She is sealed to David. Abram dies one month later.

Year	National	Church and Utah	Leonora Cannon	Elizabeth Hoagland	Amanda Mousley	Charlotte Smart	Mary Jane Lloyd	Mary Alice (Mamie) Cannon
1897	William McKinley becomes U.S. president.							
1898		Wilford Woodruff dies. Lorenzo Snow becomes the president of the Church. B.H. Roberts is elected to the U.S. House of Representatives but is never seated because he is a polygamist						Author's father, Alan M. Cannon, is born. Lewis marries Lillian for time. She is sealed to Mary Alice's brother, David.[5]
1899								
1901	Theodore Roosevelt becomes U.S. president and serves in this capacity until 1909.	Lorenzo Snow dies. Joseph F. Smith becomes the president of the Church.		George Q. dies.				
1903		Reed Smoot, a monogamous Mormon apostle, is elected to the U.S. Senate. After four years of hearings, the vote to expel him fails by one vote. He serves until 1933.						
1904		Joseph F. Smith issues the Second Manifesto in April General Conference.						
1905		Raleigh v. Wells rules that a polygamous widow cannot retain the house where she has lived and raised her family.			Amanda dies.		William dies.	

Year	National	Church and Utah	Leonora Cannon	Elizabeth Hoagland	Amanda Mousley	Charlotte Smart	Mary Jane Lloyd	Mary Alice (Mamie) Cannon
1906		Resignations of apostles Matthias Cowley and John W. Taylor from the Quorum of Twelve Apostles are announced in April General Conference. These two apostles and others oppose the termination of polygamy.[6]						
1907		"An Address: The Church of Jesus Christ of Latter-day Saints to the World" affirms the separation of church and state and the Church's abandonment of polygamy.						
1909	William Howard Taft becomes U.S. President							Mary Alice dies.
1911		John W. Taylor, John Taylor's son, claims to find a printed copy of a revelation his father received in 1886 proclaiming that polygamy should last forever. John W. leads a polygamous splinter group.						
1912		Most polygamist Saints living in Mexico relocate to the United States because of political unrest in Mexico.			Sarah, Amanda's sister and sister wife, dies			
1915					Angus dies.	Maria, Charlotte's sister and sister wife, dies		
1918		Heber J. Grant becomes the president of the Church.						
1919						Samuel Rose dies.		
1920								Lillian dies.

TIMELINE

Year	National	Church and Utah	Leonora Cannon	Elizabeth Hoagland	Amanda Mousley	Charlotte Smart	Mary Jane Lloyd	Mary Alice (Mamie) Cannon
1921								Lewis marries Annie Nielson.
1922							Mary Jane dies.	Lewis and Annie divorce.
1924								Lewis dies.
1929						Charlotte dies.		Mary Alice and Lewis' granddaughter Charlotte Cannon (author of this book) is born.
1932		President Grant announces that celestial marriage and monogamy are synonymous.						
1941		Annie Clark Tanner writes A Mormon Mother.						
1945		George Albert Smith becomes president of the Church.						
1951		David O. McKay becomes president of the Church.						
1953	The Arizona National Guard takes action against Mormon fundamentalism, an event referred to as "the Short Creek Raid."							
1995		The Church issues "The Family: A Proclamation to the World," which emphasizes the importance of families.						

TIMELINE

1 For the sake of focus, concision, and clarity, many events in my family's history, such as the births and deaths of children, are not included in this timeline.

2 Later both Sarah and Amanda marry Angus on the same day.

3 Hereafter the Church of Jesus Christ of Latter-day Saints will be referred to as "the Church."

4 A decade prior to the Civil War, one of the Republican Party's goals was fight the twin relics of barbarism: polygamy and slavery.

5 Because there is no written record of Lewis and Lillian's wedding ceremony, the date of the event can only be inferred by the timing of their first child's birth.

6 Matthias Cowley later returned to full membership. John W. Taylor continued to hold fast to his conviction that polygamy should have continued and was excommunicated. Posthumously he regained his membership.

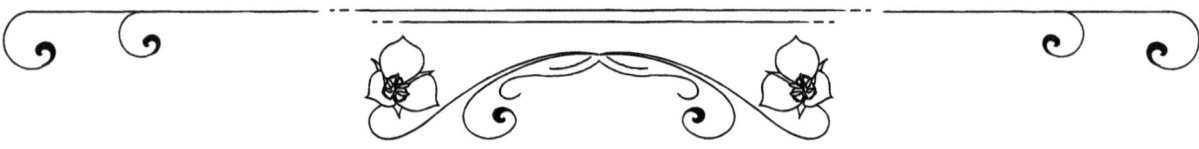

John Taylor   Leonora Cannon Taylor

Chapter One

THE BIRTH OF POLYGAMY

The Travails of Leonora Cannon Taylor

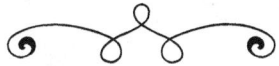

I was a stranger in a strange land. . . . The Lord often led me by a way that I knew not, and in a path that I naturally did not wish to go, every sweet has had its bitter. . . . The way seemed to me narrower every day without his almighty power to help me I cannot walk   to whom shall I go or look for succor but unto thee my Father and only Friend.

Leonora Cannon Taylor

THE MOST stressful times in the lifespan of polygamy were its birth in the 1840s and its end over fifty years later. The challenges of the early period are very evident in the life of Leonora Cannon Taylor, whose brother George was my great-great-grandfather and whose husband, John Taylor, was the third president of the Church. I have always felt an emotional tie and interest in Leonora, probably because she played such a pivotal mothering role in the lives of her nephews, George Q. and Angus Cannon (my great-grandfathers), and because she was the first Cannon to join the Church. My interest in her was whetted when my husband, Peter, and I visited Nauvoo in the fall of 1959, the year we moved to Chicago from Salt Lake City. During our visit to John Taylor's home a guide showed us a picture I had never seen before that featured John Taylor in the center with oval pictures of his seven wives encircling him. I had always known that Leonora was his first wife and that he had other wives but had heard very little about them. On that visit I also found life sketches of the original members of Relief Society, including one of Leonora. Over the years I have pieced together different snapshots of her life, including her diaries already mentioned. That we have Leonora's words that reveal her feelings and chronicle important historical happenings makes her an especially intriguing and important figure. She merits special attention because she and her husband faced the central issues of polygamy in its early years.

Leonora Cannon was born to a prosperous sea captain's family on October 6, 1796, on the Isle of Man.[93] Known for her beauty, intelligence, and wit, Leonora was hardly a likely candidate for breaking social norms and leaving the society she was born into. Her first bold move, entering the work force, was in response to her father's death. He was killed at sea trying to suppress a mutiny of his men. Left with little money, the family drastically changed their lifestyle. They moved to a much smaller home and Leonora, age fifteen, worked as a governess to help support her family. Leonora became close friends with one of her charges, the daughter of a government official, Mr. Mason. When he was offered a prominent government position in Toronto, he said he would take it only if Leonora accompanied his family as a friend and companion to his daughter. Leonora took the job and moved to Canada with the family in 1832.[94]

ADELAIDE STREET METHODIST CHURCH

Leonora Cannon and John Taylor, both of whom immigrated to Canada from England, met at this Methodist church in Toronto in 1832, the very year it was built. They married soon thereafter in January 1833. When they married, Leonora was thirty-six and John twenty-four.

---

93 Evans and Cannon, 19. The Isle of Man lies off the coast of Britain in the Irish Sea, eighty miles northwest of Liverpool.

94 Ibid., 33.

In Canada her life took another dramatic turn when she met John Taylor, who also had moved to Toronto from England that year. They first saw each other at a Methodist Church where he was the leader of the Sunday School. The description of Leonora given by B. H. Roberts, a Church historian and a member of The First Council of the Seventy, recommends her well; it is no wonder that John was drawn to her:

> Refined both by nature and education, gentle and ladylike in manner, witty, intelligent, gifted with rare conversational powers, possessed of a deep religious sentiment, and, withal, remarkable for the beauty of her person, she was a fitting companion to John Taylor.[95]

Leonora and John were both very religious. Leonora prayed for direction in important decisions. A dream prompted her to accept the job in Canada and again a dream indicated she should marry John Taylor.[96] It is evident in her writing that she had a strong sense of who she was, was committed to God, and was eager to share her convictions with other people. For example, on her boat trip from England to Canada, she wrote the following in her diary:

> *I got up early   it was a fine morning   I took my Bible on Deck   the passengers were all sitting talking, I went and got my tracts and testaments and gave them — They all began reading and a good many fetched there Bibles   it was a very pretty sight to see children and all as quiet as possible   about twelve the Clergyman read prayers and the deacons on Deck, Oh! The way the precious Sabbaths are spent here how different to Douglas   Lord help me to be thankful that I am what I am and whom I am.*[97]

Other entries reveal her yearning for "*more Love, more gratitude and more humility.*" Her entry on Sunday, July 29, 1832, reads, "*I thank God for the kindness I meet with from the Family he hath placed me in   I want to beg of the Lord that he would shine upon there Hearts bless them in there Souls. and Bodys, and bring them to the knowledge of Himself whom to know is life eternal.*"

John, also religious, joined the Methodist Church in England in 1824 when he was sixteen. In 1832 he moved to Canada to be with his parents (who had already moved to Canada), find employment, and respond to the spiritual prompting that he would one day preach the gospel in America.[98] These two Brits, Leonora thirty-six and John twenty-four, both crossed the ocean

---

95 B. H. Roberts, *Life of John Taylor* (Salt Lake City, UT: George Q. Cannon & Sons Co.), quoted in Elizabeth Taylor Morgan and Louise C. Taylor, "Leonora Cannon Taylor," in *Seven Wives of John Taylor*, 2.

96 Evans and Cannon, 310.

97 Leonora Cannon Taylor, *First Diary*. Douglas is the capital and largest town on the Isle of Man.

98 Gibbons, 9–10.

to land on foreign soil because they trusted God's promptings. On January 28, 1833, after they had known each other a few months, they acted on their love and got married—not a conventional choice given their age difference.[99]

Three years later they would meet Parley P. Pratt, a Latter-day Saint missionary. He would introduce them to a religion that would change their lives and the nature of their marriage forever. Pratt, who had been married ten years but had no children, was called in Kirtland to go on a mission to Toronto. Concerned about his wife's health and their debts, Pratt was reluctant to accept the call. He counseled with Heber C. Kimball, who gave him a reassuring blessing:

> Brother Parley thy wife shall be healed from this hour, and shall bear a son, and his name shall be Parley. . . . Arise, therefore, and go forth in the ministry, nothing doubting. Take no thought for your debt nor the necessaries of life, for the Lord will supply you with abundant means for all things. Thou shalt go to Upper Canada, even to the city of Toronto, the Capital, and there shalt thou find a people prepared for the fulness of the gospel and they shalt receive thee, and thou shalt organize the Church among them, ... and from the things growing out of the mission shall the fulness of the gospel spread into England, and cause a great work to be done in that land.[100]

Pratt spent what little money he had traveling to Hamilton, on Lake Ontario. To reach Toronto, he needed to take a boat across the lake. Nearly penniless, he did not have money for the fare. As part of the miraculous fulfillment the words of Heber C. Kimball's blessing, Pratt was approached by a stranger who offered him ten dollars and a letter of introduction to John Taylor, whose home the missionary visited upon arriving in Toronto.[101] Pratt enjoyed tea with John and Leonora and offered his message but he left discouraged because they had shown little interest. The next day, as Pratt was preparing to leave town, he passed by the Taylor home and overheard Leonora say of him to Mrs. Walton, who had stopped by their house, "He may be a man of God. I'm sorry to see him depart." Mrs. Walton then offered her large house as a place for Pratt to preach, saying that she now knew why she had felt prompted to visit the Taylors. After speaking at Mrs. Walton's home, Pratt stayed for three more weeks, during which time he met with the Taylors as well as others. John Taylor took careful notes on Elder Pratt's sermons, compared them with his understanding of the scriptures, and was impressed with the connections he discovered.[102]

---

99 Ibid., 12.

100 Evans and Cannon, 311.

101 There is no further mention of who the stranger was.

102 Evans and Cannon, 313.

On May 9, 1836, John and Leonora joined the Church, a decision they were both fully committed to but had no way knowing where it would take their lives.[103] Leonora, a well-educated, well-bred woman, was about to become part of the largest Western migration in United States history, not in the name of economics but of religion. It was a journey that took many lives; for those who survived, their faith was tested at every turn.

When Parley P. Pratt left Canada at the end of his mission, John was placed in charge of all the Saints in Upper Canada. Soon John and Leonora made plans to join the Saints in Kirtland, Ohio. They left Toronto in the middle of the winter of 1837–38 with their two small children, George John and Mary Ann, in a sled pulled by horses and piled high with blankets to keep them warm. After staying in Kirtland for a short time, they followed the body of Saints to Missouri, where John was ordained an apostle on December 9, 1838.[104] Their third child, Joseph, no doubt named for their beloved prophet, was born in Indiana en route to Missouri. From Missouri, John and Leonora moved to Montrose, Iowa, just across the Mississippi River from Nauvoo, where they joined other apostles and their families who lived in the deserted remains of Old Fort Des Moines.[105] Wilford Woodruff and his wife Phoebe, with whom Leonora became lifelong friends, lived there also. Leonora and Phoebe and their small children shared a single room part of this time.[106] Only a few months later, in 1839, John was called on a mission to England. They were fully committed to their new faith. Even though Leonora was ill with three young children and John's absence would leave the family in a precarious situation, neither John nor Leonora were reluctant for John to accept the call. Later, from England, John requested that Leonora be permitted to come to England to help with the missionary work, but Church leaders did not grant his request.[107] One wonders, given her family responsibilities, how John thought she could have made the trip.

While he was gone, Leonora lived in the barracks with her three children—ages five, three, and one. Poignant letters the couple wrote to each other tell of how devoted they were to the gospel and how much they missed each other. In Leonora's first letter to John, she catalogued her troubles: the housing shortage, five-year-old George's eye infection, the chills and fever that attacked both her and three-year-old Mary Ann, and a sickness that threatened the life of one-year-old Joseph. She ended her letter, "*I never needed more grace, patience or your prayers than I do at present.*"[108] She judiciously waited to send the letter until she could report that their health was better. John, also recuperating from illness, responded on a homemade letterhead that included

---

103 Ibid., 314.

104 *Fulness of Times*, 190.

105 Carol Cornwall Madsen, *In Their Own Words: Women and the Story of Nauvoo* (Salt Lake City, UT: Deseret Book, 1994) 6.

106 I include more about their friendship later in this chapter and in Chapter Four.

107 Gibbons, 39.

108 Leonora Taylor to John Taylor, September 9, 1839–October 1839, in "Sickness and Faith. Nauvoo Letters," ed. Ronald K. Esplin, *BYU Studies* 15 (Summer 1975): 427. Original letters in John Taylor Collection, History Department Archives.

the names of *"My Dear Nora"* and their children woven into flowers he drew. He wrote separate notes to each family member. In the letter to Leonora he wrote about his difficulties in traveling and his own illness. With deep faith he determinedly concluded,

> *You may ask me how I am going to prosecute [pursue] my journey, with my trunk a distance of 300 miles or upwardes by land, without means. I do not know, but one thing I do know, that there is a Being who clothes the lilies of the valley and feeds the ravens and he has given me to understand that all these things shall be added and that is all I need to know.*[109]

In a letter to her husband Leonora shared her faith but prefaced it with her longing for his return. "[I] want you to come back in the fall. . . . I feel as if I want to get into this Letter and go too. . . . May the Lord. . . . bring you back in safety [and] make you a blessing while you remain." She helped the children draw smudgy circle kisses on the bottom of the page.

In the midst of her own problems, Leonora wrote to John that her dear friend Phoebe Woodruff was very ill. "*I do hope she will recover, she has been a great comfort to me since you have gone.*"[110] This letter shows Leonora's determination to keep grounded by using her sewing skills to take care of her friend, family, and herself. She asked John to send *"some flannel for particular use, red and yellow, a bit; net fore lase for my self, and Quilting, checked Muslin or plain, a little; a yard 3/4 of black Silk for Apron."*[111]

In a lengthy poignant letter begun January 2, 1840, Leonora painted a vivid picture of the Saints' lives. She mentioned the frequent crossing of the Mississippi, sometimes frozen over, by the Saints between Montrose and Nauvoo; Joseph Smith's visit to Washington to ask the government for fair treatment after the Saints' expulsion from Missouri; and the growth of the Church in New York and Philadelphia. Interspersed in her account of the news of the day were her trials and how sorely she missed John:

> *I do pray for the Lord to bless and comfort you. I do praise Him for what He has done for you all ready. I wish you could see George and Mary Ann, as fat and rosy as ever. . . . Joseph is better and can run alone again, but teeth are still coming and I have to nurse him a great deal. I feel better able than I was when I last wrote. I have been sick but am better. He is still to be the baby. The Lord knows what is best for us.*[112]

---

109 John Taylor to Leonora Taylor, September 19, 1839, in Esplin, "Sickness and Faith. Nauvoo Letters," 433.

110 Carol Holindrake Nielson, *The Salt Lake 14th Ward Album Quilt, 1857: Stories of the Relief Society Women and Their Quilt* (Salt Lake City, UT: The University of Utah Press, 2004): 181.

111 Ibid. Leonora may have used scraps from this fabric years later to make her block for the Salt Lake 14th Ward Album Quilt discussed in Chapter Four.

112 Madsen, 103. Her underlining the word "sick" and her reference that Joseph is still to be the baby, Leonora was likely referring to a miscarriage in a veiled manner typical of the Victorian era, a topic explored in Chapter Three.

Later in the letter she wrote:

> *I had three Indian Women a papuce and an Elderly Man all very clean to supper with me   the[y] sat around the Fire and talked away quite comfortable   little Joseph kisst the little papuce and was delighted with It*
>
> *the Children all send there love and a hundred kisses to Father   Joseph gives me one evry day for you and points to your Old Hat. When shall we see dear Father again is my cry and the Childrens, but I do not want to hinder the work of the Lord   My comfort is not to be compared to the worth of one Soul and I do pray that many may hear & believe the truth with whome we shall yet rejoice in the presence of the Lord. . . .*
>
> *I want to hear from you very much   My Health is not good   I pray the Lord to spare me to see you once more   I feel thankfull to the Lord that I am able to do what is needfull for my dear Children   I bought them warm and Wollen frocks and had long wollen stockings knit for myself and them and all had new Shoes on at Xmas   I have made my Bed wide   G[eorge] and M[ary Ann] sleep at one end and Joseph and I at the other end   Give my love to all that ask after me on the Isle of Man. . . . May the Lord bless my dear John and bring him back safe is the prayer of your affectionate wife.*[113]

Toward the end of her poignant letter, which she finished on February 2, 1840, Leonora wrote that she hoped John had found her friends and family well and favorable to the truth. The fervent hope of Leonora's heart was realized miraculously. Leonora's sacrifices and trials yielded a priceless gift. The very month Leonora was writing this heavy-laden letter, John took the gospel to her brother George and his family in Liverpool. George and his wife, Ann Quayle, along with their older children, joined the Church on February 11, 1840.[114] After their conversion, John wrote to Leonora, "*They now stand in a nearer relationship than kindred flesh; they are brother & sister   in Jesus Christ.*"[115] George, the father of George Q. and Angus, also wrote to Leonora at this time:

> *I bless the Lord that I ever saw your husband's face, and I now see plainly that our dear mother's prayer has not only been answered for you, but extended to me and my family through you. . . . I see the hand of the Lord so visible in all that has happened to me that I cannot help telling you of it. . . . I was happy in an affectionate wife, promising children, good health, plenty of work, and always a pound to spare, but still there was a want of something which made me feel*

---

113 Leonora Cannon Taylor to John Taylor, quoted in Madsen, 105.

114 Evans and Cannon, 34.

115 John Taylor to Leonora Taylor, January 30, 1840, quoted in Richard L. Jensen, "The John Taylor Family," *Ensign,* February 1980.

> *very low-spirited at times. . . . When Bro. Taylor came to Liverpool, and I was sincerely desirous to lead a new life, he had the words whereby I might be saved, and though slow of belief at first, and not seeing the necessity of baptism, yet God in His infinite mercy opened my eyes.*[116]

When John returned in 1841, Leonora was very ill—even close to death. John gave her a special blessing and she recovered. From her *First Diary* we read:

> *Mr. Taylor returned 3rd of July, I had gone through all but death during his absence   [I] lived in an old barrack room twenty-feet square with one small window the back door of the hinges and walls so open that a skunk came in every Night. . . . Twice I found a large Snake in the room. . . . [I]n the middle of the night drunken Indians came to the door and there quarreled some to get in others keeping them back, and I alone with three small children. I had many privations and many Mercys. I never saw one of Mr. Taylors relative in my House the two years he was away.*[117]

Once the family was reunited, they crossed the Mississippi River to Nauvoo, where they made their home. Their fourth child, Leonora Agnes, named for Leonora and for John's mother Agnes, was born June 1, 1842.[118] In April 1843 Leonora's brother George and his six young children, the youngest of whom was two and a half and named for Leonora, joined them from England by way of St. Louis and a voyage up the Mississippi River. Tragically, George's wife, Ann Quayle, pregnant at the time, died as they were crossing the ocean. Leonora and John with their young family were at the riverbank in Nauvoo to meet George and his children. George Q., in his biography of Joseph Smith, writes of the experience he had that day, at age sixteen, of recognizing the Prophet among the crowd.[119] Leonora took her brother and his children into

---

116 Evans and Cannon, 36.

117 Leonora Cannon Taylor, *First Diary*. Leonora's calling her husband "Mr. Taylor" rather than "John" or "my husband" is another example of Leonora's restrained Victorian language. We have no information of the whereabouts of the Taylor family while John was gone. We do know from Leonora's later diary that his parents and three siblings crossed the plains with them.

118 I have conflicting records of when their fourth child, Leonora Agnes, was born. The current Church records indicate she was born June 1, 1840, and in her *First Diary* Leonora also gave the date as 1840. However, Gibbons states that John left Montrose en route to England on August 8, 1839, placing the birth in June 1840 eleven months after he left. Also there is no reference to the birth of a child as part of her travails while John was on his mission. In the January 1840 letter to him, she makes a veiled reference to a miscarriage. She always referred to the death of her child as a baby, not a three year old. John arrived back in Montrose in early July 1841, so the birth of a baby in June 1842 was possible. Recently I found handwritten notes I made some fifty years ago that substantiates the baby's birth as June 1, 1842, a date that seems much more likely than 1840.

119 George Q. Cannon, *The Life of Joseph Smith, the Prophet* (Salt Lake City, UT: Deseret Book Company, 1972): 20–21.

her home while they got settled. Soon George built a home for his family across the street from the Taylors.[120] In February 1844, George married Mary White, a widow living with the Taylors, another example of how intertwined the two families were.[121]

Over the years, John and Leonora remained very important to her brother's children. After her brother George died in St. Louis in August of 1844, George Q. and Ann became part of Leonora and John's family and crossed the plains with them. John Taylor taught George Q. the printing business; George Q. and his Aunt Leonora exchanged several letters while he was on his mission in Hawaii. John helped Angus, George Q.'s younger brother and my other Cannon great grandfather, get established before Angus' mission to the eastern United States. When she was sixteen years old, Mary Alice married Charles Lambert and became the surrogate mother to her younger siblings — Angus, David, and Leonora. Alice wrote of Leonora, "*To me she was all that was beautiful, and I loved her as my mother.*"[122] Later George Q. served as a counselor to John Taylor in the First Presidency and acted as a protection to him during the difficult Underground days.

At the time George and his children arrived in Nauvoo, a very difficult part of Leonora's life was beginning: accepting plural marriage. It was also difficult for John. He wrote, "*I had always entertained strict ideas of virtue and I felt as a married man that this was to me, outside of this [principle], an appalling thing to do. The idea of going and asking a young lady to be married to me when I already had a wife! It was a thing calculated to stir up feelings from the innermost depths of the human heart.*"[123] John then wrote what turned him to accepting polygamy:

> *Some time after these things [that the Prophet wanted John to practice polygamy] were made known unto me, I was riding out of Nauvoo on horseback, and met Joseph Smith coming in, he too, being on horseback. . . . I bowed to Joseph, and [he did] the same to me. He said, "Stop" and he looked at me very intently. "Look here, these things that have been spoken of must be fulfilled, and if they are not entered into right away the keys will be turned.*[124]

John interpreted this to mean that his failure to accept plural marriage would be a rejection of the Prophet and therefore of God. Both John and Leonora had struggled with the idea for some two years. In the context of the Victorian era in which they lived, their age difference

---

120 George built a home for his family on the southwest corner of Parley Street and Granger Street, diagonally across the intersection from the first home of the Taylors, which was on the northeast corner of Parley and Granger.

121 Bitton, 42.

122 Mary Alice Cannon Lambert, "Leonora Cannon Taylor," *The Young Woman's Journal* 19 (1908).

123 B. H. Roberts, *The Life of John Taylor*, 100, quoted in Gibbons, 51.

124 B. H. Roberts, *The Life of John Taylor*, 100–101, quoted in Gibbons, 51.

increased the difficulty of choosing to practice polygamy. John, age thirty-four, was in the prime of life. Leonora, age forty-six, was on the threshold of being an old woman.[125] This age difference would become more painful to Leonora if John married younger women, which indeed he did. When the Prophet confronted John directly, he answered the call and replied resolutely, "Brother Joseph, I will try and carry these things out."[126] John later wrote in his unpublished life story, "I did it with my eyes open; I counted the cost; I looked upon it as a life-long job and I considered that I was not only enlisted for time, but for eternity."[127] His testimony, as recorded in Doctrine and Covenants 135, shows the strength of his allegiance to and confidence in Joseph Smith's spiritual authority: "Joseph Smith, the Prophet and Seer of the Lord, has done more, save Jesus only, for the salvation of men in this world, than any other man that ever lived in it."[128]

We know less about Leonora's feelings at the time, but her diary reveals that it was a very stressful period for her. On May 1, 1843, she wrote, *"Mr. T[aylor] had a bad fever nigh to death.... Cut my finger with a glass it got very bad my dear Child took sick, my sweet baby died on the 9th of Sept. buried the 10th on the 14th I had the middle finger of my left hand taken off, and buried with my Baby.... I had many trials about this time but I am yet alive."*[129]

Her daughter, Leonora, died in September 1843, just three months before John married a second wife. The bereft mother was forty-seven years old and knew this would likely be her last child. She must have ached not only about sharing John's affections with other women but also at the prospect of the children the younger wives would be able to bear. She also may have relived the anguish she had felt during their recent two-year separation and realized she would never be John's only partner again. Ultimately, Leonora had consented and counseled with her husband as to who the wife would be. John married his first plural wife, thirty-two-year-old Elizabeth Kaighin, on December 12, 1843.[130] Elizabeth, who was Leonora's cousin, was also born on the Isle of Man and was baptized in Toronto by Parley P. Pratt the same day as John and Leonora.[131]

---

125 Hansen, 28–29.

126 B. H. Roberts, *The Life of John Taylor*, 101, quoted in Gibbons, 52.

127 John Taylor, "History of John Taylor," *Histories of the Twelve*. (History Department Archives): Microfilm, 274.

128 D&C 135:3. John Taylor was the author of D&C 135, which became part of the Docrine and Covenents in 1844 after the martydom of Joseph Smith..

129 Leonora Cannon Taylor, *First Diary*. The child mentioned was her namesake.

130 Gibbons, 52. Leonora probably anticipated that she and Elizabeth would be compatible as sister wives. She was soon proven wrong. I discuss the strains in their relationshipe later in this chapter.

131 John married five more women by whom he had children. I write more about these women later in this chapter: Jane Ballantyne on February 25, 1844; Mary Ann Oakley on January 14, 1846; Sophia Whitaker on April 23, 1847, and Harriet Whitaker on December 4, 1847. Nearly a decade later, after plural marriage was practiced openly in Utah, he married his seventh wife, Margaret Young, on September 26, 1856. Like many prominent early Church leaders, John was also sealed to nine other women in the spirit of creating an extensive family network and providing a celestial home for more women. There is no record of children of his being born to these women. For details of who the nine women were, see Craig L. Foster, "The Plural Wives of the Prophets."

Recently I found a copy of a blessing among the notes I had taken fifty years ago during my visit to Nauvoo. John must have given Leonora this blessing sometime after they began practicing plural marriage. It confirms John's sensitivity to Leonora's feelings of loss and his belief in the eternal nature of their marital relationship:

> Thou hast passed through trials, Nora, but thou shalt rejoice! Thou hast been driven from thy home for the truth's sake, but thou and thy children shall have a home in the Kingdom of God! . . . . The tender association [with thy husband] has been severed ¾ that others may be made partakers of endless life; but thou and thy husband shall yet reign together in the celestial kingdom of God. A few more struggles. . . . and victory will be ours.[132]

Leonora and John's story illustrates many questions that polygamy forced people to face: What does fidelity mean? How does one respond when the edicts of one's religion conflict with personal desires? How does one justify practicing polygamy in a monogamous society? Their story, unlike the others I explore, began with their taking monogamy as a given during the first years of their marriage. Perhaps for that reason, John was candid about his initial ambivalence and his taking two years to accept polygamy. Leonora, probably conforming to the expectations of the time for female decorum, veiled her pain and hesitation. In her diary we read of her sorrow—undoubtedly in reference to sharing her husband with other women—and her faith:

> *I was a stranger in a strange land. . . . The Lord often led me by a way that I knew not, and in a path that I naturally did not wish to go, every sweet has had its bitter. . . . The way seemed to me narrower every day without his almighty power to help me I cannot walk   to whom shall I go or look for succor but unto thee my Father and only Friend.*[133]

Although Leonora never referred in her diary directly to polygamy as a trial, such expressions as *"I had many trials about this time but I am yet alive"* and *"the way seemed to me narrower every day"* reveal her pain in being asked to accept polygamy. Tellingly, these and other such painful selections have been omitted from other family histories I have read about her, perhaps because reading about her struggles made the authors of these histories uncomfortable. Including them would have painted a fuller, more complex picture of her life and of a troubling period in Mormon history. I include them now in order to tell a more complete story.

---

132 B. H. Roberts, The Life of John Taylor (Salt Lake City, UT: George Q. Cannon & Sons Co.): 90, quoted in J. Lewis Taylor, "John Taylor: Family Man," in Champion of Liberty: John Taylor, ed. Mary Jane Woodger (Provo, UT: Religious Studies Center, Brigham Young University, 2009): 193–218. This reference to bereavement possibly refers to no longer being John's only wife.

133 Leonora Cannon Taylor, *First Diary*.

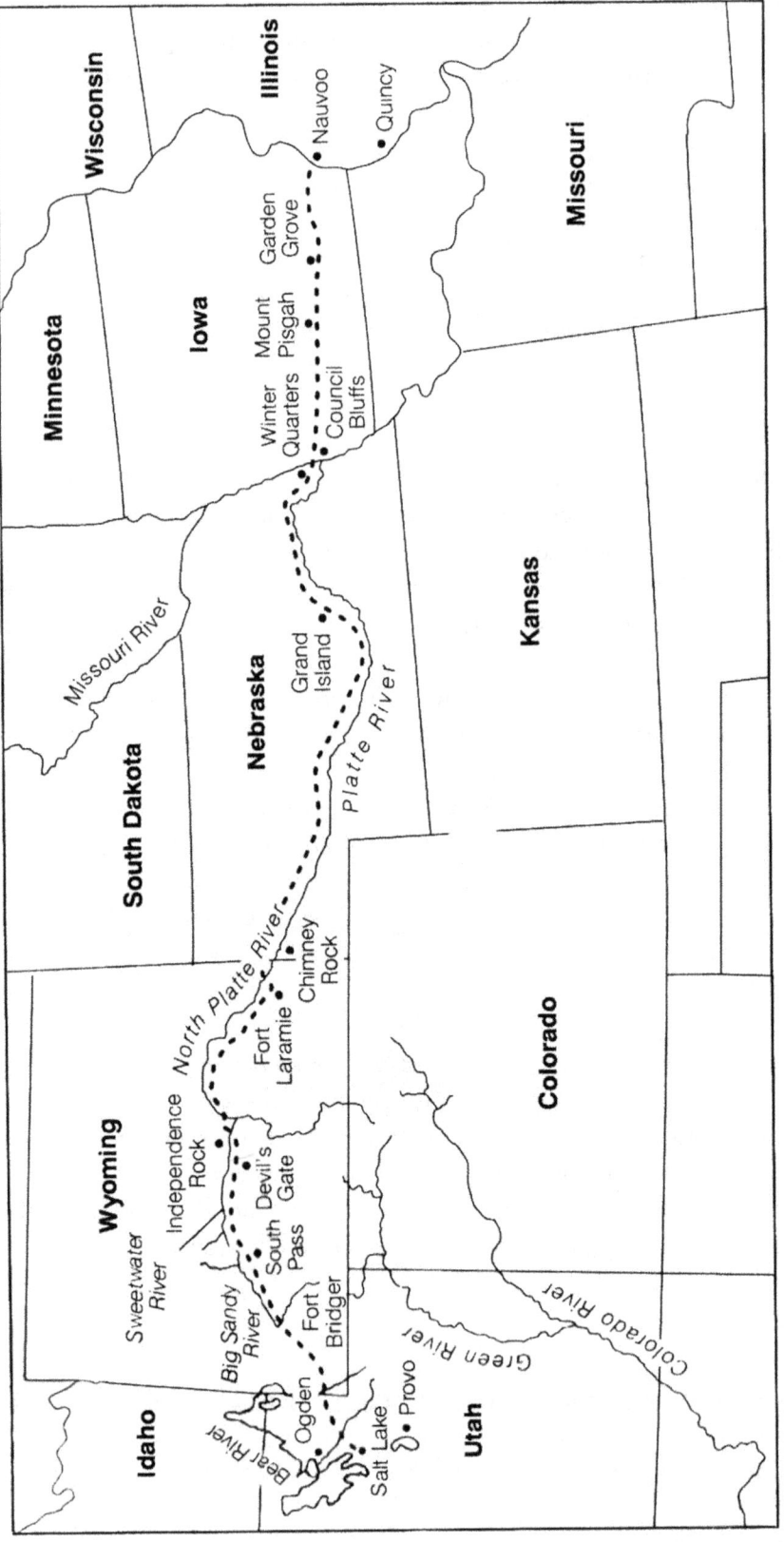

The various families mentioned in this book—the Taylors, Cannons, Hoaglands, Mousleys Maughans, Parkinsons, and Lloyds—travelled all or part of this trail. The first group traveled in 1847 in covered wagons and included Elizabeth Hoagland and George Q. with his Aunt Leonora Taylor. The latest of my ancestors was Mary Lloyd, who made the trip in 1862, riding most of the way on horseback.

Leonora had a conversation with her nephew Angus when she was fifty-seven and he was nineteen. His account says that as a young man he was disturbed to discover that a married man was asking his older sister Ann to enter plural marriage. Leonora's response to her nephew reveals how high the stakes were for her and John in accepting polygamy and how fraught with unwelcome consequences their lives would have been had they not entered plural marriage. It also shows her unwavering faith in God and allegiance to authority:

> Angus, you must not oppose this principle for the Prophet Joseph told me before his martyrdom that I must give Mr. Taylor, your uncle, other wives or he could not hold his position in the Church as one of the Twelve. To be obedient to God, having told me this in the name of the Lord, and I knowing him to be a Prophet, I did give him other wives, and have divided my scanty subsistence with them, to be obedient unto the Lord.[134]

At least as harrowing as polygamy was the trauma of her husband's near-fatal wound. On June 27, 1844, he and Willard Richards were with the Prophet and his brother Hyrum when they were killed at Carthage. John was hit with four bullets and badly wounded. It is thought that the pocket watch he was wearing saved his life.[135] The following day, Dr. Barnes extracted the bullets with no anesthetic and dressed the wounds; John's parents and Leonora came the next day.

After several days of convalescence and after both a wagon and a litter proved too painful as modes of transport,[136] concerned Saints placed John on a sleigh. It slid over the prairie grass to carry him back to Nauvoo. Later John wrote of the experience:

> Never shall I forget the difference of feeling that I experienced between the place that I had left and the one I had now arrived at. I had left a lot of reckless, blood-thirsty murderers, and had come to

---

134 Elder Angus H. Cannon, "Statement of an Interview with Joseph Smith III, President of the 'Reorganites'," October 12, 1905, quoted in Angus M. Cannon Reunion Committee, ed., *1988 Angus M. Cannon Reunion Materials* (1988): 81. Apparently Angus was persuaded; he married Amanda and Sarah, his first two plural wives, on the same day five years later in 1858 and subsequently married four other women.

135 Gibbons, 71.

136 A litter is a piece of canvas between two poles.

> the city of the Saints, the people of the living God. . . . all of whom stood there with warm, true hearts to offer their friendship and services, and to welcome my return.[137]

During this difficult time, Leonora remained strong and was not engulfed in her own turmoil. She wrote, as did other women, an eloquent appeal to Governor Ford of Illinois urging that the wrongdoers be brought to justice for the sake of the Saints' safety.[138]

Before I found Leonora's "crossing the plains" diary, which I will refer to as her trail diary, I knew little of her life after they left Nauvoo. All I had found were two snippets about her in a Young Women publication of the Church. Both reveal Leonora's strength of character. One comment refers to Leonora during the trek west: "She was a lively conversationalist and she set a fine table." The other reads, "Leonora helped other women accept polygamy."[139] The trail diary fleshes out a much more complete picture of Leonora.[140]

In her diary Leonora vividly chronicles their trek in 1846 across Iowa to Council Bluffs and then across the Missouri River to Nebraska, where they settled for the winter at Winter Quarters. Her final entries recount their continued journey the year from Winter Quarters to the Salt Lake Valley. Leonora's diary entries of encounters with Indians, thundering herds of buffalo, and stirring descriptions of the expansive landscape all offer a striking contrast to what she would have experienced on the Isle of Man, her childhood home. Her accounts of exciting and sometimes perilous travels are interesting and historically significant. Woven into these stories are details about interactions with her sister wives and the many challenges she faced in managing an extensive and complex household. Most challenging of all was that her husband was away in England for eight months to settle financial and leadership problems of the Church. As she and her fellow Saints ventured west, nothing was certain except the constancy of her love for her husband and her unwavering faith in God.

It has been difficult to decide how much of the diary to include in this chapter about Leonora and her connection to polygamy. In addition to the entries that refer to interactions with John's plural wives and directly relate to polygamy, I have chosen to include other diary excerpts with historical significance. Passages that reveal the skill with which she managed frontier life, the onerous responsibilities she shouldered while John was away, the complexities of living The Principle, and the loneliness she felt in his absence, all bring to life a complex woman whose

---

137 Samuel W. Taylor, *The Last Pioneer: John Taylor, a Mormon Prophet* (Salt Lake City, UT: Signature Books, 1999): 97. Leonora's brother George, a skilled cabinetmaker, made coffins for the Prophet and his brother Hyrum and took plaster casts of their faces, creating the death masks that provide the best evidence of the appearance of the martyrs. Bitton, 46.

138 To read a typed version of the letter, see Appendix G.

139 Excerpt from *Young Woman's Journal*, an official publication of The Church of Jesus Christ of Latter-day Saints between 1897 and 1929.

140 Leonora's trail diary, that chronicles her journey from Nauvoo to the Salt Lake Valley, is quoted extensively throughout the remainder of this chapter. A quote or reference without a footnote is from this source. The diary is located in the Church History Library in Salt Lake City, Utah.

life, like many of her time, has often been too easily summarized in a sentence or two. Reading her unabridged diary would help the reader understand the rhythm and import of her historic journey.

First I will set the scene as they left Nauvoo. Leonora was among the Saints who crossed the frozen Mississippi from Nauvoo to Sugar Creek, Iowa, in February of 1846.[141] As John Taylor's extensive family left Sugar Creek early in March, Leonora was the matriarch of a fifteen-person household. She had her own three children (twelve-year-old George John, ten-year-old Mary Ann, and eight-year-old Joseph) and two of the children of her recently deceased brother George (nineteen-year-old George Q. and fourteen-year-old Ann).[142] John's sister Elizabeth and his mother, Agnes (whom Leonora refers to her in her diary as "G Mother" and "Grandmother") were with them.[143] Two of John's siblings, William and Agnes, and their father James joined them later. Leonora also refers to "Nanny," a hired girl who helped them in various ways. Also included in the Taylor household were three of John's plural wives referred to earlier: Elizabeth Kaighin, whose baby, Josephine, was born before they reached Winter Quarters; Jane Ballantyne; and Mary Ann Oakley, whom he had married in the recently completed Nauvoo Temple. In her journal, Leonora referred to Jane and Mary Ann as "the Girls," a fitting maternal reference considering how much older she was than they and how much she enjoyed and sought out their companionship.[144] Elizabeth, with whom she had a strained relationship, was the oldest of the three sister wives and fifteen years younger than Leonora. She was never one of "the Girls."

Besides managing this large household, Leonora had many other challenges. Wind, rain, and snow beset them on their trek. On March 7, 1846, she wrote, "*Last night the wind blowing into our tent so hard Mr. T could scarse catch his breath.*" It snowed on March 23 and 25. On April 9 she wrote, "*The Cariage broke down. I had to Walk 3 miles through Mud all the way.*" Her May 1 entry reveals her frustration about how John was allocating his attention. "*Mr T pact the Girls things went with them and left the Children and I [underscored twice] to scramble through the Mud how we Could.*" John's departure for Nauvoo the next day likely fueled her sense of abandonment. That he went to settle financial affairs associated with their abrupt departure from Nauvoo and to pick up Leonora's nephew George Q. may have mitigated her frustration.[145]

---

141 Because of the hasty departure from Nauvoo the Saints were not formally organized but John Taylor was a leader of the group. When they left Winter Quarters, John Taylor and Parley P. Pratt organized the Saints into companies of hundreds, fifties, and tens to prepare for the trek west. Gibbons, John Taylor, 93. The Taylor family were one of the ten families for whom Abraham Hoagland was responsible. While traveling, Leonora's nephew George Q. and the Hoagland's daughter Elizabeth developed a lasting friendship that resulted in marriage.

142 Ann wrote a candid diary that includes memories of crossing the plains with "Aunt Taylor," which is included in Evans and Cannon, 159–183.

143 Leonora refers to three Elizabeths in her diary: Elizabeth (John's sister); Elizabeth Kaighin (John's plural wife); and Elizabeth Whitaker Cain (the sister of Sophia and Harriet Whitaker, John's plural wives).

144 Leonora occasionally referred to them by name or initial.

145 Bitton, 50. George Q. was too ill to leave Nauvoo with the Taylors; he probably stayed with his sister Mary Alice. John and George Q. joined the Saints a month later in Mount Pisgah, well on the way to Winter Quarters

On May 6, four days after John's departure, she met yet another challenge: a hurricane that *"blew down the tents and trees and wreaked heavy damage.... We fled to the wagons and gathered in the children. The men diverted the direction of a tree that was falling or it would have crushed the wagon and carriage."*[146] In a letter to John the following day, Leonora made no mention of the storm but reported, *"Duchman Stable Horse taken sick, cost 300 Dollars, sprained my knee getting out of the Cariage."* Her knee gave her trouble for several weeks. She often had trouble sleeping because of the pain and struggled to get in and out of her tent. She wrote of a sister saint rubbing her knee and also sitting awhile *"with the Girls when knee was very bad."* Juxtaposed with accounts of her pain is her appreciation of beauty and pleasure: *"a fine Moon light Night a Violin playing & a Dance by Gen Richs tent, this place is called Garden Grove and a lovely place it is."*

C.C.A. Christensen, a Danish painter who joined the Church in 1850, painted this scene of Winter Quarters.

During her trek west Leonora turned to her three children for support. Though they were young, she and others expected them to assume adult responsibilities. On April 11 she wrote of her seven year old's heroism. Brother Benson, one of the Saints in the company, came on horseback to the Taylor camp to borrow two oxen. After sizing up Joseph, Brother Benson also borrowed him so he could later return the oxen. Leonora wrote that Brother Benson

> *Put him [Joseph] on his leader horse and made him ride 2 Miles to the Camp where Brother Benson made use of the oxen   then sent him home with the Oxen through Mud that would take a man to his knees   they [the oxen] run in the*

---

146 Having a carriage was probably the mark of John's being the leader of the group. In a later entry she recorded that the carriage had a glass through which she watched the buffalo. We know that the carriage was drawn by horses because of references to a carriage horse being sick.

wood he followed them, and cried all the way home the dear Child was cover'd with Mud from head to foot, he several times lost sight of the road but would not leave his oxen.*

Ten-year-old Mary Ann also helped out. Leonora's entry on April 11, the same date as Joseph's incident with horses, reads, "*Mary Ann Cook'd some Artichokes with potatoes & onions and found them very good.*" Her oldest child, George John, played a significant role in the trek that is described later in this chapter.

One month after leaving the company to go back to Nauvoo, John returned to the company with his nephew, George Q. He met Leonora and the rest of his family at Mt. Pisgah in western Iowa.

Leonora had several interactions with the Indians, more often positive than negative; she found them fascinating:

> *June 11th one of the Pottawatamy Chiefes came to us on a lovely little pony black as Jet and dresed as fine as it could be, so was the Chiefs we gave him some biscute and Tabaco he let the children ride on his poney he said he lived 4 miles of[f].*
>
> *Frid 12th June we Moved at 8 oclock went through a lovely Praiarie about noon came in sight of an Indian Village on a hill it look like a town. . . . I was delighted to see the Indians, Squaes & papooses, all dressed up so smart painted Feathers, beads, Blankets & every thing fantastical the[y] could put on, there was a kickapoo present who talked a little English a very good looking Man & dressd in a large Shawl Nanny fell in love with him, his wigwam was 18 miles of[f].*

Later in Winter Quarters the Saints lived very close to what Leonora interchangeably called the Omehaw and the Ottaw tribe. Adept at living amicably with them, on August 27 she wrote, "*30 Indians of the Omehaw Tribe came Pitche'd a large & small tent on the Hill for them oposite our Tent the Girls George and John went with me to see them ate there Sup[p]er.*[147] *I was very sick all night and am still.*" Though she was sick, the next day "*Six Ottaw Chiefes Dined on a Large Veale Pie I made for them.*" She also wrote about making bread for them. Unfortunately, relationships with the Indians temporarily and unexpectedly deteriorated that fall. On October 18 in Winter Quarters she wrote, "*[W]ent to a meeting all about how we could Guard against the Indians who are Stealing everything the[y] can and killing our Cattle it is proposed to build a wall around the Houses.*"

Toward the end of June, before some of Leonora's entries about the Indians, they reached a village on the Missouri River.[148] Leonora wrote how much she appreciated coming to signs of civilization after being deprived of much she was accustomed to:

---

147 "George" refers to Leonora's nephew George Q., and "John" refers to her son George John.

148 Probably Council Bluffs, Iowa.

Married on the 25th of Jan in 1833 in York Upper Canada by the Revd Lockhart George Born Decr 31st 1834 quarter past five in the evening Fridays came to York to live June 12th 1837 with us 13 Weeks moved Aug to _____ Street _____ Mary Anne born Jan 23 Joind the Mormon Church 1838 Moved to Missouri 1838, Joseph born in indiana June 8th 1838 left the 12th of August 1838 for Missori _____ Mob had to leave in Sept 1839 Stopd at Quincy in June went to Montrose Mr L went to England 8th of August had to leave brother Young's House & livd in the House with Mr O. Prat took chills and feaver second Joseph, he took sick, George took chills had a convulsion. Joseph was sick all winter children had scarlet feaver in the summer

Two pages from Leonora's *First Diary*

Mr Taylor returned 3d of July. I had gone through all but death. during his absence lived in an old barack Room twenty feet square with one small window the lock gone of the hinges and walls so open that a Skunk came in every Night one Winter twice I found a large Snake in the room, naturally nervous and tended my sleep nearly left me—twice when my children were sick, and I had a light in the middle of the night drunken Indians came to the door and there quarreled some to get in others keeping them back, and I alone with three small children I had many privations and many Mercys. I never saw one of Mr Taylors rellations in my House the two years he was away the knew I was a stranger in strange

> *June Sat 20th Mr. T drove Mary Ann I & the Girls to a Concert at the Trading Village.... the Villige is situated on the banks of the Missouri River it did me good to look upon Houses & a good wide river once more after living in a tent or Waggon   going on five Months through Rain frost & Snow   deprived of many comforts we had been acustomed too suffering with pain, and the knowledge that others was a great deal worse of[f], without necessary foods or warm clothing! how long oh! Lord! how long are the Wicked to bear rule and thy afflicted people to be oppresed.*

A week later Leonora recorded her harrowing memories of the martyrdom two years earlier and her concern about the future:

> *Sat [June] 27 this year two Years since poor Br Joseph & Hyrum were Murdered & Father Shot allmost to death in Carthage jail, where shall we be or how situated, this time next year the Lord only knows.*

> *Sun 28. . . . Doct [Willard] Richards said that day two years [ago] he brought the bodys of Br J & H into a people fild with mourning & woe.*[149]

Her relationship with John remained strong and sweet despite their many separations, the difficulties of the trek, and the challenge of sharing his affections with other women. Two days after recalling the sorrows of the martyrdom, she wrote, "*I Knit & Sew'd in the tent all day   took a long walk in the evening with Father   a lovely Night.*" The next morning the Saints loaded their wagons and began crossing the Missouri River to the Nebraska side of the river, where they established Winter Quarters for the winter months before resuming their journey to the Salt Lake Valley. Faced with violent rainstorms and broken wagons, the Saints were delayed in crossing the Missouri for several days.[150] Times were very uncertain. On July 5 Leonora wrote,

> *We are now in the Wilderness   our Property which was worth ten thousand Dollars is gone, all except the Necessaries we have with us, we have been obliged to Sacrafice it to the Mob   if the Lord will Suply us with food & Raiment I care nothing about what we have left. Br Stewart lent us 50 Dollars for which I sincerely thank the Lord.*

On July 25, Leonora wrote that they "*had a dreadfull Storm   a Cow kild by lightning   Grand Mother Children and all dripping wet in our Waggon   all Night there Tents blew down and evry thing scaterd by the Wind.*" On July 29 in the midst of all this turmoil Leonora wrote, almost as an aside, "*heard of Fathers Mission to England   very stormy.*" From other sources we learn that John, along with

---

149 Willard Richards was also with the Prophet when he was killed. Richards, however, was not injured.

150 In the ensuing months the Saints maintained settlements on both sides of the Missouri River, Council Bluffs or Kanesville on the Iowa side and Winter Quarters on the Nebraska side. Leonora makes frequent references to the Saints crossing the river.

Parley P. Pratt and Orson Hyde, was abruptly called to England to settle some serious Church financial and leadership issues.[151] These three men knew the purpose of their trip but not its length, a considerable burden for them and their families.[152]

John managed to keep in touch with Leonora the first months that he was away, mostly through letters carried by missionaries returning to Winter Quarters from New York or England. She received letters dated September 9, October 5, and October 30. John also sent a trunk of clothes and other gifts, which arrived on August 27, before the letters. A diary entry from this time period reflects the complexities of Leonora's life and her appreciation of the clothes John sent to her and her children and niece.[153]

> *[Aug 27th] 30 Indians of the Omehaw Tribe came. Pitche'd a large & small tent on the Hill for them oposite our Tent. . . . I was very sick all night   Br Kimball brought a trunk from the bluffs that Father sent the Children a pair of Shoes a piece, Calico for a Dress for myself M[ary] Ann and Anne. . . . trowsers for the boys & some Tea. I thank the Lord, and him for remembering us.*[154]

Her October 1 entry reads, "*got some Onions, Potatoes, Aples Box of Rasins from Father.*"[155] Her diary reflects the slowness of communication, how out of touch she felt from John on his birthday, and how she relied on a message read in church to know how he was faring: "*E. Babbitt brought me a Letter from Mr. Taylor dated New York September 3, he was to sail for Liverpool on September 8.*" That same entry includes "*wrote him a long letter by Br. Orson Spencer who is going to England on a Mission.*" On November 1, John's birthday, she wrote, "*[It's] Fathers Birthday   I would give some thing to know where & how he is this day.*" Two weeks later she wrote, "*Mr. Taylors letter was read by Br. O. Pratt from the Stand.*" She recorded no further news of or from John until February, almost three months later. While he was gone, Leonora assumed heavy responsibilities including settling into Winter Quarters.

---

151 *Fulness of Times*, 317. Reuben Hedlock, a temporary presiding authority of the Church in England, was channeling money originally earmarked for emigration purposes into schemes for his own financial gain.

152 Gibbons, 87. John Taylor and his companions left July 31 from Winter Quarters. However, Leonora's diary and other sources indicate they were still on the Iowa side. Leonora's diary indicates they crossed on August 4. She wrote; "*Tuesday [Aug 4]. . . . the sand burning hot   Joseph went away down the River & made me very anxious   we crosed in the Evg & Walkd up the Hill to the Prairie.*"

153 That he sent nothing for the sister wives indicates that he regarded them differently.

154 Mary Ann and Anne refer to Leonora's daughter and niece.

155 There is no mention of how he got the food to her.

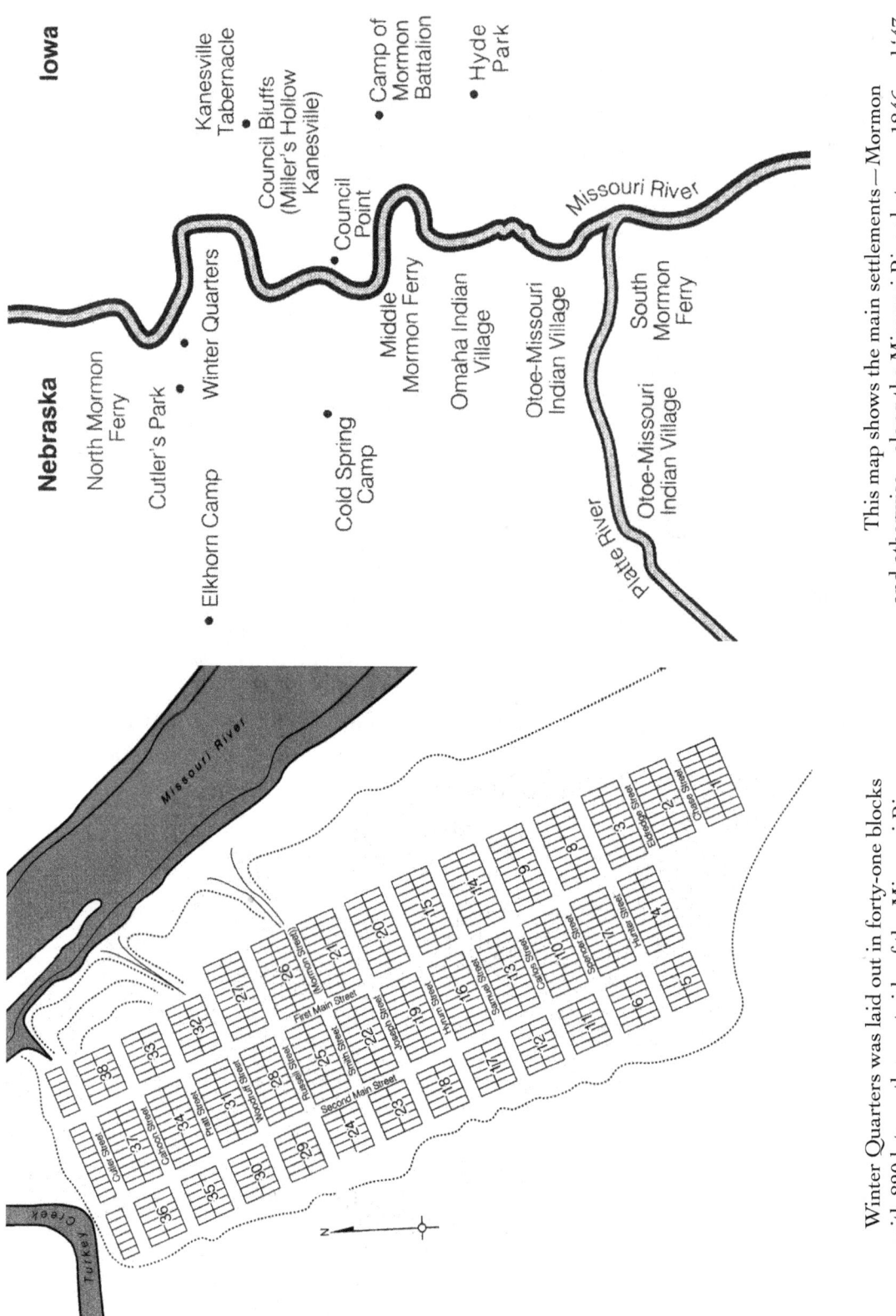

This map shows the main settlements—Mormon and otherwise—along the Missouri River between 1846 and '47. There were about twelve thousand Church members in the area; approximately four thousand were in Winter Quarters.

Winter Quarters was laid out in forty-one blocks with 820 lots on the west side of the Missouri River.

Because of the imminence of winter and the departure of five hundred of their ablest men who had recently joined the Mormon Battalion, the Saints decided to stay at Winter Quarters through the cold months rather than continue to travel west.[156] While in Winter Quarters the Saints followed their usual pattern of creating a cohesive well planned community for themselves and for those who would follow. By the end of September, plots for 820 houses were laid out.[157]

Her November 8 entry captured the rhythm of her life during her time in Winter Quarters: "*I went to see Sis Nobles who had buried her babe..... agre'ed with Chancy West to send our Cattle with him to winter on the.... bottoms at 2$ a head for the Winter. I feel thankfull to night for the Mercys of the Lord. the Omehaws set of[f] on there Winter hunt to day.*"

In the midst of helping others and finding ways to sustain her family, her most pressing responsibility was to supervise the construction of her house; as with other tasks, she enlisted the help of her children. Twelve-year-old George John, whom she usually referred to as John when her husband was away, took on the responsibilities of a man. On October 12 she wrote, "*John set off again to cut logs this week.*"[158] We learn that nine days later "*John went with the Bretheren to raft down the Logs.*" On October 30 "*John Hawling Hay*" and on November 13, "*John began to split the logs for the house.*" The following Monday "*John & William put up the House. it is 20 feet long by 16. we build our Chimney outside of Sod & line them with Brick. I got 4 hundred [bricks] for 3 fire places.*"[159] Three days later Leonora showed her practical ingenuity by paying for the work with material goods. "*Nov. 19th got 50 cts worth of Nails to put the Roof on the house and traded a Coat of Mr Taylors his old grey, for 7 Dollars worth of Clap Boards.*" On December 2 she wrote, "*Boys saming [sawing] the Flooring for The House*" and "*George & William comenced to make the window Sash at night.*"

A week later they moved into the House: "*[Dec. 15th] our change is greatly for the better   the house is very comfortable indeed considering.*" Just before Christmas Leonora wrote, "*Wed 23d I have been Sick two days   our House is so warm and comfortable that I take cold if I go into anny of my neighboures.*" Three days later, the warm comfort turned out to be a hazard because the house smoked excessively. Concerned about the safety of her home, Leonora directed efforts to pull the chimney down and build it up again.

A continuing challenge that Leonora faced while John was away was procuring food to feed her household of fifteen. At the end of the diary, Leonora included detailed accounts of what she paid for food, building supplies for the house, and other necessities, an illustration of her prudent management of the family's finances. In mid-fall, her cattle wandered off while she

---

156 Leonora makes a reference to the Mormon Battalion in her diary. The Mormom Battalion was a group of Latter-day Saint men who, at the request of President James K. Polk, enlisted in the U.S. Army to serve in the Mexican-American War. They marched from Council Bluffs, Iowa to San Diego, California, a journey on today's roads of 1,600 miles.

157 "Before Christmas 700 log homes, roofed over with clapboards or with willows and dirt, were occupied by about 3,500 people." Allen and Leonard, *The Story of the Latter-day Saints*, 234.

158 Reflecting how much Leonora depends on her son when her husband is gone, she refers to her son as George when her husband is present and as John when he is away.

159 William probably refers either to John's brother William, who had joined them, or possibly to William Farrer. Leonora got her bricks from Brother Patten, something she mentioned in her October 27 entry.

and the Girls were on an overnight trip to pick grapes. Leonora responded to this and other challenges by praying to God and enlisting the help of her son George John as well as her sister wives, Jane and Mary Ann:

> *I went off in the woods & prayed that the[y] [the cattle] might be found. John walkd all day & could not find them. it was near Sundown. he gave them up & went to borrow a Yolk of Cattle to take the Wagon.... when he was gone I asked the Girls to go into the woods to look for them. we found them without any trouble.*[160]

Just as he did with building their house, John, now almost thirteen, assumed an adult role in procuring food for the family. On December 21 he started to Missouri for provisions and did not return until January 11.

The constant struggle to find ways to feed her household was particularly difficult because people betrayed her trust. On October 30 Leonora wrote, "*What shall I do for bread for the Family this winter my Father only knows.*" A fellow saint, R. Ballantine, had kept money that John had given him to give to Leonora.[161] "*I should have had 8 Barrels of Flour purchased with that money,*" her diary reads. Still angry two weeks later about Ballantine's letting her down, Leonora wrote, "*[Nov 17] Br. Balantine Calld I spoke to him about the Money He said if Mr Taylor had been at home he [Br. Balantine] would not have given up any of the things he bought but kept them to remunerate him for his trouble. oh! honesty & honour where art thou fled.*"

Leonora wrote of disappointments with another Saint and how overwhelmed she felt about tending to ailing people under her care with John away:

> *Wed [Nov] 11th Br Peirce cald he has returnd from Philadelphia Mr T arranged with him to bring me a Stove and some grocires he brought me nothing I have had William Farer Sick 10 weeks Br Wright is here Sick and a daughter of [Jim?] Cowlas She is here sick & no where to go I have a Family of 15 to Provide for I pray the Lord to helpe me and enable me to Provide for so many untile my Husband returns.*

Interwoven with these problems of people letting her down and not having enough food are her dealings with Elizabeth Kaighin, a sister-wife. Though Leonora participated in choosing her cousin Elizabeth as John's first plural wife, the two developed a troubled relationship as early as Nauvoo. We know this because of Leonora's reference in the following excerpt to Elizabeth's "old ways." Leonora does not fully explain the details of their differences but does convey their mutual animosity:

---

160 The John referred to here is her fourteen-year-old son, George John.

161 Richard Ballantyne was Jane Ballantyne's brother. He later organized the first Sunday School in the Salt Lake Valley. As far as I can tell the correct spelling is Ballantyne. Leonora uses Ballantine which I use when I quote her.

> *Fri [Dec] 4th Elizabeth began her Old ways   I took her in to keep her Tounge still, for my own & familys Sake that if possible we might not be abused through the whole Camp, I had expected her House had been ready long ago, She ordered me to give them two tables cloths that She left here when She left and a muff that She gave me   I told her when I took it [the muff] on account of my hand I would send for one to England for her   I did so, but it never came   She declared She never gave it   so much for veracity   I cannot live with her after what She has said before my Family, all the abuse & insinuations her Evill nature could devise.*[162]

Two days later Leonora's diary reads, "*Sund 6th I was Ill all night   E[lizabeth] got up Drest & went of[f] with her babe   She stay at Br Cooliges a few days   She came back to Sister Horns.*" Six days later Elizabeth returned to Leonora for help. Given the dynamics of their relationship, it must have been very difficult for Elizabeth to ask Leonora for help. "*Sat [Dec 12th] E[lizabeth] came in the Night for Honey   her Child had the Croup   She startled me out of my Sleep   I got up and gave her what I could for it   I ment it for the Childs sake   it is quite well again.*"

As mentioned earlier, Leonora had much more compatible relationships on the trek with her other sister wives. She often looked to them for company and comfort. Early in the journey she wrote, "*Sunday [April] 12th [1846]. . . . I sat in the Girls tent all the afternoon.*" She also mentioned two excursions they took together. "*Th [June 18th] went with the. . . . Girls & Children about two Miles in the Cariage to an encampment of the Brethren to get Strawberrys   the[y] were more plentyfull there than anny place I ever saw   the[y] gathered them by Bushels[.]*"

Leonora took care of the Girls' needs. "*Tusd Dec 1st sent Jane [Ballantyne] Rice Sugar Coffy Apples   the Girls have got Mrs pinkhams Stove.*" In a maternal fashion she expressed concern about their emotional well-being and the kind of company they kept. When Leonora expressed how much she missed her husband on his birthday she also wrote, "*I felt as if I could weep all the time of Meeting   that unfortunate Girl of Ballantines came over the River to Meetting   I am Sory to see Mary Anne Oakley Seen with such a one.*"[163] Although Leonora is compatible with Jane Ballantyne, her sister-wife, she had a strained relationship with some of the Ballantynes; as mentioned earlier, Brother Ballantyne failed to deliver food and money as he had promised he would. From the entry just cited, it seems that Ann, their sister, was influencing Mary Anne in ways that displeased Leonora.

Another entry indicates that Leonora was hurt that Sister Ballantyne did not invite her to a social gathering. Although the details of what happened are unclear, her heartache as well as her desire to overcome hurt feelings and to practice The Principle well are evident: "*Sun [Dec

---

162 This reference to her hand is likely regarding her recovery from the amputation of her finger.

163 Foster, "The Plural Wives of the Prophets." "Over the river" is a reference to the settlement on the Iowa side of the Missouri River. Leonora was no doubt referring to Richard and Jane Ballantyne's sister Annie, who later was sealed to John but didn't become part of the extended household. John being sealed to Annie must have been particularly painful to Leonora.

28]. . . . *I was too sick to go when the[y] eat I went a short time in the evening took a violent Cold had to keep my bed next day, why I was not invited when the Girls were I cannot tell She [the hostess] knows well that I have been Friendly with them [the Girls] all the time.*"[164]

She also reported negative emotions when she felt that she or others had been treated unjustly. For example, when her husband returned to Nauvoo to settle their property, she wrote, "*14th [May]. . . . I hope while there, he will do me Justice and contradict the Stories his B.W. and Robins has told which he himself knows to be false, on Thee my blessed Savior I would cast my care my deep Sorrow and distress thy eye alone has seen it all.*"[165]

Clearly, living The Principle was a continuing challenge for Leonora. One thing that helped her cope with the complexities of dealing with her sister wives was that they were clearly an adjunct to her position as the first wife. When Leonora went on a carriage ride with John, she wrote of her children and the Girls coming along. When John sent a trunk of clothes and other gifts for her family, it included nothing for the sister wives. When she hosted a party, Jane and Mary Ann, her sister wives, were her guests.

Although it is unclear how much of the time Leonora's sister wives were sharing her living quarters, it appears that most of the time the Girls were in separate quarters from her as well as from Elizabeth Kaighin. On June 7, 1846, Leonora wrote that "*Sister O [Oakley] Mary Ann & Jane & Maggy took supper with us,*" an indication Mary Ann Oakley and Jane Ballantyne were living in another tent as they crossed Iowa.[166] At the end of December she wrote, "*Wed [Dec] 30th my Head very bad Girls moveing into their house.*" As mentioned earlier, Elizabeth, with whom she had a strained relationship, lived with her temporarily in early December in Winter Quarters. Leonora makes no reference to when Elizabeth moved into separate quarters.

After Leonora's house was finished, her diary indicates her home was often used as an infirmary and for Church meetings as well as a gathering place for the Saints, including Leonora's sister wives. During John's absence, Leonora mentioned a festive family dinner that she hosted soon after moving into her new house. "*Mond [January 4, 1847] preparing to have a party of our own Family G. Father G. Mother Elizabeth Agnes [John's parents and two sisters] R. Ballantine, Jane, Mary Anne, Elizabeth [Kaighin & Child]. . . . [George] & Annie Cannon. [Leonora's nephew and niece]. . . . George, Mary Ann, Joseph [and several neighbors]. . . . a goodly company, very cheerfull and pleasant.*"[167] In all she had a party of forty-two that day.

Eventually, even with John gone, her life in Winter Quarters gradually assumed a rhythm and sense of normalcy. Entries from the time period after her house was finished include references to her nephew George Q. teaching the school-aged children, her picking up her children from dancing lessons, and attending a ball with her daughter Mary Ann.

---

164 The hostess is probably Sister Ballantyne.

165 It is unclear who B.W. and Robins are.

166 Apparently Mary Ann Oakley's family was part of the company. I don't know who Maggy is. There are other references to Mary Ann and Jane having a separate tent.

167 Her "own family" included John's parents, his sisters—Elizabeth and Agnes—her sister wives, her own children, and her brother's children. In the margins of the appropriate page in her diary she noted that the party was held on Old Christmas Day, a holiday she had celebrated in England.

Unfortunately, part of the normalcy was sickness and death. She wrote of her own "dreadful" headaches and being unable to sleep because of the pain in her knee, an ailment that sometimes kept her from Sunday meetings. Even while she was in pain, Leonora often offered relief to others who were sick. During this time she wrote, "*I visited the sick and gave medicine.*" On another occasion she promised to go back to an ill person in the evening, but "*my Head ached so I could not think of it.*" On August 24, 1846, she wrote, "*vissited the Sick a great many Sick in the Camp I am very unwell myself [with a] headach all the time.*" Leonora extended her healing to the animals. She applied "*oil & poltice of Salt & Onions to a Cariage Horse bitten badly by a RattleSnake.*"

Leonora made repeated references to caring for Sister Benbow. "*[Nov 6]. . . . I made Calves feet Jelly for Sister Benbow.*" The following day she wrote, "*I made Gingerbread for S. Benbow.*" Then in late November, "*I was at Sis. Benbows, most of the Week on Friday [Nov] 27th made her Cap She died that night at 12 Oclock Sat. 28 made her Garment laid her out on Sund 29 we went to the Funeral.*"[168]

Later that winter she wrote of more difficulties with the weather and with the Indians: "*very high Winds. . . . the Souix Indians were killing our Cattle and had stolen 13, Horses the[y] quareled about them and Shot them all but one I sent 3 Yoke of Cattle to fetch the Poor from Nauvoo.*" The spare details Leonora records might lead a reader to conclude she was detached and unemotional. A more accurate assessment is that losing family members and friends was a frequent occurrence and that the demands of daily lives did not afford time for reflecting on and recording her thoughts.

All of the events described after the end of July 1846 took place during the eight months John was away in England. She lamented his absence several times and sometimes did not receive word from him for weeks at a time. About the time the Indians killed some of her cattle, February 1, 1847, she finally "*got a letter from Father dated 4th of Nov for which I am very thankfull.*" and ended the entry with "*Sister Sheets Died I went with Sister Woodsforth to Vissit S. Bringhurst.*"

Until receiving the February 1st letter, she had not heard from John directly since October 31. Three weeks later she noted, "*Thursday [Feb 25]. . . . I expect Father back from England in April*" with no mention of the source of the news. A month later, she wrote, "*Mon [March] 22d. . . . All Sick, I feell very unwell myself but am thankfull to the Lord for the measure of health I injoy and that my Children are kept in health I hope soon to see Father.*"

Though Leonora wrote many times and in many ways how much she missed John, she made no reference in her diary to his return or who returned with him. Unbeknownst to her, two weeks before her February 25 entry, John sailed from England with a small group of Saints that included the Whitaker sisters—Sophia, Elizabeth, and Harriet. Either on the ocean voyage or in Council Bluffs three days after his return, John married twenty-two-year-old Sophia as his fifth wife.[169]

Having John return after his long absence with yet another attractive young bride must have caused Leonora deep pain. This portion of her diary ends at the top of an otherwise blank page and leaves the back side of the page blank. After the last entry in her diary from Winter

---

168 The cap and garment are references to temple clothes that Sister Benbow was to be buried in.

169 Gibbons, 92. Gibbons states that Joseph Cain married Elizabeth Whitaker and that John married Sophia Whitaker as they travelled on the ocean. In contrast, Miller, "Sophia Whitaker Taylor," places John and Sophia's marriage as April 23, 1847, in Council Bluffs, three days after their arrival. John married Harriet Whitaker December 4, 1847, soon after they reached the Salt Lake Valley.

Quarters, April 1, shortly before John's return with Sophia, Leonora did not touch pen to paper until their departure from Winter Quarters in early June. Terse and unemotional, her first entry in June, along with her lengthy break from writing, indicates she was struggling to keep her composure. "*June [blank space] left Winter Quarters at ½ past 3 oclock. traveled 4 miles broke the tounge in a Waggon Campt on a beautyfull Prairy.*"

Some subsequent entries affirm Leonora's position as John's first wife:

> *Wed [July 14] went out hunting Buffalow again & saw thousands Mr T rode I took grandmother in the cariage*[170] *our Company kil'd 9 evry person bussy drying Buffalow I like it much better than Beef, more tender and pleasand truly the Lord Has spread a Table for us in the Wilderness we have not seen one Indian since we left winter Quarters.*

> *Sat [July] 17 Mr. T in the Waggons all afternoon. . . . I sat up to prepare for Elizabeth Taylors wedding about 11 Oclock we heard a dreadfull roaring of Bufalow the gaurd cald evry man to arise Thousand of Bufalow were crosing the River. . . . great fear least the[y] Should land & run over our Wagons. . . .*[171]

> *Sunday [July 19] went to meeting in Cariage took M. A. O [Mary Anne Oakley] Sophia [Whittaker], Anny & Mary Ann after Meetting Mr T. Babtised Joseph and 10, other children. . . . [Tues] 20th. . . . went hunting Buffalow in the Cariage along with Mr. Taylor.*[172]

It is noteworthy that Leonora mentioned Sophia by name as traveling with them—an indication that Leonora was able to acknowledge Sophia as a member of the family.

The absence of Indians since leaving Winter Quarters was unusual. After the early positive references to Indians, Leonora reported their cattle being taken and property stolen as well as her fear of the Indians capturing her children. However, as the following diary entry indicates, she was ready to interact with the Indians in good faith and participate in joint activities. Her openness, curiosity, and respect are apparent: "*Frid [July] 23rd Br Prat sent a messenger to the Camp to let us know that 100 Indians had been at there camp the next morning we were vissited by a number of them the[y] Danced 14 Weomen & 3 Men, traded for Buffalow Robes with a good Manny smoked the Pipe of Peace gave them food our foulks danced had musick.*" A few days later, Leonora reported

---

170 Probably a reference to John's mother

171 Elizabeth is John's younger sister for whom Leonora made the wedding dress. FamilySearch.org indicates the marriage date as July 16, 1847.

172 Mary Ann Oakley and Sophia Whitaker, John's plural wives. Anny refers to Leonora's niece Ann. The second "Mary Ann" mentioned is John and Leonora's daughter. "Joseph" refers to their younger son.

her anxiety that the Indians had come close to taking her daughter, Mary Ann. *"Tues [July] 27 M.A. rode the Mare & stopt behind I felt very much frightened lest the Indians had got both her and the horse.... her Father rode back and found her we crose'd a Creek and some Sand Hills."*[173]

The same entry includes a moving report of a potentially heartbreaking accident involving her son George John, age thirteen. *"I don't know how I got to him"* captures the depth of her consternation and concern. The passage referring to Mary Ann's whereabouts continues,

> *Soon after we Started at Noon. there was a cry that a Child was run over and the next cry that it was George Taylor I don't know how I got to him he lay on his back the first word he said was I am not hurt mother his poor breast & back was bruised black he [had] stood on the toung[ue] to whip his oxen his feet sliped & he fell on his face both wheels of a heavy loaded wagon run over his back I road with him in Br. Hogelins [Hoagland] wagon to our Camping place had him bled, put on a poultice of wormwood and vinegar had hands laid on and trust in the Lord, he will soon be well.*[174]

After reporting this wrenching experience, Leonora ended the day's entry with a matter-of-fact statement about how far they had traveled: *"found a board left by the Pioneres[:] from Winter Quarters 409 miles."*

In early September the company reached South Pass in Wyoming, three hundred miles east of Salt Lake.[175] There they met Brigham Young, who had just finished establishing the initial settlement in the Salt Lake Valley. He was leading a group back to Winter Quarters to help Saints prepare to move west. It was an important time for the leaders to reassess their settlement plans and to determine how best to bring the remaining Saints to the Valley. When Brigham Young joined them at South Pass, Leonora was in charge of a meal that set the stage for the leaders' meeting. Gibbons, John Taylor's biographer, reports the lavish affair, later remembered as the "Feast in the Wilderness":

> As the leaders parlayed, the sisters, aided by some of the other brethren[,] selected a nearby grassy spot, out of the sight of the camp, where makeshift tables were set up. On these were placed snow-white linens, gleaming silverware, and treasured dishes, the remnants of gracious living in Nauvoo, which had been stored in trunks. Meanwhile, others were busy preparing fish, game, veal, and hot biscuits and loading the tables with fruits, vegetables, jams, jellies,

---

173 This is one of the few times Leonora refers to John indirectly as the father to their children, rather than by his name or as her husband.

174 Abraham Hoagland was Leonora's bishop then and later in the 14th Ward in Salt Lake. He was also the father of Elizabeth Hoagland, George Q. Cannon's wife and my great-grandmother.

175 By today's paved roads the trip is 249 miles and by trail it is 300.

and condiments that had been bottled at the other end of the trail. . . . Their appetites were satisfied by a feast they would savor and reflect upon for years afterward.[176]

Leonora was in charge of preparing and serving the food as well as setting up the tables. She reported the event more simply in her diary:

Tud. morng [Sept 7th] had a meetting of the Sisters   apointed S. Hunter, S. Thomas & I to regulate a Diner for the Pioners an[d] Volunteers   had a splendid Diner for them in the Grove   about a hundred sat down, the[y] had a dance after, the 12 met in Counsel, until 1 oclock   it snowed untill the afternoon when it became fine   the 12 Breakfasted with us and started for Winter Quarters.

Like Leonora, John introduced a touch of class and culture into the wilderness.[177] He also understated the opulence of the event in his journal: "*We mutually felt edified and rejoiced; we praised the Lord, and blessed one another.*"[178]

Less than a month after this festive occasion, the goal of reaching the Valley was in sight. Leonora ended her diary as she began it, objectively relating recurring mishaps and acknowledging the depth of her trials, but with a strong affirmation of the goodness and power of God: "*Sund. Started late. an ox was missing   went up & down a steep hill   Rob Gardners child ran over   Tra[veled] 13 mi[les]   I feel & know in all my trials [trials underlined three times] that the Lord is near and that he blesses and Comforts my Heart   they that trust in the Lord shall never be Confounded.*" On October 6, 1847, they entered the Salt Lake Valley, blessed and comforted by the faith that they would never be confounded because of their trust in the Lord.[179]

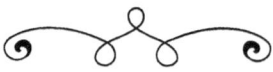

---

176 Gibbons, 95.

177 Ibid., 92. That John Taylor was aware of what was needed to create a viable settlement is evident in what he brough a map of John C. Fremont's recent expedition to the Western territories as well as instruments for determining latitude, elevation, temperature, and barometric pressure.

178 *Millennial Star* 10: 325, quoted in Gibbons, 95.

179 There are discrepancies among accounts of when they arrived in the Valley. Elizabeth Kaighin's biographer says September 29, 1847; Harriet Whitaker's indicates October 2, 1847.

After arriving in the Valley, the Taylors rented a portion of the old pioneer fort from members of the Mormon Battalion, who had reached the Valley ahead of the pioneers.[180] The Taylors lived in the old Pioneer Fort for at least the first winter.[181] By Christmas of that year, they had built and covered a ninety-foot-long building made of split logs. They used planks to separate the different wives' living quarters.[182]

John and Leonora Taylor's first home in Salt Lake Valley. They lived here from 1847 to 1848. It was located close to 300 South and present-day 300 West.

We see the practical sharing side of Leonora while living at the Fort in excerpts from the diary of Isabella Horne, who was her friend while crossing the plains and who now lived by her at the Fort. Isabella reminisced that Leonora *"brought a piece of bolting cloth with her. One of the men made a frame, tacked the cloth to it making a sieve, which was borrowed [lent] all around the Fort when the Sisters wanted to make a few white biscuits."*[183] Isabella also remembered that *"Sister Leonora Taylor was among the first. . . . to plant apple and fruit seeds. The trees were transplanted on their [the Horne or the Taylor] lot in the 14th Ward, where they grew to be very large trees, and produced fine large fruit of excellent flavor."*[184]

---

180 The log fort was located on the block bounded by 300 South, 400 South, 300 West, and 400 West. This block is currently Pioneer Park.

181 Ann Cannon Woodbury's account in Evans and Cannon, 169. Leonora's brother George's children Ann and George Q. Cannon lived with them. According to Ann's account, at some point after the first winter they moved to the south fort and lived there until moving to Taylor Row.

182 Florence T. Miller, "Sophia Whitaker Taylor," in *Seven Wives of John Taylor*. In Family History Library Salt Lake City Utah.

183 M. Isabella Horne, "In Early Days. Home Life in the Pioneer Fort," *Juvenile Instructor* 29 (March 15, 1894): 183, quoted in Nielson, 182. This may have been the "muslin" Leonora asked John to send her when she wrote him from Montrose in 1839, while he was serving a mission in England.

184 Ibid.

As they coped with the problems of settling on a new frontier, the family continued to grow. On December 4, 1847, John married his sixth plural wife, Sophia's sister, Harriet Whitaker.[185] After marrying Harriet, John built a row of houses called Taylor Row with a unit for each wife, on the western half of the block bounded by South Temple, First South, West Temple, and present-day Second West, one block southwest of where the temple would be built.[186] He also built a nail factory on the southern portion of the property. The Taylors moved to Taylor Row sometime in the early 1850s. One record indicates that the Row existed from 1850 to 1887.[187]

As part of the ongoing effort to spread the gospel throughout the world, in 1849 Brigham Young called John to serve a mission to France and Germany, which he did from October 1849 to March 1852.[188] Leonora and her sister wives could have engineered a move to their new home while he was gone; it seems more likely they moved after he returned. The biographer of John's plural wife Mary Ann Oakley supports this view; she writes that Mary Ann and her newborn son, Henry, were living in a wagon box when John's sister, Elizabeth Boyce, had them come to live with her in Cottonwood until John returned from his mission to France.[189]

John's writings indicate that he had an exalted view of what family life could be. "Books and musical instruments are now so cheap as to be within the reach of the most humble. By furnishing means of instruction, amusement, and enjoyment at home parents can. . . . tie their children to them by bonds of affection that can never be broken."[190] In a letter to George John, his oldest son, he wrote, "*I wish you to pay attention to your studies and I have sent you two French books. . . . Don't forget or neglect the German, but perfect that and learn the French also. If Joseph [James] can learn it you can teach him and baby Anna [Marie]. . . . Until I see you again, and forever I remain, Your affectionate father.*"[191] These passages are reminiscent of the tenderness John expressed in the notes and drawings he sent from England in 1840 to Leonora, to this same son, George John, and to daughter Mary Ann. However, now, as before, he was seldom able to spend time with his children in such pleasurable activities because of his many calls to serve missions and other Church duties as well as his responsibility for multiple households.

---

185 Gibbons, 53.

186 Leonora's dear friend Phoebe Woodruff lived on the northeast corner of the same block, where the Abravanel Hall now stands.

187 "Homes of the Prophets: John Taylor," Moroni's Latter-day Saint Page, accessed April 4, 2014, http://www.moroni10.com/prophets_homes/John_Taylor.html.

188 Gibbons, 106–27. A main accomplishment was his translation of the Book of Mormon into French. He returned sometime before August 22, 1852, when he referred to this translation as "as good a one as it is possible for anybody to make." Franklin D. Richards was called to Great Britain; Lorenzo Snow to Italy; and Erastus Snow to Denmark. Gibbons, 106, 121.

189 Ruth C. Smith, "Mary Ann Oakley Taylor," in *Seven Wives of John Taylor*. Elizabeth is John's sister for whom Leonora made the wedding dress as they crossed the plains.

190 "Homes of the Prophets: John Taylor," Moroni's Latter-day Saint Page, accessed April 4, 2014. http://www.moroni10.com/prophets_homes/John_Taylor.html

191 John Taylor Collection, reel 1, folder 3, item 2; from St. Louis, February 11, 1850, quoted in J. Lewis Taylor, "John Taylor: Family Man," in *Champion of Liberty: John Taylor*, ed. Mary Jane Woodger (Provo, UT: Religious Studies Center, Brigham Young University, 2009): 193–218.

Taylor Row was located in the 14th Ward, where many Church leaders lived. The Taylors had crossed the plains with several members of the ward, including the Hoagland, Horne, Ballantyne, Woodruff, and Richards families. These families had been and continued to be intertwined. Abraham Hoagland (who had been such a help when the wagon crushed her son George John while crossing the plains) was Leonora's bishop, both as they crossed the plains and in the 14th Ward. He and his first wife, Margaret Quick, were parents to Elizabeth Hoagland, who married Leonora's nephew George Q. Cannon in 1854.[192] Agnes Taylor, John Taylor's sister who crossed the plains with the Taylors, was one of Bishop Hoagland's plural wives.[193] Another member of the ward was Mary Edwards White Cannon, the widow of Leonora's brother George.[194]

In 1852, while the Taylors were living in their new quarters in the 14th Ward, Apostle Orson Pratt, under the direction of Brigham Young, made the public announcement that the Church was practicing plural marriage under commandment of God.[195] Adverse reactions to the public announcement that Mormons were openly practicing polygamy rallied the anti-polygamist forces nationwide. In 1854, to neutralize the groundswell of anti-Mormon feeling that had grew after the practice of plural marriage was made public, Brigham Young called John Taylor to preside over the Eastern States Mission. One of his chief tasks was to publish a newspaper, *The Mormon*, to present the doctrine in a favorable manner.[196] While on this mission, he met Margaret Young, the attractive nineteen-year-old daughter of a prosperous local Church leader, and married her September 27, 1856, in Connecticut.[197] A year later John returned to Utah with Margaret, the last wife with whom he had children. We have no record of Leonora's or the other wives' feelings about this attractive young wife becoming part of the family.[198]

---

192 The map of the 14th Ward indicates that George Q. owned a piece of property; perhaps he and Elizabeth lived there for a time.

193 Agnes later divorced Bishop Hoagland, remained active in the ward, and married William Schwartz. Later when John Taylor lived in the Gardo House as president of the Church, Agnes lived there and served as his hostess when rigorous enforcement of the Edmunds-Tucker Act made it prudent for his wives to live elsewhere.

194 Nielson, 176–178. George married Mary Edwards White February 24, 1844 after his wife Ann Quayle died while crossing the ocean. After George's death in St. Louis in August 1844 Mary had a child, Elizabeth Edwards Cannon, on February 21, 1845. After reaching the Valley, Mary married Charles Barber Taylor, no known relation to John Taylor.

195 *Fulness of Times*, 424.

196 Gibbons, 138. Brigham Young called other key leaders to publish favorable press in other areas: Orson Pratt to Washington, DC, Erastus Snow and Orson Spencer to St. Louis, and George Q. Cannon to San Francisco.

197 Mary Gibbs Merrill, "Margaret Young Taylor," in *Seven Wives of John Taylor*.

198 John was forty-eight when he married nineteen-year-old Margaret; Leonora was sixty.

Margaret joined Leonora and her sister wives in Taylor Row. There was much to occupy the minds of these women besides their challenging polygamous marriages. On May 13, 1857, Apostle Parley P. Pratt was murdered in Arkansas.[199] Parley's death would have been a severe loss to the Taylors. He had been an integral part of their lives since he introduced them to the Church in Toronto. Four months later, a tragedy occurred in southern Utah. Emigrants traveling from Arkansas to California stopped in Salt Lake City and then traveled south about 300 miles to Mountain Meadow, thirty-five miles southwest of present-day Cedar City, Utah. The Latter-day Saints who had recently settled in this area were anxious to protect their communities, having suffered multiple attacks as they crossed the plains. Recent heated debates with the federal government turned their anxiety to paranoia.

Though the Arkansas emigrants posed no threat to the Saints' religious practices or to their livelihoods, local Church leaders planned an attack on them and persuaded the Paiute Indians that they should be afraid as well. The results were disastrous: 120 innocent emigrants were killed and multiple Saints—Church leaders among them—were caught red-handed in what came to be called the Mountain Meadow Massacre. Causing further anxiety for the Taylor wives was that federal government seemed close to success in its efforts to govern the Territory directly by sending an army under the direction of Colonel Albert Sidney Johnston to occupy Salt Lake City and try to eliminate polygamy[200].

Tensions ran high. To help quell these uncertainties swirling around them, the Relief Society women in the Salt Lake 14th Ward, with Phoebe Woodruff as their president, turned to their needles and made an heirloom American Album quilt. What had begun as making a quilt to celebrate the tenth anniversary of the Saints' entry into the Valley became an avenue for dealing with their present anxieties.[201] Each woman designed and did creative needle work to create a square.[202] Leonora's block consisted of many small pieces of fabric.[203] The message on the square that Leonora contributed assertively addressed the threat of Johnston's Army occupying Salt Lake. More importantly it embodied the underpinnings of her life. In bold block letters she emphatically stated in crewel embroidery "IN GOD IS OUR TRUST," under which she signed her name in an unassuming, small script. It seems significant that with the choice of writing "our

---

199 Nielson, 151. Parley had proposed to a married woman, who then left her drunkard husband and married Parley as a polygamous wife; the husband took his revenge and killed Pratt.

200 Allen and Leonard, 306.

201 Nielson, 14.

202 For a fascinating insightful article on the interplay between the 14th Ward album quilt and historical events see Laurel Thatcher Ulrich, "An American Album, 1857," *The American Historical Review* 115, no. 1 (February 2010): 1–25.

203 "In the five blocked letters of the first two words, 'In God,' there are eighty-nine separate pieces of cloth; the finished size of the smallest is only one-quarter inch." Nielson, *The Salt Lake 14th Ward Album Quilt*, 33. She may have saved some of the pieces from the fabric she requested John to send to Montrose for her in 1839 when she was ill and alone with her babies while he served the mission to England and he introduced her brother George and his family to the gospel.

trust," rather than "my trust." Leonora was encouraging not just herself or the women of the 14th Ward but all of the Saints in the Valley to put their trust in God as they tried to live their own beliefs peacefully while beginning to join the wider American society.

Leonora Cannon Taylor's Quilt Block for the 14th Ward Album Quilt 1857

The federal army did not make it to Utah in 1857 because of the efforts of the Saints to prevent the Army coming through the canyon.[204] The following spring, under Brigham Young's direction, the Saints evacuated Salt Lake, leaving nothing to occupy when the army did arrive. The Saints left no trace of their community or the eleven years they had spent making the desert "blossom as a rose." Leaving her home must have been especially difficult for Leonora, who had been forced to move from Kirtland, Far West, Nauvoo, and now Taylor's Row in Salt Lake. The Taylor family got as far as Provo when they learned Johnston's Army had not come into the Valley and that residents could now return to their homes.

We have little knowledge of the remaining ten years of Leonora's life. We know she remained a stalwart member of the Church and never sought a public role or prominence. We know that she remained close to her brother George's children and wrote letters to them; however, we have no diary from this time period. The original account I have of her life states simply that she "made her home in Salt Lake City, where her history follows that of the church."[205]

---

204 Allen and Leonard, 306.

205 Morgan and Taylor, "Leonora Cannon Taylor."

At the time of her death, Leonora was still the matriarch of the family clan; her word was final in matters among the wives. Although John had loved and married others, none could ever occupy Leonora's special place, either in the patriarchal order of the family or in his heart.[206] She died of pneumonia December 9, 1868, four years after her nephew Angus' son Lewis, my grandfather, was born; one year after her nephew George Q.'s daughter Mary Alice, my grandmother, was born; one year after the Relief Society was officially reestablished; one year before the east and west railroads were joined (an event that signaled the beginning of Utah's opening to the outside world); and twelve years before her husband became president of the Church. Leonora missed the gala reception at the Gardo House, where two thousand Saints came to give their good wishes to John and his wives in their new home.[207] She also missed the uncertainty and heartache of John's last four years, when he directed the affairs of the Church from the Underground in a secluded home in Kaysville, where he died.[208]

With the help of my Aunt Marge—Marjorie, my father's sister—I found Leonora's grave in the Salt Lake City Cemetery in the Avenues neighborhood of Salt Lake City. I was very happy to see her name in big letters with an account of her life on one side of the large family vertical monument and details of John's life on another side. The other wives' gravestones are arranged, somewhat haphazardly, on the ground beside the large headstone. I am sorry that the other wives are shortchanged in the placement of the gravestones and perhaps in their marriages, but I am grateful that Leonora is recognized as a full and equal partner to John. My heart aches for how difficult her life was. I am sure her descendants are grateful for their heritage.[209] I know her brother George's numerous descendants are profoundly grateful to her for being the conduit that brought the gospel into our lives.

---

[206] Samuel Taylor, 230.

[207] Gibbons, 222. The Gardo House was the 1880 residence of the President of the Church.

[208] Ibid., 269. Together plural wives Mary Ann Oakley and Margaret Young visited John Taylor together during the final week of his life. Sophia and Harriet Whitaker, like Leonora, preceded him in death.

[209] George John never married; Leonora Agnes died as a baby in 1843; Mary Ann Taylor Redfield has descendants living largely in California and Hawaii; Joseph James's descendants live mostly in Utah and southern Alberta, Canada.

Elizabeth Hoagland Cannon, 1862

George Q. Cannon, 1862

Chapter Two

Hierarchy in Polygamy

The Preeminent Position of Elizabeth Hoagland, a First Wife

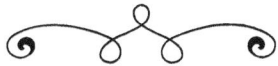

I am Mrs. George Q. Cannon.
Elizabeth Hoagland Cannon

THE ARRANGEMENT of a polygamous family's headstones may shed light on the structure and dynamics of various polygamous families. Elizabeth Hoagland Cannon (my great-grandmother and the first wife of George Q. Cannon) and Leonora Cannon Taylor each shared with her husband a headstone that emphasizes the importance each had as a first wife in the hierarchy of a polygamous family. On each headstone, a full side of the obelisk is devoted to commemorative details of their lives. In contrast, their sister wives have small, inconspicuous graves nearby. I say more about Elizabeth below.

The arrangement of the headstones of Angus Cannon (my great-grandfather and George Q. Cannon's brother) and his wives, the first two of whom he married on the same day, doesn't follow such a hierarchical pattern. A large stone marks the site with Angus' information; nearby are Sarah and Amanda's stones placed side by side. The headstones of the other wives are placed in random fashion on the family plot. The plots of my other two great-grandfathers, Samuel Rose Parkinson and William H. Maughan, and their wives suggest an equal status among the wives rather than indicating a hierarchical one. The Parkinson monument is a large granite four-sided rectangle with the details of Samuel Rose's life on one side; each of the remaining three sides has the chronology of one of his three wives; a round ball sits atop the rectangular stone, an additional symbol of unity. The headstone marking the burial place for William H. Maughan and his six wives is a tall handsome granite obelisk with only the surname Maughan inscribed on the stone. On the ground to the far right of the column is a simple rectangular stone for William H. Maughan and with the same sized stone for each wife that is equidistant from William and from each of the other wives.[210] The layout of these latter three families could indicate a lack of a formal hierarchy among the wives.

In truth, we do not know who chose the size, placement, or wording of the headstones for any of these families. Was it the patriarch of the family? The wives? The children? A combination? We simply do not know. Using the configurations of these stones as reliable metaphors of how the adults related to and envisioned each other is very tempting because doing so helps bring order to complexity. A more accurate metaphor, however, is likely that these polygamous families were like a moving dance, the steps and rhythms of which changed throughout the story of each complex polygamous family network. Their static headstones likely capture one perspective but not the full choreography of their lives.

The gravestones of George Q. Cannon and his family are in the Salt Lake City Cemetery, not far from Leonora Cannon Taylor and her family. The primary Cannon gravestone follows the same pattern as the Taylor family's. The details of Elizabeth's life are given on one side of the vertical stone and those of George are on another. The tombstones of the other wives are not organized in a meaningful order. This equal partner to George Q., Elizabeth Hoagland, was born November 3, 1835, eighteen years after Leonora was born and eight years before John Taylor took a second wife. The Hoaglands lived in Royal Oak, Michigan. Upon hearing about the Church they joined and moved to Nauvoo, where they met the Taylors. In fact, in 1846 when Elizabeth was eleven, she and her family left Nauvoo in a company led by John Taylor. Traveling with John and Leonora was her nephew, nineteen-year-old George Q. Cannon.[211]

A deep friendship developed between George Q. and Elizabeth as they crossed the plains. Soon after they arrived in the Salt Lake Valley in the fall of 1847, George Q. was called to California and then to Hawaii on what became a five-year mission.[212] Though Elizabeth was just a young girl, they knew they wanted to marry and kept in touch during his lengthy mission. That they married on December 11, 1854—less than two weeks after George's return—indicates that they became engaged some time during their separation.[213] Unlike their older relatives, John Taylor and Leonora Cannon, George and Elizabeth entered matrimony knowing other wives could follow. They had signed on not just to be loyal to each other but also to a religion that would ask them to redefine marriage.

---

210 The descendants of William H. Maughan who wrote the Maughan family history assembled the life sketches of his grandchildren in birth order of the entire family, not in a family group of each wife. Such a decision mirrors the arrangement of the gravestones.

211 Actually George Q. stayed behind in Nauvoo for a short time because he was sick. John returned later to retrieve George Q., who was likely living with his sister Mary Alice.

212 Before leaving Utah for his mission, George Q. raised a crop of corn on a lot he had purchased in the 14th Ward and made the adobe bricks for a house on the lot for his sister Mary Alice and her husband, Charles Lambert, and their two children. Mary Alice's family also included her sister Leonora and two younger brothers, Angus (my grandfather's father) and David, whom Mary Alice had assumed the care of when all of these children were orphaned. This hardy group arrived in the Valley in 1849 shortly after George Q. had left on his mission. Bitton, 60.

213 Bitton, 69–70. George Q. returned to Salt Lake City, UT, on November 28, 1854.

Because of the many responsibilities and opportunities given to George Q., Elizabeth's life constantly took unexpected turns. From these experiences, which took place before and during the practice of polygamy, George Q. and Elizabeth became very close. Reading about the many sorrows and challenges the couple endured before other wives joined the family makes it understandable and appropriate that Elizabeth retained a special position. Their first year together included moving to Sacramento, California, where George Q., under the direction of Brigham Young, edited *The Western Standard*, a publication intended to present favorable views of the Church, including the teaching of plural marriage. Elizabeth helped in proofreading the Book of Mormon, which he had translated (with Jonathan Napela) into Hawaiian during his mission.[214] While in California, they had their first child, George Q. Cannon, Jr., born January 29, 1856.[215] The baby died in November; there is no record of what caused his death. Elizabeth, pregnant at the time, gave birth to John Q. six months later. The couple, in addition to shouldering their grief, was desperately poor. George's younger brother David, who lived with them, recalled that many mornings George Q. left the house without eating and with little in the cupboards for Elizabeth and the baby.

Aware of George Q.'s plight, a wealthy Hawaiian planter gave him three thousand dollars. Though he was concerned about his family's needs, George felt that the Church's need was more urgent and he sent the entire gift to the First Presidency. This was the first of many instances of George's putting his allegiance to the Church ahead of his family's physical needs. As far as we know, he did not confer with Elizabeth about these decisions and there is no indication she ever asked him to turn down a calling, not give money to the Church, or not marry other women. She was committed both to him and to the patriarchal religion they had joined. At least in this instance, Elizabeth and George knew that the sacrifice had made a difference. President Young later told them that the money had saved the Church from a serious financial crisis.[216]

Another critical situation in Utah was the anticipated approach of Johnston's Army; Brigham Young called the Saints in outlying areas back to Utah. Elizabeth left California immediately with George Q.'s brother David and her baby John; she insisted they take with them the body of their baby George Q., Jr. to be buried in Utah. The trip home was arduous and cold. When they arrived New Year's Day, 1857, John's feet were frostbitten.[217] George Q. remained in California to publish the final issue of the *Western Standard*. He later returned to Utah, leaving this final declaration in the *Western Standard*:

> The cannon are not cast, the muskets or rifles not made, the powder and ball not manufactured, nor the men to use them either born or conceived, that will destroy Mormonism. Mark our words, gentlemen, it will live, though all earth and hell array themselves against it.[218]

---

214 Ibid., 25, 76.

215 Ibid., 76.

216 Evans and Cannon, 92.

217 Ibid., 88.

218 George Q. Cannon, *Western Standard*, September 18, 1857, quoted in Bitton, 88.

The following year, just as many Saints were leaving Salt Lake City because Johnston's Army was soon to arrive, George Q. was given the assignment of transporting the printing press to Fillmore, the Territory's capital at the time, to edit *The Deseret News*, the official publication of the Church. As the couple was preparing to move with their baby, George met eighteen-year-old Sarah Jane Jenne and received the strong impression that she should become his wife. Sarah Jane was similarly impressed. According to Bitton, "Elizabeth was not enthusiastic about the whirlwind courtship, but she had known of plural marriage for many years, had probably talked about it with her husband, and gave her consent."[219] Brigham Young performed the marriage of George Q. and Sarah Jane April 11, 1858.[220]

George Q. and his expanded family, which still included George Q.'s brother David, immediately set out for Fillmore, where he published the first issue of *The Deseret News* just four days later. Once the threat of Johnston's Army passed, the Cannon family returned to Salt Lake City with all the printing press equipment in tow in September 1858.[221] En route, John Bollwinkle, a driver of a mule-drawn carriage, met them with a letter from Brigham Young, which asked George Q. to leave immediately for the East on a special mission. He was to serve as president of the Eastern States Mission, provide a more fair representation of the Church with the press, and help make arrangements for Saints to make the journey to the Salt Lake Valley. As always, George Q. accepted the call. Elizabeth and Sarah Jane saw it as a given that they would obey the Prophet and in turn support their husband.

Because there wasn't room for everyone in Bollwinkle's carriage, the family needed to split up. Sarah Jane, now nineteen years old and five months pregnant, insisted that baby John Q. and Elizabeth, three months pregnant, return with George to Salt Lake City while she remained behind with David to deal with the printing equipment and heavy wagons.[222] Assuming a supportive, deferential role was often expected of wives that followed the first wife. Sarah Jane filled the role with grace and dignity. Later George wrote in his journal,

> Before starting [for the East coast], I prayed with and blessed Elizabeth and John Q., committing them and Sarah Jane, and all that belonged to me into the hands of the Lord. . . . My family had no place to live [and] I had not time to do anything in relation to a house and they were left to shift for themselves.[223]

That Sarah Jane did not receive an independent blessing is an indication that George Q. saw Elizabeth as the principal wife.

---

219 Bitton, 90.

220 Ibid.

221 Ibid., 93.

222 Ibid., 94.

223 Evans and Cannon, 94–95.

The thought of another separation must have been very difficult for Elizabeth. Later in a journal entry, George remembered that prior to his leaving he "*found her [Elizabeth] crying many times alone.*"[224] When George Q. returned two years later on August 13, 1860, Elizabeth and Sarah Jane were there to greet him, each with a son who had been born in his absence.[225] On August 25, less than two weeks later, George Q. was ordained as a new apostle.[226] The very next day he was called to serve as the president of the British Mission.[227] When Church authorities traveled and lived abroad, they often took family members with them. Not surprisingly, it was usually the first wife who went along. Sometimes their children went as well; usually the sister wives tended the first wife's children in her absence. Such was the case with the Cannon family. Within weeks of the calling, George and Elizabeth were making plans to leave for England to preside over the British Mission. They left their two little boys, John Q. and Abram, in the care of Sarah Jane.

George and Elizabeth left Salt Lake City early in October for New York, where they boarded the steamship *Argo* in December. Elizabeth, now four months pregnant, was seasick much of the way. She gave birth to Georgiana May 19, 1861, in Liverpool, the mission headquarters.[228] Soon after arriving in England, George Q. became the president of the European Mission, which included the Continent as well as the British Isles. He continued supervising missionaries and local branches, overseeing finances, editing the *Millennial Star*, and organizing emigration.[229]

That same May, as mentioned in the introduction, George learned that he had been selected by Utah's general assembly to be the senator from the Territory.[230] George was just settling in as the mission president when he received this very surprising news. He wrote, "*This unexpected news literally took my breath away and caused such a tremor to come over me that I could scarcely stand without clinging to the desk for support.*"[231] The new senator's principal commission was to obtain statehood for the Territory. However, rather than gaining statehood, he saw the escalating Civil War, the press for emancipation of the slaves, and the enactment of the Morrill Anti-Bigamy

---

224 *George Q. Cannon Journal*, May 1, 1881, quoted in Bitton, 94.

225 Elizabeth's son Abraham H. (March 12, 1859–July 19, 1896) became an apostle and kept a comprehensive journal of Church activities during polygamous times. He was usually known as Abram, the name I will use in this book. In Chapter Six we will see that Abram played an important role in the family that involved my Cannon grandparents. Sarah Jane's son Franklin (Frank) Jenne (January 25, 1859 – July 25, 1933) was an able defender of his father and polygamy. He served as U.S. senator from Utah 1896–1899. After that time, however, he became a vigorous and influential opponent of the Church.

226 Bitton, 101–4. George Q. had been selected in October 1859 and informed by Brigham Young in a November 1859 letter. He was to take the place left by the death of Parley P. Pratt in 1857. He was ordained an apostle when he returned from serving the Church in the East.

227 Ibid., 107.

228 Evans and Cannon, 122.

229 Bitton, 125. When signing documents, he identified himself as "President of The Church of Jesus Christ of Latter-day Saints in the British Isles and adjacent countries," an indication of how seriously he took his responsibilities.

230 Ibid., 117. The other senator was William H. Hooper. Soon thereafter, Brigham Young was elected governor and Heber C. Kimball lieutenant-governor of the Territory.

231 *George Q. Cannon Journal*, May 5, 1862, quoted in Bitton, 119.

Act. This law, signed into law July 8, 1862, by Abraham Lincoln, outlawed bigamy in the Territory, annulled the territorial legislature's incorporation of The Church of Jesus Christ of Latter-day Saints, and prohibited any religious organization in the territories from owning real estate valued at more than fifty thousand dollars.[232] President Lincoln chose not to enforce the Morrill Act. The story is told that he said to T. B. H. Stenhouse, a journalist from Utah, "When I was a boy on the farm in Illinois. . . . Occasionally we would come to a fallen log that was too hard to split, too wet to burn and too heavy to move, so we plowed around it. That's what I intend to do with the Mormons. You go back and tell Brigham Young that if he will let me alone, I will let him alone."[233] Lincoln's forbearance postponed antagonism between the Church and the government. Though the Morrill Act was not enforced, George must have felt very frustrated and disappointed that it passed.

While George was in Washington, DC, Elizabeth, fragile in health, remained in Liverpool with their daughter Georgiana. We do not know the nature of Elizabeth's illness, but we do know that her health had been poor ever since they left Utah.[234] While George was away, a woman named Alice helped Elizabeth with Georgiana, a luxury that Sarah Jane did not have.

While in Europe, Elizabeth kept a journal for six weeks. It covered an interesting and important time of their mission and gives insight into how important her children were to her as well as how deeply connected she was to her husband.[235] The first entry is dated July 20, 1862, less than two weeks after the Morrill Act passed. Interestingly, Elizabeth made no mention of this and other tumultuous political events that so dramatically affected their lives. Instead, she focused on her deep love for her husband and her deep love for her children and husband and how happy she was to have him return from Washington, her commitment to the gospel, and the details of their missionary travels.

I have included journal excerpts that illustrate Elizabeth and George Q.'s pleasure as a married couple. Elizabeth repeatedly expressed joy at having Georgina with her, concern for her daughter's health, and in later entries anxiety about being separated from her. Her health problems were also an underlying concern:

> *July 20th Received a letter from Mr. Cannon   [H]e does not know whether he will return on the next steamer or not but rather thinks not, seems to be enjoying himself, how glad I shall be to see him home again, my health is better*
>
> *July 22nd Alice took Georgy out for a walk   the little dear she is a great comfort to me in the absence of my dear husband. I could not content myself were it not for her. I pray the Lord will continue to bless her as he has done.*[236]

---

232 Bitton, 123.

233 T.B.H. Stenhouse, *Rocky Mountain Saints* (New York: Appleton and Company, 1878): 601, quoted in Bitton, 124.

234 Elizabeth continued to have health problems the rest of her life.

235 As with Leonora's diary in Chapter One, only the first quotation from Elizabeth's England journal is footnoted.

236 Georgy is Elizabeth's term of affection for her daughter Georgiana.

23rd Rosa sitting with Georgy at the Editors window when she sang out here comes Mr Cannon. I said you must be mistaken she replied he is in a cab at the door. The next moment I heard that well known footstep on the stairs my heart almost leaped out of place in beholding my dear Husband again. I could scarcely speak for awhile I was overcome with joy. Mr C was afraid the surprise was to sudden and it would overcome me not being very strong from my late illness. I recovered myself after a little and felt so happy in seeing Mr Cannon looking so well. Our dear little Georgy went to her Pa at once and would not allow him to leave her for a moment how pleased he was to see her looking so well. . . . Mr Cannon came home looking very well indeed. his health had been very good while he was away[237]

25th After so long a separation our home was happy again, even our dear little Georgy seemed as happy and joyous as though she understood it all perfectly [B]less her. What a comfort she has been to me in the absence of my dearly Beloved Husband. It should have been wretched without her.

July 29th I have been taking more outdoor exercise which has had a tendency to improve my health and the pleasure of my dear companion's society has greatly added to lightness in Spirit. May I long be blessed with his dear society to comfort me through life's uncertain ways. This is my earnest desire.

Later she wrote, "*Just got a pair of worked slippers soled and lined to present to Mr. Cannon the forth pair I have done since our arrival.*" On August 11 she wrote, "*Georgy is very well but makes no effort to walk yet, she seems too heavy to stand on her feet much yet. I trust her health may be good that she may be spared to comfort us, in the absence of our dear boys.*"[238]

Less than a month after George's return from Washington, Elizabeth wrote in her journal about a pleasure trip she and George took to London to see the sights. This must have felt like a honeymoon to them after the austere year in California, the hectic travel to Fillmore to print *The Deseret News,* and the two-year separation while George Q. was president of the Eastern States Mission. While they were in London she wrote that they "*passed through a portion of the Exhibition, so beautiful that it is beyond my description. . . . you can see articles from almost all parts of the world, among the numerous things I saw a milking machine.*" At Hampton Court she "*saw a great many paintings and rooms that were inhabited years ago by the great men of England*" and "*went to Madame Tosand [Tussaud] to see the wax figures, they were as lifelike as ever I saw.*" They also saw the Tower of

---

237 Rosa is probably a reference to Rosina Mathews, the eleven-year-old orphan who traveled with Elizabeth to America and whom George and Elizabeth later adopted. The window mentioned is probably a reference to the window by George's desk.

238 Georgiana would have been sixteen months old; Elizabeth had reason to be concerned about her not walking. Her "dear boys" were Abram and John in Utah being cared for by Sarah Jane.

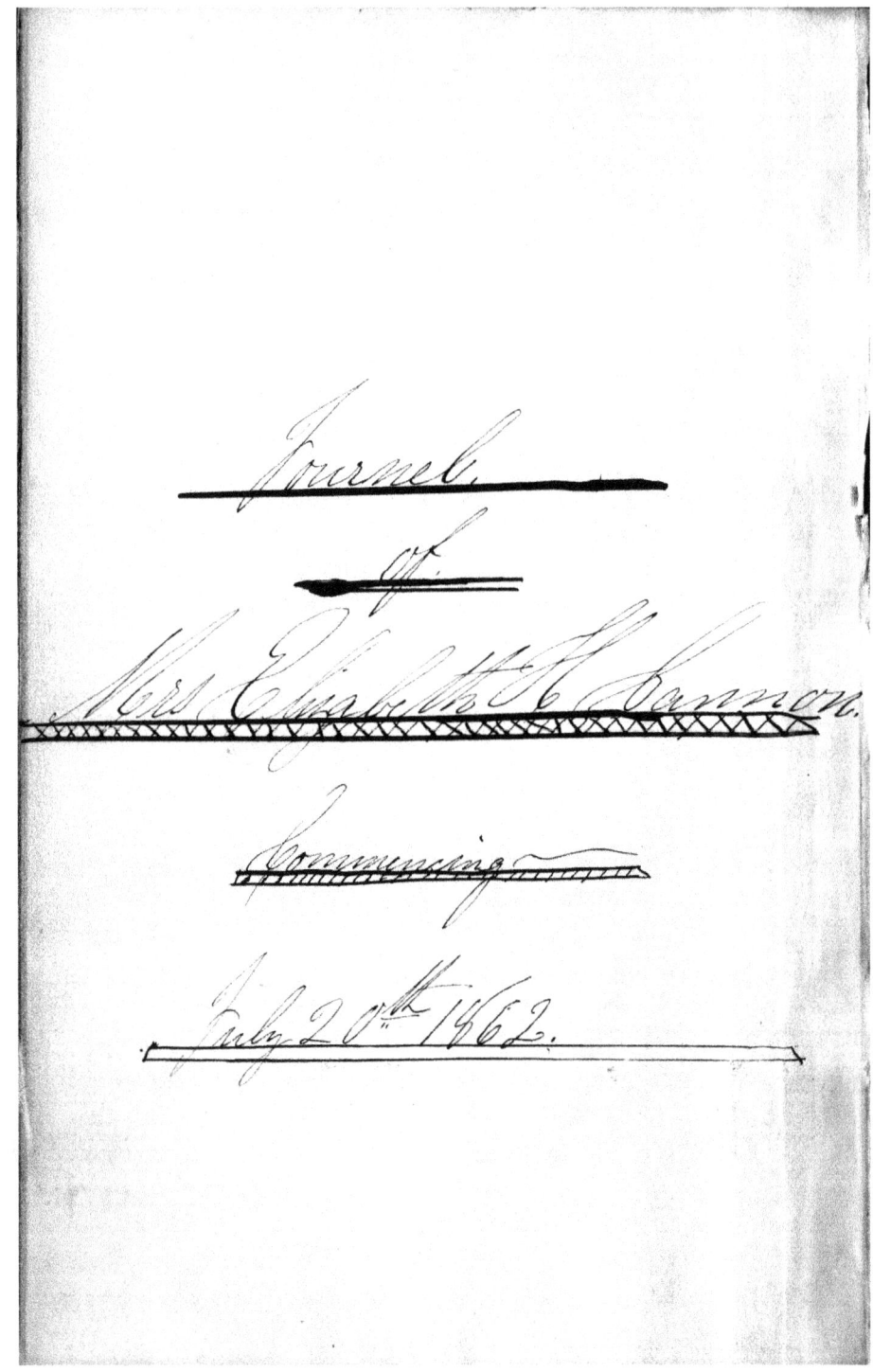

The opening pages of Elizabeth Hoagland Cannon's journal, which begins with her joyful declaration that George Q. is returning to London from Washington, DC, after the disappointing passage of the Morrill Anti-Bigamy Act of 1862. Most of the journal is a record of the couple's experiences touring the European Mission over which he presided.

July 20th Received a letter from Mr Cannon he does not know wheather he will return on the next steamer or not, but rather think not, seems to be enjoying himself, how glad I shall be to see him home again, my health is better

21st Today took the buss and went up to Kirkdale, Sister Edwards & Georgy were with me when we got out of the buss we went upon the hill where we could overlook the Town, and had a beautiful view, Georgy was delighted with it, and would lie down upon the grass, it was a treat to her

22nd Engaged in household duties, taking music lessons, &c. Alice took Georgy out for a walk the little dear, she is a great comfort to me, in the absence of my dear Husband, I could not content myself were it not for her, I pray the Lord will continue to bless her, as he has done,

23 Engaged in tidying up the house. Sister Mary Jones finishes her weeks work to day being Saturday Rosa sitting with Georgy at the Parlors window when she sung out here comes pa, I says you must be mistaken, she replied he is in a cab at the door the next moment I heard that well known footstep on the stairs, my heart almost leaped out

CHAPTER TWO

London, St. Paul's Cathedral, Westminster Abbey, Zoological Gardens, and the Crystal Palace. At the end of day four of the week-long trip, Elizabeth wrote, "*I require a little rest, not being very strong yet.*" When they returned from London August 28, Elizabeth wrote, "*Georgy looked well, she did not know me the evening I got home but next day was all right.*"

Their next trip was not for pleasure. On September 1, 1862, they left Liverpool to tour the Continent as the new mission president and his wife. That day Elizabeth wrote in her journal, "*I felt very bad in leaving my dear little girl yet I can realize she will be better off at home with Sister Edwards and Jones.*" We learn from Elizabeth's entries that they traveled to Hamburg, Copenhagen, Holland, Cologne, Switzerland, and France. Everywhere they went Saints welcomed them warmly. One entry reads, "*Mr. C. addressed the congregation, he had the Spirit and spoke well.*" Regarding the challenge of dealing with a new language, she explained, "*It is now that I can realize the feelings of a Foreigner in a strange land unable to communicate his thoughts.*" On September 19 she wrote, "*went in accordance with Bro. Smith's request to get a bust likeness.*" Later, in reference to that portrait, she reported, "*Bro. Cluff sent us some likeness of myself and Mr. C. Mr. Cannon was very good but mine did not suit me at all. I looked very bad.*"[239]

A week later she recorded, "*Mr. Cannon went out this morning and purchased me a sash to wear around my neck. Mr. C. and myself have had the best of health thus far on our tour. The Lord has blessed me with kind friends everywhere. We have enjoyed ourselves beyond expression although I am often longing to see our dearest little girl.*" Two days later she added, "*They say our darling little girl seems perfectly happy and contented and is doing nicely, how anxious I am to see the little dear. My Prayer to the Lord is that she may be continually in his holy keeping with our other dear ones.*"[240]

After they returned from their tour, Elizabeth gave birth to their third boy, George Hoagland, May 21, 1863. In July, George Q. decided that Elizabeth and the children should return to Utah ahead of him. In his journal he explained why:

> *I have deemed it wise to send my family home in advance of myself, having been led by the Spirit to do so. I have thought that in the event of any difficulty arising between England & America, or anything else arising to cause my instant return home, together with her own impaired health, it would be wise and safe perhaps to send her home. It was not, however, without painful feelings that I thus parted with her and the children.*[241]

---

239 The picture of her and the one of George are included at the beginning of this chapter. I agree that the picture doesn't compliment her.

240 The journal ends in mid-sentence when they were visiting Paris on their way back to England.

241 *George Q. Cannon Journal*, May 19, 1863, quoted in Bitton, 128.

Elizabeth with one-month-old baby George, two-year-old Georgiana, and eleven-year-old Rosina Mathews, left Liverpool in June 1863.[242] They sailed on *The City of Washington,* one of the ships on which George Q. arranged for the Saints to travel.[243] In fact, under his direction, over thirteen thousand converts emigrated to America.[244]

The journey was long and full of heartbreak for Elizabeth. The group was detained six weeks in Florence, Nebraska, by an epidemic of whooping cough. Elizabeth's continual concern and forebodings for her little girl were warranted. Her beloved Georgy died on the plains at Sweetwater River, likely from the epidemic. As when she lost her first baby in California, Elizabeth journeyed home with the body of a child she refused to bury in a strange place. A churn was made into a coffin and completely closed for Georgiana to travel home with her mother.[245] George Peacock, who was traveling in the same company, conveyed the unfortunate news to George Q.: "It becomes my painful duty to inform you of the death of your daughter Georgiana. She died on the Platte (last Company) on the night of the 2nd [Sept.] at 9 p.m.... You may be assured that Sister C. is much fatigued and worn down, seems to sink under the trial we try to comfort her all we can."[246] George Q. was devastated and wrote the following in his journal:

> *After this torpor passed off, my feelings overpowered me, and my distress was terrible. It seemed as though I had lost all control of myself. I remained for a few hours alone in this condition; but my feelings actually became so wrought up that I thought I would lose my senses unless I had relief and something to divert me from the thought which oppressed me. I rang for Bro. Shearman, who came up, thinking his society would help me; but I continued to get worse and I then started downstairs to the Office as near crazed as I well could be and retain my senses. I knew not what to do for relief; but, bethought me of being administered to. As soon as the brethren laid their hands upon me I felt soothed and by the time they had finished speaking and took their hands off I was quite calm.... It will be a very severe blow to Elizabeth deprived as she is of my society. I would feel far worse than I do, if I did not know that my motive in sending my family away was pure and that I had been led to do so by the prompting of the Spirit.*[247]

---

242 Evans and Cannon, 96. They later adopted Rosina, who later married George Q.'s sister Mary Alice's son, George Lambert. Appendix H is a letter that ten-year-old Mary Alice, George Q.'s daughter and my grandmother, wrote from Washington, DC, to Rosina in Utah.

243 One of George Q.'s main duties was making arrangements for the Saints to emigrate to the Salt Lake Valley.

244 Charles Dickens described George Q. Cannon as follows: "A compactly-made handsome man in black, rather short, with rich brown hair and beard, and clear bright eyes. From his speech, I should set him down as American. Probably, a man who had 'knocked about the world' pretty much. A man with a frank open manner, and unshrinking look; withal a man of great quickness." Charles Dickens, "The Uncommercial Traveler: Bound for the Great Salt Lake," *All The Year Round* 21 (July 4, 1863): 446.

245 Elizabeth Cannon Sauls, *The Life of George Q. Cannon* (Provo, UT, 1956): 17.

246 Bitton, 129.

247 *George Q. Cannon Journal,* October 9, 1863, quoted in Bitton, 129.

Both Elizabeth and George seemed to have known that they would lose Georgiana. From George's journal entry on October 8, the day before receiving news of her death, we learn that he could not get his mind off Georgiana and Elizabeth. *"I caught myself thinking how she would look as a child in the resurrection. I fancied my wife Elizabeth was in my room and when I lit my candle which stood on the stool by the bedside I looked round the room almost expecting to find her there."*[248] Both parents were devastated by Georgiana's death. George missed Elizabeth as sorely as she missed him. Elizabeth and George needed to be with each other.

Another tragedy awaited. In December of the same year, 1863, they lost George H.; their baby boy died of the whooping cough and measles. George learned the unhappy news while he was still in Liverpool. In his diary that evening he wrote, *"My poor dear wife, how deeply I sympathize with her in this affliction."* He thought of Job who had lost all his children as well as his flocks and herds. *"I still have three—half of mine—and I pray that they may be spared unto me."*[249] The three children who had died all bore their father's first name or a variation. Losing their children so young continued to be a source of pain for them.[250] George Q. returned to Utah from his arduous duties as president of the European mission in October 1864. On being reunited with his family he wrote, "My feelings were very peculiar and for weeks I felt it would be a relief for me to get off into a corner and weep for joy."[251]

Life resumed for George with his two wives, Elizabeth and Sarah Jane, who were soon joined by a third. While visiting settlements in southern Utah, George met twenty-year-old Eliza Tenney in Payson, where she was a partner in a millinery store. They were married in August 1865. We have no written record of how Elizabeth felt about this third marriage, but we do know it was difficult for her. Elizabeth's granddaughter Margaret Clayton told me, "Polygamy was hard for Elizabeth. When George married another wife, she would go stay with Uncle Angus for a few days."[252] Elizabeth probably first felt the full impact of plural marriage with George Q.'s marriage to Eliza. In a sense, Sarah Jane had been an adjunct to George Q. and Elizabeth's family. While the two boys were under Sarah Jane's care during George Q.'s and Elizabeth's time in Europe, Elizabeth wrote in her journal that her children were being cared for by an *"indulgent grandmother."*[253] Perhaps Elizabeth could not acknowledge, even to herself, that Sarah Jane was not just a caretaker but a sister wife as well.

---

248 *George Q. Cannon Journal*, October 8, 1863, quoted in Bitton, 129.

249 Bitton, 134–135. The third was Sarah Jane's son Frank.

250 Evans and Cannon, 142. In December 1865 Elizabeth gave birth to a daughter named Elizabeth, who died fourteen months later. In October 1869 she bore Lillian Ann, who lived only a year. In between these babies, my grandmother, Mary Alice, was born October 16, 1867. She lived to maturity and was a joy to both of her parents. In the 1870s Elizabeth had three other children who lived to maturity: David in 1871, Emily in 1874, and Sylvester in 1877.

251 Bitton, 140.

252 Margaret Clayton, John Q. Cannon's daughter, conversation with author, 1970s.

253 Elizabeth Hoagland Cannon, *Personal Journal*.

According to an account written by my father's sister Elizabeth, who in the family went by Aunt Ips, the couple wanted to take their children with them on their mission to England, but Brigham Young advised otherwise.²⁵⁴ We have no record of how Sarah Jane felt about being asked to assume the responsibility of caring for Elizabeth's children for three years when they were young or for a shorter time when the boys were teenagers while George and Elizabeth were in Washington, DC. We also don't know how Sarah Jane felt about saying goodbye to them upon their mother's return. We do know that it was heart wrenching for Elizabeth to leave her children. An excerpt from the journal she kept as they toured the mission reads as follows:

> *It is two years today we left our mountain home to come to Europe, how many times have I thought of that sad day, leaving my darling boys behind, yet I have felt that it was my duty so to do, and the Lord has greatly strengthened me in obeying his commands. I feel they will [be] blessed of the Lord for this has been promised to me, if I am faithful, and I shall have the privilege of beholding them again.*²⁵⁵

Tension erupted when George Q. married a fourth wife, twenty-two-year-old schoolteacher Martha Telle, on March 16, 1868. When the bride was brought to Elizabeth's home after the ceremony, she received her "with a storm."²⁵⁶ Anger surfaced more subtly during daily life. The story is told that some groceries for Martha were delivered to the farm. The package was addressed to "Mrs. George Q. Cannon." Martha, who knew they were for her, picked up the food. Elizabeth confronted her saying, "I am Mrs. George Q. Cannon." But so was Martha. What Elizabeth likely meant but did not articulate was that she was the *first* Mrs. George Q. Cannon and that anyone who followed her could not take her place.

Of course the family dynamics varied from one polygamous family to another, but the pattern was that when the first wife had been the sole focus of her husband's attention for a stretch of time, she earned a status that included special attention from him and respect from the other wives. Annie Clark Tanner wrote that in her case supplies were distributed from the home of the first wife and that correspondence to and from her husband also went through Mary, the first wife.²⁵⁷ We don't know how George Q. addressed the letters he wrote to his wives as a collective group, but we do know that he sent them to Elizabeth, who then shared the news with the other wives.²⁵⁸ George's sending Elizabeth the letters and her delivering the news to the other wives illustrates this status and respect. Occasionally he wrote personal letters addressed to only one wife such as his correspondence with Martha about the education of the Cannon children.

---

254 Sauls, 19.

255 Elizabeth Hoagland Cannon, *Personal Journal*.

256 Bitton, 155. Joseph J. is Sarah Jane's son.

257 Johnston, "A Mormon Mother," 9.

258 Bitton, 185.

In an effort to unify his family, the year he married Martha, George built an imposing home, the second largest in the Territory, on South Temple and present-day Second West.²⁵⁹ Called the Big House, it was the main scene of family activity for the next few years. Each of George Q.'s four wives had her own quarters. Elizabeth and Sarah Jane were on the first floor; Eliza and Martha on the top floor. All four families used the lowest semi-basement floor.²⁶⁰

George Q. Cannon's "Big House" in Salt Lake had separate quarters for his four families at the time. They lived here until 1878 when they moved to the Cannon Farm.

In 1878, George Q. made a more dramatic decision about ways to connect the Cannon clan: he asked his four families to move to the Cannon Farm, located in an isolated area a couple of miles southwest of the center of Salt Lake.²⁶¹ It was here he wanted his children and wives to become a community; they would eat in a common dining room, have their own school, and be surrounded by their brothers, sisters and "aunties."²⁶² George Q.'s children did in fact become a tight knit group.

---

259 There is a discrepancy about the location of the Big House. Evans and Cannon, 97, and Sauls, 29, place it at South Temple and First West; Bitton, 155, at South Temple and Second West. This difference is probably because the current Second West was called First West at the time the Cannons lived there.

260 Sauls, 29.

261 The Cannon Farm was between 13th and 15th South and west of present day 9th West to the Jordan River.

262 See Appendix J for an informative account of the Cannon Farm.

George Q. Cannon's family school on the Cannon Farm.
Mary Alice (Mamie) Cannon, author's grandmother, is seated fourth from left.

A painting of the Cannon Farm by C. Eisele, where George Q. Cannon and his families lived after 1878. From the left are Eliza's, Sarah Jane's, and Martha's homes; then comes the smaller dining hall/schoolhouse followed by Elizabeth's home, the original farmhouse with an addition to the right. At the far right is Carlie's home.

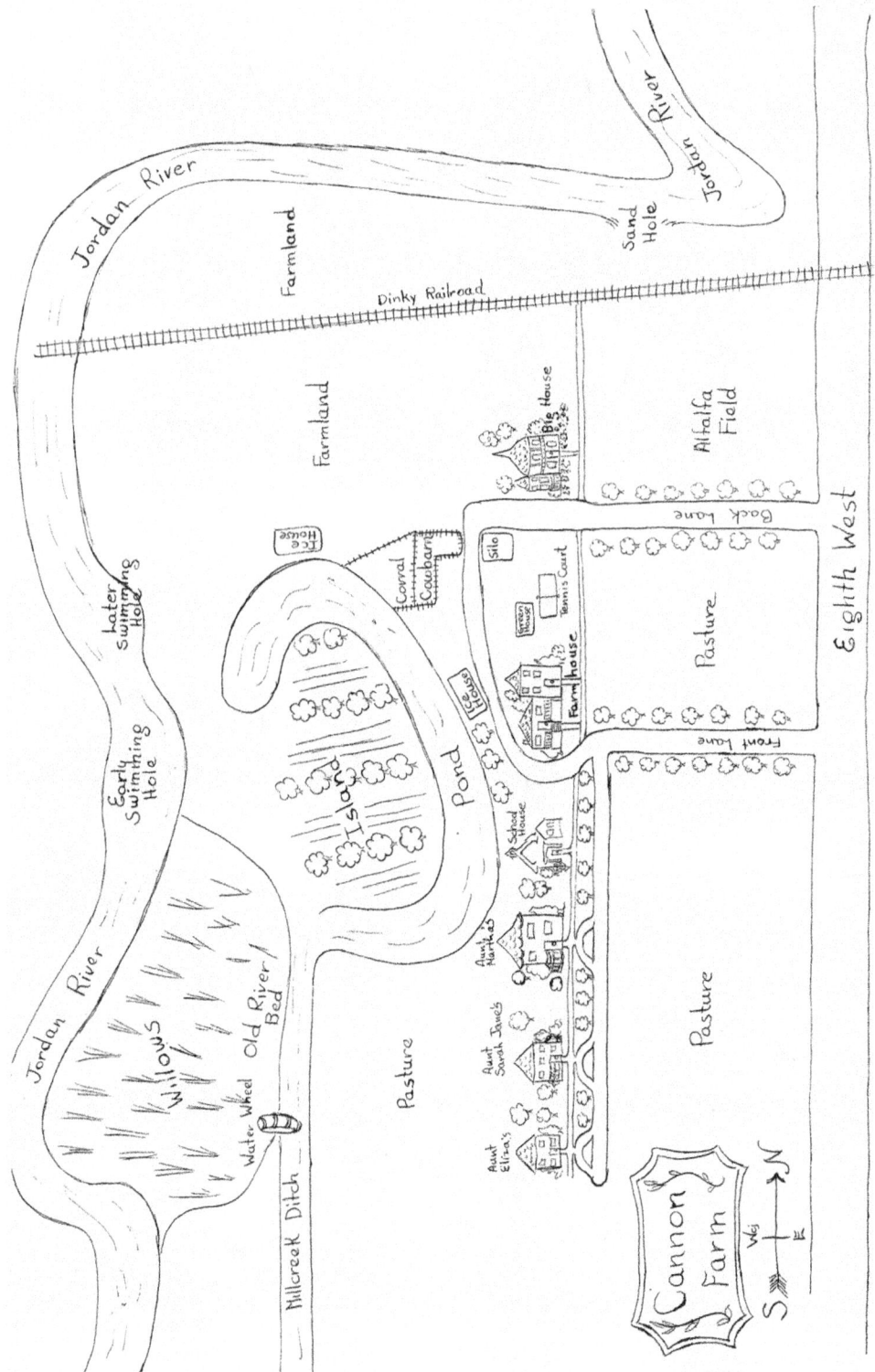

Sketch of the Cannon Farm, by Winnifred Cannon Jardine, who wrote "The Life on the Cannon Farm" found in Appendix I

First, George built a two-story addition to the existing farmhouse, where Elizabeth lived for her final four years of life.[263] For a time, Martha lived in the same house with Elizabeth and then had rooms next door in the schoolhouse. Eventually each wife had a substantial house of her own. While his four wives lived on the farm, George Q., as a delegate to Congress from 1872 to 1882, was the central person representing the Church to the government on positions of states' rights and the separation of church and state. The right to practice plural marriage was the heart of his crusade. In 1876 Elizabeth and their daughter, nine-year-old Mary Alice, my grandmother, accompanied him to Washington, DC. They observed meetings of Congress, attended receptions, and visited Arlington Cemetery, Mount Vernon, and other sites. George took Elizabeth and Mary Alice to the official opening on May 10, 1876, of the Centennial Exhibition in Philadelphia. One of the exhibitions they saw was the travel exhibit of the Crystal Palace, which Elizabeth had recorded in her journal seeing fourteen years earlier in London with George.

For the next session of Congress, Elizabeth stayed home because of poor health; George Q. took their nineteen-year-old son John Q. to act as his secretary. It is noteworthy that George took Elizabeth's son rather than another wife or another wife's child.[264] In 1878, George took Elizabeth and three of their children: Mary Alice, now ten years old; seven-year-old David; and baby Sylvester to Washington, DC. During their time in Washington, the Supreme Court ruled in the Reynolds case that a man couldn't practice polygamy on the grounds that it was part of his religion. The decision was devastating to George Q.'s efforts to defend states' rights and the right to practice polygamy as a religious principle.

An interview George Q. had with a reporter points out the tenor of the times as well as George's forthrightness:

> "What in your opinion is the main object of this anti-Mormon crusade?" the reporter asked.
>
> "It means plunder—nothing else," Cannon answered. "The combined effect of the three bills now before Congress will be to disfranchise nine tenths of the people of the Territory, and place all political power and all control of the revenues in the hands of the minority."
>
> "Pardon my apparent impertinence, Mr. Cannon, but I have heard that it is reported that the Mrs. Cannon here with you is not your first or legal wife."

---

263 Some accounts state the two-story frame structure was built first.

264 He probably wanted to portray himself as a conventional man with one wife with whom he had children.

> "The whole story is utterly false. She [Elizabeth] is my legal wife in every sense of the word. We were engaged five years and married in 1854. She is the mother of 11 children, one of whom, her oldest son, was with me in Washington last winter acting as my private secretary."
>
> "Pardon me, but may I inquire how many wives you acknowledge?"
>
> "Yes sir; I have four. If I was disposed to treat the subject lightly, I would say I have enough to keep me from meddling with the wives and daughters of other men."[265]

George and Elizabeth returned to Utah with Mary Alice, David, and Sylvester later that same year. In November of the following year, 1879, George and Elizabeth once again traveled to Washington, DC, this time with Mary Alice and their younger daughter Emily. While there, the couple celebrated their twenty-fifth wedding anniversary. Part of his motivation in taking his daughters was to present a more normal public image. A reporter from the *Baltimore Evening Bulletin* wrote that he was "cordially welcomed by the able and genial Mormon, and presented to a part of his lovely family, consisting of one of his attractive and refined wives and two bright and handsome little girls. If institutions were rated by their refining and intelligent results, there should be no prejudices against polygamy."[266]

Though George introduced his family widely and many were impressed, they themselves suffered from poor health. Mary Alice caught a cold and Emily had the croup and a high fever. Elizabeth's own health was far from robust. Concerned about Elizabeth's health, George and his family returned to Utah at the adjournment of Congress in June 1880.

Probably at Elizabeth's request, George married Elizabeth's recently divorced sister, Emily Hoagland, on July 11, 1881.[267] Elizabeth was concerned for her sister's welfare. Also, as Elizabeth's health continued to deteriorate, she and George may have thought Emily could help care for Elizabeth's children. That fall George returned again to Congress, this time alone, and once again fought for the survival of the teachings of his Church and to retain his position in Congress. While George was desperately trying to prevent the passage of the Edmunds Act in Washington DC, Elizabeth was gravely ill in Salt Lake City. George, very conflicted, wanted to come home to be by her side but knew that he must stay in Washington to defend the Church. Throughout George Q.'s life he was asked to fulfill Church responsibilities that took

---

265 Bitton, 215–16.

266 *Baltimore Evening Bulliten*, January 17, 1880, quoted in Bitton, 235.

267 Bitton, 264. I didn't grow up hearing about Emily. She never was integrated into the larger Cannon family but received equal treatment in the will with the other wives. George paid a price for marrying Emily because she became a prime example of willful violation of the law. He had married his other wives between 1854 and 1868, whereas he married Emily after the Poland Act, after the Reynolds decision, and just a few months before passage of the Edmunds Act. No mention was made of Elizabeth's sister Emily caring for Elizabeth's children in Evans and Cannon, *Historical Treasury*, or in Annie Wells Cannon, "Elizabeth Hoagland Cannon," a privately published document.

him away from his family, sometimes for extended periods of time. It is clear from his letters and journal entries that he not only understood the burden his obligations put on his family but also mourned his own absence from those dearest to him. When George heard that Elizabeth had contracted pneumonia, an illness that was nearly always fatal before antibiotics, he wrote the following in his journal:

> *For her, with her weak lungs and bad cough and general debility, it will be a serious matter. Were I to yield to my feelings I would be plunged in grief and if I were here on private business I would start for home by the first train, but I cannot desert my post. All I can do is cry unto the Lord. He knoweth all things, and neither she nor I is overlooked. We are in his keeping. . . . Her constant devotion to me, her unceasing love and self-sacrifice, never thinking she could do enough for me, as ready to do me any service and to deny herself any pleasures as she was the first months or weeks of our marriage, and never sparing herself if she could add to my comfort, have been beyond all praise.*[268]

The telegram Elizabeth sent to George Q. has become part of Cannon family "scripture": "Remain at your post. God can raise me up, if it is His will, in answer to your prayers there as well as if you were here. All is being done for me that can be done."[269]

Later that day she had her four youngest children, Mary Alice, David, Emily, and Sylvester, brought to her bedside.[270] Commending five-year-old Sylvester to the care of fifteen-year-old Mary Alice, Elizabeth kissed them all and blessed them before she died January 25, 1882, at her sister Emily's home on Second South and First West.[271] The next day his brother Angus telegraphed George, "Elizabeth has just left us. God comfort you. Any instructions?" In answering, the sorrowing husband wired his desires concerning the kind of coffin and burial place and included the following, "Keep the children constantly in company; must not yield to grief. Have no gloomy trappings at funeral, no black about coffin."[272]

George felt very isolated and alone in Washington. Not mentioning his despair to others, he went to New York for a weekend to be by himself. George wrote in his journal, "*It might be made, when my back was turned, a subject of ribald mirth about my wives. We are not supposed to feel as other people do, so I hold my tongue and keep my feelings to myself.*"[273] Later he added, "*I bow to His will, receive with submission and resignation this affliction. I must carry out for myself that which I have so often taught*

---

268 George Q. Cannon to Daniel H. Wells, December, 7, 1864, quoted in Bitton, 250–251.

269 Evans and Cannon, 122.

270 Abram and John Q. were married and serving foreign missions for the Church.

271 See Chapter Six for Mary Alice's account of her mother's visit to her six weeks after her death.

272 Sauls, 28.

273 Bitton, 251.

others."[274] After Elizabeth's death, George returned to Utah a broken man. He had not only lost his wife but also his seat in Congress. What's more, a severe law against the Church's position on polygamy had been enacted.

Even after Elizabeth died, George continued to regard her as his first wife. At family meals each wife sat at a table with her children; George sat at the head table with Elizabeth's children.[275] Mary Alice, their eldest child, accompanied him on trips visiting the Saints in southern Utah after Elizabeth's death. He didn't recognize another wife as his legal wife until he married Caroline (Carlie) Young Croxall in November 1884.[276]

Given the depth of the connection George and Elizabeth had, the reason for his allegiance to her undoubtedly reached beyond her position in the polygamous hierarchy. She was a remarkable woman in her own right as well as a steadfast, loving wife. In her account of Elizabeth's life, her son John Q.'s wife, Annie, aptly captures the focus of her mother-in-law's life:

> The main desire and ambition of Elizabeth Cannon's life was to build a real home and make it the most desirable place in all the world for her husband and children. . . . She was always the same—the perfect lady to the manor born. Never at any time was she unequal to the occasion, whether at official dinners in the nation's capital, at homes of distinguished people in large cities, or entertaining some of the most noted people in the world, her dignified and easy manner gave one in her presence a feeling of ease and security.[277]

Despite all of George Q.'s travels, preoccupation with heavy Church responsibilities, and duties to other wives and their children, his relationship with Elizabeth held a special place in both of their hearts. They met multiple challenges together and remained sweethearts to the end.

---

274 Sauls, 28.

275 Ibid., 30.

276 Bitton, 268.

277 Cannon, "Elizabeth Hoagland Cannon," 7–9.

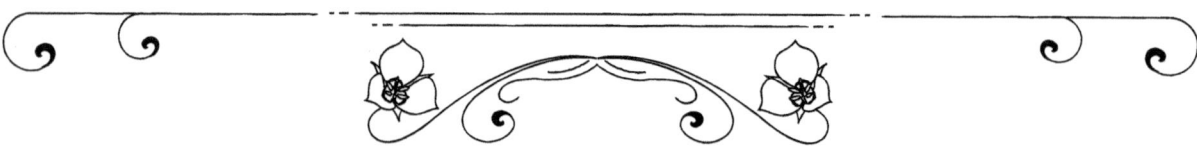

Angus M. Cannon

Ann Amanda Mousley Cannon

Chapter Three

MEN'S AND WOMEN'S PLACES IN POLYGAMY'S PATRIARCHAL ORDER

Each Gender's Unique Power

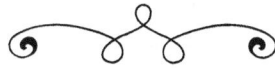

Our sisters should be prepared to take their position in Zion. Our sisters are really one with us, and when the brethren go into the Temples to officiate for the males, the sisters will go for the females; we operate together for the good of the whole, that we may be united together for time and all eternity.

John Taylor

AS WE SAW in the previous chapter, being the first wife gave Elizabeth a significant place in the family structure. The marriage of Ann Amanda Mousley and Angus Cannon (the parents of my father's father) further illustrates the importance of having this position.[278] In Amanda's case it was uncertain which wife, she or her older sister Sarah, was the first wife. Before we explore how this unusual marriage arrangement illustrates the importance of being the first wife, let's become better acquainted with the Mousley family.

Amanda and Sarah were two of ten children in the family of Titus and Ann McMenemy Mousley. They were a prosperous family with roots dating back to pre-Revolutionary War times, living in northern Delaware when Mormon missionaries approached them with the gospel.[279] Ann McMenemy Mousley and some of the older children, including Sarah, joined

---

278 Hereafter, Ann Amanda will be referred to as Amanda, the name by which she most commonly went.

279 *1990 Angus M. Cannon Reunion Materials*, edited by Angus M. Cannon Reunion Committee (1990): 10. The Mousley property adjoined where the DuPont Winterthur Museum now stands.

the Church in 1840.²⁸⁰ Ann had no further contact with the Church for fifteen years but kept the teachings alive in her home. In 1854, Angus, who was serving a mission to the eastern United States, was one of the elders who reestablished contact with the Mousley family. In his journal he records his pleasure at visiting with the warm and hospitable family.²⁸¹ When the family decided to join the Saints in Utah, Angus helped them with their travel arrangements.²⁸² Their mode of travel reflects their comfortable financial status. Rather than traveling in the customary covered wagon pulled by oxen, the Mousleys arrived in Utah in early October 1857 in a carriage and a two-seated buggy drawn by teams of fine horses. Amanda and Sarah likely stepped from the buggy, not grubby and faded from the long trail, but resplendent in elegant bonnets and hooped skirts.²⁸³

Angus M. Cannon

Angus returned home from his mission on June 21 of the next year;²⁸⁴ his marriage to Sarah and Amanda took place a month later, July 18, 1858.²⁸⁵ When President Brigham Young, who was scheduled to perform Angus Cannon's wedding to Amanda, learned that Angus planned to marry Amanda and then at a later date Sarah, Brigham Young counseled Angus that he should

---

280 Titus Mousley didn't join the Church until late in life in Utah but went to Utah with his wife and supported her activity in the Church.

281 *1990 Angus M. Cannon Reunion Materials*, 16–17.

282 Ibid., 27.

283 Evans and Cannon, 220. Sarah had fourteen silk dresses in her trousseau. *1990 Angus M. Cannon Reunion Materials*, 72.

284 *1990 Angus M. Cannon Reunion Materials*, 29.

285 Evans and Cannon, 221. Angus' younger brother David married Sarah and Amanda's younger sister, Wilhemina.

marry the two women on the same day and that Sarah should be his first wife. Amanda shed tears of disappointment; however, Angus promised Amanda that she would never lose by giving up the privilege of being the first wife. She consented and the ceremony took place under the new arrangement.[286] Though this counsel came only hours before the scheduled ceremony and Angus' true sweetheart was Amanda, he and the two sisters did as the Prophet directed.

Angus M. Cannon with his older sons. Standing: George M., Quayle, Angus M. Jr., Jesse F., Lewis M, the author's paternal grandfather. Seated: Eugene M., John M., Angus M. Cannon, Charles M., Clarence M.

Angus was a towering figure in his own right, though sometimes overshadowed by his older brother, George Q. He served as prosecuting attorney during the 1860s in St. George and as president of the Salt Lake Stake from 1876 to 1904, during which time the stake included fifty wards.[287] He showed dignity and fairness in these positions. In his personal life, Angus brought his fairness to finding a way for Sarah and Amanda to share the role of being the first wife. All signs are that the three of them cooperated and made it work.

He was a beloved figure in his family. The writings of Mary Cannon Peck, a granddaughter, show he was an important person in her life:

---

286 Ibid., 224. When Angus returned to Salt Lake after eight years in St. George, Amanda and her children accompanied him, a customary role for the first wife. Sarah and her children remained in St. George for a time to close the households. Also Amanda was the official hostess for the many events Angus held throughout their marriage. In later life she said that Angus had remained true to his word to have a high regard for Amanda's feelings.

287 Ibid., 203, 212.

[Because of his church position] Grandpa always occupied a special armchair provided for him, just beside the pulpit. . . . Grandpa was a patriarch to his family and blessed each grandchild on their eighth birthday. He visited our home often and greeted each child affectionately.[288] He was fond of fresh buttermilk, and mother churned from time to time, so he came for a drink of buttermilk. He was carefully dressed, with a stiff white shirt front, swallow tails, and a stove-pipe hat. The only time I saw him in anything but a starched white shirt was in the canyon. I once saw him riding on his own mare named Fanny wearing a black shirt."[289]

From its beginning to its end, polygamy was a patriarchal system. Men chose which men would practice it. Men chose which women to marry. In addition, it was men who spoke out in defense of it among people of their own faith as well as to the nation's legislature and even to the President of the United States.[290] As the Prophet, Joseph Smith was the conduit from the Lord to institute plural marriage; he called men to take plural wives, sometimes even directing them to marry particular women. The next two presidents of the Church, Brigham Young and John Taylor, followed the same practices. Finally, it was a man, Wilford Woodruff, the fourth president of the Church, who received the revelation for its official termination in 1890.[291]

For Latter-day Saints, the line of authority in the Church and in the family is clear. The Prophet receives revelation for the entire Church. Members believe that the Prophet is the representative of the Lord on the earth and they follow his direction willingly. Just as both male and female Church members follow the counsel of the Prophet, so too are wives told to trust in and follow the righteous counsel of their husbands. Also integral to the Mormon faith then as well as now is the belief that individual members are entitled to revelations about their Church callings, their personal lives, and the lives of people for whom they are responsible.

Brigham Young's counsel that Angus should marry Sarah first illustrates that following certain protocols was important. Just as lines of priesthood authority are followed in the correct order in delegating responsibility, so should Sarah, because she is the older sister, be married

---

288 My father often said with a smile, "Angus was a kisser."

289 Lorin Cannon Peck, "Personal History of Mary Cannon Peck," in *1990 Angus M. Cannon Reunion Materials*, 45. Mary Cannon Peck was the daughter of John B. and Zina Bennion Cannon and the granddaughter of Angus and Sarah Mousley Cannon.

290 As we will see later in the book, women also defended The Principle.

291 The first seven presidents of the Church, through Heber J. Grant, practiced plural marriage. They were all married to their wives before the 1890 Manifesto.

first and be regarded as the first wife. Also, in the context of polygamy, the first wife had special authority. Subsequent wives showed deference to her because of her position in the family structure.

Eighteen years later, Brigham Young was again involved in the inner workings of Angus' family. Ann, Sarah's daughter, wrote the following in her account of her mother's life:

> Once as a little child I remember a two-seated carriage drawn by a span of beautiful horses stopping in front of our house. . . . Years later she [Mother] told me it had been President Young; he came to ask if she were willing for Father to marry Aunt Clara [as a third wife] and also if Father were so situated financially as to go on another mission. She told me she consented to the marriage and that she then said,
> "We have no income but what he earns."[292]

Angus did marry Clara and was not called to go on a mission. From this story we learn that even years after the unusual wedding of the two sisters, Brigham Young still regarded Sarah as the first wife, the woman in the family who had the authority to make certain kinds of decisions. It also shows that he took Sarah's feelings into consideration in making financial family decisions and that both Angus and his wives respected and followed the authority of Brigham Young.

During the Underground and after the 1890 Manifesto, the laws required that a man live with only his first wife—the one who was regarded as legal. My great-grandfather Angus' marriage on the same day to Amanda and Sarah points up how they solved the dilemma before and after the Manifesto. Although Sarah, the older sister, was actually married to Angus first, Amanda served many of the functions of the first wife in keeping with Angus' promise to Amanda that she would never be sorry she had consented to the change in the order the sisters were married. Sarah's daughter Ann, who was a keeper of Cannon family stories, wrote,

> For many years neither told which was the first wife. Old deeds of record in the office of the County Recorder of Salt Lake County show the names of both joining in deeds to real estate owned by Father. Not until the days when men were being prosecuted for polygamy did either tell which was first. They would simple say: "We were married the same day."

> When Father's case was under consideration before the Grand Jury, both women were required to testify. They had no chance to consult, yet both, when questioned, answered that Sarah M. was first. They had never done so before and they felt they had been especially guided when they learned afterward that the Jury was intending to

---

[292] *1990 Angus M. Cannon Reunion Materials*, 68. Angus married Clarissa Cordelia Moses Mason Cannon on June 16, 1875.

pronounce Aunt Clara the legal wife on the grounds that the other two marriages were illegal, both having been, as they supposed, performed at the same time.²⁹³

It is striking that over the years, Amanda and Sarah did not refer to whose marriage occurred first until they testified before the government, when that information was of critical importance. The two sisters were a team in fulfilling the function of first wife. Though sometimes they had their differences, Sarah and Amanda remained close throughout their lives.

Brigham Young exercised authority about small personal matters as well. As mentioned earlier, when George Q. was called as the president of the British Isles Mission, he and Elizabeth wanted to take their two young sons with them but followed Brigham Young's counsel to leave them with Sarah Jane, George Q.'s second wife. Brigham Young's organizational skills and visionary, authoritarian leadership were crucial not only for the successful migration of the Saints from Nauvoo to the Salt Lake Valley but also for the subsequent settlement of the West. However, making decisions for people in their private lives seems intrusive and inappropriate. But, because of Brigham Young's position, neither he nor Church members questioned his authority to issue directives about personal matters.

Sometimes it was male family members, not Church leaders, who gave directives. For example, after Elizabeth Hoagland, George Q.'s first wife, died, Sarah Jane's son, Joseph, advised his mother to support George Q. in taking a fifth wife, Caroline (Carlie) Young Croxall, as his legal wife rather than following the custom of the second wife becoming the legal one. Joseph said, "Now Mother, you're getting along in years. Father is also getting old and he needs someone to take care of him. I think you should tell Father to make Aunt Carlie his legal wife. She can take care of him and can do his entertaining and travel with him."²⁹⁴ We have no record of Sarah Jane's feelings at relinquishing a position that was rightfully hers as the second wife. We do know that she followed her son's advice and that from all indications she adjusted in her usual supportive manner to that course of events.

Given the patriarchal role that men played in their families, it is not surprising that the family was defined by them. During the men's lifetimes, family members hosted annual parties to celebrate their birthdays, not those of their wives. For years after their deaths, the descendants of my four grandfathers, George Q. and Angus Cannon, William Maughan, and Samuel Rose Parkinson, gathered to celebrate their respective birthdays.²⁹⁵ As participants in these birthday parties and other family reunions, we descendants came to know these men as beloved individuals. For example, I have memories of one Parkinson reunion where Mother

---

293 *1990 Angus M. Cannon Reunion Materials*, 68. Aunt Clara is the third wife, whom Angus married in 1875, eighteen years after he married Sarah and Amanda. Ann, a chronicler of Cannon family events, is an invaluable resource. Because she is Sarah's daughter, we have much more information about Sarah than about Amanda.

294 Evans and Cannon, 327.

295 For the Geroge Q. Cannon parties, "each family home had the honor of housing at least one of these gala events. One held at Aunt Carlie's included the general authorities and only the married sons and daughters. The most elaborate was held in 1900 at Aunt Sarah Jane's. And in 1901, the last birthday party during George Q. Cannon's life was held at Aunt Martha's." Evans and Cannon, 338.

read a poem she had written based on her Grandfather Parkinson's sayings. At several George Q. Cannon reunions descendants presented clever skits portraying each of the five wives.[296] On a more serious note, at one Cannon reunion George Albert Smith, president of the Church at the time, spoke to the Cannons assembled saying that some Cannon ancestors had visited him in a dream and had told him to come to the Cannon reunion to urge us to be more diligent in our devotion to the Church. It was a memorable evening.

At a much earlier reunion, an Angus Cannon birthday party in 1909, my grandparents, Lewis and Mary Alice Cannon, and their six children were part of a large group picture taken at the occasion. In the 1980s my brother John, attending an Angus Cannon reunion with my father Alan, looked at this large photograph and spotted Lewis and Mary Alice in it, seated with their children, including my father who was nine. Mary Alice, not yet sick at the time of the photo, died about eight months later. My father was delighted to have this picture, the last one taken of his whole family. He gave framed copies of his family's photograph (excerpted from the larger photograph), to all of his descendants and the descendants of his brothers and sisters.

These reunions indicate not just filial loyalty but that these men were truly extraordinary. Each had a successful career, fathered and supported dozens of children, and served as a religious leader his whole adult life. Samuel Rose Parkinson, my mother's paternal grandfather, was counselor in a bishopric for thirty years and a patriarch for seventeen.[297] William H. Maughan, my mother's maternal grandfather, served as the bishop of the Wellsville Ward for nearly forty-one years, a record in the Church.[298] Angus M. Cannon was president of the Salt Lake Stake for twenty-eight years, during which time the stake encompassed the entire Valley. George Q. Cannon, in addition to the political and religious positions he held described in Chapter Two, was secretary to Brigham Young, a role that included settling his complicated estate. He also served as a counselor to three presidents of the Church. Leonora's husband, John Taylor, served as president of the Church from 1880 to 1887.

These men's stability and standing made them appealing candidates for marriage for many reasons, some temporal and others spiritual. Upon entering a family with one of these men as the patriarch, a woman became part of a network that provided economic security and social support. For some women such a marriage was lifesaving. When the practice of polygamy began, women had little economic power; being part of a family, whether by marriage or by returning to their own kin, was a necessity. Women could not own property and had few ways to support themselves. For women who did not come from well-to-do families, getting married was a welcomed answer. Such was the case for several in my ancestors' extended families. When Angus married thirty-six-year-old Clarissa Cordelia Moses Mason, affectionately known as Aunt Clara, she had been recently widowed with five children. The first husband of William Maughan's second wife, Elizabeth Brice Hill, froze to death traveling in the canyon to get to

---

[296] One funny memory I have of a reunion dinner at the Lion House was a Cannon cousin being wide-eyed with envy that I was a "double Cannon." My grandparents, Lewis and Mary Alice Cannon, were first cousins since their fathers were brothers.

[297] Lester Parkinson Taylor, *Samuel Rose Parkinson: Portrait of a Pioneer* (Provo, UT: The Claymont Co., 1977): 155, 161.

[298] Janice Maughan, 179.

Wellsville, and his fourth wife, Mary Jane Lloyd, my great-grandmother, was an orphan who had been adopted by a Church family in Wales.[299] As mentioned earlier, upon Elizabeth's request, George Q. married her recently divorced sister, Emily, during the last year of Elizabeth's life and provided financial security for her in his will.

Though there are many examples of women in dire straits entering polygamy, my direct female forbears, except for Mary Lloyd, were, like their prospective husbands, from prominent, stable families. They entered marriage having received a strong religious and secular education and had experienced economic security and stability. Abraham Hoagland, Elizabeth's father, was a bishop in Nauvoo and later in Salt Lake; Titus Mousley, Ann Amanda's father, not a member of the Church until his later years, was wealthy and supported his wife in her acceptance of Mormonism and came to Utah with her and their children. Thomas Smart, Charlotte's father, was a fellow settler of Franklin, Idaho, with Samuel Rose Parkinson and was well established in the area; Charlotte's two brothers, Thomas and William, were prominent and financially secure. No matter what their age or dowry, these women brought to their marriages valuable attributes and skills that greatly benefitted their entire family network. A biographer in the *Cannon Family Historical Treasury* wrote, "George Q. Cannon's remarkable insight was never better demonstrated than in his choice of the ladies he courted and married. They must be spiritual, intelligent, pleasing, and strong—strong enough to live and to die, to bear, rear, and bury their children without their husband if necessary."[300] My other great-grandfathers showed similar acuity in choosing their wives.[301]

One attribute shared by all of the wives and their husbands in my family was their commitment to their new religion. Many, in joining the Church, had not only left behind a secure and stable life but also family members who loved them. Whether born into the faith or converted, they all devoted their lives to a cause greater than themselves and showed resilience and adaptability in meeting the rigorous demands posed by living their faith on the frontier.

Marrying and having children was integral to their religion. Section 132 of the Doctrine and Covenants stresses the importance of the new and everlasting covenant—eternal marriage. The revelation also sheds light on a main reason plural marriage was introduced: "for they [wives] are given unto him [a husband] to multiply and replenish the earth, according to my commandment, and to fulfill the promise which was given by my Father before the foundation of the world, and for their exaltation in the eternal worlds, that they may bear the souls of men."[302] Because of the young ages at which many of these women married and the number of wives the men had, these husbands and their wives did indeed multiply and replenish the earth. George Q. fathered thirty-four children and adopted five of Carlie's from a previous marriage; Angus fathered twenty children and adopted Clara's three living children whose father had

---

299 For a biographical sketch of Mary Jane Lloyd, see Appendix E.

300 Evans and Cannon, 97.

301 In addition to bringing various strengths and assets to their marriages to fellow Church members, women benefitted from these unions. By marrying in the fold, a woman's spiritual salvation and social acceptance were ensured. If a woman married outside the fold, she jeopardized her spiritual and social standing as well as that of her children.

302 D&C 132:63.

died; William Maughan fathered forty-eight children, and Samuel Rose Parkinson thirty-two. At a recent Parkinson reunion it was estimated that more than twelve thousand people have been born to the descendants of Samuel Rose and his three wives.[303] Descendants of all four of my great-grandparents as well as other polygamous families living in all parts of the world carry not only the name of their forbears but often their religious commitment and leadership skills as well. These descendants have been instrumental in strengthening the Church and spreading the gospel.

In recent years Church leaders have done a better job recognizing what has been true since the Church's inception: that women play a central role in the Church. When the Relief Society was organized in the spring of 1842, Joseph Smith gave women "a portion of the keys of the kingdom,"[304] making them "legal administrators holding the keys of presidency."[305] He said that the Society was patterned after the priesthood and that the women needed "to elect a president who would choose counselors to preside over the society, just as the First Presidency presided over the Church."[306] Elizabeth Ann Whitney nominated Emma Smith, the Prophet's wife, to serve as president.[307] Joseph rejoiced in the formation of Relief Society, which enabled women, as they wrote in their minutes, to "improve upon our talents and to prepare for those blessings which God is soon to bestow upon us."[308] He spoke regarding those blessings at the Relief Society's first meeting:

> In the beginning God created man, male and female, and bestowed upon man certain blessings peculiar to a man of God, of which women partook.... [I]t takes all to restore the Priesthood. It is the intent of the Society, by humility and faithfulness [to receive such blessings] in connexion with those husbands that are found worthy.... It is our privilege as that of the ancient saints to receive grace for grace, light and intelligence—if we have intelligence we have power—knowledge is power.[309]

---

303 Parkinson Family Reunion Brochure, 2012.

304 Bruce R. McConkie, "The Relief Society and the Keys of the Kingdom," *Relief Society Magazine* 37 (March 1950): 151, quoted in Carol Cornwall Madsen, "Mormon Women and The Temple," 80.

305 Nauvoo Relief Society Minutes, August 13, 1843, quoted in Madsen, "Mormon Women and The Temple," 80.

306 Richard Lyman Bushman, *Joseph Smith: Rough Stone Rolling* (New York: Vintage Books, 2007): 446.

307 Derr, Cannon, and Beecher, 28.

308 Nauvoo Relief Society Minutes, May 27, 1842, quoted in Derr, Cannon, and Beecher, 54.

309 Ibid.

Women embraced the opportunity to lead and be led by women. At the request of Sarah Granger Kimball, Eliza R. Snow, one of the Society's first members, wrote a constitution and bylaws for the Society, which Joseph said was "the best he had ever seen."[310] A year after the Society was formed came an event that gave women the power to bring salvation to themselves and their dead female kin: they received their temple endowments in ways that mirrored what the men had received. When women joined men in the sessions, it was for many as the Prophet Joseph promised Mercy Fielding Thompson it would be. He said that the endowment "will bring you out of darkness into marvelous light."[311] Joseph Smith also received and established by revelation the temple ordinances that sealed husband and wife together in marriage "for time and all eternity." If a marriage between a man and a woman is performed by priesthood authority in the temple, the marriage partners are promised that if they do not violate their obligations, their marriage covenants will last through the eternities. They are sealed to each other and to their children forever.

Women played an essential role in these ordinances. First they received them for themselves and then acted as officiators and proxies for other women who had died. While these ordinances were applicable to both men and women and promised the same level of exaltation to both, they had particular significance to women because "they opened up a new concept of spiritual participation relating to the 'privileges, blessings and gifts of the priesthood,' which not only enhanced their position in the Church but offered limitless potential in the hereafter."[312] As wife of the Prophet, Emma Smith was the first woman to receive the temple ordinances and to preside over the Relief Society and over the women ordained to perform temple ordinances. Had the Nauvoo temple been completed before her husband's death in June 1844, Emma and Joseph may well have presided there as president and "presidentess," a commonly used nineteenth-century term for the position now known as temple matron.[313]

Members of the Relief Society were grateful to experience the sealing powers of the priesthood, which linked them to their husbands in eternal marriage and bound families together from generation to generation. Women entered into covenants and received the keys that would lead them to exaltation; they performed their portion of these saving ordinances, officiating at the temple alongside men. At a Relief Society conference in Juab, Utah, in 1879, President John Taylor explained this partnership: "Our sisters should be prepared to take their position in Zion. Our sisters are really one with us, and when the brethren go into the Temples to officiate for the males, the sisters will go for the females; we operate together for the good of the whole, that we may be united together for time and all eternity."[314]

---

310 Female Relief Society Minutes, March 17, 30, 1842, quoted in Bushman, *Rough Stone Rolling*, 446.

311 Mercy Fielding Thompson, "Recollections of the Prophet Joseph Smith," 400, quoted in Derr, Cannon, and Beecher, 55.

312 Madsen, "Mormon Women and the Temple," 83–84.

313 Ibid., 86.

314 *Woman's Exponent* 8, (June 1, 1879): 2.

These ordinances, including baptisms for the dead followed by vicarious endowments and sealings, made possible the reuniting of families for eternity. Originally no gender distinctions were made in the performance of vicarious ordinances, but in 1845 Brigham Young explained, "all men must be redeemed by men, that are found worthy and the women are to be redeemed, women acting for and in their behalf."[315] After 1845 women had the authority to officiate in ordinances for women as men did for men. James E. Talmage explains,

> It is a precept of the Church that women of the Church share the authority of the Priesthood with their husbands, actual or prospective; and therefore women, whether taking the endowment for themselves or for the dead, are not ordained to specific rank in the Priesthood. Nevertheless, there is no grade, rank, or phase of the temple endowment to which women are not eligible on an equality with man.[316]

Talmage's conviction was echoed by Spencer W. Kimball in 1979 when he said that women "had full equality as his [the Lord's] spirit children." Then, quoting John A. Widstoe, he continued,

> The place of women in the Church is to walk beside the man, not in front of him nor behind him. In the Church there is full equality between man and woman. The gospel, which is the only concern of the Church, was devised by the Lord for men and women alike.[317]

When we see the lofty promises in the temple ordinance, it is much easier to understand the Saints' wholehearted acceptance of The Principle. With its inclusion of multiple families in celestial exaltation, plural marriage was the ultimate of eternal possibilities. Value was placed on creating connections between families; women, usually single, were sealed to prominent men to guarantee them a place in celestial glory.[318]

The high esteem in which Mormon women were held had favorable political consequences. Paradoxically, Utah, the state populated primarily by a religious group that was seen as being backward and oppressive to women, was the first of the states and territories to give women the right to vote. Starting in February 1870, a Utah woman could cast her vote. Elizabeth Hoagland Cannon, my father's grandmother, was included in a group of leading women who

---

315 Brigham Young, Minutes and General Record of the First Council of Seventies, 1844–1847, February 10, 1845, 66, quoted in Madsen, "Mormon Women and the Temple," 82.

316 James E. Talmage, "Be Thou an Example," *The House of the Lord: A Study of Holy Sanctuaries, Ancient and Modern* (Salt Lake City, UT: Covenant Communications, 2006): 94, quoted in Madsen, "Mormon Women and the Temple," 90.

317 Spencer W. Kimball, *My Beloved Sisters* (Salt Lake City, UT: Deseret Book, 1979): 35–45, quoted in Madsen, "Mormon Women and the Temple," 93.

318 Allen and Leonard, 242.

wrote a letter thanking Acting Governor S. A. Mann for signing the bill.[319] A remarkably long fifty years passed before the ratification of the Nineteenth Amendment that gave the right to vote to women across the United States. As related in my introduction, Mormon women used the right to vote and the power of assembly to *support* rather than to object to polygamy, much to the consternation of other suffragettes. It also took outsiders by surprise to learn that members of this new church that relied on patriarchal authority were at the forefront of the fight for women's equality. We learn of George Q.'s views on the role of women in an editorial he wrote for the *Millennial Star*:

> With women to aid in the great cause of reform, what wonderful changes can be effected! Without her aid how slow the progress! Give her responsibility, and she will prove that she is capable of great things; but deprive her of opportunities, make a doll of her, leave her nothing to occupy her mind but the reading of novels, gossip, the fashions and all the frivolity of this frivolous age, and her influence is lost, and instead of being a help meet to man, as originally intended, she becomes a drag and an encumbrance. Such women may answer in other places and among other people; but they would be out of place here [in Utah].[320]

Brigham Young's oft-quoted vision of women at work, which he offered in 1869 in the Tabernacle, stands out as unusual for his time:

> We have sisters here who, if they had the privilege of studying, would make as good mathematicians or accountants as any man. . . . We believe that women are useful, not only to sweep houses, wash dishes, make beds, and raise babies, but that they should stand behind the counter, study law or physics, or become good bookkeepers and be able to do the business in any counting house, and all this to enlarge their sphere of usefulness for the benefit of society at large. In following these things they but answer the design of their creation.[321]

---

319 Bitton, 163. Wyoming adopted a similar measure in December 1869, but the women in Utah were the first to vote.

320 Thomas G. Alexander, "An Experiment in Progressive Legislation: The Granting of Woman Suffrage in Utah in 1870," *Utah Historical Quarterly* 38 (Winter 1970): 20–30, quoted in Bitton, 164.

321 John A. Widstoe, *Discourses of Brigham Young: Second President of The Church of Jesus Christ of Latter Day Saints* (Salt Lake City, UT: Deseret Book Company): 216–17, quoted in Claudia Lauper Bushman, "Women in Dialogue: An Introduction," *Dialogue: A Journal of Mormon Thought* 6, no. 2 (Summer 1971): 7.

It was Brigham Young who sent women from Utah to the East to get the best medical training available. In 1869 he started the Retrenchment Movement, originally for his daughters, to encourage women to "spend more time in moral, mental and spiritual cultivation, and less upon fashion and the vanities of the world."[322]

The reason for Brigham Young's concern is unclear because there is little evidence that Mormon pioneer women were vain or frivolous. More apt adjectives would be industrious and independent. For example, from 1872 to 1914, a group of Mormon women published their own newspaper, *Woman's Exponent*, the masthead of which read, "The Rights of the Women of Zion, and the Rights of the Women of all Nations." The paper covered many topics including a strong support of women's suffrage as well as plural marriage. The fact that the original editor, Louisa Lula Green, accepted the position with the approval of her great uncle, Brigham Young, indicates Church approval of the publication. She was succeeded as editor in 1878 by Emmeline B. Wells, a polygamist, who later became general president of Relief Society. Wells served as the editor for thirty-seven years until the publication ended in 1914.[323] Initially the newspaper was allied with the Relief Society. In its closing years, some Church authorities were uncomfortable with the existence of a publication outside the official channels of the Church. After *Woman's Exponent* shut down its press, *The Relief Society Magazine* was instituted as the official organ of Relief Society.

Not surprisingly, the public emphasis put on equality also influenced the homefront. Notwithstanding the preferential treatment the first wife received under the law and the unique status she held in the family, husbands made many efforts to treat their wives equally and fairly—sometimes to comical extremes such as as when George Q. bought identical dishes and dress material for his wives. A letter from George Q. to Eliza, his third wife, reveals the way he balanced his effort to please and be conciliatory yet stating his own preferences:

> *I would very much like to have Sarah Jane and you and Martha get together and take this matter up, and decide upon what you think is best, seeking the counsel and aid of the Spirit of the Lord.* [324] *If you feel unitedly that you would prefer having your houses separate and not too far apart, I will endeavor to comply with your wish. If on the other hand you would like them connected and yet separate, all right. If you would like them to be made one building each to have her separate apartments for herself and children, all right. . . .*
>
> *You expressed a wish to have a place in the city. Unless there is some stronger reason than I heard you advance for this, I think you will find living near each other advantageous, but I do not wish to bring my pressure to bear upon you,*

---

322 *Woman's Exponent* 11, no. 8 (September 15, 1882): 59.

323 Sherilyn Cox Bennion, "The Woman's Exponent: Forty-two years of Speaking for Women," *Utah Historical Quarterly* 44, no. 3 (Summer 1976): 222–39. Wells and other Mormon women were acquainted with Susan B. Anthony and attended events at the Women's Building at the 1893 World's Fair in Chicago.

324 George Q.'s suggestion to "take this matter up" refers to the proposed living arrangements at the Cannon Farm.

> *to force a compliance with what I consider best. I will do as I said I would, that if you insisted on having a place in the city I should do my best to procure it for you.*[325]

The women did all agree to move to the "farm," where ultimately each had her own separate house.[326]

Another example of George Q.'s being solicitous of a wife's feelings, while clearly stating his own wishes, is evident in a letter he wrote to Martha regarding the timing of their child's baptism:

> *Lewis will be eight years old this month, and my principal thought in writing this letter is to urge you to have him baptized on his birthday. . . . That grey hair came safely to hand. You are fortunate in only having one. I had more when I was 12 years younger than you, but yet I sympathize with you, for I expect that hair was only changed after much anxiety and perhaps tribulation. When one has six children and has to be father and mother both to them and has only one room to live in, and that with mud-colored walls and ceiling, and has difficulty in procuring coal to keep warm and kindling wood and then has dirt tramped in all over the room, they are a combination of troubles and vexations sufficient to turn more than one hair grey. I am very glad you endure these trials so patiently.*[327]

When one considers the size of George Q.'s family and the weight of his professional, ecclesiastical, and politcal responsibilities, the tenderness and care he showed in familial matters as illustrated in these letters becomes even more remarkable. His playful humor and his attention to small details, such as the appearance of a gray hair and when a child will be baptized, help us recognize his capacity to live such a full life.

Husbands' private expressions of love and concern were accompanied by public ones. At a celebration of his seventieth birthday, a year before his death, my great-grandfather, Bishop Maughan, said,

> I wish to express from the depth of my heart my gratitude to my Heavenly Father for these noble women who for so many years have shared in my burdens, my sorrows and my trials, as well as participating in my joys. They have not only all been true, good,

---

325 Evans and Cannon, 324.

326 Winnifred Jardine, a granddaughter of George Q. and Carlie, wrote a delightful essay, "Life on the Cannon Farm," in Evans and Cannon, *Historical Treasury*. It is referred to in Chapter Two and is included in Apendix I.

327 Evans and Cannon, 133. Martha must have sent a gray hair with her letter or referred to it in an earlier letter or conversation.

faithful, loyal wives to me, but, what is of equally infinite importance, they have been, in very truth, sisters to one another in all which that name truly implies.[328]

Samuel Rose Parkinson, my mother's grandfather, was also famous for the devotion and impartiality he showed his three wives. The story goes that one day while in the Idaho State Penitentiary, the warden asked him, "Mr. Parkinson, which one of your wives are you going to live with when you leave here? You can't go home to all of them." My great-grandfather replied, "When I leave, I am going home to all of them." Then the warden asked, "Which one do you like the best?" Samuel made a circle in the dust with his cane and said," You see this circle? Put me in the center and my wives any place on the edge of it. I like the one nearest me."[329]

The role that these men's faith played in their devotion to their families and their willingness to passionately express their love in public would be difficult to exaggerate. When the prosecutions began for violation of the Edmunds-Tucker Law that prohibited plural marriage, Angus Cannon was one of the first to be arrested, tried, and convicted. He refused to have his wives undergo the ordeal of testifying at his trial for co-habitation; rather, he furnished evidence against himself on which he was convicted and sent to prison.[330] To help determine the length of the sentence, the judge asked what his intentions were regarding the law in the future. Angus' dignified and forthright answer was as follows:

> I cannot state what I will do in the future. I love the country. I love its institutions, and I have become a citizen. When I did so I had no idea that a statute would be passed making my faith and religion a crime; but having made that allegiance, I can only say that I have used the utmost of my power to honor my God, my family and my country. In eating with my children day by day, and showing an impartiality in meeting with them around the board, with the mother who was wont to wait upon them, I was unconscious of any crime. I did not think I would be made a criminal for that. My record is before my country; the consciousness of my heart is visible to the God who created me, and the rectitude that has marked my life and conduct with this people bears me up to receive such a sentence as your Honor shall see fit to impose upon me.[331]

---

328 Peter Maughan Family Organization, *Peter Maughan Family History* (Logan, UT: Unique Printing Service, 1971): 94.

329 Preston Woolley Parkinson, ed. *The Family of Samuel Rose Parkinson: Roots and Branches* (Salt Lake City, UT, 2001): 110.

330 Evans and Cannon, 210.

331 Ibid., 210–11.

Later, Angus went into voluntary exile because he could not legally live with his wives, two of whom had been his wives for more than a quarter of a century.³³² To renounce any part of his family that he had taken in good faith was to him and many others unthinkable. On July 15, 1890, he wrote the following entry in his journal: *"As I prayed this morning, I felt free in my submission unto the will of God. After arising from my knees I felt rather to go to prison than to be exiled from my loved ones, not knowing how long. I feel I would rather die in prison than live in exile with only part of those I love. In prison they will know I love all!!!"*³³³

The letters, journals, and public statements by my ancestors provide ample evidence that these men took their responsibilities as husbands and fathers very seriously and their hearts were fully attached to their whole clan. Unlike Thomas Jefferson, who wrote and spoke out against slavery but owned and even fathered slaves, these men lived lives that were consistent with their stated beliefs. One cannot assume that such was the case in all polygamous families. Unfortunately, the paucity of personal accounts, especially from women, makes it impossible to measure how happy and functional other families were. We do know from *A Mormon Mother*, Annie Clark Tanner's account of her polygamous marriage to Joseph Marion Tanner, that an inconsiderate, negligent husband had a negative influence on how his wives treated each other as well as how they viewed themselves. Indeed, many polygamous wives suffered from acute neglect and loneliness. Thanks to congenial relationships with their sister wives as well as fair and kind treatment from their husbands, my direct female polygamous ancestors had harmonious families.

Like Annie Clark Tanner, Esther Parkinson, a daughter of Samuel Rose and Arabella, had a very unhappy experience with polygamy.³³⁴ She was married New Year's day 1885 in the Logan Temple to John A. Hendrickson.³³⁵ Without Esther's knowledge, he married Mary D. Lloyd later that same day.³³⁶ This was a great shock to Esther; she returned to her parents' home, never to live with Hendrickson. In 1889 she was served a subpoena to testify against her husband which, following Church counsel, she refused to do. After much litigation Esther was sentenced to serve one year in the Utah State Penitentiary. Prison life was so unbearable that Church officials released her from the obligation to remain silent. She received a temple divorce

---

332 Ibid., 211.

333 Ibid.

334 Aunt Luella was the only child of Charlotte or Maria to practice plural marriage. Three of the sons of Arabella (the first wife), Samuel, William, and George, were polygamists. Two of her daughters, Charlotte and Esther, were.

335 Parkinson, 183.

336 I have found no blood relationship between my great-grandmother, Mary Jane Lloyd, and Mary D. Lloyd, who also lived in Wellsville.

from John Hendrickson July 25, 1889.[337] Esther's life then took a turn for the better. In 1893 she was sealed to Henry Tooles Rogers, a monogamist who had lost two wives in childbirth. Esther and Henry had six children.[338]

In contrast to Annie Clark Tanner and Esther, Luella Parkinson Cowley, Esther's half-sister, had a very positive attitude toward plural marriage.[339] Of her polygamous marriage to Matthias Cowley, in 1889, she wrote,

> I was reared in the patriarchal order of celestial marriage. My father [Samuel Rose Parkinson] had three wives and 32 children. He was a just and upright man, always treating his wives and children with consideration and equality. . . . I readily imbibed a love for this system of marriage. . . . so much so that I felt impressed that if I had a place in the Kingdom of Heaven, where I could be with my parents and enjoy the same glory and exaltation with them, I must obey the same principles to which they had rendered obedience. I therefore made up my mind that I would never marry a man who would not obey the principle of celestial marriage, including plural marriage. . . . In harmony with these ideals, I became the wife of Matthias F. Cowley when I was 19 years old. . . . We were married in the old Endowment House in Salt Lake City, the same place that my father and mother were married, and by the same person, President Daniel H. Wells.[340]

In another part of her story she wrote, "May the Lord bless my dear children with an appreciation of this principle lived by three generations of their ancestry on their mother's line: myself[;] my mother, Maria Smart Parkinson[;] and her mother, Ann Hayter Smart. May they always uphold the divine principle which gave them birth."[341] Aunt Luella conveyed this respect and belief in polygamy to her children. Her daughter Elna, born in 1901, remembered feeling sorry for her cousins who were not raised in polygamous homes.[342]

---

337 Parkinson, 183.

338 Ibid.

339 Aunt Luella (1870–1962) was Samuel Rose and Maria's oldest child. She was a half-sister to my grandfather Joe Parkinson, who was the son of Charlotte Smart, Maria's sister.

340 Luella Parkinson Cowley, "Birth and Early Family Life," an article obtained from Joanne Cowley Austin Linford, Aunt Luella's granddaughter.

341 Luella Parkinson Cowley, "About Polygamy," another article from Joanne Cowley Austin Linford. For thirty-six years Aunt Luella was a temple worker, performed endowments for 2,500 persons, and kept family genealogical records forty-five years. The quotation on her funeral program was "I am off to the Temple and my heart is singing for joy!"

342 Joanne Cowley Austin Linford, conversation with author, 2011. Joanne is the daughter of Elna Parkinson Cowley Austin.

Aunt Luella's life, however, certainly had difficulties. In the early years of her marriage she needed to keep her identity secret. Matthias was absent from Aunt Luella and their five children a good deal of the time. She would gather her children around her to read his loving letters, which he signed "Papa." His youngest daughter, Elna, called him her "Paper Papa."[343] In many ways the lives of Annie Clark Tanner and Aunt Luella are similar. They were contemporaries and both grew up in respected polygamous families with a positive attitude toward polygamy and other church teachings. In addition, they both married as second wives before the Manifesto. However, they differed in how they experienced and viewed plural marriage. In contrast to Aunt Luella's positive global endorsement of plural marriage, we know more of Annie's specific negative feelings of living in the Underground, not having a home to call her own, not having financial or moral support from her husband in rearing ten children, and finally separating from him and from her belief in plural marriage.

Both Annie Clark Tanner's experience and Aunt Luella's experience reveal how much influence and power men had in shaping a family culture. Matthias was a warm sustaining presence in Aunt Luella's life; Marion Tanner was not in Annie's life. When a patriarchal family network operated with love and mutual respect, all involved held spiritual, social and political power. When men did not respect their wives, the cost was great not only for women but also for their children, topics I explore in later chapters. Because my ancestors' accounts of their lives reflect their ability to live The Principle with grace and dignity, learning of the pain of other polygamous families, such as the Tanners, was initially surprising to me and is still sobering.

---

343 Ray Linford, email message to author, February 26, 2015.

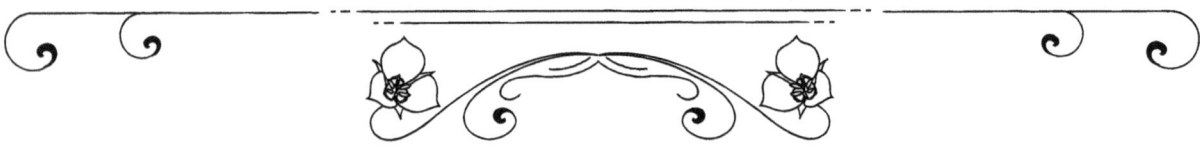

Charlotte Smart Parkinson   Samuel Rose Parkinson

Chapter Four

Sisterhood

Networking Among Sister Wives

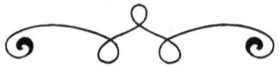

I wish to express from the depth of my heart my gratitude to my Heavenly Father for these noble women who for so many years have shared in my burdens, my sorrows and my trials, as well as participating in my joys. They have not only all been true, good, faithful, loyal wives to me, but, what is of equally infinite importance, they have been, in very truth, sisters to one another in all which that name truly implies.

William H. Maughan

OFTEN POLYGAMOUS WIVES extended themselves to other women in a warm sisterly fashion. When Leonora's neighbor Jane Snyder Richards, the first wife of Franklin Richards, was involved in a misunderstanding with her sister wives, Leonora (who was considerably older than Jane) advised her that she had "too much pride and grit to let anyone know of your domestic trials."[344] She encouraged Jane to make herself happy whether or not her husband was there and not to think about where he was or whom he was with. She also promised Jane that she would eventually outgrow these concerns. We can presume that Leonora had been similarly troubled and had ultimately found peace. The suggestions she gave to Jane to help her live plural marriage harmoniously are an example of what I first knew about Leonora: that she helped women accept polygamy.

---

344 Connie Duncan Cannon, "Jane S. Richard," in *Sister Saints*, ed. Vicky Burgess-Olson and James B. Allen (Provo, UT: Brigham Young University Press, 1978): 185. Jane Richards and Sarah Jane Jenne Cannon, one of George Q.'s plural wives, were biological sisters, another example of the intertwining of polygamous families.

Leonora Cannon and John Taylor were the only couple among my ancestors who had no foreknowledge of polygamy when they married. When Elizabeth Hoagland and George Q. married, polygamy had just recently been introduced. They were married for five years before a sister-wife joined the family. When the marriages of my other great-grandparents occurred, plural marriage was more established.

As we have seen in previous chapters, polygamy changed the definition of marriage. Rather than a traditional union of one man and one woman finding emotional intimacy and mutual sexual satisfaction in marriage, one man and his wives and children became a community that supported and sustained each other in a cause larger than themselves. The women focused on having children to build the Kingdom and being part of a network of wives who, together with their husband, worked toward becoming an eternal celestial family.

When polygamy was introduced to America in the mid 1830s, there were multiple roles that a woman filled to help her household function: seamstress, farmer, educator, mother, wife, cook, and nurse among them. What happened to these multiple roles when one household was loosely or tightly conjoined with other households that shared the same husband? Just as with the gravestones discussed in Chapter Three, there were multiple configurations—not just from one family to the next but within the lifespan of the same family network.

In many families, distinct roles developed among the wives, some by virtue of seniority. Leonora was older than the three wives with whom she crossed the plains: there were fifteen years between her and Elizabeth Kaighin, seventeen between her and Jane Ballantyne, and twenty between her and Mary Ann Oakley.[345] As the first wife and head matriarch, Leonora shouldered taking responsibility not only for her own children but also for the other households and John's parents. In fact, for a few months, the three other wives and their children lived in Leonora's home while their quarters were being built.

In contrast to Leonora, whose first-wife status meant increased responsibilities, Elizabeth Hoagland as first wife enjoyed unique opportunities to travel abroad to various parts of the European Mission including Germany, Denmark, and France. Elizabeth often wrote about how much she missed her boys, but the thrill of traveling abroad and having so many wonderful experiences with her beloved husband is also very evident.[346]

Some roles women played were determined by training. Martha, George Q.'s fourth wife, taught elementary school before she married. When the George Q. clan moved from the "Big House" (at present day 200 West and South Temple) to the flat, isolated strip of land (southwest of the central city) that became the Cannon Farm, Martha initially taught at the school for all of George Q. Cannon's school-aged children, which likely numbered about sixteen at the time. This position brought with it the opportunity to confer and collaborate with her husband about curriculum and discipline, a rare privilege. Other roles were determined by assignment. For example, Eliza, George's third wife, rode the rail car, referred to as the "Dinky," from the

---

345 The age gap between Leonora and subsequent wives was even greater. She was twenty-nine years older than Sophia, the fifth wife; twenty years older than Harriet the sixth wife and forty-one years older than Margaret Young, the seventh wife.

346 Elizabeth had Georgiana May 19, 1861, in Liverpool before the European tour. Elizabeth also makes several references to how much she misses her daughter, who stayed in Liverpool with a sister saint.

farm to town to buy everyone's groceries at ZCMI.[347] When Sarah and Amanda lived in the same house, Sarah was responsible for the meals and Amanda for sewing the clothes for the children.[348] Unlike roles determined by position or training, assigned roles were likely arbitrary or requested by the woman herself.

Some polygamous women temporarily left their children and husbands to pursue schooling. In their absence, other sister wives cared for their children. For example, Margaret (Maggie) Curtis, one of Milford Bard Shipp's wives, left Salt Lake City to attend the Women's Medical College of Pennsylvania. Not long after starting, she returned home because she was homesick. That year's tuition must have been paid already because Milford's first wife, Ellis Reynolds Shipp, immediately took Margaret's place. When Ellis lacked money, her husband and sister wives sent it to her. When that wasn't enough, she sewed and sold dresses. Three years later, Ellis returned home with a medical degree. She practiced medicine and opened a school that trained nurses and midwives.[349] The first Dr. Shipp was soon joined by three other doctors in the same family: Maggie, who returned to medical school; another sister-wife, Elizabeth; and Ellis's husband, Milford Bard Shipp.[350]

We can see that for families such as the Shipps, polygamy provided the support necessary for women to leave their households, pursue their professional interests, and return home not only to continue raising their own and other women's children but also to practice their professions. This liberty also allowed them to develop personal interests, get involved in local politics, and make significant contributions to their church to a degree that was likely harder for their monogamous peers. In her master's thesis about polygamy, Gail Casterline wrote,

> the reinstitution of the ancient custom of polygamy may have in its own subtle ways served as a liberating force for women. This may have occurred by default, with restless or dissatisfied plural wives looking for places to direct their energies, or it may have occurred through the necessity of a wife supporting her family. Some women may have welcomed polygamy as a great boon, as it decreased some of the demands and divided the duties of the wife role, allowing them more time to develop personal talents.... [P]lural marriage did in some cases provide a working method for women to achieve independence from men.[351]

---

347 ZCMI stands for Zion's Cooperative Mercantile Institution. Samuel Rose Parkinson ran a store in Franklin, Idaho, that was a subsidiary of this system.

348 *1990 Angus M. Cannon Reunion Materials*, 77.

349 "The Ellis Reynolds Shipp Papers, 1875–1955," A Register of the Collection at the Utah State Historical Society, accessed September 10, 2012, http://history.utah.gov/findAids/B00004/ b0004.html.

350 Janice Maughan, 134–35. One of my relatives, Angus' fourth wife, Martha Hughes Cannon, was also a doctor. I will tell more about her life in Chapter Five.

351 Gail Casterline, master's thesis, Utah State University, 1974, quoted in Janice Maughan, 134.

Though polygamy opened the door for women to experience greater flexibility and freedom, the majority of wives devoted all of their time to filling the many roles associated with running a household and participating in a communal family. Numerous tasks besides rearing their children called for their attention: carding, spinning, and knitting wool; milking cows and goats; making soap, candles, and quilts; raising, killing, and dressing chickens; baking bread and preparing meals; planting, gardening, and bottling produce; running cottage industries; and helping their husbands run family businesses. For instance, Charlotte, my mother's paternal grandmother, kept the books for her husband Samuel Rose Parkinson's dry goods store.

In many ways families who shared the same patriarch relied on and interacted with each other, so it is not surprising that sister wives and their children became well acquainted. Intimate intermingling of various families was especially likely when the wives were biological sisters. In all four of my great-grandparents families, as well as in John Taylor's family, biological sisters became sister wives: John Taylor's wives Sophia and Harriet Whitaker; George Q.'s wives Elizabeth and Emily Hoagland; Angus' wives Amanda and Sarah Mousley; William Maughan's wives Margaret Wilson Nibley and Euphemia Nibley; and Samuel Rose Parkinson's wives Charlotte and Maria Smart.[352] How being related by blood influenced their relationship as sister wives is hard to pin down, but we do know that a number of these sister pairs lived together for extended periods of time. Charlotte and Maria Smart shared a home until they had seventeen children between them. Amanda and Sarah Mousley lived in the same house in St. George early in their marriages and close to each other most of their lives in Salt Lake. During their first winter as sister wives in St. George, they created a home by placing two covered wagons about twenty feet apart and stretching a tent between them; the tent served as their living quarters and the wagons as the two bedrooms. "Under these circumstances our brother George was born to Aunt Sarah on Christmas day 1861," wrote Virginia Cannon Nelson, Amanda's granddaughter.[353] In such situations the line between one family and another was virtually indistinguishable.

Sometimes friendships existed between women as if they were biological sisters. For example, sister wives Mary Lloyd and Rachel Barnes, William Maughan's fourth and fifth wives, lived in neighboring homes on a farm east of the center of Wellsville while the other wives lived in separate units of a common building in the center of town.

The friendship of the women in the 14th Ward in Salt Lake City is very evident in an album quilt they made, discussed earlier in Chapter One. Leonora was especially close to Phoebe Woodruff, the president of Relief Society in the 14th Ward when the sisters made the quilt. Phoebe and Leonora had been dear friends since they first met in 1839 in Montrose, Iowa, where they lived sometimes together in the same room and sometimes in adjoining rooms of an abandoned army barracks, while their husbands served missions in England. While they were gone, Leonora wrote to John of Phoebe's serious illness. *"I do hope she will recover, she has been a great comfort to me since you have gone."*[354] In 1845, when the Taylors were living in Nauvoo,

---

352 In the cases of Sophia and Harriet as well as Elizabeth and Emily, the original wife requested the husband to marry her sister.

353 1988 Angus Cannon Reunion, 5. This George was the first white child born in St. George.

354 Nielson, 181.

Leonora wrote a letter to Phoebe, who was serving a British mission with her husband, to tell her how much she missed her, to request that Phoebe send some drawing paper for George John (Leonora's son), and to report that Phoebe's five-year-old son, whom his parents had left in Nauvoo, was doing well.[355] We know how much Phoebe meant to Leonora in Winter Quarters by her diary entry July 9, 1846: *"moved our Camp a mile nearer the River. . . . Br Woodruffe came on and Campt near us which is a great Comfort."*[356] Leonora was there for Phoebe when she lost a baby later that year. "*[Dec 13, 1846] Cald at Br. Youngs & to see S. Woodruff who is confined & her babe Dead.*" After they reached the Valley, Phoebe and Leonora continued their friendship when they lived on the same block in the 14th Ward when they made the Album Quilt.[357]

Whether or not sister wives were related by blood, their families interacted in ways that identified them as a family unit. The three Parkinson families met once a month for "Family Night" at Arabella's home. "On this occasion," wrote Carmen Daines Fredrickson, Maria's granddaughter, "business was taken care of, a program given by the family members in turn, and refreshments served. These occasions were pleasantly anticipated and proved helpful to uniting the families."[358] George Q. created his own small society on his farm—each of his four wives at the time living in a different house but all eating dinner together in the building that was also used as the school that all of his children attended.

Wellsville, settled by William Maughan and other families, with a population of about twelve hundred in 1880, was a larger-scale community than the Cannon Farm.[359] Like the Farm, Wellsville was physically isolated, but unlike George Q.'s isolated living situation, people other than family lived in Wellsville. William was the bishop of this small farming community for over forty years. *Windows of Wellsville* describes the town as a close-knit community.[360] Much like Wellsville, though about half the size and somewhat less isolated, Franklin, Idaho, was also a small, cohesive community. It was settled by Thomas Smart and Samuel Rose Parkinson, my forbears, as well as other Mormon leaders.

With communal living, families experienced a predictable set of strains, including competition among the wives. For example, as mentioned in Chapter Two, when Eliza and later Martha joined the family, Elizabeth Hoagland left her home to live with Angus, her brother-in-law, for a few days.[361] Although Leonora helped her husband choose Elizabeth Kaighin as his second wife, later, as we have already learned in Chapter One, she wished that Elizabeth were not part of the family. Arabella was initially reluctant for Samuel to enter plural marriage. She consented

---

355 Madsen, *In Their Own Words*, 106–7.

356 No doubt Phoebe was with him. As is typical of her and the era, Leonora refrains from using familiar language.

357 The Woodruffs lived where the Utah Symphony Center now stands. Taylor Row was directly west on present-day Second West between South Temple and First South.

358 Parkinson, 106.

359 *U.S. Census, 1880,* Washington: Government Printing Office, found in the Family History Library.

360 LaRayne B. Christensen, Wilma J. Hall, and Ruth H. Maughan, *Windows of Wellsville* (Wellsville, UT: Wellsville History Committee, 1985).

361 Margaret Clayton, interview by author, early 1970s. Margaret Clayton is Elizabeth Hoagland's granddaughter.

to the idea only under certain conditions. According to Samuel's daughter Luella Parkinson Cowley, when her father lost his team of mules and could not find them after searching for two days, Samuel and Arabella

> went to see a man who had a peep stone. Father described his mules and the man looked into a large glass ball and saw the mules lying under a tree about four miles away.... To Father's great surprise he could see his mules lying under the tree. Father then turned to his wife and said, "Is there anything you would like me to inquire about?" She answered, "Ask to see your other wife, if there is one for you.".... Immediately he saw two young girls dressed just alike, and they stood arm in arm. He called his wife to come and look and to her surprise she saw the two girls.... Going home, Father said to his wife, "If you ever see those two girls will you consent for me to marry them?" And she answered, "Yes, but never until then."[362]

At a church meeting five years later, Samuel and Arabella saw the very same girls walking arm in arm. As promised, Arabella then consented to Samuel entering plural marriage.

Charlotte became Samuel Rose Parkinson's plural wife December 8, 1866, soon after her seventeenth birthday. Arabella, almost forty-three, had just given birth to her ninth and last child. Charlotte's younger sister, Maria, became Samuel's third wife fourteen months later. Arabella, like Leonora, had the challenge of accepting much younger women as sister-wives. However, records indicate that the three women were compatible. We know, for example that when Arabella developed cataracts, her children had married and moved to their own homes. She needed help. Charlotte had her sons, Joe and Fred, cut Arabella's firewood to keep her wood box filled. Each week Charlotte dispatched her daughters, Annie and Lucy, to do Arabella's laundry by hand on a scrubbing board.[363]

An account of how sister wives looked after each other's interests would not be complete without a story from the family of my late husband, Peter Budge Johnston. Peter's great-grandfather William Budge, a colonizer and prominent Church leader in the Bear Lake area, married his first wife, Julia Stratford, in London in 1856 before emigrating to Utah in 1860. Julia bore twelve children, eight of whom died in infancy or as young children.[364] William married a second wife, Elizabeth Pritchard, in 1861; she bore nine children, five of whom lived to adulthood.[365] In 1868 William married his third wife, fifteen-year-old Ann Hyer, my husband's

---

362 Luella Parkinson Cowley, "Mormon Folklore," in Kate B. Carter, ed. *Our Pioneer Heritage* (Salt Lake City, UT: Daughters of Utah Pioneers, 1958): 7:576–77.

363 Taylor, *Samuel Rose Parkinson*, 174.

364 Joan Balderree, interview by author, 2013. An inherited blood condition probably caused the deaths. Julia's only son to survive to adulthood, Jesse, became a prominent attorney. He has written an absorbing biography of his father.

365 Elizabeth's three sons became a dentist, a stockman-farmer, and a state Supreme Court Judge in Idaho.

great-grandmother. Ann had fifteen children, all of whom reached adulthood.[366] When Julia's health failed, she had no children at home to help her. Elizabeth's and Ann's boys regularly took care of feeding Julia's animals, doing other outside chores, and filling her wood box so that she would have plenty of fuel for the cold Bear Lake winters. These chores often ended long after dark. In turn, Julia watched at her front window to make sure her sister wives' sons were safely home before she went to bed. My heart has ached for Julia for the many deaths of her children and I have admired how she looked after the interests of her sister wives' children.

Sarah Maria Mousley Cannon (left) and Ann Amanda Mousley Cannon (right), biological sisters and sister wives

While most accounts we have indicated that wives usually found mutually satisfying ways to settle their differences without involving other people, not all of the sister-wife relationships were compatible and self-contained. When conflicts arose, sometimes the husbands entered the fray when women could not resolve the matter. One time Angus, tired of hearing Amanda and Sarah bicker over who got how many eggs, did as he had earlier said he would if they could not resolve the dispute. He went into the chicken yard and wrung the heads off half a dozen hens before Amanda ran into the yard, threw her arms around his neck, and exclaimed, "Let Sarah have all the eggs, Angus, but please don't kill any more chickens."[367] That Angus took such destructive measures to quell an ongoing fight is sobering and may reveal more about his impetuosity than the seriousness of the contention.

Another time the problem was not overtly between wives but with discouragement. When President Young called on Angus and his families to go settle southwestern Utah (Dixie), they traveled with cattle, horses and a number of camp wagons. After a particularly trying day,

---

366 Ann Hyer had eight sons, six of whom were doctors and dentists, including those who founded the Budge Clinic in Logan. The other two were successful farmers. The seven daughters filled their roles as homemakers equally well.

367 *1990 Angus M. Cannon Reunion Materials*, 74.

Amanda sat on a rock and wept. I want to go home to my father where I can get things out of the store," she cried. Angus replied, "All right, Amanda. Get your things together. We'll hitch the team to one of the wagons in the morning and you can go back." "What are you going to do?" she asked curiously as she wiped her eyes. "Sarah and I will go and settle Dixie!" he said triumphantly. The next morning Amanda went forward with the others.[368]

Martha Hughes Cannon's daughter, Elizabeth, wrote other stories about Angus' interactions with his wives, including one about Sarah and Amanda, each of whom inherited $850 from their father's estate. Amanda bought herself a gold watch and chain, silk dresses, and other luxuries with her money. With her inheritance, Sarah had a small house built on land she had previously purchased. When Amanda found out about Sarah's new home she "threw a fit." Did Amanda regret how she had spent her money? We don't know, but we can safely conclude that she was jealous that Sarah had something she did not. When Amanda "threw her fit," Angus told his wife Martha, "I just made it up to her. I feel like my life is going out of me." Martha responded, "I should think it would. I saw you shake hands with nine people as you crossed the street."[369] It is important to note that Sarah could also be reactive and possessive. Once Martha wondered whether she could borrow Aunt Sarah's rake. "Aunt Sarah's rake!" Angus exclaimed. "Nobody borrows Sarah's rake."[370] Clearly, managing multiple marital relationships and cultivating relationships with members of the stake he led were ongoing challenges at every turn.

Other conversations with Martha show Angus' tactics in managing relationships with his wives. When Angus asked Martha to go with him when he went to preside over the mission in Mexico, she declined, saying if she had to leave, "I want to hide in a civilized country." It was after this decision that Angus told her, "I am going to marry Maria Bennion. I want a young wife."[371] He married Maria the next year, though Maria was not younger than Martha.[372]

Another instance that shows Angus' tongue-in-cheek humor occurred when he and Martha were visiting the Palace Hotel in San Francisco. As they walked along the waterfront, he took a deep breath of sea air and said, "It reminds me of when I courted Clara here."[373] Such humor probably helped their unusual marital relationships.

Sister wives had many occasions to interact, including taking care of one another's children. One might suppose that one wife taking care of another wife's children was a strong indicator of a positive relationship between the two mothers. However, there were reasons other than

---

368 Ibid.

369 Ibid., 77.

370 Ibid., 75.

371 *1990 Angus M. Cannon Reunion Materials*, 74.

372 Evans and Cannon, 230–235. Maria was born the same year as Martha, 1857, and was twenty-nine years old when she and Angus were married.

373 *1990 Angus M. Cannon Reunion Materials*, 76.

conviviality that explain why these exchanges took place. For example, Leonora helped Elizabeth with her ailing child out of concern for the feverish girl and despite her differences with Elizabeth. Other times the younger, less senior wives were given the responsibility to care for the children of more senior wives. In many families, taking care of each other's children was a natural and ongoing exchange. Such was the case with Sarah's and Amanda's children as well as Charlotte's and Maria's. In these two families the status of the sister wives was the same. With Elizabeth and Sarah Jane it was not; there is no record of Elizabeth caring for Sarah's children.

Given the propensity of women to be jealous, have hurt feelings, or to take advantage of each other, it is truly remarkable that the diary entries, biographies, and letters we have of my ancestors reveal associations that are for the most part collaborative and supportive. An oft-repeated story among the Parkinsons, as an illustration of Charlotte Smart's generosity and adaptability, is that Charlotte cared for Arabella's children so that Arabella could attend the wedding of Charlotte's sister Maria and Samuel Rose Parkinson.

Many of the children of polygamous families have written accounts that reveal that they saw no difference between their half-siblings and their full siblings. This likely happened not only because of the time logged together but also the convivial relationships between the children's mothers. Espey, son of George Q. and Martha, wrote, "My mother and Aunt Eliza were very good friends. We children were in and out of both houses interchangeably. If mother was occupied, we would go to Aunt Eliza. The relationships among all Father's family were pleasant and friendly."[374] Virginia Nelson, in her biography of her grandmother Amanda Mousley Cannon, wrote, "Amanda always kept a cook, and the highlight of each day was when her family came home at noon to the hot meal around the big table. She dressed for the occasion in a black silk dress, over which she had tied a white [apron] trimmed with handmade lace from St. George, After the meal, she would usually go calling—often to see Aunt Sarah."[375]

Quayle, youngest child of Amanda and Angus, wrote, "Aunt Sarah, having lost her firstborn, made a good deal of our sister, Mina, and brother, Angus . . . [T]hey grew to love [Aunt Sarah] very much; almost as much as their own mother."[376] In fact, in his account of his childhood, Quayle sees no difference between the children born to his Aunt Sarah and those born to his own mother. This lack of distinction held true in other families as well. In Aunt Luella's account of the accident her full sister Belle suffered, she refers to Annie, who led out in applying salve on Belle's burns, as her sister, not her half-sister. It is likely that the mothers, more than the children, were responsible for these harmonious relationships. The husbands, as we saw in Chapter Three, also made serious efforts to keep things equal between the wives. In many cases, the women relied on each other not only for childcare and assistance after birthing a child but also for their own needs not associated with motherhood. Elizabeth Hoagland named one of

---

374 Jardine, 327.

375 Evans and Cannon, 225–26.

376 *1988 Angus M. Cannon Reunion Materials*, 10.

her daughters after Emily, her biological sister who was also her sister-wife. Emily, in turn, was Elizabeth's caretaker in her last days. This is evidence that the two sisters were deeply bonded before the marriage occurred and that the close connection continued to the end of Elizabeth's life.

Charlotte Smart Parkinson (left) and Maria Smart Parkinson (right), biological sisters and sister wives

Learning of the kind gestures these women consistently extended to each other would make even the most ardent critic of polygamy pause. The woman for whom I am named, Charlotte Smart, was especially gracious and generous. Aunt Vivian Taylor Hales, her daughter, wrote,

> Charlotte lived polygamy in spirit as well as in deed. She was always solicitous of the other wives' needs. During sickness in one of their homes, she was ever there to nurse and comfort, day or night. For example, during a smallpox epidemic, she left her own family of small children to help out in the homes of the other wives and relatives. When death struck among their children, she stayed to prepare them for burial—with never a question to her own safety.... She was a peacemaker in her parents' home, in her own, those of her husband's other wives, and in the homes of her children.[377]

Such a laudatory description is not uncommon in the annals of my polygamous ancestors. Is it any wonder, then, that when I read Annie Clark Tanner's negative experiences as a polygamous wife I was taken aback?

---

[377] Vivian Parkinson Taylor Hales and Deanne Taylor Harrison, "Charlotte Smart Parkinson," in *The Family of Samuel Rose Parkinson: Roots and Branches*, Preston Woolley Parkinson, ed. (Salt Lake City, UT, 2001): 132–33.

Samuel Rose and Charlotte Smart Parkinson family, 1903.
Back from left: Eva, Fred, Annie, Joe (the author's maternal grandfather), Bertha.
Center: Leona, Samuel Rose, Charlotte, Lucy. Front: Nettie, Vivian, Hazel.

What did living so intimately and interchangeably do to a woman's personal identity? How did they distinguish themselves from each other? After all, sister wives all shared the same last name since they shared the same husband. Soon after Eliza, George Q.'s fourth wife, joined the family, Sarah Jane (the second wife) said, upon meeting Eliza, "Do you know who I am?" "Yes," answered Eliza, nonplussed. "I suppose you are one of the Mrs. Cannons." The exchange reveals Eliza's confidence and the complicated feelings that accompanied sharing not only a husband but also a name.[378] Cannons love to tell the story of Sarah Jane and Eliza tricking the federal authorities, or "the Feds" as they were called during the underground days. The Feds sought pregnant plural wives to testify against their husbands. They arrested Eliza, George Q. Cannon's third wife, because she was pregnant. Before questioning her, they left her sitting on a witness chair in Sarah Jane's house while they looked for other likely suspects. Sarah Jane, who was not pregnant and therefore a less implicating witness, put on Eliza's clothes and took her place on the witness chair. By the time the Feds realized they had the wrong woman, Eliza was on her way to her hometown of Payson with her father.[379]

---

378 Bitton, 143.

379 Margaret Clayton, interview with the author, 1970s. Payson is a town south of Salt Lake.

As mentioned in Chapter Three, husbands made an effort to be fair and keep the peace. For example, George Q., while in Europe, had Haviland china sent to each of his five wives. On another occasion he sent five sets of silk brocaded furniture. For his daughters in each family he bought Steinway grand pianos.[380] Collins Telle Cannon (son of George Q. and his fifth wife, Martha Telle) wrote about a time when his father's identical gifts became conspicuous, and likely amusing, to the community at large. Utah's inaugural ball was to be celebrated soon after it became a state. George Q. wanted his wives to be dressed appropriately for the event. He brought back from the East the necessary dress goods suitable in style and quality. The family dressmaker set to work to prepare the gowns. Perhaps in an attempt at humor, she arranged for each wife to meet with her separately. It was not until the night of the gala that the five wives learned that their dresses were all made with fabric from the same bolt. A fashionable lady from the Eagle Gate District was heard to say, "Wasn't it quaint of Brother George Q. to dress his wives all alike!"[381]

Such a story, though amusing, may have given the wives the impression that they were interchangeable and replaceable, rather than unique. In fact, several pairs of women were seen as units. For example, in multiple accounts Charlotte and Maria are referred to as a unit, likely in part because that is how they were first seen in the peep stone referred to earlier. The sisters, married to Samuel just fourteen months apart, went underground together at least twice and lived in the same house for almost two decades. When Samuel Rose Parkinson was exploring Arizona as a place to settle at Brigham Young's request, he wrote in his diary about receiving two letters—one from Arabella and a joint one from Charlotte and Maria.[382] The William Maughan family was exceptionally close; most descendants continued to live in nearby areas.[383] The organizers of the *William Maughan Family History* emphasized that the six wives' families were all members of the same family. One indication of this is that the lives of the forty-six children are chronicled in birth order rather than in family groups.

The clearest example of overall family cohesion that I know of is the funeral of Arabella Chandler Parkinson, the first wife of Samuel Rose Parkinson. She died August 9, 1894, four years after the Manifesto. From the laudatory obituary we read that she "received during her last illness . . . the most kind and tender treatment that the loving hands of her husband, family and sister wives could render." In the funeral procession, the casket was followed by "the bereaved husband, who was accompanied by the eldest and the youngest daughters of the deceased. Next came in the order of age her other children with their families, followed by Brother Parkinson's two plural wives and their respective families."[384] This procession account illustrates the solicitude of her sister wives as well as their willingness to follow a hierarchical

---

380 Evans and Cannon, 328.

381 Ibid., 328–29.

382 Taylor, *Samuel Rose Parkinson*, 86.

383 Mary Lloyd's daughter Ida, my mother's mother, was one of the few of William Maughan's forty-six children to leave the Cache Valley area. In 1900 Ida married my grandfather, Joseph Smart Parkinson from neighboring Franklin. Soon they moved to Rexburg, Idaho, about 180 miles north of Wellsville, a considerable distance in horse and buggy days.

384 Parkinson, 118–120.

order in a ceremony such as a funeral. For Arabella's service, Thomas S. Smart, a brother to Charlotte and Maria, gave the opening prayer; the concluding speaker was William H. Smart, another brother—more indications of the closeness of the three families.[385]

The bonds that the wives and their children enjoyed and the complex, multiple loyalties the husbands demonstrated helped create funeral services such as Arabella's. These bonds also helped them prosper in a desert—raising dozens of children, making significant contributions to their communities, and feeling the sustaining force of their faith. These families needed all of these attributes to carry them through the difficult times that lay ahead.

---

385 Ibid., 120.

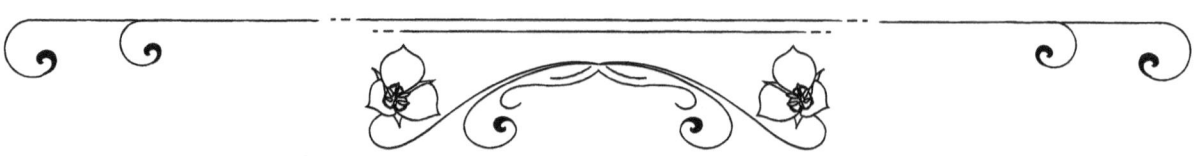

Mary Lloyd Maughan

William Harrison Maughan

Chapter Five

THE UNDERGROUND

Polygamy Goes Under Cover

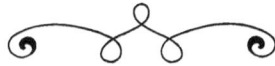

We are governed by the law of God, which is not in violation of [the] Constitution. Our revelation, given in August 1831, specifically states that if we keep the laws of God, we need not break the laws of the land. Congress has ... placed us in antagonism to what we term the unconstitutional law, and now it becomes a question whether we should obey God or man.

President John Taylor

PART OF WHAT sustained the Saints amidst the challenging physical conditions of pioneer life and the complex relationships integral to polygamous families was that they did not face their feelings directly. This way of navigating the world was customary for the Victorian era in which they lived. That the Saints were practicing a religious principle that ran counter to social norms pushed their feelings even deeper undercover. Years before anti-polygamous laws drove the Saints into hiding, many of their feelings were already underground.

Characteristic of the era, my ancestors' journals and personal correspondence did not include informal or familiar language even toward family members. For example, John Taylor referred to Leonora as "Mrs. Taylor" in reference to her caring for him in the wagon on the road from Carthage to Nauvoo after the martyrdom.[386] Leonora in turn referred to him as "Mr. Taylor" or "my husband." In her journal Elizabeth referred to her husband as "Mr. Cannon," never "George." Samuel Rose Parkinson referred to each wife as "Missus." The story goes that as he

---

386 Taylor, *The Last Pioneer*, 96.

was leaving one wife to go to be with another, he would say with a twinkle in his eye, "Won't the Missus be glad to see me!" Samuel Rose's wives always referred to him as "Mr. Parkinson" or "your father."[387]

Also characteristic of this time period was that people rarely complained or made direct references to jealousy or anger. Because mention of such matters was veiled, we have to look closely to find subtle expressions of these intense emotions. The few feelings that we do learn about are often expressed through other people. For example, when extolling Elizabeth's virtues as his wife after her death, George wrote,

> *My obedience to celestial marriage tried her [Elizabeth's] faith, and it made her unhappy at times. But she rose superior to this, and for many years, she thanked the Lord for revealing it and has been a very happy woman. For the three years and four months that we lived together until I married Sarah Jane, no couple could have been more happy unless they could have had greater capacity for happiness than we. We never had an unpleasant or cross look pass between us much less an unpleasant or cross word. Our lives were heavenly in peace and love.*[388]

From George's comment, we learn that polygamy was difficult for Elizabeth, and we can infer that he saw life as much simpler and perhaps more satisfying with just Elizabeth as his wife. As noted in Chapter One, John and Leonora also made similiar references to the difficulties of polygamy.

Feelings of pleasure were just as veiled as those of pain. We learn from Eva, Mary Lloyd Maughan's daughter, that her mother "fixed herself up in her best in anticipation of a buggy trip alone with her husband to visit his brother John and his family in Weston."[389] Clearly having time alone with her husband was an unusual and special experience.

Not surprisingly, in public and private discourse about polygamy, emotional intimacy and mutual sexual satisfaction were not spoken of or written about. The milieu of the era as well as the doctrinal nature of polygamy contributed to this silence. Church authorities made it clear that marriage, whether polygamous or monogamous, was not about romance and sexual fulfillment but about giving birth to children and creating a kingdom of God on earth. This anti-romantic view of marriage, like the veiled approach to expressing emotion, helped polygamists manage their complex lives. The counsel that Brigham Young gave men as to the importance of putting their devotion to God and commitment to the Church ahead of marriage illuminates

---

387 Parkinson, 113.

388 *George Q. Cannon Journal*, January 18, 1882, quoted in Bitton, 251.

389 Mary Parkinson Cannon, personal conversation with author, early 1970s. Weston is a small town about twenty miles north of Wellsville named for Mary Ann Weston, Peter Maughan's second wife, who raised William and John after their mother died in England. Mary Ann drove the first wagon train into Cache Valley. She kept one of the best journals available of a woman's view of pioneer times including the many babies she delivered.

how intimacy and deep attachment were not priorities. "Elders, never love your wives one hair's breadth further than they adorn the gospel, never love them so but that you can leave them at a moment's warning without shedding a tear."[390]

It is easy to lose sight of the fact that the Saints' rules and views concerning sexual behavior within a marriage mirrored those of the Victorian era. For one, the rules against sexual relations outside of marriage were strict. George Q. Cannon wrote, "We believe in marriage. We have opened the door in that direction. . . . but we close the door in the other direction, and say, you shall not commit adultery, defile, prostitute or lead astray innocent beings."[391]

At the time, it was a commonly held belief that men's sexual drives are greater than women's. Polygamy offered a solution. George Q. argued that "polygamy allowed the 'demands of nature' to be met with 'decency and propriety,' an implicit indictment of the prostitution flourishing in monogamous society."[392] A corollary to this thinking was the view, held in society at large, that a woman's thoughts and sexual activities affected the health of the children she carried in her womb or nursed. It was believed that refraining from sexual intercourse during both pregnancy and lactation promoted the "'sound health and morals in the constitutions of their offspring."[393] Apostle Heber C. Kimball urged husbands not to "weary the tree while it is maturing fruit" or "excite adultery" by having sexual intercourse at "improper and unwise times and thereby seriously injure their offspring."[394] Victorian mores advocated that men practice self-control. For Latter-day Saint men polygamy offered another solution. "Men, having no such 'drawback on their strength,' could have their needs met by practicing plural marriage while protecting their unborn and infant children from unwanted influences."[395]

Setting Church rhetoric and uninformed attitudes about female sexuality aside, it is difficult to fathom how a wife could achieve sexual satisfaction with a husband she knew she was sharing with other wives. Under these circumstances, it would have been emotionally risky for a woman to connect deeply with her husband. Instead, women usually invested their feelings in their children, a topic I say more about later in this chapter.

In addition, being judicious about the depth of a husband's attachment to his wives was likely made easier because male polygamists were frequently called away from home on Church business or missions for extended periods of time. Even when they were home, they faced complex problems of managing several households that made expressions of romantic love difficult. They tried to avoid favoritism toward any plural wife in order to maintain family

---

390 Brigham Young advice to wives was similar, given in the same talk: "And when a man has passed through the veil, and secured to himself an eternal exaltation, he is then worthy of the love of his wife and children, and not until then, unless he has received the promise of and is sealed up unto eternal lives. Then he may be an object fully worthy of their affections and love on the earth, and not before." *Journal of Discourses* 3:360 (June 15, 1856), quoted in B. Carmon Hardy, *Solemn Covenant: The Mormon Polygamous Passage* (Urbana, IL: University of Illinois Press).

391 *Journal of Discourses* 24:40 (June 25, 1882), quoted in Daynes, *More Wives than One*, 196.

392 Daynes, 39.

393 Ibid.

394 *Journal of Discourse* 4:278 (January 25, 1857), quoted in Daynes, 39.

395 Ibid.

harmony and needed to make an equitable distribution of their time, money, and affections.[396] Zina Diantha Huntington Jacobs wrote, "A successful polygamous wife must regard her husband with indifference, and with no other feeling than that of reverence, for love we regard as a false sentiment: a feeling which should have no existence in polygamy."[397]

The tenuousness of marital relationships increased as the federal government increased its legal response. The Edmunds Act of 1882 made it illegal for a husband to visit his families, further straining the emotional bonds between husbands and wives. Everyone involved had already needed to hold in check many emotions; now they had to pretend they did not even know each other. Although visits were not allowed by the law, a husband sometimes came to have a meal with one of his plural wives. On such occasions, a wife couldn't exhibit behavior that indicated that he was her husband.

A polygamous wife's limited contact with her husband (because of her sister wives, his frequent absence, the law, or the de-emphasis on intimacy) necessitated her being more independent than her monogamous counterpart. Eliza, George Q.'s third wife, is a case in point. She chose to discipline her children rather than wait for George to be there. Against George's wishes, twice she took their youngest boy, Eddie, on trips east to visit older sons attending medical school or returning from a mission. To make things fair, George Q. then needed to take other sons on similar trips.[398] Eliza showed a similar independent spirit on other occasions such as when she hid in the willows with her baby Edwin and chose not to testify against her husband.

George's brother Angus also married independent women. Martha Hughes, an accomplished twenty-seven-year-old, married Angus in 1884. Martha was an intriguing figure. She graduated from the University of Michigan Medical School in 1880 and received additional training at the University of Pennsylvania in 1882 and was a physician at the Deseret Hospital.[399] The two met when Angus was president of the board of the hospital. When their first child, Elizabeth, was born, Martha took the initiative to go into exile to England and again in 1890 to California with five-year-old Elizabeth and newborn James. Both times she went into hiding to avoid persecution and being forced to give evidence against her husband as well as families for whom she had delivered babies. While in England, she researched advanced gynecological practices that had not yet been introduced in the Utah Territory. As an adult, her daughter Elizabeth wrote about their leaving Utah for England:

---

396 Janice Maughan, 112.

397 *New York World*, November 19, 1869, quoted in Eugene England, "Fidelity, Polygamy, and Celestial Marriage," in *Multiply and Replenish the Earth: Mormon Essays on Sex and Family*, ed. Brent Corcoran (Salt Lake City, UT: Signature Books, 1994): 112. Zina was sealed to Joseph Smith and later Brigham Young while married to her husband, Henry Bailey Jacobs. She was a strong advocate of polygamy and women's rights and served as the third general president of Relief Society from 1888 until her death in 1901.

398 Evans and Cannon, 130. It was Eliza to whom he wrote the conciliatory letter about wives being included in the decision to move to the Cannon Farm.

399 *Utah Historical Quarterly* 10: 30, quoted in *1988 Angus M. Cannon Reunion Materials*, 13.

When she left with me, seven months old, her baggage was piled at the station in Centerville. At the last minute it was reported the place was being watched. We were rushed with fast horses to another train stop. All of our clothes were left behind [at the first station]. Mother never did recover them. Mother visited European hospitals and brought home textbooks for the Deseret hospital and the first nursing school in the intermountain country[,] which she started.[400]

In 1896, ten years after her exile in England, Martha was elected in Utah as the first female state senator in the United States. She ran as one of several at-large candidates, as did her husband Angus. She won a seat; he did not.[401] In 1899, amid all of these activities, Martha bore her last child, Gwendolyn, who was also Angus' last child.[402] Everything about Martha—her profession, mobility, and readiness to run against her own husband—reveals an unusual level of confidence and independence. It is hard to imagine a monogamous wife in the 1880s having this degree of autonomy.

Annie Clark Tanner agreed that the polygamous wife developed "an independence that women in monogamy never know. . . . The plural wife, in time, becomes conscious of her own power to make decisions. . . . Her lack of contact with and attachment to her husband makes her independent of him and closely aligned with her children."[403] She argued that a plural wife's lone position compels her to make a confidant of her children. Another plural wife wrote, "I have worshipped my children all my life, as I have no husband to love so all my love has been for them."[404] The authors of The Windows of Wellsville concur:

> While these plural wives were forced to shoulder the responsibility of farms and family, their comfort was in their children. Polygamy was a heavy load in one sense; in another sense it was a bond of strength. They were forced to lay aside all interest or thought of what their husband was doing while he was away from them [in hiding] and simply to be as pleased to see him when he came in as she was pleased to see any friend.[405]

---

400 *1988 Angus M. Cannon Reunion Materials*, 20. The quotation is from a photocopy of an article titled "Dr. Martha Hughes Cannon: First Woman State Senator in America," by Elizabeth C. McCrimmon. It was published in the *Seydell Quarterly* of an unknown date. The *Seydell Quarterly* was published by Mildred Seydell from 1948 to 1967.

401 Angus M. Cannon Reunion Committee, ed., *1989 Angus M. Cannon Reunion Materials* (1989): 199.

402 Evans and Cannon, 230–232. *Historical Treasury* and other sources say Gwendolyn was born in 1900. The Utah birth certificate record indicates 1899. See "Utah, Births and Christenings, 1892–1941," index, *FamilySearch*, https://familysearch.org/pal:/MM9.1.1/F823-H9M.

403 Ibid.

404 Compton, xiv .

405 Christensen, Hall, and Maughan, 378.

Though this independence served polygamous families well, when the federal government became more serious about terminating the practice of plural marriage, the Underground years still posed considerable challenges for the Saints. By the time the Edmunds Act was passed in 1882, the Saints had already been legally prohibited from practicing polygamy for twenty years. In 1879, the Supreme Court ruled in the George Reynolds case that the Constitution did not protect the religious right of a person to practice plural marriage, a devastating decision for the Saints. They had pinned their hopes on the Supreme Court protecting that right. Now they had to choose between obeying the law of the land and obeying what they saw as the law of God. John Taylor, after thirty-nine years of stoutly defending the faith as an apostle, became president of the Church in 1880, the October following the Reynolds decision. His wife Leonora's nephew, George Q. Cannon, was his first counselor and Joseph F. Smith was his second counselor. John Taylor eloquently described the dilemma:

> We are not the parties who produce this antagonism. It is men who place themselves in antagonism to the Constitution of the United States. We are governed by the law of God, which is not in violation of that Constitution. Our revelation, given in August 1831, specifically states that if we keep the laws of God, we need not break the laws of the land. Congress has since, by its act, placed us in antagonism to what we term the unconstitutional law, and now it becomes a question whether we should obey God or man.[406]

The Saints followed President Taylor's injunction to continue obeying the law of God rather than the law of the land.

During the early years of his presidency, John was a vigorous, effective leader. Known for being a fearless defender of Mormonism, John Taylor often shared his personal creed: "The Kingdom of God or nothing."[407] However, because the pressure from the government against the practice of plural marriage intensified during his tenure, his dynamic leadership was short-lived. One of the first manifestations of his strong leadership took place soon after the Edmunds Act passed in March 1882. One month later the Saints convened for April General Conference amid gusting winds and pelting sleet. President Taylor talked to the Saints of the nation's bitter prejudice against them and warned that a "storm was coming, and that it would break with

---

406 Janice Maughan, 151.

407 *Fulness of Times*, 423. Under his leadership more than one hundred settlements were founded in outlying areas. In addition, missionary work was expanded in the United States and extended to Mexico, New Zealand, and Turkey. The Book of Mormon as well as the Doctrine and Covenants were reissued with extensive cross-references and explanatory notes. He pushed for the completion of the Logan Temple and dedicated it in 1884. He forgave half of the money owed by some Saints to the Perpetual Emigrating Fund and took other steps to alleviate poverty in the Territory.

its fury upon them." Then he added half humorously, "Let us treat it the same as we did this morning coming in through the snowstorm—put up our coat collars and wait till the storm subsides. After the storm comes sunshine. While the storm lasts it is useless to reason with the world; when it subsides we can talk with them."[408] In his conference address the following day he said that the Saints would "contend inch by inch for their liberties and rights as American citizens."[409]

Committed to keeping their marital covenants and following their prophet, many polygamous men and women went underground to avoid arrest. Individuals and sometimes whole families fled to Mexico and Canada to be beyond the reach of the law. John Taylor continued to tour the stakes—teaching, counseling, and encouraging the Saints with great energy. His encouraging words helped them cultivate courage and strength in the midst of turmoil. He also fiercely defended freedom of religion and the separation of church and state. On January 3, 1885, he left Salt Lake City for a lengthy trip to the southern Church settlements, chiefly in Arizona. His trip included northern Mexico, where he purchased land in Chihuahua to serve as a refuge for Saints from the harassment of the government.[410] After traveling almost five thousand miles, President Taylor returned to Salt Lake City three and a half weeks later on January 27, 1885, under heavy guard. He gave his last public address on February 1 to a capacity audience in the Tabernacle. His speech began with a blistering attack on the injustices of the government against the Saints. Then he said,

> When little children are set in array against their fathers and mothers, and women and children are badgered before courts, and made to submit, unprotected, to the gibes of libertines and corrupt men; when wives and husbands are pitted against each other and threatened with pains, penalties and imprisonments, if they do not disclose that which among decent people is considered sacred, and which no man of delicacy, whose sensibilities have not been blunted by low associations, would ever ask; when such a condition of affairs exists, it is no longer a land of liberty, and it is certainly no longer a land of equal rights.[411]

He concluded with, "We must take care of ourselves as best we may, and avoid being caught in their snares."[412] Soon after this address, he went underground and was never again seen or heard by a congregation of the Saints. His extreme isolation must have been very difficult for him; he valued freedom almost more than life itself.

---

408 Ibid., 427.

409 Ibid.

410 Gibbons, 244.

411 Ibid., 249.

412 Ibid.

In early spring President Taylor sent a letter to a new apostle, Heber J. Grant, who read it to the Saints at April 1885 General Conference. The apostle then explained the reasons for the First Presidency's absence at the conference:

> The prophet deemed it wise, under the circumstances, to withdraw for awhile to attend to his business in a more private manner. . . . This he has continued to do. . . . writing, receiving and answering letters, giving counsel and instructions, and devoting himself assiduously to all the duties of his calling, except in delivering public addresses from the stand.[413]

President Taylor's letter alludes to the "deadly hostility" of the federal officers, which had produced a "reign of terror" and a consequent flight to the Underground, where he and other polygamists expected to remain until there was "a prospect of receiving impartial treatment by the courts and juries. . . . We are as ready today, as ever, to submit our cases to a properly organized court and jury of our peers, to decide upon."[414] Noting that only about two percent of the male membership practiced plural marriage,[415] the message continued:

> We consider it an act of great injustice to the ninety-eight percent to be abused and outraged, and have all their business relations disturbed, values of every kind, unsettled, neighborhoods agitated and alarmed, and the property of the people generally jeopardized, because of this "raid" upon these alleged breakers of the law. . . . We exhort you, therefore, to preserve your bodies and spirits pure, to protect the virtue and honor of your wives and daughters, to live your religion, to deal honestly and honorably with all men, and to maintain inviolate these glorious principles which have been revealed unto you.[416]

President Taylor moved many times in the next two and a half years to avoid detection and directed the affairs of the Church from these locations. In November 1886 he moved to the Roueche farm located in an open flat area east of Kaysville, where it was easy to see approaching federal agents. He remained there for the last seven months of his life. During this time his counselor George Q. Cannon was the main liaison between him and the Saints.

---

413 Ibid., 356.

414 Gibbons, 256–57. At the time, the law prohibited Mormons from serving on juries. A jury of peers would include Mormons and others.

415 As discussed elsewhere in this book, sources vary on what the actual percentage was of those practicing polygamy.

416 Gibbons, 257.

In early 1887, the Edmunds-Tucker Act disincorporated the Church as a legal entity and expanded the repressive measures of the Edmunds Act. With this law, the Church lost control of its funds and temples and the Territory's courts and schools were run by the federal government. In addition, women lost their right to vote and couples married polygamously no longer had spousal privileges.[417] In response to this act, the First Presidency composed a letter that was read at the April 1887 General Conference. It stated that the Church was experiencing a period "of transition or evolution" which appeared "to be necessary in the progress and perfecting of all created things." The tone and content of the letter reveal the beginning of a change of attitude toward the practice of plural marriage. It explained that such periods of transition generally had "their pains, perplexities and sufferings" and that the present was "no exception to the rule." The letter, signed by John Taylor, assured the Saints that "out of apparent evil, Providence will bring abundant good, and the lesson which the signs of the times should teach us is one of patience, endurance and calm reliance on the Lord. . . . The final victory of the Saints is certain; after the trial comes the reward."[418] This pronouncement indicates that John Taylor was moderating his views. Even more noteworthy is that he gave his support to a proposal for statehood advanced by John T. Caine, a Mormon representative to Congress. Caine's proposal included a provision outlawing plural marriage. Though giving up the practice of polygamy was a heartbreaking concept for John to support, he approved Caine's proposal.[419]

Soon after President Taylor issued this transition statement, his physical condition deteriorated markedly, perhaps in part because of how stressful it was for him to support Caine's proposed bill. He also sorely missed seeing his wives and children and having freedom to move about. Sensing the gravity of John's illness, George Q. Cannon called his fellow counselor, Joseph F. Smith, to return from Hawaii where he was in hiding. They and two of John's wives, Mary Ann Oakley and Margaret Young, were among those at John Taylor's bedside when he died July 25, 1887.[420][421] At his funeral service, Angus Cannon (John Taylor's stake president and nephew to his wife Leonora) conducted the service. In his closing remarks, Angus said, "I saw him in enfeebled health, and when I asked him if he would have me bear a message to his loved ones—to his family, his wives and children—he said, 'Yes, say unto them I remember them always. I love them individually, and never cease to plead with God for them.'"[422] At the time of his death, John Taylor had thirty-four children and four of his seven wives were still living. Leonora had been gone for nineteen years. His counselors and many of the apostles could not attend his funeral because they also were in hiding.

---

417 Ibid., 258.

418 "An Epistle of the First Presidency," *Deseret Evening News*, April 8, 1887, quoted in Gibbons, *John Taylor*, 258–59.

419 Despite his public conciliation, John Taylor was sealed to the daughter of the man who housed him while he was in hiding.

420 Gibbons, 266. Shortly after John Taylor's death, the Utah legislature almost unanimously approved the proposed constitution that would have outlawed polygamy.

421 Ibid., 270.

422 B. H. Roberts, *The Life of John Taylor*, 459, quoted in Gibbons, 275.

The centrality of John Taylor to the story of polygamy deserves special mention. I see him as a heroic tragic figure participating in the practice from the beginning to the end. He was on stage at the beginning of plural marriage with his painful and reluctant acceptance of the practice and eventually became one of its most ardent advocates. Polygamy, among other issues, landed John, as well as Willard Richards and Joseph and Hyrum Smith, in Carthage Jail, where John was severely injured and Joseph and Hyrum were killed. Later, as president of the Church, John's effectiveness was crippled by the struggle with the federal government over whether plural marriage would continue. He moved with great ambivalence toward accepting the end of polygamy, dying on the Underground away from his beloved family. After his death, his son John W. Taylor lost his apostleship and later his membership in the Church because he couldn't let go of the practice. John would have been heartbroken that this son had an active role in leading a group away from the central Church. John epitomizes the struggle of many Saints to accept and then reject The Principle that had become a cornerstone of their lives.

The tumultuous Underground years included running from the enforcers of the law, serving prison time, and sustaining families without the presence of father and husband. The efforts of William H. Maughan (my mother's maternal grandfather) to evade federal authorities—the "Feds" as the Saints contemptuously call them in the Underground days—were similar to the efforts of many polygamists, including those of my other great-grandfathers. William had many escapades, some humorous, in evading the law. According to one account, Joseph B. Woodward, a constable who chose to help rather than turn in polygamists, hid Bishop Maughan in the loft of his barn. On another occasion Woodward helped Bishop Maughan dress in women's clothing and escape on a horse. The Feds saw William about the time he got on the horse, but it was too late. He was on his way, and they could not catch up with him.[423]

Robert W. Baxter, a polygamist from Wellsville, records another example of evading the law that involved William Maughan:

> In May 1886 Bishop W. H. Maughan, Francis Gunnell, Levi Minerly, Charles Bailey and myself went to Rexburg, Idaho, as we learned we had been indicted for unlawful cohabitation and the marshals were hunting for us and we returned [to Wellsville] the latter end of the same month and kept out of the way, by laying in the fields etc. until Sept. 19, 1886. . . . On the 6th of Oct. 1886 Bishop W. H. Maughan [names five others] and I started from Salt Lake for Old Mexico and traveled to Draperville eighteen miles south of Salt Lake and camped

---

423 Christensen, Hall, and Maughan, *377*.

for the night. . . . The 8th we traveled to Santa Quin and as soon as
we arrived there we were informed that there was a posse of marshals
on our track.[424]

This group arrived in Mexico in February 1887. Robert Baxter decided to return home and risk the consequences of being arrested, "as our food was worse than we would have in the penitentiary."[425] Bishop William H. Maughan did not return until the spring of 1888, when he went directly to Bear Lake County to live with his daughter Agnes and her husband, Norman G. Allan.

Though he knew it could cost him his freedom, William left his daughter's home in Bear Lake for the funeral of Barbara Morgan, his first wife, an indication of his love and respect for her and the institution of marriage.[426] He then turned himself in to the First District Court in Ogden, where he was sentenced to prison for two and a half years. He served a shorter time, from January 3, 1889 to October 15, 1889, because he was pardoned by President Benjamin Harrison, as were many others.[427] Eva, his youngest child with his wife Mary Lloyd, was conceived after William returned from Rexburg in May 1886 and before he left for Mexico in October. Eva was born May 4, 1887, while her father was in hiding in Mexico. I have often thought about how difficult it must have been for Mary Lloyd to bear a child under such uncertain circumstances.

Some women went underground in order to prevent their husbands from being found and identified as polygamists. In the Parkinson family, my great-grandmother Charlotte and her sister Maria were initially the ones to go into hiding. In 1877, to avoid their being detected as plural wives by federal authorities, Samuel Rose Parkinson moved them to Richmond, Utah, just over the Idaho line, and there Maria's fourth daughter, Olive, was born. Charlotte's daughter, Leona, whom she no doubt took with her, had been born three months before in Franklin.[428]

Charlotte's oldest child, Ann, would have been ten when caring for three younger siblings, one of them my grandfather; Maria's oldest children, Thomas (eight years old) and Luella (seven), were responsible for two younger siblings.[429] My Aunt Luella, Maria's daughter, wrote about how difficult life was while her mother and Charlotte were on the Underground in Richmond:

> I remember a sad incident occurred while [our mothers were]
> in Richmond. It was on a wash day. My older sister, Charlotte's
> daughter Ann, made the starch and was carrying it to the table, when
> my younger sister, Belle, came running in from outside where she

---

424 Ibid.

425 Ibid.

426 Janice Maughan, 2. William married Barbara Morgan in 1853 at age nineteen; they had entered Cache Valley in 1856 as two of the original settlers. She died September 19, 1888.

427 Janice Maughan, 178.

428 Parkinson, 134.

429 Ibid. Presumably their father, Samuel Rose, would have been with them, but they probably had no other help.

had been playing. She struck the pan and the boiling starch burned her from her chin down. They immediately sent for a doctor who lived nearby. As we took off her clothes the skin came with them. The doctor laid her on a sheet and covered her with molasses and soda and rolled her in a sheet. She screamed with pain, said it was like a bed of fire. They went to Franklin and brought Sister Molly Thomas, a midwife and doctor. She took chicken feathers and washed the molasses off with linseed oil, then mixed linseed oil and lime water, which was cooling and healing. Belle soon fell asleep. The burns left scars all down her body, which she carried to her grave.[430]

The details we have of these Underground years are mostly about who was where when—not about how people were feeling. Eight years later Charlotte and Maria went into hiding for a second time for three months—less than a year after Hazel, Charlotte's daughter, and Hazen, Maria's son, were born. One wonders how the other children managed. When their mothers went this time into hiding with their babies, Hazel and Hazen, the girls left behind and responsible for younger siblings were again Annie and Luella. During the intervening eight years, Charlotte had borne two more children and Maria had borne three more; in all, Charlotte left seven children at home in Franklin and Maria left eight. Samuel could see that Annie and Luella needed much more help for these heavy responsibilities, so he decided it would be better for him to go into hiding than his wives. He was arrested in 1886 and served about a year in the Idaho penitentiary.[431]

As I have suggested, it is difficult to measure the effects of polygamy on children, including how it felt to have their mothers or fathers go underground and be sent to prison. We do know that a code of silence concealed the whereabouts of the polygamous men and the existence and the living situations of the wives and children. Any expression of emotion went underground as well. In 2009 I witnessed this silence firsthand when I talked in person or by phone with three grandsons of William H. Maughan, all of whom were clear-thinking eighty-eight-year-olds eager to share their memories and their love of Wellsville. My hope was to figure out which of three possible houses my maternal great-grandmother, Mary Lloyd, had lived in to raise her family.[432] Surely the two grandsons of Mary Lloyd would know in which house she had raised their fathers. They did not. Ken, Frank's son, said, "My father did not like to talk about his childhood. I didn't ask him and he didn't tell me."[433] When I asked Webster, Mary Lloyd's other grandson, how he felt about polygamy he replied, "They were all my uncles and aunts. We

---

430 Luella Parkinson Cowley, "Maria Smart Parkinson (1851–1915)," 3. In the text it is unclear where the unfortunate incident occurred. My hypothesis is that the mothers were in Richmond with their two infants and that the other children were in Franklin, probably with their father where the accident would have happened.

431 Parkinson, 110. In Chapter Four I tell of Samuel's experiences with the warden while serving in the Idaho penitentiary.

432 Where Mary Lloyd had raised her family was of particular interest to me because my mother and her mother, Ida, were both born in that home.

433 Ken Maughan, phone coversation with author, 2009.

were all one family."[434] The third cousin I spoke with, Clarke, a grandson of William Maughan's second wife, also could not tell me in which Wellsville house his grandmother, Elizabeth Brice Hill, had raised his father.

Mary Lloyd and her seven living children. Standing: Frank, Eva, Millie, Dave. Sitting: Fannie, Mary Lloyd, Heber, Ida, the author's maternal grandmother. This picture was taken after William died in 1905.

Mary Lloyd [left] in front of Wellsville home she owned with her son Dave. Ida and her children were staying with her mother while her husband, Joe Parkinson, was serving a mission in England. Ida is holding Seth. Joe, Mary and Gretta are standing in front of the fence.

---

434 Webster Maughan, phone conversation with author, 2009.

It was apparent that these men were not withholding information about where their fathers lived while growing up; they simply did not know the answer to my question. Their fathers must have had stressful and painful childhoods. Between not knowing the whereabouts of their father and keeping secret the details of where they were living with their mothers, life was uncertain. However, since Wellsville was a tightknit, isolated community and because none of William's wives left Wellsville during the Underground, the Maughans probably experienced less dislocation and pain than many other polygamous wives and children. The living arrangements during the Underground were enveloped in a code of silence that extended to many particulars of life on the Underground, as well as to the sporadic post-Manifesto marriages. In some ways this silence continues today, a topic I discuss in Chapter Six.

Even before the Saints had to go into hiding because of intense persecution, they secluded themselves from the world in order to create a strong and safe religious community. As early as the 1860s, Angus M. Cannon, in one of his homesteading ventures, built a ten-room rock house in Bluffdale, a desolate area near the Point of the Mountain at the southern end of the Salt Lake Valley. Even before the Underground, it was dangerous for Saints to put anything in writing regarding their loved ones' whereabouts. However, we know from the writings of Ann (Angus and Sarah's daughter) that Sarah and her children lived in Bluffdale for more than a year starting in 1880. In 1939, sixty years later, Ann wrote a nostalgic essay about the year they lived in Bluffdale, entitled "Christmas at the Point of the Mountain."[435]

Her happy memories, told through the eyes of her eleven-year-old self, are a testament to her mother's ability to create and maintain Christmas traditions despite the tumultuous events swirling around the family. An excerpt shows the close interaction the family enjoyed. "In the morning Father would come on the train from business in the city. And Mina and George would be with him, George, the big brother who taught [at] Uncle George Q's private school on the Cannon Farm. . . . Mina, the big sister who was Aunt Amanda's and yet Mother's, and without whom no celebration would have been complete."[436] Ann's reference to Mina as "the big sister" illustrates how close the children in the two families were.

During the transition years leading up to the 1890 Manifesto, the Saints became adept at making the Underground work as well as possible. We have a copy of Angus' journal that he kept from July to December 1886, written after his 1885 imprisonment and after his marriage to Maria Bennion on March 11, 1886.[437] From it we learn of Angus' going about his daily life attending to his farms and business affairs, performing his duties as a stake president, and having contact with his wives. We also learn that he usually slept at one of the Saints' homes

---

435 We know the year was 1880 from her mention of her brother "John, our fifteen year old brother, had gone to the hills about two miles away and chosen the most perfect little juniper tree he could find." John was born in 1865. Ann Cannon, "Christmas at the Point of the Mountain," in *1990 Angus M. Cannon Reunion Materials*, 33.

436 Ibid.

437 "Angus M. Cannon Bluffdale Diary," in *1990 Angus M. Cannon Reunion Materials*, 42–48.

or at the Gardo House and that he remained under surveillance.[438][439] On Tuesday, July 27, 1886, Angus recorded a cryptic message concealing the whereabouts of his wife Martha. "*I wrote letters, but again got no news from my one over the water.*"[440] He clearly was under surveillance by federal authorities. His entry on Friday, August 27 reads, "*rec'd message telling me to look out as 10 marshals have ten warrants to arrest me on sight.*" On Wednesday, November 10, he wrote, "*I reached home about 2:30 p.m. and enterd my house without being seen by putting my wife's shawl over my head. I got my wife Amanda to sit in front of me to prevent me being seen.*"[441] A month later he was arrested. The closing sentence of his entry on Monday, December 13 indicates that he took his arrest in stride:

> *I enter the Commissioner's office today, feeling I am a servant of the most High God, and am accompanied by Franklin S. Richards and Ben Hocks as Counselors at Law.*
>
> *I was immediately put under arrest and charged with having married Miss Maria Bennion, Mrs. Hattie Harker and co-habited with Mrs. Clara Cannon, Sarah M. Cannon, Amanda Cannon, [and] Mattie Hughes. This makes four charges I am charged with. I was amazed with the result of the investigation, considering how very bitter the prosecution seemed. They separated their 3 witnesses, and after examining, a recess was taken until 2 p.m., when I went before the Lord and thanked Him for His goodness unto me. About 2 p.m. we again convened, and at night they had nothing more than in the morning.*
>
> *I ate oysters with Bro. B. Haven, and I had a good sleep at night.*[442]

Refusing to sever ties with any of his wives after his imprisonment, Angus chose to stay in touch with all of them and not to take any as a legal wife, perhaps because of the ambiguity of who had first-wife status when he married Sarah and Amanda on the same day.

The pressure for polygamous men to identify which of their wives was legal posed a problem when the first wife died. At least in my family, there was not a consistent pattern in how families chose to handle this. We know what occurred in only some of the marriages. John Taylor followed the usual practice of marrying Elizabeth Kaighin, his second wife, as his official wife after Leonora's death in 1868.[443] After Elizabeth's death in 1882, initially George Q. sat with her children in the dining hall where each wife presided at a table, an indication that Elizabeth still had first wife status. Given the political climate at the time, it was especially important

---

438 Angus M. Cannon Journals May 8, 1885 to July 6, 1886. Owned by author.

439 The Gardo House, which had served as the home for the president of the Church when John Taylor was president, apparently later served other functions.

440 Martha was in exile in England with her baby Elizabeth because of polygamy.

441 "Angus M. Cannon Bluffdale Diary," 45.

442 Ibid., 48. I don't know who Hattie Harker refers to. Apparently they released Angus without a conviction.

443 Taylor, *The Last Pioneer*, 230.

for George Q. to publicly have a legal wife because of his prominence. With the permission of his other wives, George Q. took a fifth wife, Caroline Young Croxall on November 3, 1884, as his legal wife.[444] She traveled with him extensively and was his official hostess.[445] I have no information about who, if anyone, became William Maughan's legal wife after Barbara Morgan died in 1888. As stated previously, Angus lived with his children rather than take one of his wives to be his legal wife. As far as I know Samuel Rose Parkinson took neither Charlotte nor Maria as a legal wife after Arabella's death. Instead he rotated living between their two homes, a decision that concurs with his declaration to the Idaho judge in 1887 that he would go home to all three of his wives. Our knowing only this minimal information about the status of these marital relationships is another example of the code of silence surrounding plural marriage.

The position of the "unofficial" wives was precarious. In court they were called to say whether or not they had lived with their husbands. All of George Q.'s living wives testified against their husband except Eliza. Hoping to avoid being called to the witness stand, she hid in the willows on the outskirts of the Cannon Farm by the Jordan River with her baby Edwin.[446] As a precaution against being identified, some wives changed their names. Others moved. In 1888 George Q.'s wife Martha moved to Manassa, Colorado, with eight of her nine children and lived under the assumed name of Lawrence.[447] Although there were restrictions on their mobility and interactions, men found ways to visit their wives. We know this because several children were born in my progenitors' families during the Underground days of the 1880s.

During this time, polygamists went to prison—either because they were arrested or because they turned themselves in. All four of my great-grandfathers served in the penitentiary. Serving a prison sentence had all the aura and honor of a mission.[448] A photograph that has had wide circulation shows George Q. in prison garb holding a bouquet of flowers sitting in the center of a group of fellow prisoners. After one week in prison, George Q., in an attempt to bring humor to the situation, told a fresh arrival that he "would not miss it [prison] for anything."[449] His brother Angus, my other Cannon great-grandfather, was one of the first Mormon officials to go to prison. He exhibited a particular flair regarding his imprisonment. My father told me, "When my grandfather Angus went to the penitentiary it was like a parade. He was in the first carriage. Then his wives, all dressed up, followed him in other carriages."[450] This description of Angus' trip to prison resembles this story of how he left the penitentiary:

---

444 Bitton, 268.

445 Evans and Cannon, 135. Four children were born to this marriage. His last child by any previous wife was Collins, born in 1888 to Martha Telle, his fourth wife.

446 Ibid., 130.

447 Ibid., 134.

448 Imprisonment wore others down. Annie Clark Tanner was struck by how haggard and old her father looked when he came home after being in prison.

449 Janice Maughan, 177.

450 Alan M. Cannon, conversation with the author, 1990s.

Upon his release after eight months in the Utah Penitentiary in Sugarhouse he [Angus] ordered his tall silk hat and cut-away coat brought to him. Angus and Rudger Clawson left the prison dressed in their finery, riding in an open surrey down 12th South, which is now 21st South. All the Sunday school children in the valley lined the sidewalks waving little flags and singing, "In Our Lovely Deseret" to celebrate the release of their Stake President who doffed his hat to them.[451]

Angus' statement of innocence, quoted in Chapter Four, is evidence of his strong allegiance to polygamy as are his marriages to Maria Bennion, his fifth wife, in 1886 after he was released from the penitentiary and to Johanna Cristina Danielson in 1887.[452] My great-grandfather Samuel Rose Parkinson's similar commitment to the practice is clear from the statement he made when brought before the court in Idaho:

> I married my wives after I understood the principle of plural marriage and for the love I had for them and I did this for my own free will and choice and not because someone counseled me to do it, and my wives did the same. There was no compulsion on either side, and I have been married to my plural wives about twenty years, and I have twenty-seven living children, and I am willing to compare them with the average of monogamist families.
>
> My credit is good any place where I have lived and I teach my children to always live in this way: that their word is as good as their bond.
>
> I have a farm and get a living by farming. . . . I superintend the Franklin Co-op Store, and I cannot make any promise to disregard my family and turn them out in the cold world; and before I would do it, I would suffer myself to hang between the Heavens and the earth right here in Blackfoot, but your Honor, I am here to pay the penalty your Honor sees fit to place upon me.[453]

---

451 This story was told to T. Quentin Cannon by his father, Jesse Fox Cannon, son of Angus and Ann Amanda. *1991 Angus M. Cannon Reunion Materials* (1991): 10.

452 Evans and Cannon, 234–37. Johanna had one child who died very young.

453 Parkinson, 110.

Two of the author's great grandfathers are pictured here at the Utah Territorial Penitentiary. William H. Maughan is the fourth from left. George Q. Cannon is standing behind him.

The Utah Territorial Penitentiary was built in 1855 and torn down in 1951. It is the present location of Sugar House Park, which is at 2100 South in Salt Lake City. Three of the author's great-grandfathers—Angus M. Cannon, George Q. Cannon and William H. Maughan—served time here in the 1880s.

Elder M. B. Wheelwright,
   Dear Brother:
           Freedom or Imprisonment? You were given your choice. A few words spoken by you would have secured the former. Your refusal to speak them has brought you the latter and made you a convict. But you have kept your honor. You have been true to God, to your family and to your convictions. For this all true men will respect you and God will love and crown you his.   Your Fellow prisoner
Utah Penitentiary,
Feby. 4th, 1889   Geo. Q. Cannon

                                   Penitentiary, Feb. 8, 1889.
Elder M. B. Wheelright,
   Dear Bro.: Jesus the Son of the Living God said, He counted it no robery to be equal with His Father inasmuch as He did the works that He saw His Father do. As brethren and Latter Day Saints it will be no robery for us to be equal with Abraham inasmuch as we do the works that he did.
   May this be our happy lot is the prayer of your fellow prisoner. Bp. Wm. H. Maughan,
Sentenced by Judge Henderson,   of Wellsville
at Ogden, Jan. 3, 1889, to three &   Cache Co.,
a half years, and $200 00/100 & costs.   Utah

William H. Maughan's and George Q. Cannon's entries in the autograph book of M.B. Wheelwright, a fellow prisoner.

Bingham County Courthouse, where Samuel Rose Parkinson was sentenced to the Idaho Penitentiary in Boise for six months in 1886.

None of my great-grandfathers married women after the Manifesto of 1890, but they did remain steadfast in their determination to care for and keep in touch with all of their families. In fact, they all fathered children after the Manifesto with their existing wives. George Q.'s legal wife, Caroline, bore Georgius in 1892.[454] Angus' fourth wife, Martha, bore Gwendolyn in 1900.[455] His fifth wife, Maria, bore Eleanor in 1891 and Glenn in 1897.[456] William Maughan's sixth wife, Euphemia, bore George in 1896.[457] Samuel Rose Parkinson's wife, Charlotte, bore Vivian in 1892 and his wife Maria bore Glenn a few months earlier the same year.[458] These births are evidence not only of their continued contact but also of their belief that polygamy was good and right. As we will continue to see in the next chapter, letting go of polygamy was even more difficult than accepting it had been, something that John and Leonora could scarcely have imagined when Joseph Smith first asked them to enter the practice.

---

454 Evans and Cannon, 140.

455 Ibid., 233.

456 Ibid., 236.

457 Janice Maughan, 172.

458 Parkinson, 134.

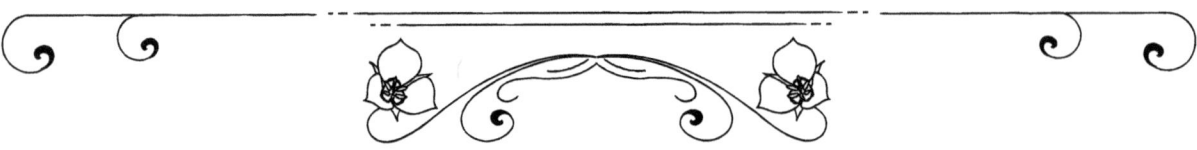

Lewis M. Cannon   Mary Alice (Mamie) Cannon

Chapter Six

LIFE AFTER POLYGAMY

Strains of the Post-Manifesto Period

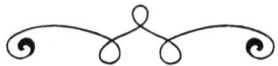

Neither side [the federal government or the Church] seemed to comprehend the magnitude of theological dysfunction then afflicting the church. Mormonism was, in fact, in the throes of doctrinal reformation.... When one considers how deeply imbedded the belief in polygamy had become in Mormon theological consciousness, the fifteen-year period of indirection and awkward posing associated with its arrest is remarkably brief.

Victor W. Jorgenson and B Cannon Hardy[458]

AFTER JOHN TAYLOR'S DEATH in 1887, Wilford Woodruff led the Church as president of the Quorum of Twelve Apostles for two years and was sustained as the prophet, seer, and revelator of the Church at the April 1889 General Conference. George Q. Cannon and Joseph F. Smith were sustained as his counselors.[459] As a result of the enforcement of the Edmunds-Tucker Act, George Q. Cannon made two trips to Washington, DC in the spring and summer of 1890. His purpose was to ask several legislators he knew well to support measures that would allow husbands contact with their plural wives and would support Utah in its effort to gain statehood.[460] He returned to Utah confident that the prospects for Utah for becoming a state were brighter.

---

458 Victor W. Jorgenson and B. Carmon Hardy. "Taylor Cowley Affair and the Watershed of Mormon History," *Utah Historical Quarterly* 48, No. 1 (Winter 1980): 35.

459 *Fulness of Times*, 436.

460 Ibid., 439. Among them was Secretary of State, James G. Blaine.

Concerned about how the Edmunds-Tucker Act was affecting the Saints, President Woodruff traveled through the principal Mormon settlements in Wyoming, Colorado, Arizona, and New Mexico. In the month of August 1890, he covered 2,400 miles.[461] Next he went by rail to California, where he met for two weeks with Isaac Trumbo and other influential business and political leaders who were friendly to the Mormons and supportive of the Utah Territory becoming part of the Union.[462] Given the actions he took upon returning from this trip, we can infer that President Woodruff saw that the Edmunds-Tucker Act was having widespread negative effects on the Saints. He held a historic meeting with the First Presidency, the Quorum of the Twelve, and other general authorities, during which he explained that the Church must stop practicing plural marriage and issue the 1890 Manifesto.

Frank Cannon, a journalist and the son of Sarah Jenne and George Q., was present at this meeting, probably to report on his conversations with national leaders.[463] His compassionate and melodramatic account captures the emotional blow the Manifesto was to those who had sacrificed and suffered in a cause they believed in to their core:

> A sort of ghastly stillness accepted what he [President Woodruff] said as a confirmation of the worst fears of the men there who had evidently some knowledge of what they were to hear. I glanced at the faces of those opposite me. . . . I was conscious of a chill of heart that seemed communicated to me from them. My brother Abraham was sitting beside me; I knew his deep affection for his family. I knew with what a clutch of misery this edict of separation [from his family] was crushing his hope. I felt myself growing as pale and tense as he.[464]

Twenty years later, after Frank Cannon had become estranged from the Church, he wrote about this 1890 meeting to show the discrepancy between the leadership's promise in 1890 to forsake polygamy and the subsequent efforts of some Church leaders to keep the practice in place. When the apostles and other men present asked President Woodruff what discontinuing the practice of polygamy meant, he replied that husbands must cut off relations with all wives except the one recognized as legal. Frank described what happened next:

> I saw their faces flush and then slowly pale again—and the storm broke. One after another they rose and protested, hoarsely, in a voice of tears, that they were willing to suffer "persecution unto death"

---

461 Reminiscent of John Taylor's extensive trip to assess conditions in outlying areas. As far as I know, Wilford Woodruff did not travel to Mexico.

462 *Fulness of Times*, 439. Trumbo, a wealthy influential political leader whose mother was a Mormon, had helped the Saints over a period of years try to gain statehood. President Woodruff also met with Leland Stanford, senator from California; Morris M. Estee, the chairman of the Republican convention in 1888; and John S. Clarkson, chairman of the Republican National Committee.

463 Bitton, 313.

464 Ibid. At this point Abram had three wives.

rather than to violate the covenants which they had made "in holy places" with the women who had trusted them. One after another they offered themselves for any sacrifice but this betrayal of the women and children to whom they owed an everlasting faith.[465]

George Q. Cannon spoke next. He, more than any other Church leader, had fought in Congress for Mormons to have the right to practice their religion, plural marriage in particular. Though he still did not believe what the federal government was asking was constitutional, at this meeting he knew "the end of the road had been reached"; the fight was over. The nation's laws, having been found constitutional, must be obeyed.[466] When George Q. was finished explaining his willingness to acquiesce to the federal government and to support the Manifesto, Joseph F. Smith, President Woodruff's other counselor, responded to George Q.'s remarks. Frank wrote,

> [W]ith a face like wax, his [Joseph's] hands outstretched, in an intensity of passion that seemed as if it must sweep the assembly, he declared that he had covenanted, at the altar of God's house, in the presence of his Father, to cherish the wives and children whom the Lord had given him. They were more to him than life. They were dearer to him than happiness. He would rather choose to stand, with them, alone—persecuted—proscribed—outlawed—to wait until God in His anger should break the nation with His avenging stroke....
>
> He dropped his arms. He seemed to shrink in his commanding stature like a man stricken with a paralysis of despair. The tears came to the pained construction of his eyelids.
>
> "I have never disobeyed a revelation from God," he said. "I cannot—I dare not—now."
>
> He announced—with his head up, though his body swayed—that he would accept and abide by the revelation. When he sank in his chair and covered his face with his hands, there was a gasp of sympathy and relief, as if we had been hearing the pain of a man in agony.[467]

---

465 Ibid.

466 Ibid.

467 Frank J. Cannon and Harvey J. O'Higgins, *Under the Prophet in Utah* (Teddington, UK: Echo Library, 2007): 102–11, quoted in Bitton, 314.

The Prophet, the bearer of the momentous news, made the following poignant entry in his journal:

> *I have arrived at a point in the history of my life as the President of the Church of Jesus Christ of Latter-day Saints where I am in the necessity of acting for the Temporal Salvation of the Church. The United States government has taken a stand and passed laws to destroy the Latter-day Saints upon the subject of polygamy or patriarchal order of marriage. And after praying to the Lord and feeling inspired by his spirit I have issued the following proclamation.*[468]

The next day, September 25, Wilford Woodruff issued the Manifesto of 1890, which stated that the Church no longer taught the doctrine of plural marriage nor permitted anyone to practice it. In it he also admonished Church members to "refrain from contracting any marriage forbidden by the law of the land."[469] On October 6, 1890, the Manifesto was presented and approved at general conference. In an address at this general conference George Q. Cannon supported President Woodruff's action, saying that what is required at one point in time is not required in another. He reminded the Saints that in 1838 Joseph Smith had taught that the Lord would not require them to follow the commandment to develop Jackson County as the center of Zion because of the fatal persecution that would result.[470] George Q. acknowledged that the Saints had suffered to support plural marriage and that he had defended plural marriage as a religious right in Congress. Now, however, he said it was time to follow the law of the land. President Woodruff closed the meeting once again strongly defending the issuance of the Manifesto.

The comments President Woodruff made about polygamy at a stake conference in November 1891 in Logan, Utah, indicate the strong feelings he had encountered against giving up polygamy during the previous year:

> The Lord showed me by vision and revelation exactly what would take place if we did not stop this practice. If we had not stopped it, you would have had no use for. . . . any of the men in this temple at Logan; for all ordinances would be stopped throughout the land of Zion. Confusion would reign throughout Israel, and many men would be made prisoners. This trouble would have come upon the whole Church, and we should have been compelled to stop the practice. Now, the question is, whether it should be stopped in this manner, or in the way the Lord has manifested to us, and leave our Prophets and Apostles and fathers free men, and the temples in the hands of the people, so that the dead may be redeemed. A large number has already been delivered from the prison house in the spirit world by

---

468 Allen and Leonard, 414.

469 D&C OD 1, 292.

470 D&C 124:49.

this people, and shall the work go on or stop? This is the question I lay before the Latter-day Saints. You have to judge for yourselves. I want you to answer it for yourselves. I shall not answer it; but I say to you that that is exactly the condition we as a people would have been in had we not taken the course we have.

. . . I saw exactly what would come to pass if there was not something done. I have had this spirit upon me for a long time. But I want to say this: I should have let all the temples go out of our hands; I should have gone to prison myself, and let every other man go there, had not the God of heaven commanded me to do what I did do; and when the hour came that I was commanded to do that, it was all clear to me. I went before the Lord, and I wrote what the Lord told me to write. . . . I leave this with you, for you to contemplate and consider. The Lord is at work with us.[471]

The President of the Church apparently felt the need to make this strong statement defending issuing the Manifesto because many Church leaders and members wanted to continue with plural marriage.

Clearly letting go of polygamy was even more difficult than embracing it had been fifty years earlier. It was excruciatingly difficult to drop a practice that was a cornerstone of their religion that they had fought to preserve with all their energy. However the Saints knew that forsaking The Principle was necessary for the survival of the Church. They also knew that for Utah to join the Union, they needed to obey federal law and discontinue the practice of polygamy and also agree to a clearer separation between church and state, a topic I discuss in Chapter Seven.

The year 1890 was a watershed year for the Church. Giving up plural marriage moved the Saints toward a less isolated existence. President Woodruff's public declaration and the majority of the membership's compliance was probably the reason the Mormon Tabernacle Choir was invited to participate in the Columbian Exposition of 1893 in Chicago. In addition, several Mormon women were invited to the Exposition to participate in activities geared towards women being enfranchised. Also, Saints who were not invited participants attended on their own, including my grandparents, Lewis and Mary Alice Cannon. My relatives and their fellow Saints apparently now felt comfortable mingling with mainstream America. Because the Church stepped away from polygamy, the government did not take the Church temples or financial assets. The Saints were energized to finish the Salt Lake Temple and they dedicated it on April 6, 1893. They had begun it forty years earlier, just five years after entering the Valley.

---

471 D&C OD 1, 293.

The following year, Church authorities addressed the second obstacle to obtaining statehood, the separation of church and state, by disbanding the People's Party, to which every Church member had belonged. Afterward, members were assigned to join either the Democratic or the Republican Party.[472] George Q. Cannon's unending efforts for Utah to become a state finally bore fruit. On January 4, 1896, Utah joined the Union as the forty-fifth state.

The response of most polygamists to the Manifesto, including my great-grandfathers, was to follow it even though doing so was a challenge. How could a man have no contact with wives and children with whom he had close emotional bonds and for whom he was financially responsible? The men were ingenious in finding ways to keep in touch with and to support their plural wives and children.

The story of how William Maughan financially took care of my great-grandmother, Mary Lloyd, his fourth wife, is a case in point. As I mentioned in Chapter Five, while I was researching in which of three Maughan houses in Wellsville my mother and her mother, Ida, Mary Lloyd's daughter, were born, LuAnn Bates, a former resident of the most likely house, unearthed a deed her father had kept that was very revealing. The deed shows that William Maughan sold the house to Mary Lloyd in 1904 for five hundred dollars. At first I was puzzled. Why would William sell a house to Mary Lloyd, whom he had married thirty-seven years earlier? She had lived in this house essentially all of her married life. It was here she raised their nine children. The house was already hers. Then the answer came to me. In the eyes of the law, Mary was not his legal wife, so the house was not hers; no mention could be made of their relationship in the deed of sale. Likely anticipating his death, William sold the house to Mary to protect her right to keep it. William died six months later on August 29, 1905.[473] According to the deed, Mary sold the house a year later for fourteen hundred dollars—nine hundred dollars more than she had paid for it. This money helped defray the expense of living with her son Dave and his family until her death on November 4, 1922.[474]

Over the years, the state and federal courts struggled with what polygamous spouses and their children should inherit from a polygamous father's estate. One of the first acts passed by the Utah Territorial Legislature in 1852 provided that children of polygamous unions and their mothers could inherit from the father in the same manner as "legitimate" children.[475] In 1862, Congress passed the Morrill Anti-Polygamy Law, which indicated that all acts or statues passed by the Utah Legislature that "establish, support, maintain, shield, or countenance polygamy" were annulled. On the basis of this law, in 1890, the Utah Supreme Court, on which Mormons were ineligible to serve, ruled that children born through plural marriages were no longer legal

---

472 Allen and Leonard, 417.

473 Janice Maughan, 1.

474 Ibid., 4.

475 Territorial Act of March 3, 1852.

heirs.[476] However, when this decision was cited in an appeal to the United States Supreme Court the year after the 1890 Manifesto had been announced, the Court ruled that the Anti-Polygamy Law of 1862 did not annul the previous statute passed by the Territorial Legislature of 1852 regarding what children of plural wives inherited.[477] However, the plural wives of polygamous unions did not fare as well as the children did. In 1905 (the year after William Maughan deeded the house to Mary Lloyd) in Raleigh v. Wells the court ruled that a polygamous wife could not retain the house where she had lived and raised her family, saying that it could grant her no inheritance since under the law she did not have the status of legal wife.[478]

The federal law mandated that each man could have only one legal wife. Many of my ancestors were creative about how they dealt with this law after the first wife died. As characteristic of the silence surrounding polygamy, in my family little has been said about who was the legal wife after the first wife died. I don't know who became William Maughan's legal wife after Barbara Morgan died or with whom he lived. In the Parkinson family I do not know whether Charlotte, Maria, or neither of them became the lawful wife after Arabella died in 1894. Under the usual practice my great-grandmother Charlotte, as the second wife, would have become the lawful wife. At one time I thought Maria, the third wife, did instead of Charlotte, because Aunt Luella, Maria's daughter, wrote about several trips Samuel and Maria took with various members of their family.[479] In addition, the closing paragraph from a biography of Charlotte supported this conclusion: "She [Charlotte] was a peacemaker.... Often she deprived herself of her husband's rightful company in order to bring more peace and happiness to a sister-wife."[480] I also remembered that it was Charlotte who moved when she and Maria's joint household was bursting at the seams. However, after I read more Parkinson family history and remembered Samuel Rose's declaration to the Idaho warden that he would return from prison to all three of his wives and that he held them all in equal esteem, it became clear to me that when Arabella died, he probably took neither Charlotte nor Maria as his legal wife. After all, Samuel had also taken at least one trip with Charlotte and members of her family and showed impartiality in many ways.[481]

---

476 "Real Estate of George Handley," *Utah Reports* 7 (1890): 49 quoted in Leonard J. Arrington, *David Eccles: Pioneer Western Industrialist* (Logan, UT: Utah State University, 1988).

477 *Cope v. Cope*, 137 Supreme Court 833 (1891).

478 *Utah Reports* 29 (1905): 221 quoted in Arrington, *David Eccles*, 186.

479 Cowley, "Maria Smart Parkinson (1851–1915)."

480 Parkinson, 132–33.

481 Taylor, *Samuel Rose Parkinson*, 152.

The author's grandfather Joe Parkinson's crew harvesting grain on Rexburg Bench. Joe's father, Samuel Rose Parkinson, is standing to the left of his wife, Charlotte Smart Parkinson, who is wearing a white long-sleeved blouse.

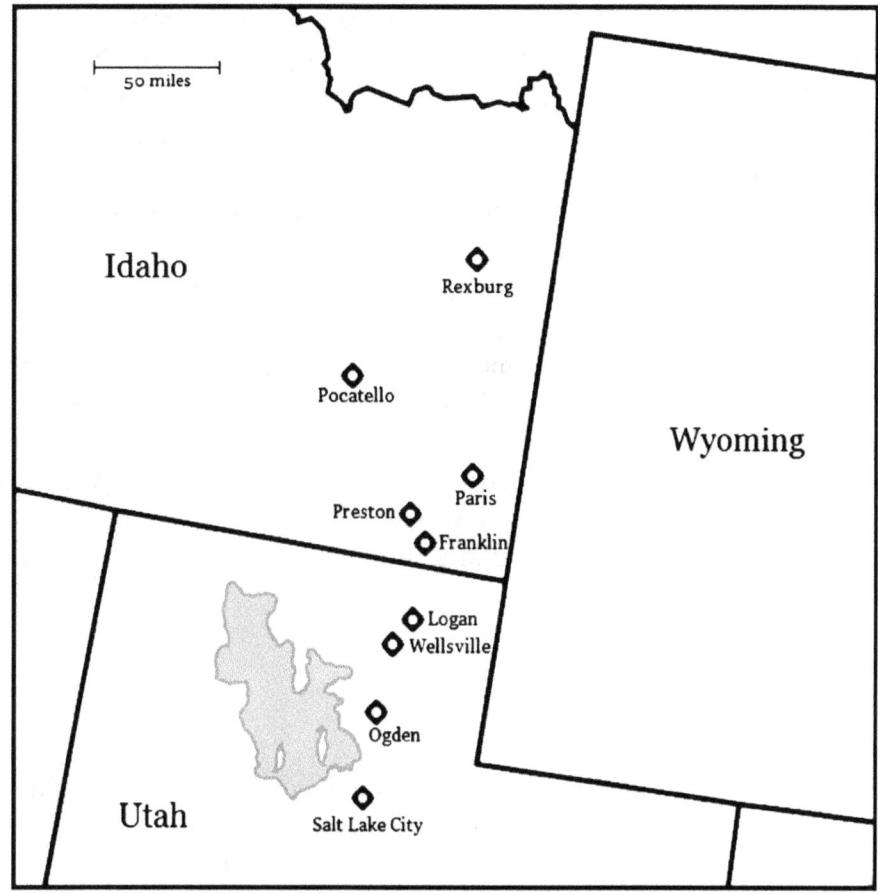

This map illustrates the relationship of the towns in the history of the Maughan and Parkinson families.

Charlotte and Maria enjoyed flexibility as to where they lived during these post-Manifesto years; this shows that they were on equal footing and were part of a united family. Sometime after Arabella's death in 1894, Charlotte's house burned down. Samuel then moved Charlotte into the big house where Arabella had lived. Later he built Maria a home on the site where Charlotte's house had been.[482] A few years later, when the sisters' children were teenagers, Charlotte lived in a rented house in Logan so that children from both families could live with her while they attended Logan High School. (There was no high school in Franklin.) During this arrangement, Samuel lived with Maria the first part of the week in Franklin, where he attended to his bishopric duties. In the latter part of the week he lived twenty miles away with Charlotte in Logan, where he and Charlotte did temple work. Later Samuel built Charlotte a home in Preston, eight miles north of Franklin. Preston was larger than Franklin and was a town where many Parkinsons moved. He built Maria a home in Logan, probably because she had children living there.[483] Such details illustrate the great care Samuel took to keep things equal.

---

482 Ibid., 174.

483 Ibid.

After Maria's death in 1915, Samuel Rose and Charlotte lived in Preston. They celebrated their golden wedding anniversary in July 1916 in their home at 129 East 100 South in Preston; he died there on May 23, 1919.[484] Charlotte lived another ten years. She died June 14, 1929.[485]

After the Manifesto of 1890, on the Cannon side of my family, Angus M. Cannon lived with his children, probably most often with Sarah's son George M. and his family, rather than choose one of his wives as his legal one and live with her. Perhaps he did not live with any wife because of the complexity and sensitivity surrounding how his marriage to Sarah and Amanda began. After Amanda died in 1905 and Sarah in 1912, Angus lived in Sarah's home in Forest Dale with their daughter Ann until his death in 1915.[486]

Because of George Q. Cannon's prominence as a counselor in the First Presidency and as the leading spokesman for polygamy as a religious right before Congress, his obedience to the Manifesto was imperative. He resided with Carlie, his legal wife, and saw Sarah Jane, Eliza, and Martha only in carefully supervised settings such as meals with one of their children and their family.[487] He had no children with these women after the Manifesto. As mentioned at the end of Chapter Five, my other great-grandfathers did father children with their plural wives after the Manifesto.

We know some of the difficulties that polygamous husbands and wives faced during this confusing time of transition, but little is known about how being raised in a polygamous home felt to children. The story of eight-year-old Collins Cannon (Martha and George Q.'s youngest) is an important window into a child's world. George Q. had called a group of his younger sons together for an accounting of some misdeeds. Collins wrote,

> I was the youngest, I was little, I was but a lamb. . . . No, there was nothing to confess but there was an opportunity to right all the wrongs that had been heaped on me and mine during the seven or eight years of my life. . . . I had been neglected; my mother had too. She hadn't fine clothes nor jewels. She didn't go a-traveling to far away places in fine style and take me along. She didn't have a

---

484 Parkinson, 130. My mother was deeply attached to Samuel Rose and Charlotte. She often talked about the summer she lived with her grandparents in a small Salt Lake City, Utah, apartment in 1917. Two years later, when Mother was a junior at Westlake School for Girls in California preparing to enter a spelling bee, she learned her grandfather had died. She was heartbroken at the loss and distressed that she would not be at the funeral. See a picture of Samuel Rose and Charlotte and their descendants in Parkinson, 129.

485 Ibid., 132. I, her namesake, was born three weeks later. Charlotte was aware and pleased that my mother, her granddaughter, was planning to name me Charlotte.

486 Evans and Cannon, 216, 223, and 226. Angus died June 7, 1915; Sarah died March 12, 1912; Amanda died March 18, 1905.

487 Bitton, 356.

sideboard in her dining room and she wanted one. In short, she and I didn't belong—we were not wanted. This was my confession. It all came out of me in soul-tearing sobs.[488]

Collins went home dejected, sure that his father would summons him back for a severe reprimand. As anticipated, George Q. did ask Collins to come in for a talk. The boy mounted the long steps to the Farm House. His account continues,

> I was so alone. It was to be unique—the only time I was ever to be with my father alone. . . . He spoke gently—as a gentleman to a gentleman. He didn't descend to my level, but raised me to his. . . . He recounted patiently some of the trials he had lived down through the years. He told me of the cruel Edmunds-Tucker Act, a thing I had never heard of. He told of the houndings of the U. S. Marshals, of being a fugitive with a price on his head like a common criminal. . . . of his capture and incarceration. He told me of the Manifesto which he hoped would ameliorate a situation in Utah that had become intolerable. . . . I remember he told me exactly why he decided to live out the rest of his days . . . with one wife only. I was so small to be told these things I could hardly grasp them, but how completely soul-satisfying it all was! . . . I knew now that I wasn't just so much polygamous spawn. I was George Q. Cannon's little boy.[489]

In sharing the burdens of polygamy, George Q. created a link with Collins. Besides revealing some of the complicated feelings of a child raised in a polygamous home, a striking feature of Collins' poignant story is that this was the only time he had been alone with his father.[490]

In contrast to the typically infrequent encounters between children and their polygamous fathers, much is known about the close relationship that my grandmother Mary Alice (sixteen years older than Collins, her half-brother) had with her father. As the first daughter to survive after George Q. and Elizabeth lost their beloved Georgiana as well as another daughter named Elizabeth, Mary Alice had a special place in her parents' hearts.[491] She was the only child who traveled with her mother each time Elizabeth went to Washington, DC with her husband. One senses George Q.'s and Mary Alice's closeness in his journal entry about their visit to the Centennial in Philadelphia in 1876. "*Every place was crowded. There was no order maintained. . . . I never saw such disorder and jamming except in the streets of London at the illumination in honor of the marriage*

---

488 Jardine, 336. For the complete text of Collins' moving story, see Appendix J.

489 Ibid., 337.

490 It reminds me of a joke told in the family. George Q. saw a little boy on a Salt Lake City, UT, sidewalk and asked, "Whose little boy are you?" The youngster replied, "Oh Dad, you know me. I'm Rad, Martha's little boy."

491 After Georgiana's death in 1863 George Q. and Elizabeth also lost Elizabeth (1865–1867) a few months before Mary Alice's birth in 1867. Another daughter, Lillian, born in 1869, died a year later.

of the Prince of Wales. I had to exert my strength to the utmost to keep my daughter Mary Alice from being crushed."[492] For the next session of Congress, Elizabeth and Mary Alice stayed in Utah;[493] it was difficult for the family to be separated. George wrote that before he left he "*visited the farm in the evening, and had my feelings considerably stirred up by the grief of my wife [Elizabeth] and especially of Mary Alice my little daughter, who wept sorely at parting with me.*"[494]

Mary Alice's family's positive experience with polygamy, her close relationship with her father, and her trips with him to the very place where the battle to defend polygamy was taking place, all cultivated in Mary Alice a deep loyalty to plural marriage. In fact, my father told me that as a teenager she protested the intrusion of a federal agent into her family's home by waving a gun in his face. He added, "I can believe it. She was a staunch supporter of her father."[495]

Her strong bond with her extended family played an important role in her marrying her cousin Lewis Cannon. He was born in St. George on April 1, 1866, to Angus M. and Amanda Mousley Cannon. Lewis' family returned to Salt Lake City a year or two after his birth. After attending public school, he went to Brigham Young University before going on a mission to Germany at age twenty-one. His beautifully penned journal from the early months of his mission reveals a sensitive young man who loved and missed his family, enjoyed the cultural offerings of Germany, and believed deeply in the importance of doing missionary work.

Despite his convictions, being away from home was hard. Early in his mission Lewis wrote,

> *Mother is the same fond mother she was seven months ago and continues to think as much of me as ever. She says there is hardly ever an hour passes but what she thinks of me and that I am always remembered in her prayers. . . . I cannot help but feel that I am not worthy of the love I receive from her, but with the help of God I intend to try to make her life more pleasant when I return.*[496]

In his missionary journal Lewis also refers to receiving numerous Christmas cards from family members, including one from Mamie, the family name for Mary Alice, and the name I usually use in the remainder of the book. Although little mention is made of Mamie in his missionary journal, he did write of his visit with someone who had arrived from Utah. "*Some way or other our conversation drifted on to the girl subject and as there was none other that I loved to talk of more than Mamie C. she was accordingly discussed.*"[497]

---

492 Bitton, 200.

493 George took their nineteen-year-old son, John Q., to act as his secretary.

494 Bitton, 202.

495 Alan M. Cannon, conversation with author, 1990s. This incident may be the same one reported by Bitton, when George Q. took a circuitous route home to avoid detection. Upon arriving home, he found his daughter Mary Alice "aroused to anger." *George Q. Cannon Journal*, October 15, 1884, quoted in Bitton, 268.

496 Lewis M. Cannon, *Missionary Journal*. Volume 2, November 27, 1887 – July 7, 1888, privately published. The passage also illustrates the close relationship Amanda had with her children.

497 Lewis M. Cannon, 78.

After Lewis returned from his mission in 1889, Lewis and Mamie began dating. They were married in the Logan Temple on October 1, 1890, the very year the Manifesto was signed.[498] Very much in love and from strong prominent families, they were off to an auspicious start. We know much of their story from the tender memories their son Alan, my father, had of his growing up years. In a series of interviews I conducted with him, he shared some of his childhood memories. In one conversation he explained, "Everything we owned in that house was wedding gifts. The house was completely furnished with wedding gifts from the family. Many of them became family heirlooms."[499] Clearly the couple was well loved.

Early in their marriage, Mamie and Lewis wrote letters to Lewis' brother Eugene, who was serving a mission in Tahiti. These letters show a contented couple focused on creating a life together before the complications associated with plural marriage became part of their lives. (See Appendix I.) Early on, they experienced a harrowing loss. Their first baby, Lewmar, named after both of them, was born January 16, 1892, and died July 6 the following year. The only letter from Mamie to Eugene, written from Saltair on June 27, 1843, foreshadows the baby's death.[500]

> *We are here for the sole purpose of benefitting Lewmar who has never recovered his strength since that severe sick spell he had in the winter, we think, however, that he will soon regain his strength here, as the salt air has given him an appitite and he already seems much better by the change.*[501]

That same day Lewis also wrote a letter to Eugene that shows tender affection and concern for their little boy.

> *My dear Brother, ... Very many thanks for the picture you sent Lewmar. He thinks it very nice and wishes to send "Gene kiss." He chatters like a parrot and as I write he is lying on the table driving his horse Pete as he calls him. He says Mama-town get papa Pete.... He can say nearly everything but does not connect his sentences very well. He has been very sick so sick that he could hardly sit up. It is for his sake that we are at Saltair, having come here thinking a change of air would do him good. We have now been here nearly two weeks and he has greatly improved, although he is still very weak."*[502]

---

498 George Q. left work early to prepare the Cannon School House for the wedding reception, which was in fact for two of his children who were married the same day: Mary Alice (Mamie) to Lewis and Hugh Cannon (Sarah Jenne's son) to May Wilken. Bitton, 311–12. That same month Mary Alice was proxy for her grandmother, Ann Quayle, in the Cannon family sealing, which I cover later in this chapter.

499 For a full acount of his memories, see Mary Parkinson Cannon, "Alan Munn Cannon," in *Remember Who You Are: Alan and Mary Cannon Family History* (1981): 5–10a, privately published.

500 Saltair was a resort on the Great Salt Lake.

501 Mamie's letter to Eugene June 27, 1843

502 Lewis' letter to his brother Eugene June 27, 1893.

Lewmar died just ten days later.[503] Two and a half months later, perhaps to help themselves heal, Lewis and Mamie attended the Columbian Exposition in Chicago, as did many other Saints.[504] One of Lewis' letters included in Appendix I to Eugene makes the wonders of their time in Chicago immediate.

In a letter to Eugene a year and a half later it is clear that Lewis retains tender memories of Lewmar. He writes that Mamie is feeling better and that *"our little daughter Elizabeth is healthy and grows very nicely. She favors Lewmar considerably although she is inclined to be darker than he."*[505] He then shares his efforts to create a welcoming landscape for their new home as well as his warmth and humor.

> *I have had a grove of about 100 trees, (lindens, ash, and elm) set out just south of the house and they are beginning to show up very nicely. By the time you return they will be large enough for you to eat water melon, with your girl, under their branches.*[506]

Their first home was close to Mamie's extended family and the Cannon Farm, just south of a bend in the Jordan River close to present-day Ninth West and Ninth South. My father shared many happy memories of life with his family in this home. He loved to point out in a vintage photograph the various family members on the generous lawn of this home. One photograph shows him and his siblings Doug (riding on a pony led by his father), Ips (the family's name for Elizabeth), Bob, and Marge (Marjorie), as well as their mother. The youngest, Jo (Josephine), had not yet been born.

In 1905, when my father was six, his father bought Martha Telle's twelve-room home just south of the original Cannon schoolhouse on the Cannon Farm and moved his family there. According to Marjorie's account, they moved because their home burned down.[507] My father, on the other hand, told me building the railroad near their property forced them to move.[508] In her life sketch Marjorie, my father's younger sister, shared positive memories of living in Aunt Martha's spacious, high-ceilinged home and playing on the grounds of the Cannon Farm. However, according to my father's memory, "Father said that buying it was one of the biggest mistakes he ever made; it was too big and hard to heat. My sister Josephine was born

---

503 FamilySearch: Family Group Record.

504 For over forty years, my husband and I owned a home in Chicago, just five blocks from the Columbian Exposition. Our home was built in 1892, reportedly as housing for the event. I have always imagined Lewis and Mary Alice could have stayed in our home.

505 Elizabeth was born March 2, 1894. Lewis wrote the letter on May 28.

506 Lewis' letter to brother Eugene May 28, 1894.

507 Allison Pingree, ed., *Marjorie Cannon Pingree: A Personal History* (1990): 5.

508 Alan M. Cannon, conversations with author, 1970s.

in this home on March 7, 1908. Uncle William was Mother's doctor and Margaret Clayton her nurse."[509] The most important memories for my father had little to do with which house he lived in; they coalesced around his mother.

> I remember my mother with nothing but love. I have a very intense feeling of love toward her. I remember her very clearly—her animation, her sparkle when she talked. I remember her loyalty and devotion to her family, her keen sense of humor. I remember her as being very capable, democratic, and able to converse well. She was a beautiful penman. She was known for her ability to mimic people. I remember going to church with Mother and in the pony cart to Primary. I have nothing but good feelings when I think of her.[510]

Everyone agreed she was an extraordinary woman. Who can say whether her strength and grace came because of or in spite of the challenges she faced. When she was only fourteen, her mother died, and she became as a mother to her three younger siblings: David, Emily, and Sylvester. Mamie was up for the challenge. After her mother's death, she essentially took her mother's place, sitting in Elizabeth's seat at the dinner table, helping raise her siblings, and stepping in as her father's companion on various trips in Utah as he was representing the Church.

The central role Mamie played in her family is confirmed by the fact that she was proxy for her grandmother, Ann Quayle, in a sacred family temple ceremony that occurred in the Logan Temple in October 1890. Abram, her older brother, reported in his diary that he stood proxy for their grandfather, George the Immigrant, and May Alice stood proxy for their grandmother, Ann Quayle, as they were sealed to their six living children and to two children who had died as infants in England. The living children—George Q., Mary Alice Cannon Lambert, Ann Cannon Woodbury, Angus M., David M., and Leonora Cannon Gardner—were all at this memorable event to be sealed to their parents.[511]

In 1892 another beloved family member with a promising future died. While serving a mission in Germany, Mamie's brother David, who was betrothed to Lillian Hamlin, died of pneumonia. The family was devastated. As he often did, David's father, George Q., turned to his son Abram, a fellow apostle, with family concerns. Abram, thirty-five at the time, wrote in his diary that his father asked him to marry a woman for time (that is, for this life only, not eternity)

---

509 Uncle William was William Tenney Cannon, Eliza's son. Margaret Clayton was the daugther of John, Mary Alice's brother. These two people helping with the delivery illustrates how integral the Cannons were to each other's lives.

510 Mary Cannon, *Remember Who You Are*, 6.

511 Kenneth L. Cannon II, review of *Candid Insights of a Mormon Apostle: The Diaries of Abraham H. Cannon, 1889–1895*, ed. Edward Leo Lyman, in Significant Mormon Diaries Series, no. 12. *Journal of Mormon History* 38, no. 1 (Winter 2012): 251.

to whom David would be sealed for eternity in order to "raise seed" for David.[512] This request shows the strength of George Q.'s belief in an afterlife and his belief in the Old Testament teaching that a family member should marry a deceased brother's widow to care for her and most importantly to provide an eternal posterity for the deceased brother.[513]

George and Ann Quayle Cannon's six children. Standing: Ann, David M., Mary Alice. Sitting: Leonora; George Q., Angus M., and Elizabeth (a half-sister)

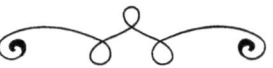

---

512 Ibid., 248. The word "sealed" here means married for eternity. Abram H. Cannon's diaries 1889–95 provide a window into Abram's life and an indispensible insider's view of Utah, the interactions among Church leaders, business development and personalities, and politics during a pivotal period of Utah and Church history. Ken Cannon calls it the single most valuable primary document of the time period.

513 George Q. seems to have asked Abram to violate the Manifesto by asking him to marry a plural wife after 1890. Abram already had three wives from before 1890. In George Q.'s and Abram's minds, the fact that the marriage to Lillian was for time only might have lessened the violation. It is thought that George Q. sanctioned other post-Manifesto marriages. Jorgenson and Hardy, 16.

Mamie and Lewis Cannon, the author's paternal grandparents, are standing on the porch of their first home. Their oldest five children and cousins are in the group.

George Q. Cannon's plural wife Martha's home where Lewis and Mamie moved in about 1905. This home was where Josephine was born in 1908 and where Mamie died one year later. Josephine is sitting on her mother's lap. Other family members are clustered on the porch.

Abram's diary entry of October 24, 1894, indicates that after receiving his Uncle Angus' approval, Abram proposed to Sarah and Angus' unmarried daughter, Ann, to carry out his father's wishes; she, however, chose to remain single.[514] Two years later, Abram did carry out his father's wish when he married Lillian Hamlin, David's betrothed. On June 17, 1896, Lillian was sealed to David H. Cannon and married to Abram for time only.[515] Joseph F. Smith performed the ceremony; J. Nicholson and A. Burt were witnesses.[516] Just one month after the marriage, Abram died unexpectedly on July 19, leaving Lillian widowed and pregnant with their child, Marba.[517][518]

Sometime after Abram's death, Lewis married Lillian for time only, just as Abram had done, to produce seed for David. We have no written record of Lewis and Lillian's marriage. Lillian's granddaughter and namesake thinks they were married in 1899, which is consistent with the view of Lewis' daughter, Irene Cannon Salahor (I'll say more about Irene later in this chapter). Irene remembers that Matthew, Lillian's first child with Lewis, was born about the time Mamie gave birth to Bob, August 16, 1901.[519] If Lewis' marriage to Lillian was in 1899, Lewis and Mamie would have then been married nine years and had two or possibly three living children: Elizabeth was born in 1894; Douglas in 1896; and Alan (my father) in 1899. Lewis and Mamie went on to have three more children: Robert in 1901, Marjorie in 1903, and Josephine in 1908.

Lewis and Lillian had six children: Matthew, Warren, Victor, twins Aaron and Moses, and Leah. Counting Marba, Abram and Lillian's child, Lewis was responsible for supporting two households that had thirteen children between them. Earlier polygamous families had larger quivers and had flourished and been very happy; Lewis' situation differed in three critical ways.

---

514 Ann M. Cannon made it her mission in life to chronicle Cannon history and care for her parents as they aged. In addition, for decades she served as a board member and general officer in the Young Ladies Improvement Association. Unfortunately, the pages from the diary that would have included details of her relationship with Abram were torn out of the diaries before they were donated to BYU.

515 Temple records in Family History Library. Ken Cannon, email message to author, February 3, 2016. Why Abram waited four years to fulfill his father's wish is an unanswered question.

516 In 1911 Lillian maintained that Joseph F. Smith had not performed the ceremony. She said nothing about who did perform it. *Deseret News*, March 2, 1911.

517 Aunt Mini, Abram's second wife and Lewis' oldest sister, testified at the Smoot hearings that Abram caught a fatal cold while swimming in the ocean on his honeymoon with Lillian. However, a more likely cause of his death was a form of meningitis he had contracted before marrying Lillian. Ken Cannon, email message to author, February 3, 2012.

518 Marba Cannon Josephson, born March 22, 1897, in Philadelphia, became an important bridge in the family. She was close to Lillian and Lewis' children, with whom she grew up as an older sister. Marba was a very good friend of Marjorie from Lewis' first family. She was also close to Irene Cannon Salahor, the daughter of Lewis' third wife, whom he married after Lillian's death in 1920. Marba was recognized for her literary abilities as an editor for the *Improvement Era*.

519 Family Search, the usual source for birthdates, is unreliable in this case. For example, it lists the birth date of Matthew (Lewis and Lillian's oldest child) as March 2, 1894, two years before Lillian married Abram. This date is actually when Mary Alice's oldest daughter, Elizabeth, was born, probably explaining the Family Search error. Moses and Aaron, who were twins, are listed as being born in 1908 and 1909. Only Leah's birthdate, August 18, 1911, is certain from a conversation with her daughter, Lillian.

First of all, Lewis had difficulty providing financially for his two large families.[520] Though he worked hard, there was never enough money to go around. Second, his marriage to Lillian violated the law as well as Church policy, so the familial, religious, and national climates were not supportive. Finally and certainly most importantly, his beloved Mamie died in 1909 after a brief struggle with pneumonia, leaving six children; her oldest was fifteen and her youngest not even one.

The family's grief was intense and lifelong. My father told me, "I remember her body at the home of Aunt Emily (Mamie's sister). Her casket was pulled by a team of horses to the Pioneer Stake House for the funeral service. We never did get over it. We used to get out her diary and read it and cry."[521] Mamie's death was also a severe blow to her siblings, who had already suffered so many losses. Margaret Clayton, the daughter of Mamie's brother John Q., said, "Father adored her. When she was so sick and dying and he was administering to her, he couldn't speak. When he came in from being with her, my mother said, 'How is Mamie?' he just shook his head, crying."[522]

Mamie's death devastated Lewis.[523] My father said, "My father was never the same after my mother died. After her death, he asked Will Clawson, a respected portrait painter, to do her portrait."[524]

Marjorie wrote,

> I will never forget when my father brought Mother's portrait home. It was an experience which was moving to all of us. . . . The artist had had a slight acquaintance with Mother. Father had given him a large group photograph from a summer family reunion, where Mother was just one of several hundred. We all felt that Mr. Clawson did very well, considering what he had to work with. . . . [It] hung in the most prominent place in the house. The family eventually decided that it

---

520 Lewis tells of mining ventures he planned to enter with his father in one of the letters to his brother Eugene in Appendix I. As a young man, Lewis worked in Zion's Savings Bank. Later he became interested in the sheep business. When he entered the building business in later years, my father helped him construct many homes in Cannon Ward. When he was older he worked as an accountant in the City and County Building for Uncle Sylvester, Mary Alice's brother.

521 Cannon, *Remember Who You Are*, 6. Mary Alice's diary has been lost. A letter she sent from Washington, DC at age ten to her adopted sister, Rosa, is precious because it captures her voice and is the only writing of hers that we have besides her letter to Eugene, Lewis' brother.

522 Margaret Clayton, interview with author, 1970s. Margaret Clayton also remembered that Mary Alice made beautiful embroidered baby dresses with tiny fine tucks and petticoats to match.

523 Some say that Mamie died of a broken heart.

524 Cannon, *Remember Who You Are*, 5–10.

should belong to the youngest, our sister Jo. She, however, expressed little desire to have it, so it became mine and it has always hung in my living room for these many years.[525]

Lewis and Mamie (Mary Alice) Cannon and their six children at an Angus M. Cannon reunion in 1908. Left to right: Douglas, Elizabeth, Marjorie, Josephine, Alan (author's father) and Robert. Mamie died less than a year after the photo was taken.

To the children, their mother took on a mythic stature. Near the end of her life Marjorie wrote,

> Although (or perhaps because) I was only five then, my mother's death deeply affected me.... The sympathy and love expressed continually has.... become more effusive as time passes....
> [E]ven now, eighty years after her death, relatives continue to remember what a great woman she was. Her wonderful personal character has been made more perfect in the passage of time, while her negative qualities (if she had any) have long since been forgotten. Our family, which ranged in age from one to fifteen years, always

---

[525] Pingree, 4. George, Marjorie's (Aunt Marge) son, now owns the portrait. My father had special feelings for the picture of his parents and their six children extracted from the family reunion group photograph referred to by Aunt Marge. My father had copies of the picture made for all of his children, grandchildren, nieces, and nephews.

thought of her as a person without any negative characteristics. Because we all had such reverence for her, the absence of her physical being had a profound effect on the life of each of her children. We would feel her influence in decisions we would make. . . . because she was elevated to near sainthood, we usually thought twice before doing anything wrong. This influence became greater as we grew older and more mature. The loss of a mother becomes more heartbreaking to a person as time passes.[526]

Undoubtedly, this grief intensified existing negative feelings about Lillian, making it difficult to distinguish which feelings came from where. Given the weight of the negative feelings connected to Lewis' marriage to Lillian and all of the reasons it should never have occurred, an important question needs to be addressed: Who made the decision that Lewis and Lillian should marry? During Lewis' lifetime, many held him responsible not only for the decision but also the financial as well as emotional struggles that resulted. Being surrounded by Mamie's family, Mamie and Lewis' children often heard critical comments about the second marriage.

Not until Mamie's daughter Marjorie was an adult did she learn about her mother's role in the marriage. After Marjorie graduated from college, she taught school and lived with her mother's brother Sylvester and his wife, Winifred. One evening Marjorie complained to her aunt and uncle about her father's decision to marry Lillian and the consequent neglect her family experienced. Uncle Sylvester sat her down and said, "As an apostle and as Mamie's brother, there is something that [I feel] you need to know. Your mother encouraged your father to marry Abram's widow. It was on her initiative that Lewis married Lillian."[527] In a conversation with me toward the end of her life, Marjorie told me she had come to a more generous view of her father's actions. In her personal history recorded in 1990, Marjorie recorded her version of the second marriage, which corroborates what she told her son John and me:

> It was only after my marriage and after Father's death that one of Father's sisters told me the reason for my father marrying Aunt Lillian while mother was still alive. It sounded like a story from the Bible. My mother had a full brother, who died while on his mission in Germany. . . . David was betrothed to a woman named Lillian Hamlin before he left for his mission. . . . After David's death, his brother Abram—an apostle with three wives already—decided with the permission of Church authorities to marry Lillian and raise an earthly family for his dead brother David. Within months of this marriage, Abram died, leaving Lillian pregnant with Marba. According to what I was told, within a few years' time [after Abram's death] my mother—who was a full sister to both David and Abram—felt that

---

526 Ibid.

527 John Pingree, conversation with author, 2013. My Aunt Marge relayed this information to her son John Pingree a few years before she died on March 26, 1998.

Lillian should have more children for David. So she decided that her husband should marry Lillian and follow the biblical injunction to raise up seed for David. I was told that Church authorities agreed to sanction this plural marriage as they did the prior one to Abram.[528]

If this interpretation is true, one wonders how family dynamics would have been different had Mamie's probable role been known and acknowledged.

That George Q. Cannon's oldest living daughter had a fierce loyalty to polygamy is not surprising given that she had been very close to her father while he battled for the Church's right to practice polygamy. She had been schooled in the Old Testament principle that a family member should care for the widow of a brother who dies and produce seed for him. Also, just before Elizabeth died, she gave her daughter Mamie the responsibility of caring for her siblings; soon after her death, Elizabeth visited Mamie twice. Mamie told Abram about these experiences, which he recorded in his diary.[529] Mamie's desire was to fulfill her mother's wishes to care for her siblings. Also, Mamie was grief stricken that two of her adult brothers, David and Abram, had died unexpectedly.

When evaluating Lewis' second marriage, it is important to remember that Lewis and Mamie both came from homes in which plural marriage had been successfully practiced. It's also important to remember that according to Abram's diary, George Q. approached Abram about marrying Lillian for time. After Abram died, perhaps he asked the same of Lewis. Both of these factors help explain why a happily married couple chose to break the law as well as the Church's policy.

Lewis and Mamie were caught between two worlds. On the one hand, their generation had seen having more than one wife as a status symbol and had experienced polygamy as a cornerstone of their religion. They both had personally witnessed their families live The Principle successfully and happily. They also felt a responsibility to Lillian and to her deceased intended, David. On the other hand, practicing polygamy in the late 1890s put them at odds not only with the law but also with Church policy. What should they do? In the end, the strength of Lewis and Mamie's concern for producing seed for David and the intensity of their belief in polygamy trumped their following the law and the Manifesto. Lewis was a bishop at the time and continued to hold that calling until 1918, which indicates that at least some members of the Church and their leaders had very ambivalent feelings about giving up plural marriage. Other Cannon post-Manifesto marriages in my extended family show the strength of their

---

528 Pingree, 4. Aunt Marge and Uncle Fred Pingree were married August 10, 1928. Aunt Marge was very close to Lewis' sister, Aunt Mina, a plural wife of Abram. In all probability she was the one who talked with Aunt Marge. Abram actually died a month and two days after marrying Lillian. They were married June 17, 1896; Abram died July 19, 1896.

529 Quoting from Abram's diary, "*On one occasion Mother stood at the foot of the bed, and upon Mamie* [Mary Alice] *saying, 'Oh Ma, don't come in the night, you scare us.' Mother replied, 'Why Mamie, I come every night, don't be frightened.' On the other occasion Mother stood by the bedroom door, and as Mamie awoke, she said, 'Don't be frightened, Mamie. I merely came to kiss Sylvester.' At this point she moved across the room and vanished at the window. Mamie says she heard no audible voice, but still communicated spiritually; she was not frightened.*" This visit occurred about two months after Elizabeth's death. Cannon, *The Diaries of Abraham H. Cannon*, 141–42.

continued belief in The Principle. Both prominent men in the community, George M. and John M.—Lewis' half-brothers, (the two sons of Angus and Sarah)—married wives well after the 1890 Manifesto.[530] Twelve years after his marriage to Zina Bennion in 1889. John M., while a member of a stake presidency, was sealed to Margaret Peart December 23, 1901, and to Hattie Neff some time after that.[531] In an interview conducted through the Charles Redd Oral History Project, John B. Cannon spoke about his father's strong allegiance to The Principle:

> I have a very definite memory of Father talking to me in the library. I was about ten. I remember him telling me of the feeling that was prevalent and the understanding of the revelation in the Doctrine and Covenants that has to do with marriage and polygamy. He said it was a requirement. If the highest degree of standing in the celestial kingdom was to be attained it was to be attained only by keeping this commandment. He was counseled to that effect, and that was as I would infer equal to advice to marry. I feel that my Father entered into it because of his faith.[532]

John M.'s older brother George M. was sealed to Ellen Steffensen on June 17, 1901, and to Catherine Vaughan Morris (his first wife Addie's younger sister) on August 6, 1901. Both marriages likely occurred in Mexico.[533] In contrast to John apparently being counseled to marry polygamously, George wrote that the decision was entirely his own in response to an adult daughter's inquiry of why he entered into plural marriage eleven years after the Manifesto:

> No official of the Church ever directed or ordered or suggested such action. On the contrary I was told that if I entered into that relation with additional wives it must be on my own responsibility, at my own risk and at such time and place as not to bring active persecution on the Church. I can truly say that my marriage to each of my three wives was with the motives I have . . . . set forth as those of men who were leaders and real Mormons . . . . the desire of spirits in the

---

530 *1990 Angus M. Cannon Reunion Materials*, 229. John M. was counselor to Frank Y. Taylor in the Granite Stake from as early as his son Paul, born 1901, could remember until John M.'s death at age fifty-two in 1917. George M. was the founder and developer of Forest Dale, where many members of the Angus M. Cannon lived. In 1889—when John W. Young, the representative of Brigham Young's family—didn't have the funds to sign the promissary note due Zion's Saving Bank, George M. acquired the property that extended from 2100 South to 2700 South from 900 East to State Street, then known as Brigham Young Forest Farm. George M. divided the property into building lots and created the beautiful suburban town of Forest Dale. Just east of George M.'s home, today a bed and breakfast, was Brigham Young's farmhouse, which was used as a place of worship until 1912, when the farmhouse was moved to This Is the Place Village, where it is a chief attraction. *1989 Angus M. Cannon Reunion Materials*, 4.

531 Paul B. Cannon, "Letter to Lynne and Kathryn," in *1900 Angus M. Cannon Reunion Materials*, 233.

532 Ibid.

533 George M. Cannon, "George Mousley Cannon," in *1989 Angus M. Cannon Reunion Materials*, 11.

> Spirit world for an opportunity to have an experience in mortality, an intense love of posterity which is characteristic of the Latter-Day Saints, and particularly true of the Cannon family; the tradition of my own father and mother who were Orthodox Mormons of the old school . . . Did I think it my duty? . . . I must say that it was my conviction that in taking two additional wives, I expected that such action would bring the blessing of our Eternal Father upon me, my . . . wives and my posterity.[534]

George M.'s reference to himself as a "true Mormon" and his perception of his parents as "Orthodox Mormons of the old school" voiced the sentiment of those who, at some level, saw the 1890 Manifesto as nonbinding. Much secrecy surrounded when and where these marriages occurred. Although written records don't seem to have been kept, it is very likely it was in Mexico—so the participants were in accordance with a literal interpretation of the 1890 Manifesto. Apparently they were part of the group that felt the Manifesto was given as "advice," not as a commandment, and that it would be turned away from when the Territory obtained statehood and the government was no longer harassing them. Like Lewis and Mamie, my grandparents, it is clear that the depth of both of John M.'s and George M.'s commitment to The Principle overrode their commitment to the promises made to the government in the 1890 Manifesto. In Chapter Seven I tell how John M.'s son Paul broke the code of silence enveloping these marriages.

I know of no record of Mamie's feelings about Lillian, but it seems likely that it was more difficult than she had expected to share Lewis' affections with another woman, especially without the acceptance of earlier times. The women in my family who married before the 1890 Manifesto were able to raise their families harmoniously, and the children were often more like full rather than half-brothers and sisters. It did not turn out this way for Mamie and Lillian. During the time Mamie was still alive, we do not know where Lillian and her children lived. My father's and Marjorie's memories, as well as a newspaper account say that Lillian and her children lived in Canada at least part of the time to avoid legal trouble.[535] When Mamie died in 1909, Lillian and her children returned to Salt Lake. Lewis invited Lillian and her children to join my father and his siblings in Aunt Martha's home on Cannon Row, where he and Mamie had lived. We know that the arrangement did not go well because after less than a year, Lewis moved my father and his siblings to 1216 Ninth West, just south of where Mamie's sister Aunt Emily and her husband Israel Willey (Uncle Ike to the family) lived. Lewis moved Lillian and her children to the house on the other side of my father and his siblings. Aunt Emily's daughter Trix, whom I interviewed in the 1990s, had many warm memories of my father and his siblings and remembered them all playing with Lillian's children, but no lasting friendships seemed to have been formed with them. My father said, "They passed out of my life."[536]

---

534 Ibid. George M. is right. We Cannons have inordinate pride in our family heritage.

535 *Salt Lake Tribune*, April 16, 1904. This newspaper article confirmed that Lillian was in Canada in 1904, probably to avoid testifying in the Smoot hearings in 1904.

536 Alan M. Cannon, conversation with author, 1990s.

In contrast, my father's other neighbors, Aunt Emily and Uncle Ike, were crucial to him and his siblings. My father explained, "They came into my life at an important time. They were very close to us all and we loved and appreciated them."[537] Marjorie wrote that after her mother's death,

> Aunt Emily became the closest thing to a mother that we children had. Aunt Emily and Uncle Ike couldn't have been more wonderful to us. They were always sympathetic and anxious to do what they could. Uncle Ike was on the Salt Lake City School Board. During my junior year in college, the University was trying out a plan of hiring students to teach half-day who were also taking classes. Uncle Ike had me fill out an application to get a job — I needed the money. When I went to Superintendent Child for an interview, Uncle Ike sent a note with me, saying, "Treat Miss Cannon as though she were my daughter." Of course I got the job.[538]

In this instance, as in many others, Uncle Ike and Aunt Emily helped my father and his siblings.

Lillian has always been a shadowy, mysterious figure to me. Little was said in my immediate or extended family about Lewis' marriage to her. Until I was in college, I knew nothing about the marriage except joking references to our twin relatives named Aaron and Moses. My cousins report a similar silence in their homes. I learned only recently that Lillian was the valedictorian of her class at the University of Utah. I can see from a photograph of her that Ken Cannon recently sent me that she was very attractive.[539] In a recent phone conversation with Lillian Olesen, Lillian's granddaughter and namesake, I learned that her grandmother taught math as the first or one of the first female faculty members at BYU and that she was a student at the State University of New York at Oswego when Marba, Abram's daughter, was born in Philadelphia. I asked her, "How did your mother and her brothers feel toward their mother?" She replied, "They adored her."[540] My father told me she was intelligent and taught school before she married Abram. He also said his family treated her unfairly and that Lillian

---

537 Cannon, *Remember Who You Are*, 8.

538 Pingree, 5.

539 Ken Cannon, email message to author, February 2012.

540 Lillian Smith Olesen, conversation with author, October 20, 2012. Lillian Smith Olesen is Lillian Hamlin Cannon's granddaughter through Leah Hamlin Smith.

Home of Lewis, Lillian, their six children, and Lillian's child by her previous marriage to Abram.

Present day address
1224 South 900 West Salt Lake City.

One year after Mamie died, Lewis moved to this home with their grieving children.

Present day address
1216 South 900 West Salt Lake City.

Home of Mamie's sister Emily and her husband Israel Willey. They lived here with their five children.

Present day address
1208 South 900 West Salt Lake City.

and her children had a lesser standing among the extended family than his family did.[541] Even so, Lillian was acknowledged in George Q. Cannon's will and her daughter Marba was listed among Abram's children in the will, so clearly Lillian and Marba were considered to be part of the extended family.[542]

Because my side of the family has had no contact with Lillian's children until recently, we do not know how the situation affected Lillian's children. Given that the marriage was illegal, that the family sometimes lived in another country, and that Lillian was not the favored wife, the situation was likely harder for them than for my father and his siblings, for whom we know it was very difficult. The effects on Mamie's children depended on many factors including their age. Elizabeth, the eldest child, who hereafter I refer to as Aunt Ips, bore the responsibility of being the mother to her brothers and sisters after her mother's death. When Lewis stayed at Lillian's house, there was no adult in my father's house. Aunt Ips, only a teenager, was in charge of herself and her five younger siblings. She seldom talked of that period of her life but had negative feelings toward Lillian.[543] Uncle Bob voiced negative feelings and openly expressed resentment that his father married Lillian.[544] Aunt Marge told me a poignant story of her baptism in which she felt abandoned. A disappointing eighth birthday, the very day her baptism was scheduled, exemplifies this. For hours she stood alone in the kitchen of her family's home on Eighth West. Lewis did not make it home until late that night to baptize her in the Jordan River behind their house.[545] She had many other unhappy memories of her childhood and did not like to talk about that time in her life.[546]

Like Aunt Marge, my father was also baptized in the Jordan River on his birthday, but his memories were only positive. He often told his children about his mother's helping him get ready for his special day. Once he was dressed and ready to ride the Dinky to the Tabernacle, where his baptism was scheduled to take place, the family learned that the Dinky was not working. In response, the family gathered for his baptism for a beautiful, memorable event at the Jordan River, which ran behind his house. The key reason their memories of their baptisms were so different is that Mamie was with my father the day he was baptized. On Aunt Marge's baptism day, she had already been without a mother for three years. Her father's tardy entrance further emphasized how alone she was that day and likely many others.

---

541 Alan M. Cannon, conversations with author, 1990s.

542 Bitton, 446. It is curious that Lillian and Marba were included in George Q.'s will since Lillian was married to Lewis at the time of George Q.'s death. Perhaps the will was drawn before Lewis married Lillian. It is likely that they were included in the will because Lillian had been sealed to his son David. No mention is made in the will of the children of Lewis and Mary Alice or the children of Lewis and Lillian.

543 Mary Alice Collins, converstion with author, 2011. Mary Alice Collins is Elizabeth's, (my Aunt Ips's) daughter.

544 Pat Romney and Toby Pingree, conversation with author, 2000s. Pat Romney and Toby Pingree are my Aunt Marge's children.

545 My Aunt Marge shared this memory as we stood in the kitchen of her childhood home at a reunion in 1992. Aunt Marge and my father, the two then-living siblings, and many of Lewis and Mary Alice's grandchildren were in attendance.

546 I am not aware of how Doug and Jo viewed their childhoods.

I never heard my father express any bitterness about his father's marrying Lillian nor any feelings about being neglected. Perhaps this was because he did in fact spend some time with his father. My father and his father built homes together for people who lived in the Cannon Ward. In addition, my father, like his brothers, took his turn traveling with Lewis on a train to Omaha, Nebraska, to sell sheep.[547] It is also likely that my father screened out some of the painful memories. What he recounted to me and others were happy, sometimes even idyllic, memories of his childhood, most of them before his mother died. As a middle child, he did not carry the weight of being responsible for his siblings. Ten years old when his mother died, unlike Aunt Marge, who was only five, he had many clear and happy memories that he held onto his whole life. Each time he spoke of his mother, especially in his later years, he cried.

Regarding his father, my father remembers him crossing the lawn between his home and Lillian's every other night to spend equal time with each family. It seems that my father had an understanding beyond his years about his father's life. He told me,

> When it comes right down to it, my father really had a hard life. He was never the same after Mother died. He had more challenges than he could handle. He had a hard rugged life and didn't live to see the many positive results of his far-sighted efforts in rearing his children. He was such a matchmaker and a strong believer in education, but he didn't live to see any of his children married and that all of us graduated from college.[548]

He had not only compassion for his father but also gratitude for the emphasis he put on education; he was also grateful for the manner in which his siblings helped each other to get their education. My father wrote,

> Father had strong feelings about our getting an education. He insisted that we attend school every day. There were no excuses for staying out. As a result of this tradition we all graduated from college. We had to help each other to accomplish this, but we made it and grew closer as a result of this effort. Because of lack of money, my brother Bob applied for a coveted West Point appointment and got it. Marge and Jo graduated from the University of Utah, and Elizabeth, Doug, and I from Utah State. When Doug was teaching in Bunkersville, Nevada, he sent me money each month that I later repaid. We also helped Marge when she and Doug were both studying at Ames.[549]

---

547 My father took turns with his brothers, Doug and Bob, to make the trip to sell sheep.

548 Alan M. Cannon, conversation with author, 1970s.

549 Mary Cannon, *Remember Who You Are*, 9. My father, Mary Alice's last surviving child, stayed in touch with his nieces and nephews including the children of his brother Bob and his sister Jo., who both lived far from the family, until the end of his life. My Aunt Marge, who lived until 1998, also kept in touch with her nieces and nephews.

Being surrounded by his first wife's family, who bore him ill will, certainly did not help Lewis. Though Uncle Ike and Aunt Emily, to whom Mamie had been very close, served as second parents to Lewis and Mamie's children, they did not extend that warmth to Lewis. Perhaps because of Mamie's untimely death and the unwelcomed second family, their relationship was strained, a dynamic that likely influenced Lewis and Mamie's children's feelings about their father. In addition, Uncle Ike's hostility toward the Church colored my father's younger siblings' responses to the Church.[550]

After Mamie's death in 1909, Lewis did his best to raise his two families and continued to serve as bishop of the Cannon Ward until he was released in 1918 because of Lillian's poor health. In search of help for Lillian's health problems, Lewis, Lillian, and their children who were then still at home moved to Arizona and then to California. Lillian died November 28, 1920, in California.

Lewis then returned to Salt Lake. Soon after his return, he married Annie Nielson in August 1921. Lewis was fifty-five and Annie forty. Annie was born February 1, 1881, in Denmark.[551] Soon after Annie was born, her mother died. When Annie was about a year old, she came with her father and older brother to the United States as converts to the Church. His immediate family was already here.[552] When Annie met Lewis she was living in Forest Dale, where she had a connection with the Angus Cannon family.

Lewis and Annie had one child, Irene, born November 18, 1922. I recently met Irene Cannon Salahor, a spry older woman with the direct Cannon manner and quick wit, and her daughter, Yasmine Salahor Miller.[553] According to Irene, Lewis and Annie's marriage ended shortly after she was born, at the request of her mother, Annie.[554] One of their differences was that Lewis wanted more children. Annie, almost forty-two years old, did not. Clearly Lewis continued to strongly embrace the teaching that a large posterity increased his eternal standing and wanted more children despite his limited resources and his and Annie's ages. Perhaps Lewis felt shortchanged because only Mary Alice's children and Annie's child Irene were sealed to him; Lillian's seven children were sealed to his deceased brother-in-law David.

---

550 Uncle Bob and Aunt Jo left Utah and the Church. The other children remained in Idaho and Utah and close to the Church.

551 Irene Cannon Salahor, conversation with author, October 4, 2012.

552 Irene Cannon Salahor, letter to author, September 24, 2013.

553 In 2009, Irene, passing through Chicago with her daughter, approached my brother John's son, Joe Cannon (then bishop of the Hyde Park Ward), at church and introduced herself as Irene Cannon Salahor, the only living child of Lewis Cannon. Joe passed that news to me. I knew she must be the daughter of Lewis' third wife, Annie Nielsen. Aunt Marge's son, John Pingree, found that Irene was living in the Salt Lake City, Utah, area; he hosted a gathering of Mamie's grandchildren to meet Irene and her daughter. Irene has had a very interesting life. She graduated from Columbia in New York in 1947; worked in Paris on the Marshall Plan for three years; moved to Turkey, where she met and married her husband in 1952, whom she subsequently divorced. Later she worked for Copperwell Steel in Turkey and the Ford Foundation in New York. Her daughter, Yasemin Salahor Miller, was born August 20, 1960, in Salt Lake City, Utah, and is married to Steven Kay Miller, a surgeon. They have five children and are active in the Church.

554 Irene Cannon Salahor, conversation with author, October 4, 2012.

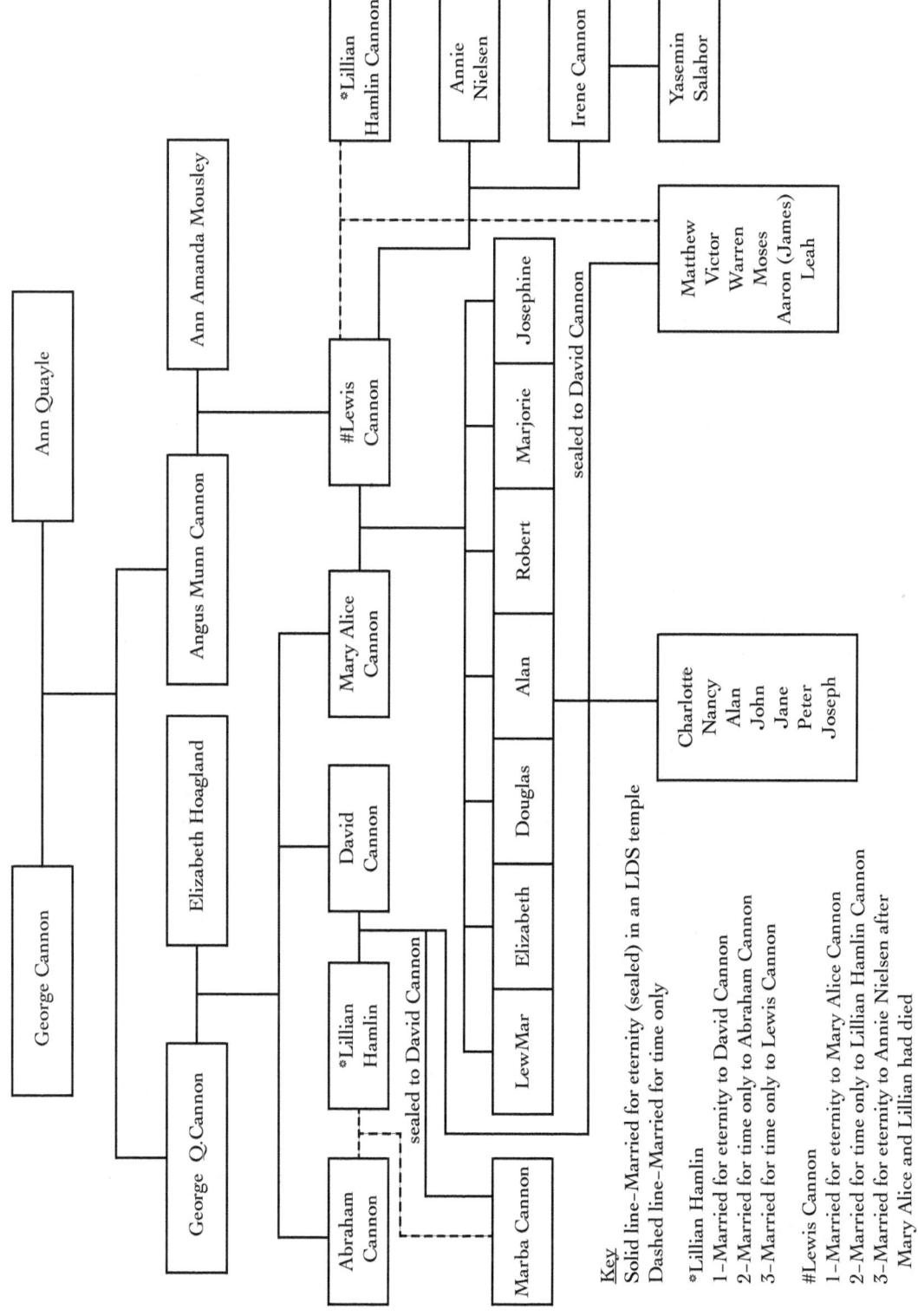

Five generations of Cannons, the second and third of which practiced polygamy. The third generation—which includes Lewis, Mary Alice, Lillian, David and Abraham—includes eternal as well as time-only marriages.

The author with her new found friend, Irene Salahor,
her father's half-sister, whom he never met

Annie supported herself and her daughter Irene by working as a seamstress at an awning factory in downtown Salt Lake. Annie died in 1976 at age ninety-five in Salt Lake. Irene now lives in her mother's home, where Annie and Lewis lived as a married couple.[555] Lewis died June 7, 1924, at his home with his first family on present-day 900 West after a short illness. The obituary reads in part:

> He is survived by Elizabeth of the BYU faculty; Douglas Q. of the Utah Agricultural college; Alan, Robert M., who is at the West Point Military Academy; Marjorie, teacher in the Salt Lake schools; Josephine; Matthew M., a missionary in Switzerland; Victor; Warren; Moses; Aaron; Leah; and Irene Cannon. . . . All of his immediate family were with him with the exception of Robert M. and Matthew.[556]

---

[555] The home is in the Forest Dale area, where Angus and his children had settled. Irene and I continue to keep in touch. In a recent conversation she said, "I want to be your friend." I replied, "And I want to be yours."

[556] *Deseret News*, June 8, 1924.

In the obituary no mention is made of his wives.[557] The contrast in the attention given to the deaths of Mamie and Lewis in their obituaries is noteworthy. Mamie, a central figure in the Cannon family who died unexpectedly at age forty-two and was sorely missed by her family, had an extensive laudatory obituary. Lewis, who had had considerable financial struggles and emotional strain, died fifteen years later at age fifty-eight with much less notice. Both, however, were important enough for Orson F. Whitney, a prominent Church leader, to speak at their funerals.

Another post-Manifesto marriage in my extended family illustrates the difficulty the Saints had in forsaking polygamy and the problems that resulted. This involves my mother's cousin, Preston Parkinson. His father, George Chandler Parkinson, son of Samuel Rose Parkinson and Arabella, was married on April 14, 1881, to Lucy Doney, with whom he had ten children.[558] George, who served as president of the Oneida Stake from 1887 to 1910, was encouraged ten years after the Manifesto by some of the Church leaders to marry a second wife.[559] His father, his brother William, and some of his sisters had entered polygamy before the Manifesto.

On January 17, 1902, George married Fannie Woolley, daughter of Bishop Edwin Dilworth Woolley and Mary Ann Olpin, as a plural wife in Colorado, where she was serving a twelve-month mission.[560] Fannie had one child, Preston, born October 22, 1903.[561] Fannie and Preston lived in hiding, first in Canada near her brother Orson Woolley and then in Salt Lake City in Forest Dale near her brother George Edwin Woolley. Preston remembers living under the assumed name of Ferrin until elementary school, when it became safe for him to use his real name.[562] Living such a secluded and secret life must have been particularly difficult for Preston's mother, whose sisters were married monogamously to Church leaders—Olive to Spencer W. Kimball's father, Andrew, and Mary Louisa to J. Reuben Clark's father, Joshua. After the early years of isolation, Fannie became less secretive; with the passage of time, she took an active role in the Church and community affairs.[563]

---

557 Bishop Charles Davey, who was Lewis' counselor for many years, conducted the service. Orson F. Whitney (of the Council of the Twelve Apostles) spoke. He had also spoken at Mary Alice's funeral. Sylvester Q. Cannon, Mary Alice's younger brother, dedicated the grave.

558 Parkinson, 164. Annie Clark Tanner lived with the Parkinsons when she was in hiding, an example of how intertwined the lives of the Saints were.

559 Ibid., 176.

560 Ibid.

561 Ibid., 179.

562 Ibid., 178.

563 Ibid., 176.

My mother told me about a poignant conversation with Preston, which began with her saying, "I was born in 1902 and you were born in 1903. We are almost the same age." He replied, "Yes, but I am a bastard."[564] The comment suggests Preston had suffered much pain. Preston rose above the negative feelings he had concerning his birth. He worked tirelessly on recording family relationships and stories of family members, perhaps in an effort to establish a sense of belonging to his mother's and father's families. In 1967 he completed a 1,150-page history of his mother's family entitled *The Utah Woolley Family*.

Then he turned his efforts to compiling a history of the Parkinsons, his father's family. The result of this prodigious effort was his publication in 2001 of *The Family of Samuel Rose Parkinson: Roots and Branches*, for which we Parkinsons are very grateful. Though Preston felt rejected and abandoned by his father and was puzzled as to why his parents married after the Manifesto, Preston dedicated the book to his father with affection. In the process of writing the book, he faced the painful truth that the Church sent conflicting messages about polygamy after 1890. The tone and content of the book make it clear that Preston has forgiven his father, Church leaders, and fellow Saints for their imperfections.

Another post-Manifesto plural marriage connected to my Parkinson forbears is that of William H. Smart, Charlotte and Maria's younger brother. In 1888, at age twenty-six, William married Anna Haines. From the beginning, the couple wholly accepted plural marriage. That same year, he planned to marry a second wife, Caroline Parkinson. Caroline agreed, but the marriage never took place because her parents—Samuel Rose Parkinson and his wife, Arabella—did not approve.[565] In 1902, after fourteen years of monogamy, William married a second wife, Mary Elizabeth Wallace, while he was serving as stake president.[566] Matthias Cowley performed the ceremony.[567] Mary, five years older than William, had three sons from a previous marriage. She and William had one child together, named May.[568]

These stories of post-Manifesto marriages within my extended family illustrate not only the difficulty the Saints and their leaders had giving up plural marriage but also the complex and compromising situations that resulted from these marriages. They occurred in the United States,

---

564 Mary Parkinson Cannon, conversation with author, 1970s.

565 Caroline, age twenty-two, was Arabella's youngest child. Samuel and Arabella may have disapproved of her becoming a plural wife because of Caroline's older sister Esther's unhappy experience with polygamy, discussed in Chapter Three.

566 William B. Smart, *Mormonism's Last Colonizer: The Life and Times of William H. Smart* (Logan, UT: Utah State University Press, 2008): 49–50. He was a stake president for several years in Vernal, an outlying area in the Uintah Basin.

567 Ibid., 142–44. Mary was the daughter of George Benjamin Wallace, a wealthy lumberman from Boston who had converted to Mormonism; George had five wives and forty-six children.

568 For a wide-ranging discussion of Church leaders, doctrine, and practice during post-Manifesto polygamy, see Smart, 140–147.

which was unusual; most post-Manifesto marriages occurred in Canada (where polygamy was also against the law after 1890 but its practitioners were never turned in) or in Mexico (where the practice was also illegal but permitted by the country's president, Porfirio Diaz).[569]

While the Church was having internal differences about how to respond to the federal pressure to give up polygamy and whether or not the Church should condone polygamous marriages outside of the United States, problems over seating Utah's representatives in Congress brought the issue to a head. B. H. Roberts, a member of The First Council of the Seventy married to three wives before the Manifesto, was elected as a Democratic representative to Congress in 1898. The fight over whether to seat him once again brought national attention to the Mormons. Questions regarding the separation of church and state and charges that the Mormons continued to take additional wives were the issues. The vote to seat Roberts was 268 against and 50 in favor.[570]

Four years later the issue again came to national attention when Reed Smoot, a monogamous apostle, won a Senate seat as a Republican. His seating was contested because people mistakenly assumed that because he was a Mormon he was also a polygamist. The hearings over whether he could retain his seat went on for over four years with several lay members and prominent Church leaders, including the president of the Church, Joseph F. Smith, testifying in Smoot's favor. After tumultuous debates in Congress, he was finally seated. The Church took several actions to ensure that Reed Smoot would hold his seat in Congress and that the thorny issue of polygamy would finally be resolved.

In 1904 President Joseph F. Smith issued what came to be called the Second Manifesto, which stated that no plural marriages had been "solemnized with the sanction, consent or knowledge of the Church" and announced that "all such marriages are prohibited, and if any officer or member of the Church shall assume to solemnize or enter into such marriage he will be deemed in transgression against the Church and will be liable to be dealt with . . . and excommunicated therefrom."[571] The president of the Council of the Twelve, Francis M. Lyman, moved that the statement be adopted as the policy of the church and those voting in the April 1904 General Conference approved the resolution unanimously.[572]

Shortly before the Second Manifesto was issued, Smoot himself expressed the feelings of some of the Twelve regarding the need for the Church to be more forthright and consistent in its position concerning polygamy. He explained that not all members of the Church had

> lived strictly to our agreements with the government and this lack
> of sincerity on our part goes farther to condemn us in the eyes of the
> public men of the nation than the mere fact of a few new polygamous

---

569 Thomas G. Alexander, *Mormonism in Transition: A History of the Latter-day Saints, 1890–1930* (Urbana, IL: University of Illinois Press, 1996): 61.

570 Allen and Leonard, 439.

571 Joseph Fielding Smith, comp., *Life of Joseph F. Smith, Sixth President of The Church of Jesus Christ of Latter-day Saints* (Salt Lake City, UT: Deseret News Press, 1938): 374–75, quoted in Alexander, 64.

572 Ibid., 64.

cases, or a polygamist before the Manifesto living in a state of unlawful cohabitation.... We must be honest with ourselves, with our fellow-men, and with our God.[573]

To give official endorsement to these promises, the Manifesto of 1890 and three excerpts from addresses that President Woodruff had given in support of the Manifesto were incorporated into the Doctrine and Covenants in 1908.[574]

As further evidence of the Church's intention to forsake the practice of plural marriage, two apostles who had performed several post-Manifesto marriages were omitted from the list of apostles sustained as members of the Quorum of the Twelve in general conference, starting in October 1904. These were Matthias F. Cowley and John W. Taylor. The First Presidency reluctantly requested Cowley's and Taylor's resignations, and these resignations were submitted to other Quorum members October 28, 1905.[575] However, members of the Quorum were divided on how to view and respond to these actions towards their fellow apostles. Some apostles were disturbed by the requested resignations, but others considered it a necessary action.[576] Dropping them from the Quorum would be a definite signal that the practice of polygamy was at an end. Feelings ran high.[577]

At a meeting preparing for the April General Conference of 1906, the Quorum, under the First Presidency's direction, decided to present the previously obtained resignations at the conference. At the same conference the First Presidency and Twelve sustained George F. Richards to fill the vacancy caused by the death of Marriner W. Merrill. Orson F. Whitney and David O. McKay were sustained to fill Taylor's and Cowley's positions.[578] A year later the First Presidency published "An Address: The Church of Jesus Christ of Latter-day Saints to the World," which, in a conciliatory tone, answered the charges brought against the Church in the Smoot hearings four years earlier. It included the basic beliefs of the Church and affirmed that it had no intention of dominating the politics of the state, was politically loyal to the government, and had abandoned plural marriage.[579]

---

573 Reed Smoot to Jesse M. Smith, March 22, 1904, quoted in Alexander, 65.

574 D&C OD 1, 291–93. See Appendix M.

575 The First Presidency had worked with and been close to these men for many years.

576 Smoot Proceedings 3:194; *Richards Journal*, April 8, 1906, quoted in Alexander, 65.

577 Alexander, 66.

578 The Quorum members experienced considerable sadness over the resignations of Taylor and Cowley. Taylor left for Canada, and Cowley, remaining in the United States, was instructed that he might "bear testimony" but was forbidden to accept invitations to preach. *Lund Journal*, April 5, 1906. The death of Marriner W. Merrill and subsequent deaths of two other members of the Quorum, Abraham O. Woodruff and George Teasdale, may have saved them from censure for ongoing defiance of the Second Manifesto. Alexander, *Mormonism in Transition*, 66. For a full discussion of the complexities of the issue, see Victor W. Jorgensen and B. Carmon Hardy, "The Taylor-Cowley Affair and the Watershed of Mormon History," *Utah Historical Quarterly* 48, no. 1 (Winter 1980).

579 Allen and Leonard, 445.

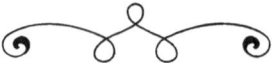

![Photo]

First Presidency and Twelve Apostles in 1898 soon after Wilford Woodruff had died and Lorenzo Snow had been sustained as the prophet with George Q. Cannon and Joseph F. Smith as his counselors. Standing, from left to right: Anthon Hendrik Lund, John Whitaker Taylor, John Henry Smith, Heber Jeddy Grant, Francis Marion Lyman, George Teasdale, Marriner Wood Merrill. Seated, from left to right: Brigham Young, Jr., George Quayle Cannon, Lorenzo Snow, Joseph F. Smith, Franklin Dewey Richards. Front row, from left to right: Matthias F. Cowley and Abraham Owen Woodruff.

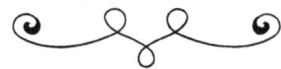

Allegations that new plural marriages were occurring continued. On November 15, 1910, Reed Smoot met with the First Presidency and Francis Lyman, president of the Quorum, before returning to Washington, DC to obtain a statement of the Church's firm prohibitive position on plural marriages to give to President Taft. The document confirmed that anyone who had taken a plural wife after 1904 Second Manifesto would be disciplined.[580] In 1911 the Church further strengthened its policy by excommunicating members who continued to marry plural wives.

To communicate its commitment to abandon polygamy once and for all, the Church disciplined Matthias Cowley and John W. Taylor, the former apostles who had performed many such marriages. Matthias Cowley's priesthood was suspended. In response, Matthias said to his fellow church leaders, "I want you to know that I am not rebellious and never have been and if I have erred it has been because of these circumstances and the example of my brethren. I am in harmony with you and I would like you to put me upon my honor to make that good in the future. I would rather die than be cut off from the Church."[581] On the other hand, John W. Taylor held firmly to the belief that the practice and doctrine should remain central to the Church. Because of his stance, he was excommunicated.[582]

The action taken against John W. Taylor needs further explanation. Most of the polygamous Saints living in Mexico lived on land his father, John Taylor, had purchased in 1885 as a safe haven for members living on the Underground. After the 1890 Manifesto, the way members of the Church used Mexico depended on how they viewed polygamy. A small group of Saints in Mexico believed that the Manifesto applied only to the United States and continued to marry plural wives. John W. Taylor (a son of John and Sophia Taylor), was a key proponent of this interpretation. As an apostle, he was very active in developing settlements in Mexico and Canada in the late 1880s for polygamous Saints seeking refuge from the Edmunds-Tucker Act. He owned a substantial home in Mexico, in Colonia Juarez.[583] He also established the first stake, named the Taylor Stake, in Alberta, Canada.[584] Many of its members were polygamous.

---

580 Those cases between the 1890 Manifesto and 1904 would be "dealt with according to circumstances." If the parties had been "drawn into [new marriages] by Apostles they would not be excommunicated" but would be released from any position in the Church where members were liable to be asked to vote for them. Though not strctly adhered to, enforecement generally followed this pattern. *Smoot Diary*, November 15, 16, 1910; *Lund Journal*, November 16, 1910; see also *Ivins Journal*, January 1911. The generalization is based on a review of numerous instances cited in the journals of participants in the decisions as cited in Alexander, 68.

581 *Charles A. Penrose Journal*, May 10, 1911, quoted in Richard S. Van Wagoner, *Mormon Polygamy: A History* (Salt Lake City, UT: Signature Books, 1989): 182. Matthias Cowley counseled his family that if they ever had to choose between him and the Church, they should choose the Church. The family never had to make that choice. Matthias stayed close to the Church. The privilege of exercising his priesthood was reinstated in 1936; later Matthias served a mission in Europe with his wife, Luella, and their daughter Laura. Matthias died in 1940. Aunt Luella lived until 1962. Matthew, Matthias Cowley's son with Abby, his first wife, later became a member of the Quorum of the Twelve Apostles. Joanne Cowley Austin Linford, interview with author, 2011.

582 John W. Taylor was granted full fellowship posthumously in 1965. Allen and Leonard, 474.

583 Nelle Spilsbury Hatch, *Colonia Juarez: An Intimate Account of a Mormon Village* (Salt Lake City, UT: Deseret Book Company, 1954): 8.

584 V. A. Wood, *The Alberta Temple: Centre and Symbol of Faith* (Calgary, AB: Detselig Enterprises, 1989): 18. The stake is no doubt named for President John Taylor, who in 1887 encouraged Charles O. Card and other polygamists from Cache Valley to settle in Canada rather than Mexico.

As already discussed, as an apostle and perhaps under the direction of those under whom he served, John W. Taylor continued to perform plural marriages after the 1890 Manifesto. In this time of transition he was certainly not the only Church leader who performed plural marriages and who believed the manifesto was issued only to appease the U.S. government and was not binding.

In 1911 John W. Taylor received further reason to continue his commitment to polygamy when he found in the basement of the Church Archives a record of a revelation that his father is said to have received in 1886. The text of this revelation contains God's answer to John Taylor's question of whether it would not be right to discontinue plural marriage in view of the high political costs to the Church and to the lives of the Saints. Part of the revelation reads,

> Thus saith the Lord, All commandments that I give must be obeyed by those calling themselves by my name unless they are revoked by me or by my authority. And how can I revoke an everlasting covenant; for I the Lord am everlasting and my everlasting covenants cannot be abrogated nor done away with; but they stand forever. . . . I have not revoked this law nor will I for it is everlasting and those who would enter into my glory must obey the conditions thereof, even so amen.[585]

John W. told the First Presidency and members of Quorum of the Twelve that he felt it was the Church's obligation to follow this revelation. For John W. and many others, this document validated their conviction that a non-negotiable cornerstone of the "true church" was plural marriage. This revelation has served and continues to serve as critical evidence in support of what is now referred to as Mormon fundamentalism.

As discussed in Chapter Five, just months before he died, John Taylor issued a transition statement that showed signs of moving toward ending plural marriage. Also, a few weeks before his death, John Taylor approved a proposed constitution—another effort to obtain statehood—which contained a provision outlawing plural marriage. A few weeks after his death, the Utah electorate approved the constitution by a wide margin. The Saints probably would have done so only if they felt their late beloved leader concurred.[586] However, in that same time period, John Taylor also chose to be sealed to another plural wife—a poignant indication of how inseparable The Principle was from his very fabric and how conflicted he was about giving up the practice.[587] His son, John W. Taylor, was unequivocal in his support of plural marriage but he lived in a time when both the government and the Church outlawed the practice. Performing plural marriages was now against the law and grounds for excommunication from the Church.

---

585 A copy of the uncanonized revelation is in the John Taylor file, LDS Archives, quoted in Van Wagoner, 128.

586 Gibbons, 265–66.

587 On December 19, 1886 John Taylor was sealed to Josephine Roueche, the daughter of Thomas F. Roueche, in whose farmhouse he lived the last seven months of his life. VanWagoner, *Mormon Polygamy*, 128.

Although some of the Saints who went to Mexico in the 1880s continued to believe that taking new plural wives was a central tenet of the Church, most of the Saints who fled to Canada and Mexico to avoid persecution stayed loyal to the Church and gave up the practice, often remaining in these countries after the 1890 Manifesto to raise their families. The Saints living in Mexico established thriving communities in the states of Chihuahua and Sonora in northern Mexican with the intention of remaining there indefinitely. Joseph Barnard Romney wrote in *The Journal of Mormon History*,

> [Eventually] they built substantial brick homes equal in quality to those in Utah. They built churches, tithing houses, a fine Relief Society building in Colonia Dublan, elementary schools with an academy (high school) in Colonia Juarez which continues to function today. Their economy was prosperous and diversified—including fruit, grain, substantial herds of cattle, lumber, gristmills, mercantile establishments, and other businesses needed to support a growing population.[588]

In 1910 the political situation in Mexico became volatile when Porfirio Diaz, who had been president for many years, was forced into exile and replaced by Francisco Madero. Mormons, trying to remain politically neutral, were caught in the middle of tensions between Madero on the one hand and Pascual Orozco and Francisco ("Pancho") Villa on the other. In the summer of 1912, 4,500 Saints evacuated the Mormon colonies and fled to the United States under the leadership of their thirty-four-year-old stake president, Junius Romney. My uncle, Antone K. Romney (married to my mother's sister Gretta) was ten years old when he fled from Mexico with his family as part of this group.[589]

While these Saints were returning to the United States, prejudice against the Church remained high in both the United States and Great Britain. Frank J. Cannon (the son of George Q. and Sarah Jane Jenne) had been a solid support to George Q. in his lifetime but later became an outspoken critic of the Church. As the editor of *The Salt Lake Tribune* (the then anti-Mormon Salt Lake City newspaper) and as a national speaker, he had wide influence. Four national magazines—*Pearson's*, *Everybody's*, *McClure's*, and *Cosmopolitan*—viciously attacked the Church. The criticism of the Church extended to Great Britain, which was experiencing great social change. Polygamy was seen as a threat to England's stability. Widely distributed anti-Mormon literature stated that polygamy was still being practiced and that missionaries were

---

[588] Joseph Barnard Romney, "The Lord, God of Israel, Brought Us Out of Mexico: Junius Romney and the 1912 Mormon Exodus," *Journal of Mormon History* 36, no. 4 (Fall 2010): 212.

[589] Ibid., 208. To read the fascinating story of the exodus that Junius saw as their miraculous deliverance, see the cited article in *The Journal of Mormon History*.

luring away British girls. In 1910, Parliament discussed the expulsion of missionaries from England. Young Winston Churchill, then Home Secretary, reported that he had found nothing against the Mormons, so no expulsions took place.[590]

An incident from my mother's life illustrates the prejudice against the Church during this time period. She often told of the experience she and two teenage cousins from rural Rexburg, Idaho, had when they attended the Westlake School for Girls in Los Angeles in 1918. The school offered the girls choices of church services to attend. When Mother explained that she and her two Smart cousins were Mormon, the administration insisted the girls be sent home; however, the quarantine imposed by the worldwide influenza epidemic prevented their immediate departure. By the time the quarantine was lifted, Mother and her cousins had made a place for themselves; they stayed until school ended in the spring. Her cousins returned to Westlake the following year. Mother was always proud that she had spoken up and acknowledged that she was a Mormon and that they were ultimately accepted.[591]

Polygamy remained a prominent issue in the Church in the early years of the twentieth century. In answering a missionary nephew's queries in 1924 about polygamy, George M. Cannon, a son of Angus and Sarah Maria referred to earlier, wanted his nephew to see that polygamy had contributed many leaders to the Church. He noted that in 1924, of the twenty-six general authorities all but five were either themselves polygamists, including the President of the Church, Heber J. Grant, or were the sons or grandsons of polygamists.[592] It is important to note that Heber J. Grant, the president of the Church from 1918 until 1945, entered plural marriage before 1890 and conscientiously encouraged the Saints to obey the Manifesto. The fact that he had been a polygamist was not an issue during his presidency, likely because only one of his three wives was alive after 1908.[593]

As late as the 1920s, secrecy still surrounded any polygamous marriage, even those performed before 1890. My mother's cousin Sam Monson, born in 1919, lived with his parents, Olive and Ezra Monson, in Logan. Olive's sister Luella, the second wife of Matthias Cowley, lived close by. Sam remembered that Aunt Luella drew the blinds in the daytime when Matthias came to visit so that no one would know he was there.[594] We continue to draw the blinds on what a

---

590 *Fulness of Times*, 472. See also, Alan K. Parrish, "Turning the Media Image of the Church in Great Britain, 1922–33," Religious Studies Center, accessed February 10, 2015, http://rsc.byu.edu/archived/regional-studies-latter-day-saint-church-history-british-isles/9-turning-media-image-church, and David S. Hoopes and Roy Hoopes, *The Making of a Mormon Apostle: The Story of Rudger Clawson* (Landham, MD: Madison Books, 1990): 263.

591 Mary Parkinson Cannon, converstions with author, through the years.

592 George M. Cannon to Elder Milton Bennion Cannon, in *1990 Angus M. Cannon Reunion Materials*, 239. Elder Milton Cannon was serving in Germany at the time. The twenty-six general authorities mentioned probably included the First Presidency, the Twelve Apostles, the Presiding Bishopric, the Patriarch, and the Seven Presidents of Seventy.

593 His first wife Lucy died in 1893. Emily, his third wife, died in 1908. His second wife Augusta died in 1951. President Grant died in 1945.

594 Samuel Monson, conversation with author, 1980s.

prominent role polygamy has played in our history. The code of silence that operated during the Underground days and squelched conversation about Lewis' marriage to Lillian continues to the present day.

Two Mormon scholars have eloquently captured the wrenching effects giving up polygamy had on the Church:

> Neither side [the federal government or the Church] seemed to comprehend the magnitude of theological dysfunction then afflicting the church. Mormonism was, in fact, in the throes of doctrinal reformation. What had commenced as a posture of expediency became an increasingly orthodox departure from the past. Those who disparaged the church were perhaps too close to appreciate the dislocations resulting from years of unyielding pressure [from the government]. Their laws and invectives wrought more than they knew. When one considers how deeply imbedded the belief in polygamy had become in Mormon theological consciousness, the fifteen-year period of indirection and awkward posing associated with its arrest is remarkably brief.[595]

As time passed, it became easier for the Church to close the chapter on plural marriage and to view monogamy as the new expression of celestial marriage.

---

595 Jorgenson and Hardy, 35.

Mary Parkinson Cannon and Alan M. Cannon married in 1927.
This photo celebrates their fiftieth wedding anniversary.

Chapter Seven

Polygamy in Contemporary Mormon Culture and Doctrine

Our Past Is in Our Present

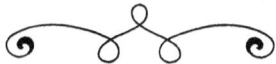

Celestial marriage—that is, marriage for time and eternity [—] and polygamous marriage are not synonymous terms. . . . Monogamous marriages solemnized in our temples are celestial marriages.

President Heber J. Grant

TO TRANSITION from polygamy to monogamy the Church focused its efforts on redefining celestial marriage. In the process, it not only gave up the practice of polygamy but also chose to be silent about it having occurred. Changing the doctrine, rhetoric, and culture surrounding eternal marriage was a major task. Plural marriage had been the Church's distinguishing doctrine and the avenue for reaching the highest degree of exaltation. Annie Clark Tanner wrote, "It was taught that a second wife opened the door of salvation in the Celestial Kingdom not only for herself, but for her husband and his first wife."[596] Joseph E. Taylor, a counselor in the Salt Lake stake presidency from 1876 to 1904, interpreted Doctrine and Covenants 132 to mean that exaltation could "only be reached by observing the patriarchal

---

596 Tanner, *A Mormon Mother*, quoted in Daynes, 76.

order of marriage," which at the time was interpreted as plural marriage.[597] George Q. Cannon's statements on the matter corroborate this interpretation. He said that he "did not feel like holding up his hand to sustain anyone as a presiding officer over any portion of the people who had not entered into the Patriarchal order of Marriage."[598] Another time he warned, "Some men think they can slip around—I have heard such men talk. They think they are going to get into the celestial kingdom without obeying the law of celestial marriage."[599]

The process of redefining celestial marriage began as early as 1899, when James Talmage, a monogamous Mormon intellectual who later became an apostle, gave a series of lectures on the principal doctrines of the Church. The lectures, later published as *The Articles of Faith*, were a profoundly influential expression of Church doctrine. In these lectures he defined celestial marriage as "the system of holy matrimony, involving covenants as to time and eternity." Celestial marriage is "the order of marriage that exists in the celestial worlds."[600] He leaves it an open question whether that order involves plural marriage. The following year, in an article Talmage wrote for *The Improvement Era*, an official LDS publication, he was explicit about what he meant: "In celestial marriage plurality of wives . . . was never an essential."[601] His interpretation became the new norm.

Ten years later, Charles W. Penrose, a counselor to President Heber J. Grant, reinforced the omission of plural marriage as essential to the definition of celestial marriage when he wrote that "the heavenly order of celestial marriage, that is matrimony, [is] for time and all eternity." Similarly, J. M. Sjodahl wrote in 1927 that the "revelation of celestial marriage" dealt solely with the "eternal duration of the marriage relation."[602] The operative word, "relation," implied that marriage involves only one man and one woman.

In 1933 President Grant made the new definition official: "Celestial marriage—that is, marriage for time and eternity [—] and polygamous marriage are not synonymous terms. . . . Monogamous marriages solemnized in our temples are celestial marriages."[603] By the 1950s, no explanation accompanied the term "celestial marriage" in LDS publications. By then it was assumed to mean an eternal union between one man and one woman in an LDS temple. By

---

597 Brian H. Stuy, ed., *Collected Discourses, Delivered by President Wilford Woodruff, His Two counselors, the Twelve Apostles and Others* (Burbank, CA: B.H.S. Publishing, 1987–92): 1:142, quoted in Daynes, 76. Joseph E. Taylor was a counselor to Angus M. Cannon. *Deseret News*, Joseph E. Taylor's obituary, February, 18, 1913.

598 Charles Lowell Walker, *Diary of Charles Lowell Walker*, eds. A. Karl Larson and Katharine Miles Larson (Logan: Utah State University Press, 1980): 2:629, quoted in Daynes, 72.

599 George Q. Cannon, October 31, 1880, in *Journal of Discourses*, 22:124, quoted in Daynes, 76.

600 James E. Talmage, *The Articles of Faith* (Salt Lake City, UT: Deseret Book Company, 1990), quoted in Stephen C. Taysom, "A Uniform and Common Recollection: Joseph Smith's Legacy, Polygamy, and the Creation of Mormon Public Memory 1852–2002," *Dialogue: A Journal of Mormon Thought* 35 No. 3 (2009): 11.

601 James E. Talmage, "The Story of Mormonism," *The Improvement Era*, October 1901, 12, quoted in Taysom, 11.

602 J. M. Sjodahl, "Temple Marriage and Antidote Against Divorce," *The Improvement Era* October 1927, 12, quoted in Taysom, 11. J. M. Sjodahl was a Swedish convert who edited several Church newspapers and translated Mormon scripture into Swedish. "Janne M. Sjodahl," Wikipedia, accessed April 2, 2014, http://en.wikipedia.org/wiki/Janne_M._Sj%C3%B6dahl.

603 "Official Statement from the First Presidency of The Church of Jesus Christ of Latter-day Saints," reprinted in *The Deseret News*, June 17, 1933, quoted in Taysom, 11.

1950, Doctrine and Covenants 132 was seen as the section on celestial marriage rather than on plural marriage. In 1995 the First Presidency's issued "The Family: A Proclamation to the World," which states that "marriage between *a* man and *a* [italics added] woman is ordained of God and that the family is central to the Creator's plan for the eternal destiny of His children."[604] The document, included as Appendix O, emphasizes the importance of a husband and a wife as equal, collaborative partners bearing and raising children in a loving home in which the husband focuses on providing protection and the necessities of life and the wife is primarily responsible for nurturing their children. The document includes not even a nod to the Church's polygamous past. In the move from polygamy to monogamy, the Church's marital practices changed, but the importance of families being sealed in the temple did not.

To shift from polygamy to monogamy, the Church needed not only to redefine marriage but also to emphasize to members as well as to the outside world that plural marriage would not be tolerated. J. Reuben Clark was sustained as a member of the First Presidency in April 1933, two months before President Grant made the official statement in June that monogamy and eternal marriage were synonymous. J. Reuben Clark brought a fresh perspective about transitioning from plural to monogamous unions. He had not risen through the ranks of Church leaders, many of whom had close personal ties to polygamy; rather, he came to Church leadership after having been a U.S. Undersecretary of State, a corporate attorney, and the U.S. ambassador to Mexico.

Perhaps even more important to his perspective than his professional experience was the home in which he grew up. His parents, Joshua Reuben Clark and Mary Louisa Woolley, were always monogamous even though they married in 1872 during the height of polygamy.[605] When Clark became a member of the First Presidency, he was troubled to discover that some Church leaders had authorized polygamous unions for several years after the 1890 Manifesto. Perhaps because of this discovery, he led out on the Church's taking a very clear and firm stance on how to respond to members in fringe groups who were still marrying plural wives. Soon the First Presidency issued a harsh warning to all who resisted the Church's new course. The statement not only claimed that "in abandoning polygamy, Mormon leaders were conforming to Divine will but that further attempts to revive The Principle were inspired by Satan, that new plural relationships were adulterous, and that the President of the Church alone had authority to approve plural unions—permission he no longer granted."[606] With similar intent to end the practice, in 1935 Utah's state legislature enacted a Church-supported criminal provision that elevated the conviction for polygamous cohabitation from a misdemeanor to a felony.[607]

---

604 The First Presidency and Council of the Twelve Apostles of The Church of Jesus Christ of Latter-day Saints, "The Family: A Proclamation to the World," (presented at the General Relief Society Meeting, Salt Lake City, UT, September 23, 1995).

605 J. Reuben Clark's mother and father, though married monogamously to each other, both came from polygamous families.

606 B. Carmon Hardy, "The Persistence of Mormon Plural Marriage," *Dialogue, A Journal of Mormon Thought* 44, no. 4 (Winter 2011): 62.

607 Ibid.

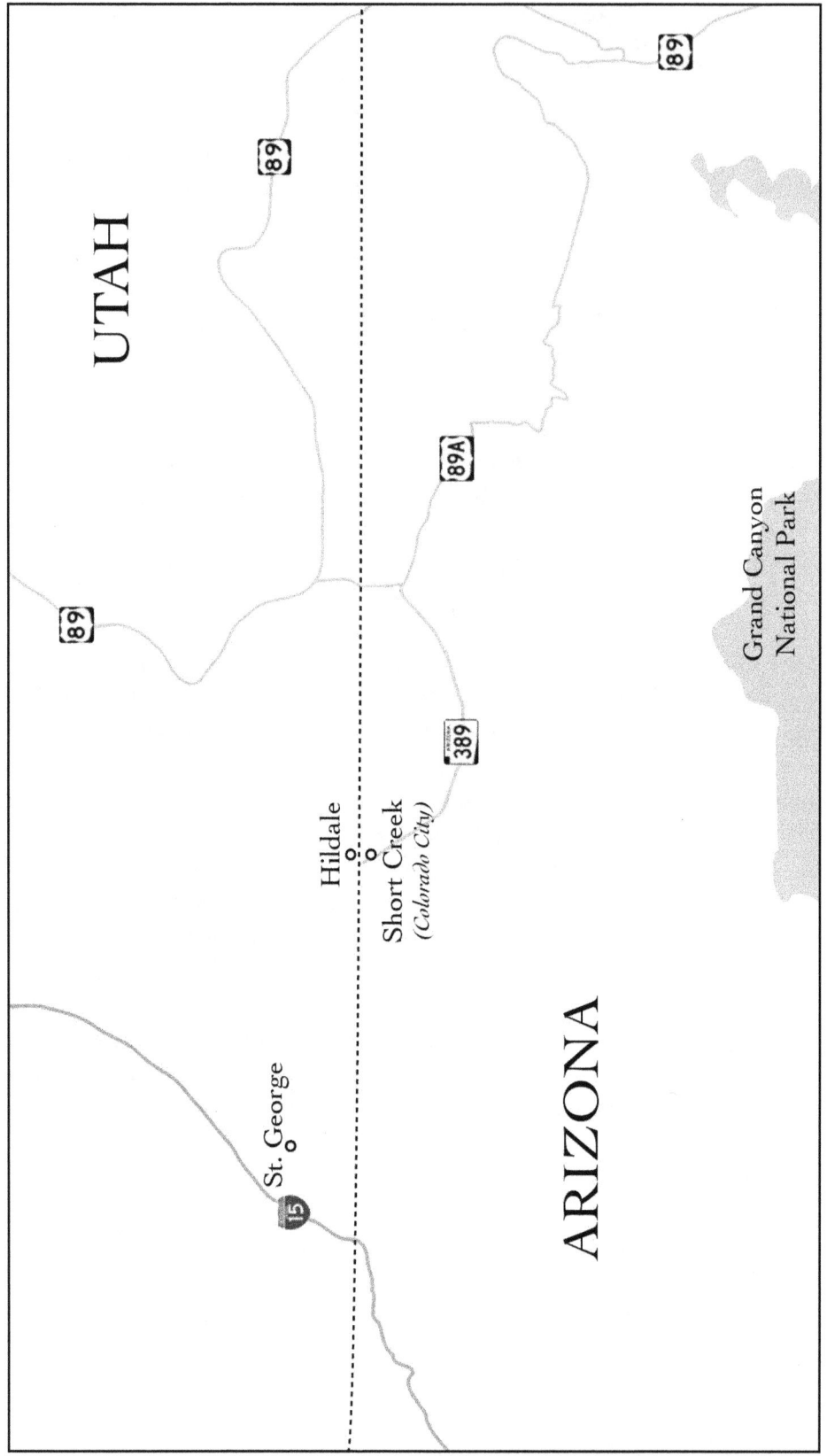

An Arizona State Route 389 map that shows the area on the southern Utah and northern Arizona border where some fundamentalist groups lived and continue to live. Short Creek was present-day Colorado City. Both Colorado City and Hildale still have many polygamous residents.

In response, fundamentalists became more outspoken in their defense of polygamy as central to the "True Church" and attracted more practitioners. This growth intensified the efforts of Church leaders to discipline Church members associating with such groups, often by excommunicating them. Several raids of fundamentalist homes occurred in Salt Lake, as well as other Utah towns, the culmination of which was the infamous 1953 siege of Short Creek, Arizona, located on the Utah-Arizona border. In the effort to end polygamy, parents were jailed and children were separated from their mothers in a heavy-handed manner under the direction of Arizona's Baptist governor, Howard Pyle. The national press showed crying children ripped from their mother's arms and police raiding school yards, which brought negative criticism to Arizona government officials as well as to the Church. Governor Pyle was not reelected.[608] After the widespread negative publicity, which stood in contrast to the Church's silence about its polygamous past, both the government and the Church backed off aggressive efforts to eradicate plural marriage.

Widespread publicity gradually led the Church to be more open about what it had kept hidden. The Church's relationship with polygamy, even when it was considered doctrinal, was enveloped in secrecy. From the beginning, a code of silence shrouded plural marriage. The unusual nature of the doctrine and the hesitancy of many Church leaders to enter the practice made Joseph Smith reluctant to talk about it openly with fellow Church members, let alone the general public. In fact, exactly when Joseph Smith first instituted plural marriage and how many wives he had are unknown.[609] The practice was never acknowledged publicly while the Saints were in Nauvoo.

The code of silence that Joseph Smith initiated gave the practice of polygamy time to take root. The martyrdom of Joseph Smith in Carthage, a town near Nauvoo, as well as continued hostility toward the Saints, forced them to leave their newly completed temple and the city they had grown to love. They traveled westward to create a kingdom of God in an isolated area outside the boundaries of the United States. Here they hoped to practice their religion, including plural marriage, without persecution or the need to be secretive.

In 1852, after the Saints had been in the Salt Lake Valley five years, Church leaders had the confidence to publicly announce the doctrine of plural marriage at that year's April general conference. Then, for some twenty years, the Saints flourished and openly practiced polygamy. Once settled in the West, they established themselves by planting crops and building homes

---

608 O. K. White and Daryl White, "Polygamy and Mormon Identity," *Journal of American Culture* 28 (2005): 170.

609 My generation grew up thinking of Brigham Young as the prophet who established plural marriage. I didn't know Joseph Smith was involved with polygamy until well into my adult years. Todd Compton's *In Sacred Loneliness: The Plural Wives of Joseph Smith* first published in 1997 sheds light on Joseph Smith's polygamous relations well.

and schools in a corridor of communities located south and north of Salt Lake, with large polygamous families at the hub of these communities. The lack of separation between church and state and the Saints' isolation meant there was nothing to hinder the practice.

The eventual end of this asylum by isolation had its roots as early as 1848 when the Treaty of Guadalupe Hidalgo ended the Mexican-American War and extended the United States' sovereignty to the Pacific coast.[610] In addition, fortune seekers went through Utah on their way to search for gold in California. The final delineation of the Canadian border was in 1846. The completion of the Union Pacific Railroad in 1869 definitively ended the isolation of the Saints from the outside world.[611]

The freedom to openly practice plural marriage lessened during the last years of Brigham Young's presidency (which ended in 1877 with his death), when the federal government began more actively to enforce laws against the practice of plural marriage. The government's efforts continued throughout John Taylor's tenure, which lasted until 1887. To preserve their right to obey God's law and to maintain ties with their family members, many polygamous men and women participated in a different code of silence: they went underground as discussed in Chapter Five. Doing so helped them avoid legal trouble and maintain privacy while cultivating the continuing hope of being admitted to the Union. During the Underground it was necessary to keep people's whereabouts secret as a matter of safety and freedom. Keeping polygamy concealed during this period also hid the discrepancy between what was being said publicly and what was being practiced, allowing Church leaders to delay deciding how to react to federal pressure.

Now, more than a century after the Manifestos of 1890 and 1904, we have different reasons for being quiet about our polygamous past. Embarrassed by the behavior of contemporary polygamists—such as the indicted Warren Jeffs and fictional characters of the popular TV drama *Big Love*, which depicts the vicissitudes of living in a polygamous family—we disassociate ourselves from fundamentalists who continue to embrace a practice that was once a cornerstone of Mormonism. The Church has difficulty being honest about its past[612] and relating civilly to

---

610 Heather Symes Cannon, "Practical Politicians," in *Mormon Sisters: Women in Early Utah*, ed. Claudia L. Bushman (Cambridge, MA: Emmeline Press Limited, 1976): 158.

611 Ibid.

612 There are eighty churches listed in the Wikipedia article entitled "List of Sects in the Latter Day Saint Movement." Of these, about seventy are now defunct or have fewer than one thousand members. In the years following the 1890 Manifesto and the 1904 Manifesto, two groups split off to continue practicing polygamy: the Short Creek Community and the Latter Day Church of Christ. The Short Creek Community and its many later splinters account for nearly all the groups known since as fundamentalist Mormons, including those led by Rulon C. Allred, Leroy S. Johnson, Joel LeBaron, Ervil LeBaron, Warren Jeffs, and Winston Blackmore.

There are two notable groups with LDS roots that practice polygamy today. The Apostolic United Brethren began in 1954 under Rulon C. Allred, as a successor to the Short Creek Community. Its headquarters are in Bluffdale, Utah. It currently has membership of about ten thousand. The Fundamentalist Church of Jesus Christ of Latter-day Saints also began in 1954 as a Short Creek successor, under Leroy S. Johnson. It is concentrated in the neighboring communities of Colorado City, Arizona (formerly known as Short Creek) and Hildale, Utah. There are eight to ten thousand members. "List of Sects in the Latter Day Saint Movement," Wikipedia, http://en.wikipedia.org/wiki/List_of_sects_in_the_Latter_Day_Saint_movement.

contemporary splinter groups. For now, Church leaders essentially do not acknowledge our common roots but instead concentrate on the fact that they are no longer a part of us, nor we of them.

Recently I became acquainted with present-day fundamentalists in a visit that touched me deeply. As I was researching the location of George Q.'s homes, I visited Joanie Wayman; she and her husband, Nephi, monogamists with eight lovely children, are the current owners of the home of George Q. Cannon's wife, Martha Telle Cannon, where my father lived for part of his childhood. Joanie was most gracious in showing me the house and sharing what she knew of its history. In a note she thanked me for coming and wrote that she hoped that we could meet again. We did just that when I visited the Cannon Farm area again with my Cannon cousins. Joanie and her husband as well as her husband's brother (a polygamist who is remodeling the home next to the home of George Q.'s wife Eliza Tenney Cannon) were generous in sharing their history and also some produce from their gardens. My cousins and I felt linked to them and they to us. How ironic that present-day polygamists live in some of my great-grandfather's homes. They look to George Q. as a mentor and as a defender of plural marriage. I and his other LDS descendants see him as a forceful, articulate leader who defended states' rights and polygamy when it was allowed, but who acknowledged the authority of President Woodruff and followed the 1890 Manifesto in his personal life.[613]

Our current code of silence reveals not only our continued ambivalence about polygamy but also helps us preserve our image of being a religion that embraces traditional family values: spouses being faithful to each other and family members spending meaningful time together. Embracing these traditional values helps Mormons sustain healthy family units and perpetuates an image of being mainstream and traditional—though our past is neither.

As a result of the Church's ambivalent relationship to its past, many ironies and complexities have emerged. One example is the Church's firm stance against gay marriage. The Church asked members in California to contribute money and canvass door to door to promote the passage of Proposition 8, which states that "only marriage between a man and a woman is valid or recognized in California."[614] This is reminiscent, in a milder form, of the way that anti-polygamists put muscle behind laws such as Edmunds-Tucker Act to prohibit polygamy. George Q. Cannon fought for decades for the Saints' right to practice plural marriage. When Elizabeth, his first wife, died in 1882 in Utah, he was in Washington, DC trying to prevent passage of laws that would prohibit his full obedience to his religion. Much like a gay politician who is wisely wary about discussing the details of his private life, George Q. did not share with his fellow politicians that he was grieving the loss of his first wife. The discriminatory treatment we fought and resented for so many years is what we are now involved in ourselves. I understand the doctrinal reasons for the Church's position on gay marriage but I am disappointed that

---

613 Jorgeson and Hardy, 16.

614 "Proposition 8," in "Text of Proposed Laws," *Official Voter Information Guide*, State of California (2008): 128.

Church leaders and members do not acknowledge the similarities between discrimination against polygamists and against gays. If we acknowledged the parallels, then we would be more compassionate and understanding about the grievances of gays.

From the time Utah drafted its first constitution and was admitted to the Union, polygamy has been prohibited in the state, as it generally was and is in all the states. Modern-day male polygamists are often living with multiple women to whom they do not claim to be legally married. So, if being *married* to multiple women is the crime, they are not committing a crime. Nineteenth-century Mormon polygamists were married, but it was hard for federal enforcers to prove these marriages had taken place. This is why the Edmunds Act (1882) was important: it added cohabitation—living with a woman outside of marriage—as a crime.

Times have changed. The social, cultural, political, and legal determination to stop consenting adults from living with each other and having sexual relations on any basis they choose has nearly evaporated. The day seems to be coming when all legal interference in relationships, whether married or not, will end.

Paradoxically, Utah and other heavily Mormon populated states have been more energetic than other states in keeping a role for government in regulating living arrangements, especially those practiced as part of a professed religious belief—another illustration of the Church's distancing itself from its polygamous roots. Did current-day Utah legislators and prosecutors forget that when Utah was a territory, its legislators, my great-grandfather among them, fought to protect people's right to practice their religion without legal censure? Perhaps as a result of the popularity of the reality TV show *Sister Wives*, (which features Kody Brown and his four polygamous wives, and that family's insistence that their lifestyle should be legal), U.S. District Judge Clark Waddoups ruled in August 2014 that the anti-cohabitation part of the Utah anti-polygamy law was unconstitutional (though Utah is still allowed to prohibit legal *marriage* to two people at once). Waddoups ruled that the state's law prohibiting "'cohabitation'—the language used in the law to restrict polygamous relations—violates the First Amendment guarantee of free exercise of religion, as well as constitutional due process."[615] On April 11, 2016 a federal appeals court overturned the Waddoups ruling and restored Utah's ban on polygamy, marking a defeat for the polygamous family on the TV show *Sister Wives*.[616] Isn't it ironic that Utah is among those most vigorously opposing the freedom of religion and privacy for which it had once fought so hard?

---

[615] "A Utah Law Prohibiting Polygamy Is Weakened," *New York Times*, December 14, 2013. The judge left standing the state's ability to prohibit multiple marriages "in the literal sense" of having two or more valid marriage licenses. This article refers to an early ruling of Judge Waddoups that he made final in 2014.

[616] Lindsay Whitehurst, "Utah Polygamy Ban Restored in Loss for 'Sister Wives' Family," *Post and Courier* (Charleston, SC), April 12, 2016.

Another problem is that the Church's current policy on polygamy is inconsistent. On the one hand, it does not allow practicing polygamists to be baptized in Africa, where the practice is legal and customary nor can children of polygamous parents be baptized.[617] On the other hand, if a man's first wife to whom he has been sealed dies, he can be married and sealed to a second wife. The understanding is that he will be married to both women in the hereafter.[618]

Not surprisingly, the Church's current public portrayal of polygamy excludes these current inconsistencies and minimizes its polygamous past. President Gordon B. Hinckley participated in an hour-long interview with Larry King on September 8, 1998.[619] He was asked many wide ranging and often sensitive questions. Larry King first asked when the Church allowed polygamy and followed with further questions. In response, President Hinckley's said,

> When our people came west they permitted it on a restricted scale. The figures I have are from . . . between two percent and five percent of our people were involved in it. It was a very limited practice; carefully safeguarded. In 1890 that practice was discontinued. . . . The president of the church prayed about it, worked on it, and received from the Lord a revelation that it was time to stop, to discontinue it then. That's 118 years ago. It's behind us. . . .There are actually no Mormon fundamentalists. . . . People mistakenly assume that this church has something to do with it. It has nothing whatever to do with it. It has had nothing to do with it for a very long time. It's outside the realm of our responsibility. These people are not members. Any man or woman who becomes involved in it is excommunicated from the church." [620]

At the Sunday morning session of the October General Conference, three weeks after the Larry King interview, President Hinckley expanded on and clarified the Church's positions on several topics covered in the interview. Regarding polygamy, he said,

> I wish to state categorically that this Church has nothing whatever to do with those practicing polygamy. They are not members of this Church. Most of them have never been members. They are in violation of the civil law. They know they are in violation of the law. They are subject to its penalties. The Church, of course, has no jurisdiction whatever in this matter. . . . If any of our members are

---

617 Sarah Jane Weaver, "Elder Christofferson Speaks about Handbook changes Affecting Same-sex Marriage," *Church News* (Salt Lake City, UT), Nov. 15, 2015.

618 However, if a woman is sealed to a man who dies, she can marry again in the temple—but only for this life.

619 Gordon B. Hinckley, interview by Larry King, *Larry King Live*, CNN, September 8, 1998

620 For insight into why President Hinckley was so adamant about distancing the Church from fundamentalist groups in Utah and surrounding states in 1998, see James Brooks, "Utah Struggles with a Renewal of Polygamy," *New York Times*, Aug. 23, 1998.

> found to be practicing plural marriage, they are excommunicated, the most serious penalty the Church can impose. Not only are those so involved in direct violation of the civil law, they are in violation of the law of this Church. . . . More than a century ago God clearly revealed unto His prophet Wilford Woodruff that the practice of plural marriage should be discontinued, which means that it is now against the law of God. Even in countries where civil or religious law allows polygamy, the Church teaches that marriage must be monogamous and does not accept into its membership those practicing plural marriage.[621]

President Hinckley's remarks highlight the dilemma Church leaders face. They want to celebrate the heroism of stalwart pioneer men and women but not draw attention to the controversial practice of polygamy. Understandably leaders and members feel strongly about distancing the Church from the extreme behaviors of present fundamentalists. Leaders have chosen in contexts such as this widely viewed interview to largely distance the Church from its polygamous past.

Clearly, the evolution in how we see polygamy is complex, confusing, and painful. In doing research for this book, I have seen more clearly than ever that in the case of polygamy, today's Church leaders are stuck between a rock and a hard place as they consider how to relate to polygamous splinter groups and how to present the Church's polygamous past to Church members and to others. Current leaders have kept their distance from polygamy and today's polygamous groups, an approach that has often included an attempt to erase it from Church history. As a result, members have found it difficult to be open about and comfortable with the Church's polygamous history.

Mitt Romney, for example, when asked during his 2012 presidential campaign how he felt about polygamy, said,

> There is nothing more awful, in my view, than the violation of the marriage covenant that one has with one's wife. The practice of polygamy is abhorrent . . . and it drives me nuts that . . . . polygamists keep pretending to use the umbrella of my church. . . . My church abhors it; it excommunicates people who practice it. It's got nothing to do with my faith.[622]

---

621 Gordon B. Hinckley, General Conference address, October 1998, quoted in "Polygamy: Latter-day Saints and the Practice of Plural Marriage," Mormon Newsroom, http://www.mormonnewsroom.org/article/polygamy-latter-day-saints-and-the-practice-of-plural-marriage

622 Douglas Kmiec, "Revising Kennedy," *National Review* (November 14, 2007), quoted in "Public Image of Mitt Romney," Wikipedia, http://en.wikipedia.org/wiki/Public_image_of_ Mitt_Romney#cite_note-78.

The truth is that Romney's paternal and maternal great-grandparents were polygamists. While he abhors the current practice of polygamy, he no doubt has positive feelings about his forbears. His reaction is a perfect example of how many Mormons disconnect themselves from their past. We Mormons find ourselves juggling a sanitized public image with our pride in our family heritage, which for many Church members includes polygamy. I am very aware that the answers to these issues are not easy; therefore we need to give ourselves and our ecclesiastical leaders space and understanding.

Evidence of the Church's silence about its past is also apparent in historical Church exhibits and lesson materials in which the practice of plural marriage is never mentioned. For example, a permanent exhibit on presidents of the Church at the Church History Museum makes no mention of the wives of the first seven presidents, likely because doing so would involve showing that they each had more than one. This omission not only masks what took place but also presents a male-oriented picture of Church history that omits women's significant sacrifices and contributions to the growth of the Church. A recent display of some of the past Relief Society presidents helps compensate for this omission.[623]

Similar omissions are evident in the Church's curriculum. In 1997 the Church began a course of study for Priesthood and Relief Society classes called *Teachings of the Presidents of the Church*.[624] The first manual was on Brigham Young and made no reference to plural marriage in the chronology of his life.[625] Only his first wife, Miriam Angeline Works, who died of tuberculosis, and his second wife, Mary Ann Angell (whom he married after Miriam died) are included in his personal narrative. It is hard to imagine how we can talk about Brigham Young without mentioning that he had multiple wives. Those responsible for the series later slightly changed the approach; subsequent manuals on Joseph F. Smith, John Taylor, Heber J. Grant, and Wilford Woodruff acknowledge the deliberate omission of important personal events of the prophets' lives, including their marriages as well as the births and deaths of their children.[626] The reason given is that the emphasis is on the given prophet's teachings, not on his personal life. However, it is important to note that personal details of prophets' lives *are* included for those who came after the practice of polygamy ended.

Sometimes such omissions create a very distorted view of what occurred. For instance, in the manual about John Taylor, little is said about polygamy and nothing is said about his directing the affairs of the Church from the Underground for the last two and a half years of

---

623 The Church History Museum closed in 2014 for major reconfiguration. When it reopened in 2015, relevant exhibits acknowledge the practice of polygamy in our history and pay more attention to women.

624 The series on the lives and teachings of the presidents of the Church began with Brigham Young in 1997 and has continued each year since in no particular chronological order.

625 *Teachings of Presidents of the Church: Brigham Young* (Salt Lake City, UT: The Church of Jesus Christ of Latter-day Saints, 1997).

626 *Teachings of Presidents of the Church: Joseph F. Smith* (Salt Lake City, UT: The Church of Jesus Christ of Latter-day Saints, 1998). *Teachings of Presidents of the Church: John Taylor* (Salt Lake City. UT: The Church of Jesus Christ of Latter-day Saints, 2001). *Teachings of Presidents of the Church: Heber J. Grant* (Salt Lake City, UT: The Church of Jesus Christ of Latter-day Saints, 2002). *Teachings of Presidents of the Church: Wilford Woodruff* (Salt Lake City, UT: The Church of Jesus Christ of Latter-day Saints, 2004): xiii. The word *polygamy* is not mentioned.

his presidency or about his dying while in hiding.⁶²⁷ Until the 2013 manual on Lorenzo Snow, the most coverage readers get about polygamy in the manuals on the presidents who practiced polygamy is in the Wilford Woodruff manual, in which we read about President Woodruff's receiving the revelation that the practice of polygamy must cease.⁶²⁸ That the 2013 manual on Lorenzo Snow, the last manual to feature a polygamous president, mentions he was a polygamist might indicate that there were complaints about these omissions and/or that the Church is now ready to be more open about polygamy. The Lorenzo Snow manual mentions polygamy several times. The historical summary of his life includes that in 1845 he "enters into plural marriage, as then practiced in the Church, by marrying Charlotte Squires and Mary Adaline Goddard."⁶²⁹ His life sketch also includes that later he was sealed to other women.⁶³⁰ In addition, the historical summary mentions not only the Edmunds Act of 1882 and the Edmunds-Tucker Act of 1887 but also Lorenzo Snow's imprisonment from March 12, 1886 to February 8, 1887, for practicing polygamy.⁶³¹ Interestingly, no mention is made of the 1890 Manifesto.

Perhaps the most conspicuous silence surrounds the Church's depiction of Joseph and Emma's marriage. The manual on Joseph Smith, which is a two-year manual and comes in the middle of the series, includes his marriage to Emma in the chronology of his life but makes no reference to the issue of plural marriage or Joseph's multiple wives.⁶³² Other Church literature, films, and monuments also depict Joseph Smith and Emma as a loving couple. There is no acknowledgement of Emma's sorrow and anger about his taking plural wives or of Joseph's denials that he did so. Consider the Hollywood-like romance movie called *Emma Smith: My Story*.⁶³³ Though it graphically captures difficult issues such as mob violence and the struggles Emma had with her parents regarding her marriage to Joseph, there are no references to other wives. There are, however, many tender, intimate scenes between what appears to be an idyllic monogamous couple. The Church has now changed course on how open to be about Joseph Smith's having polygamous wives, a development I discuss later in this chapter.

Apparently, the membership of the Church as a whole wants to forget polygamy. A 2011 survey conducted by the Pew Research Center Forum about LDS members' beliefs, values, perceptions, and political preferences indicates that modern-day Mormons have little sympathy for the practice of polygamy. In fact, eighty-four percent of those surveyed found it to be

---

627 *Teachings of Presidents of the Church: John Taylor*.

628 *Teachings of Presidents of the Church: Wilford Woodruff*, xiii.

629 *Teachings of the Presidents of the Church: Lorenzo Snow* (Salt Lake City, UT: The Church of Jesus Christ of Latter-day Saints, 2012): 17.

630 Ibid., 17.

631 Ibid., xi.

632 *Teachings of the Presidents of the Church: Joseph Smith* (Salt Lake City, UT: The Church of Jesus Christ of Latter-day Saints, 2007)

633 This 2008 movie was commissioned independently of the Church, by the Joseph Smith Historical Society. The cast includes people who also appeared in the 2005 Church-produced movie, *Joseph Smith: Prophet of the Restoration*.

morally objectionable. This figure is higher than other behaviors that Mormons view as wrong. Seventy-nine percent disapproved of sex between unmarried adults, seventy-four percent of abortion, and fifty-four percent of drinking alcohol.[634] Polygamy trumped them all.

Joanna Brooks, author of *Book of Mormon Girl: Stories from An American Faith*, has written eloquently about the cost of not being honest about the past and why contemporary Mormons shy away from their history:

> I fully understand the reasons we tell the world we don't practice polygamy. The amount of sheer revulsion directed at Mormons for polygamy is astounding, and it's ridiculous in a world where other forms of non-hetero-monogamous relationship are welcomed or winked at. We crave understanding. We want to get along with our neighbors and fit in. . . . Why should we not inform our own people about our own history? When we don't, we set up our people to feel betrayed and ashamed, and we give power to people who would like to embarrass us. What we refuse to be ashamed of, others can never hold over us.[635]

Given the current attitudes toward polygamy, not only of Mormons but of society at large, it is not surprising that breaking the silence is rare. One of the first to speak out in the twentieth century was Annie Clark Tanner, whom I referred to earlier. In 1941, when she was seventy-eight years old, she wrote about the pain and challenges of raising her ten children as a second wife in a polygamous marriage. Annie moved from being a child in a stable, prestigious polygamous home to being a second wife in a polygamous marriage fraught with pain and disillusionment. As a result, she looked less to her husband and the Church as sources of authority and more to herself and science. Her candid account opened the door to a more honest look at our polygamous past.

Laura Bush, author of *Faithful Transgressions in the American West*, described Tanner's account as "a developmental journey that begins with youthful naiveté, rigid religiosity, and unwavering obedience and ends with mature womanhood, religious tolerance, and self-determination." Bush wrote that Tanner was aware that her audience would likely include readers inside and outside the fold, so she "construct[ed] her narrative to educate [readers] about Mormon polygamy and to create space for a woman to speak as frankly as her Victorian upbringing would allow about a controversial subject that profoundly affected her life."[636] Bush's robust and insightful analysis of Tanner's evolution is more complete and measured than my initial response in 1970 and likely more complete than Tanner's own understanding was. Now, half of my lifetime later, I concur with this contemporary scholar.

---

634 Joseph Walker, Mormon Times, *Deseret News*, January 11, 2012.

635 Joanna Brooks, "I'm pretty sure Mormons still believe in polygamy. Am I wrong?" Ask Mormon Girl Blog, entry posted January 22, 2012, http://askmormongirl.wordpress.com/2012/01/22/im-pretty-sure-mormons-still-believe-in-polygamy-am-i-wrong/.

636 Bush, 61.

Forty years after Tanner published her memoir, a member of my extended family broke the code of silence by writing about a post-Manifesto plural marriage in his family. In 1981, when he was seventy-nine years old, Paul B. Cannon wrote a letter to his daughters stating that his father—John M. Cannon, the son of Angus M. Cannon and Sarah Mousley Cannon—had married two plural wives in 1900, ten years after the 1890 Manifesto.[637] In the letter he expresses his concern about

> the common and oft-repeated statement in church publications and by church authorities is that polygamy was discontinued by the Manifesto in 1890. If this were true I would have to assume that my own father's plural marriages were without church authority, and that he should have been excommunicated. I have never had any doubt but that his marriages were authorized because of certain specific and undisputable facts. The principal fact is that my father was a first counselor to Frank Y. Taylor, as President of Granite Stake from as early as I can remember until his death June 16, 1917. I was fifteen years old when father died and I have a very vivid recollection of the funeral service. My mother [Zina], his first wife, "Aunt" Margaret, his second wife, and "Aunt" Hattie, his third wife, sat side by side on the front row with family and relatives seated in the usual front section. Both President Joseph F. Smith and his counselor, Charles W. Penrose, spoke at the funeral.[638]

Paul remembered that "Aunt" Margaret had often stayed in his family's home with her children and that his family had often gone to "Aunt" Hattie's home in Millcreek for Sunday dinner. He did not realize that Margaret and Hattie were married to his father until he was twelve years old. In his letter he noted that the families lived harmoniously and then referred his family to additional evidence, summarized in the *Utah Historical Quarterly* in 1980, that at least some Church authorities approved plural marriage after 1890.[639]

Paul acknowledged that his openness about the occurrence of post-Manifesto marriages was not a comfortable position because it was contrary to the official position of the Church that polygamy ended with the 1890 Manifesto. His parents had always taught their children to be loyal to the Church and to general authorities. The fact that there was no criticism on any matter in his home caused him considerable internal conflict in acknowledging the post-Manifesto marriages of his father. "I am torn between the position of the Church as now announced and the fact that John M. Cannon did not disobey Church authority. He should

---

637 Salt Lake City temple records show that John M. Cannon was sealed to Margaret Peart December 23, 1901. *1990 Angus M. Cannon Reunion Materials*, 233. Paul has another reference that places John in Mexico for the 1900 marriage to Margaret. Paul does not include a reference to the date for his father's marriage to Hattie. It seems this may be the first time that he shared this information.

638 Paul B. Cannon to his daughters Lynne and Kathryn in *1990 Angus M. Cannon Reunion Materials*, 229.

639 Ibid., 230, 235.

have been excommunicated if the marriages were not authorized. Since it is certain that he was authorized it is not unwarranted to assume he was told to marry in polygamy."[640] After many years, Paul finally decided to be open about the timing of the marriages so that descendants of post-Manifesto marriages would realize their ancestors had acted in good faith and were not going contrary to their Church leaders.

The article "The Taylor-Cowley Affair" in the 1980 winter edition of *The Utah Historical Quarterly*, which Paul Cannon referred to, is another example of more openness.[641] The article explores the apparent approval that the Church gave John W. Taylor and Matthias Cowley to perform post-Manifesto marriages.

The Church has become more open in other ways about early Church history. In response to social media discussions about controversial Church history topics, in November 2014 the Church published two articles on its website: "Plural Marriage in Kirtland and Nauvoo" and "The Manifesto and the End of Plural Marriage." These well-researched and candid articles include details that most members had not known before, such as Joseph Smith's marriages to several women, some of whom were already married.[642] These and other details reveal that his marriage to Emma was not as idyllic as it has often been portrayed. These disclosures have been very difficult for many committed members because they have grown up with a sanitized version of Church history and feel betrayed and are now unsure of what and whom to trust.

President Uchtdorf's talk at the October 2013 General Conference perfectly captures what I see as the balm that will heal our wounds:

> We openly acknowledge that in nearly 200 years of Church history—along with an uninterrupted line of inspired, honorable, and divine events—there have been some things said and done that could cause people to question. . . . To be perfectly frank, there have been times when members or leaders in the Church have simply made mistakes. . . . I suppose the Church would be perfect only if it were run by perfect beings. God is perfect, and His doctrine is pure. But he works through us—His imperfect children—and imperfect people make mistakes.[643]

---

640 Ibid.

641 Jorgensen and Hardy, 5.

642 "Plural Marriage in Kirtland and Nauvoo," The Church of Jesus Christ of Latter-day Saints, accessed January 18, 2015, https://www.lds.org/topics/plural-marriage-in-kirtland-and-nauvoo?lang=eng. "The Manifesto and the End of Plural Marriage," The Church of Jesus Christ of Latter-day Saints, accessed January 18, 2015, https://www.lds.org/topics/the-manifesto-and-the-end-of-plural-marriage?lang=eng. For a discussion of the number and nature of Joseph Smith's plural marriages and sealings, see "A Trajectory of Plurality: An Overview of Joseph Smith's Wives," in Compton, 1–23. As stated earlier, Joseph was intent on establishing wide lateral family networks. Many of his marriages were sealings that were never consummated.

643 Uchtdorf, 22.

President Uchtdorf's acknowledgement that leaders and members have made mistakes in the past and will continue to do so is refreshing. Such an admission reduces the force of people who find fault with the Church. This acknowledgment can allow members and leaders to be less fearful about looking at our history more honestly and feel less need to revise it in an effort to cover up mistakes leaders have made. The pressure to be perfect or to appear to be perfect is a burden neither leaders nor members should bear. The relinquishment of this expectation is one of the boons of the silence being broken.

Perhaps in writing this book, I am another example of breaking the silence by taking a more nuanced, objective look at the effect of plural marriage in the lives of my forbears and exploring issues that I heard nothing about as a child or adult. At family reunions we spoke matter-of-factly about multiple families without reflecting on the intricacies that inevitably arose in such relationships. My research has exposed the emotional strains and complexities that polygamy introduced to their lives, especially those entering polygamy after 1890, and the ambivalence of leaders toward giving up the practice. In making my research public, I have tried to go deeper than the facts and to reveal my forbears' hearts. The publications listed in my bibliography are evidence that candid, even-handed information is now available. In time I hope that we will become more comfortable talking about the complexities of our polygamous past and the humanness of our leaders.

Charlotte Cannon Johnston and Peter Budge Johnston's
fortieth wedding anniversary picture.

Chapter Eight

A Personal Retrospective

Thoughts of a Contemporary Mormon Great-grandmother

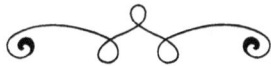

While my ancestors' writings have given me insights into their ingenuity in successfully living plural marriage, I have also become aware of how much of their experience remained unwritten and probably unspoken. Revealing the complete truth was likely either too painful or seemed too dangerous for both themselves and their families.

Charlotte Cannon Johnston

As I explained in the Preface, I began my research about polygamy in hopes of answering two questions that surfaced as I was writing my own life story. First, what were my great-grandmothers' experiences of living The Principle? Second, were any of their lives similar to that of Annie Clark Tanner, who wrote so movingly about her mistreatment as a plural wife? In the process of trying to find answers to these questions, I discovered much more. This final chapter is my reflection on the process of researching and writing this book as well as a collection of my insights, tentative conclusions, and ongoing questions about the history of polygamy and how polygamy and our response to it have shaped contemporary Mormon culture and religious practice. Some of my thoughts include looking at how polygamy has affected me personally.

I have enjoyed working on this book because learning about my family's history is important to me. I know that if we don't record and examine the stories of our ancestors, their lives will be forgotten. I hope that this book will help my children and grandchildren and others know these heroic men and women and see how well they lived a commandment that was very difficult for them.

Tracking down the details to tell their stories, I often felt like a detective. I found multiple, sometimes conflicting, clues. As I discussed in Chapter Six, such was the case for identifying the Wellsville house in which my great-grandmother, Mary Lloyd, lived with her family for thirty years. I remember my exhilaration at realizing that I had found the house where my mother and grandmother were born and learned that William Maughan had sold the house to Mary Lloyd to make sure it would be hers after he died. Because of the Edmunds-Tucker Act, Mary could have lost the house because she wasn't the legal wife.

It was very satisfying to be part of finding my father's half-sister, Irene Salahor, the only living child of my grandfather, Lewis Cannon, and becoming good friends with her. She led me to the "eureka moment" of seeing how important having a large posterity was to Lewis, her father, when she told me the major cause for her parents' divorce was his strong wish that Annie, then age forty-three, should have more children after Irene's birth. Lewis apparently felt shortchanged—perhaps because seven of the fourteen children he was responsible for rearing were sealed to his brother-in-law, David.

I especially enjoyed learning more of Leonora Cannon Taylor. I began my research for this book with only a few bits of information about her, which I had read during a trip to Nauvoo in 1959: that she was a lively conversationalist who set a fine table and that she helped other women accept polygamy. Though interesting, this information was hardly enough to get a real sense of her character but sufficient to entice me to learn more about her. Next I came upon poignant excerpts from her *First Diary*, quoted in Chapter One, in which she summarized her early life and her first years in the Church. While doing research in the new Church History Library, I found a forty-page typed copy of another diary, one of many "trail diaries" kept by pioneers. Leonora's includes a detailed record of her crossing the plains between February 1846 and September 1847. As I read her vivid account of the journey from Nauvoo, across the state of Iowa to Winter Quarters, and then on to the Salt Lake Valley, Leonora became a three-dimensional person for me; the historic journey crossing the plains also became more real.

When I saw my friend Laurel Thatcher Ulrich at the 2012 Mormon History Association meeting and told her that I was working with Leonora's trail diary, she encouraged me to track down the original, which she herself had read for her own research. When Laurel returned home, she found the trail diary's call number in her research notes and emailed it to me. I took the number to the Church History Library, where a librarian gave me a microfilm copy of Leonora's early life diary, not the trail diary, and said it was the only one available. I pressed to see the original of the early life diary and said, as Laurel had suggested, that I am related to Leonora. The librarian found the original of the early life diary and said I could look at it briefly with her by my side. Both wearing white gloves, together we looked at her five-by-seven-inch diary. Using a magnifying glass, we read much of it and were both moved to tears by Leonora's candor about the challenges of leaving her homeland and accepting a new religion. The librarian offered to copy the last two pages, which include the poignant passage of her being a stranger in a strange land, and handed me the copied pages to keep. Then she took the original diary and left me working with the microfilm copy of it.

Though I was pleased to have seen the original of Leonora's early life diary, I still had not seen the original trail diary, the one I had come to see. I approached the same librarian who had already been so helpful. After considerable research on the computer, she found its location. Her shift was about to end so she offered to leave instructions to her replacement on how to access the original diary. I was very tired and had planned to go to lunch but was willing to postpone that to get her help then. She said, "No, you need some lunch. I will leave clear instructions for the next person on how to access it."

After enjoying a meal at the Lion House, I returned to the library and asked the first librarian's replacement for the original of Leonora's trail diary. He said matter-of-factly, "A family history missionary is waiting in the Reading Room to show it to you." As I walked into the Reading Room, the missionary handed me the requisite white gloves, invited me to sit down, and opened a beige folder that held Leonora's trail diary. I could not believe what I saw. It was so small! Leonora's 169-year-old diary was only three inches by five inches, the size of a small index card, a shocking contrast to the typed forty-two page, full size copy of the diary I had been working with for several weeks. Leonora had covered every inch of the unlined sheets in tiny script. I counted forty thin leaves, each of which was filled front and back except for one and a half-blank pages, which came after an entry she wrote before her husband John Taylor's return from an eight-month calling to England. In her diary Leonora made no mention of John's bringing home a new plural wife, about whom she had had no forewarning as far as we know. The silence of those blank pages told me of her pain more than any words she could have written.[644] Reverently handling this tiny, fragile diary brought the reality of Leonora and her trials and strength very close; it was a significant spiritual and emotional experience to hold and read Leonora's original words. I felt I had been guided to them.

While writing this book has been satisfying and sometimes even thrilling, it has also been difficult. First, though I enjoy writing, it does not come easily to me; finding the right words to express a thought, deciding how to organize material, keeping track of different strands, and deciding how to interweave the lives of my ancestors with the history of polygamy have all been challenging. While the ease of modifying text on the computer and my daughter Mary's edits have helped me move from draft to draft, I have still found it hard to decide what to emphasize, what to put where, and what information to discard. I was surprised and often discouraged at the number of drafts that it took before my portrayal of an event, person, or idea felt right.

Second, there have been a number of logistical challenges. I spend part of the year in Idaho and part in Chicago and could not have all of my resources in both places. I needed to keep track of what was where and remember the tasks I had to accomplish when I returned to either place. Third, Mary lives in Charleston, South Carolina, many miles from both of my homes. She read every draft I wrote. We emailed revisions back and forth, spent time together for extended periods on three occasions, and held a couple of phone meetings every month across seven years.

---

644 Two months later as they left Winter Quarters for the Valley, Leonora resumed writing in the diary.

Fourth, it seemed that nearly every day more information about polygamy surfaced. During the time I worked on this book, I kept finding new primary sources from family members and was always uncovering more information from published scholars. The project became a much bigger enterprise than I had originally intended. While making the discoveries has been satisfying, the seemingly endless avalanche of information was often daunting.

More concerning than any of these challenges was the effect that the research has had on me emotionally. Each new chunk of information was part of an ever-growing tapestry of insights and impressions, some comforting and others upsetting. In short, immersing myself in the polygamous world of my ancestors has taken me on an emotional roller coaster ride. The drive to understand and honor my ancestors has sustained me as have their remarkable examples of dignity and faith.

Now, as I close this book, let me share some insights I have gleaned in the process of writing it. As I read first-person accounts of some relatives and life sketches of others, again and again I found expressions of pain and confusion. Their eloquence and candor drew me closer to them and helped me put myself in their shoes. Very wrenching to me was the anger and pain Leonora and Elizabeth experienced each time a new wife joined their families. I thought about how difficult it must have been for Arabella, another first wife, when Charlotte, my great-grandmother (who was only four years older than Arabella's oldest child), married Samuel Rose Parkinson just a month after Arabella had borne her last child. I have also wondered how it was for my Grandpa Joe Parkinson when his mother went underground for eight months when he was a young child. I empathize with Preston Parkinson's sorrow regarding his problematic birth and his lifelong efforts to establish an identity for himself. I also now have a clearer sense of the difficulties involved in the adjustment period before and after the Manifesto as people had to hide their families, see loved ones go to prison, and deal with society's castigation and with the uncertainty of their futures. The pressure to hide who you were and to conceal your own as well as your siblings' and your mother's relationship with your father certainly compromised children's identities, sense of security, and willingness to speak honestly. Nothing was safe, free, or open.

Now I better understand how difficult it was for Lewis, Mamie, and Lillian to manage their post-Manifesto polygamous family as well as why my father and his siblings said so little about their childhood or their half-siblings. For example, my father rarely mentioned his own painful experiences with polygamy. He often jumped over his parents' generation and concentrated on how much he admired his grandfathers, Angus M. and George Q. He also emphasized that his mother was George Q.'s oldest living daughter and that she was very important to her father.

In addition to having a greater sense of my forbears' emotional lives, I also have a greater appreciation for how ingenious they were as polygamists. For example, putting together pieces of information about the marriages of sisters Ann Amanda and Sarah Maria Mousley to Angus M. Cannon on the same day gave me fresh insight of how creative the two sisters and Angus were in finding ways for the women to share the role of being the first wife. Angus also showed inventiveness and diplomacy in living with one of his children after the Manifesto to avoid forcing the issue of which of the sisters would be regarded as his legal wife.

I also now see how ingenious George Q. was to take Elizabeth and their daughters to Washington to present a positive picture of Mormon family life when he represented the Territory in Congress. I also appreciate the impartiality Samuel Rose Parkinson showed to Charlotte and Maria after Arabella died. The first part of the week he lived with Charlotte in Preston, Idaho, where he performed his bishopric duties and lived with Maria the other part of the week in Logan, Utah, where they worked in the temple.

While my ancestors' writings have given me insights into their ingenuity in successfully living plural marriage, I have also become aware of how much of their experience remained unwritten and probably unspoken. Revealing the complete truth was probably either too painful or too dangerous for both themselves and their families. To whom could Leonora or Elizabeth or Arabella express their emotions about sharing their husbands with other women? What were the subsequent wives' feelings about coming into an established marriage? What did Mary Lloyd feel as she faced giving birth to her ninth and last child alone, with the child's father in hiding at an undisclosed location? She was not certain when or if she would see him again. I see more clearly than ever that we will never know the whole story; we do know that my ancestors and others who practiced polygamy did not speak or write about much of what they experienced and felt.

Conversely, the power of what *is* written affects how we remember and understand. For instance, what has been recorded about Sarah and Amanda as wives of Angus affects how we see that family's structure. Because Ann Mousley Cannon, Sarah's daughter, wrote of family events with her mother as the central figure, readers see those events with Sarah as the focus. In the spiral-bound materials gathered for the 1990 Angus Cannon Reunion there are two biographies of Sarah as well as her trail diary. None of Amanda's descendants wrote a corresponding account of her in that publication. Given this emphasis, a reader is more likely to focus on Sarah as Angus' wife rather than her sister Amanda or the other wives.

I became aware of another example of the power of the printed word to affect interpretation of events. At the 2011 Parkinson family reunion it was mentioned several times that Arabella had agreed with Samuel Rose Parkinson before their marriage to later enter into polygamy if called to do so. When I questioned the source of the information, I discovered that the basis for the statement was a passage in Lester Taylor's biography of Samuel Rose Parkinson in which Lester *imagined* a conversation between Samuel and Arabella before their marriage in St. Louis in January of 1852. Although Lester acknowledged in the book that he only imagined that conversation, seeing it in print carries great weight nevertheless.[645] We have no written record of such a conversation, and in my mind it is very unlikely that such a conversation took place.

---

645 Taylor, *Samuel Rose Parkinson*, 40.

The twenty-year-old groom (a recent convert) and his bride were married in St. Louis far from the Utah Territory. The doctrine was not made public in Utah until four months after their marriage in St. Louis. Even so, because the imagined conversation is printed in Lester's book, it has gained a factual status for many family members.

We humans have the capacity to choose what we remember, based partly on what is compatible with what we currently believe. At the same time, our interpretation of the past shapes what we currently believe. An example from my mother's life offers a good example of how past events and current beliefs affect each other. Born in 1902, twelve years after the 1890 Manifesto, to parents who both grew up in well-functioning polygamous homes, my mother was surrounded, though she may not have consciously realized it, by competing interpretations of how completely the practice of polygamy ended in 1890. Mother had great affection for her father's half-sister, Luella, who was Maria Smart Parkinson's oldest daughter and Matthias Cowley's second wife. Mother often talked about the fact that Aunt Luella was a polygamist and a firm believer in plural marriage.[646]

Less often Mother shared that Matthias was dropped from the Quorum of the Twelve Apostles and his priesthood was suspended because he performed plural marriages after the 1890 Manifesto and opposed the 1904 Manifesto. Little was said openly in my family about the possibility of such discipline being part of the Church's efforts to extricate itself from its part in post-Manifesto marriages. I remember her saying in a private conversation with me that my father believed that Matthias F. Cowley and John W. Taylor were scapegoats—that the Church had disciplined them to emphasize that polygamy had ended. I think Mother gave serious consideration to my father's interpretation of the events, but she wouldn't have come to or voiced such a conclusion herself, for to do so would be to admit that Church leaders were disciplining people to save face. Her fervent support of authority and her strong testimony of the truthfulness of the Church were central to who she was. Without looking to the right or left, she chose to fully support the Church authorities, including their decision to stop practicing polygamy in 1890. She also kept the love of her polygamous forbears active in her own life and in the lives of her children, who carry on both her strong allegiance to the authority of the Church and her love of our forbears.

A recent conversation about polygamy with my cousin Joanne Linford, also my college roommate and a dear friend, is another example of how we select certain facts or aspects of the past to strongly bolster our version of what we believe to be true. Joanne is Matthias and Luella Cowley's granddaughter. She regards the 1904 Manifesto as the "real" Manifesto. She grew up hearing that her grandfather, whom she knew well and loved dearly, had been asked by Church authorities to perform selected plural marriages after the 1890 Manifesto to illustrate that plural marriage remained the correct doctrine. To her, the 1890 Manifesto was issued to appease the government and was not binding on the Saints. I, on the other hand, grew up believing that the 1890 Manifesto was the revelation that marked the end of polygamy. As discussed earlier, my paternal grandfather Lewis Cannon, a bishop at the time, married a plural wife in the late 1890s,

---

646 Luella was the only child of Charlotte or Maria to enter polygamy. Several of Arabella's children were polygamists.

a decision that had always troubled me. Though my mother spoke openly and positively about her polygamous ancestors, I don't recall her talking about Lewis' marriage to Lillian. My father had little to say about it either.

Before I started the research for this book, I had heard very little about the 1904 Manifesto. In working with family group sheets in earlier years, I remember my relief on learning that Matthias Cowley and Aunt Luella had married in 1889, before the 1890 Manifesto. For Joanne, the fact that they had married before the 1890 Manifesto was incidental. As I have said, to her the Second Manifesto, issued in 1904, not the First Manifesto issued fourteen years earlier, marked the end of polygamy. Her version is more sympathetic to her grandfather's actions and fits with her interpretation of what occurred. With my background of Mother's allegiance to authority and my belief that the first manifesto was to be taken literally, I am more comfortable viewing the 1890 Manifesto as the revelation that terminated the practice of plural marriage. Our conversation gave both of us a broader understanding of that difficult period and helped us see the possible reasons for our divergent viewpoints. We both saw the task of giving up the practice as very difficult for our forbears.

The research I did for this book has helped me see that I had underestimated the strength of the Saints' belief in polygamy and the ongoing struggles of how to respond to its termination. Studying the long and painful transition from polygamy to monogamy detailed in Chapter Seven has reinforced for me a principle of the Church that was very important to my late husband, Peter: the Church evolves. Peter saw the Church's ability to change as a sign of its divinity and believed that changes in its teachings were evidence of continuing revelation, a fundamental Mormon doctrine.[647]

As a stake high councilor and as a branch president, Peter often gave talks detailing the multiple changes the Church has made since it began in 1830. Among his favorite examples were the Church's dramatic shift toward being regionally organized, the changes in the structure of the Church to accommodate growth in membership, the changed role of the Seventy, and the changed and expanded ways the Church accomplishes its three missions—to perfect the saints, proclaim the gospel, and redeem the dead. Perhaps most important to Peter and to me was the revelation in 1978 that gave the priesthood to all worthy male members. In my mind, changing from polygamy to monogamy as the prerequisite for the highest degree of celestial glory, and changing from creating the expansive lateral family relationships initiated by Joseph Smith to tracing family connections only to direct ancestors, are two additional examples of continuing revelation.

---

[647] The Ninth Article of Faith reads, "We believe all that God has revealed, all that He does now reveal, and we believe that He will yet reveal many great and important things pertaining to the Kingdom of God." The Articles of Faith are a fundamental expression of Mormon doctrine.

In 1879 the Supreme Court ruled that the practice of plural marriage was unconstitutional. In response, President John Taylor declared that despite this ruling, the Saints would continue to practice plural marriage because it was God's law and so overrode the law of the land. Today, using the same argument, Church leaders defend traditional marriage between one man and one woman as God's revealed law.[648] Our leaders and most members strongly oppose and are even offended by the Supreme Court ruling of June 2015, which recognizes same-sex marriage as legal. The intensity of our feelings about the rightness of traditional marriage should alert us to the intense feelings our polygamous forbears felt about the rightness of practicing plural marriage despite the practice being against the law of the land.

The scriptures lend support to both polygamy and monogamy as God's will at various times. The authorized practice of polygamy in the Old Testament was an important precedent for the early Saints.[649] On the other hand, Jacob's writings in the Book of Mormon support our current rejection of polygamy.[650]

Has God's law actually been different in ancient Israel, in 1879, and in 2015? Can God's will for us and his revealed law change, based on the circumstances of the time? Both in the late 1800s and today, in both belief and practice, most Church members have followed the counsel of their leaders. However, in the early days of the Church and also recently, members have left the Church when they differ with positions leaders have taken. Some have started splinter groups. These responses sadden me. My ancestors accepted a big change in God's law when polygamy was revealed and gave The Principle their full support for fifty years. When Wilford Woodruff had the revelation that it was time to stop the practice, my ancestors, even when ambivalent, followed the prophet.

I feel that we should work for change as committed members from within the Church. We are counseled to follow our leaders; we are also given the Holy Ghost when we are baptized to help us discern truth for ourselves regarding our own lives and callings in the Church. How to balance differences between the two approaches is a continuing challenge for me.

Another insight gained in writing this book is the less-than-satisfying role of sexuality in a plural wife's life. One contributing factor was that she lived in the propriety-conscious Victorian age. For any Victorian woman, stifling of personal expression undoubtedly included clamping down on her sexual feelings. While not expressing sexual feelings is generally thought of as being part of the reticence and propriety of the Victorian age, for a woman participating in polygamy, this restraint took on special meaning. A plural wife saw herself as part of a celestial eternal family; if she was of childbearing age, her main function was to have as many children as possible, rather than to have an intimate monogamous relationship with her husband. With new

---

648 Dallin H. Oaks, "No Other Gods," *Ensign*, November 2013. Russell M. Nelson, "Decisions for Eternity," *Ensign*, November 2013.

649 Genesis 26:34, 28:6–9, 29:15–28, and 2 Samuel 5:13–16

650 Jacob 2:24–29.

vividness I have realized how impossible it must have felt to a woman in a polygamous family to be truly sexually intimate with and express her love to a man whom she knew had multiple partners.[651] Rather than being romantically attached, it would be much less risky emotionally to emphasize to herself her relationship to her children and her pleasure in being part of a successful communal living unit that functioned well under a patriarch who was a generous, fair-minded religious leader. A wife's focus had to be on having many children and investing herself in them, not on her relationship with her husband.[652]

Immersing myself in my ancestors' stories has brought me to another set of insights related to sexuality and how polygamy has a left an imprint on contemporary Mormon culture and practice. Just as having many children was linked to a woman's sexual identity in polygamous days, today there remains a premium on a woman bearing many children. Members still take great pride in creating a large number of intergenerational relationships.[653]

I am an example of being affected by a premium being placed on having numerous children. When I was in my twenties and early thirties, I felt the importance of having a large family. If I wasn't pregnant, hadn't recently given birth, or was not planning to be pregnant, I felt I wasn't really a woman. After bearing three sons in four years, the third one a full-term stillborn baby, we moved from Salt Lake City to Chicago, where I had a baby daughter, Mary, a year later. About a year after her birth, my period was late; I was certain I was pregnant and began to prepare for another baby. When I went to the doctor, I learned that there was no baby. I was surprised and disappointed. I had been certain that I was pregnant. In therapy I realized I was conflating being a woman with having children. Apparently my definition of womanhood included having babies to create a large posterity. Four years after Mary's birth, David, my last child, was born. With four children, I felt I had few enough to hold my head high both in Hyde Park, a neighborhood concerned about overpopulation , and an adequate number to be accepted in the West with my Mormon friends and family. Now, with my fifteen grandchildren (of whom I am very proud) I am the envy of my Hyde Park friends who have few grandchildren. Fortunately, I am also quietly comfortable with my friends and family in the West who have much more progeny than I.

---

651 In the case of my great-grandmothers, Amanda and Charlotte, I have wondered if it was easier or more difficult to have a woman with whom you shared your husband be your biological sister.

652 Today, in Church settings, young women are counseled to regard their bodies as sacred and to have no sexual relationships before marriage. They hear little about enjoying their bodies or the pleasures and satisfaction of sexual activity they can look forward to in marriage. Our current circumspect attitude toward sex and marriage could very well be in part a reaction to our polygamous history; it seems we need to prove how conservative we have become.

653 During a recent visit with school friends in Idaho, several proudly shared that their descendants numbered over one hundred. My son David, thirty-five years my junior, thinks the emphasis placed on having a large family has diminished significantly. The fact that he lived in Philadelphia at the time, away from the center of the Church, and is a generation younger than I am no doubt contributes to his different perspective. Conducting a study of size of Mormon families across time and in different parts of the world would be an interesting and worthy pursuit.

Peter Budge and Charlotte Cannon Johnston and their family at Christmastime in 1997, five months after Peter received his cancer diagnosis.

Charlotte and thirteen of fifteen of her grandchildren at the 2006 Johnston family reunion

I see the possible effect of polygamy on me in other ways. Like my mother did with her children, I insist on things being fair and equal among my children. Our female polygamous ancestors were legitimately concerned about their husbands giving them and their children fair and equal treatment. In researching whether Charlotte or Maria was the legal wife after Arabella's death, I felt disappointment and resentment when I saw indications that Maria was the legal or at least the favored wife. Since Charlotte, my great-grandmother, was the second wife and entitled to become the "first" wife when Arabella died, I bristled at the idea that Maria, the third wife, may have taken Charlotte's rightful place when Arabella died. Charlotte was the wife who moved when she and Maria's home was overflowing with children, and Charlotte's daughter had written in the biography of her mother, "Often she deprived herself of her husband's rightful company in order to bring more peace and happiness to a sister-wife."[654] In my concern for Charlotte having her just dues, I had lost track of how much effort Samuel and his wives put into having things equal before and after Arabella died.

When I mentioned to Joanne Linford that my mother lived with Samuel Rose and Charlotte in Salt Lake City for a summer, Joanne said emphatically, "That would have been after Maria died," inferring that when Maria, her great-grandmother, was alive, Samuel was living with her in Logan. Joanne was emphasizing Maria's place in Samuel Rose's affection just as I was emphasizing Charlotte's. As in our discussion about which manifesto to recognize as binding, how we *wanted* to view the past influenced how we saw the past. Looking at how invested I have been in defending my great grandmother's position in the Parkinson family has helped me understand that they probably experienced turf battles similar to the ones I have waged with various women in my own life.

The process of researching and wrestling with this history has affected me intellectually, emotionally, and spiritually. I have learned how to respond more effectively to unsettling information about polygamy. Integral to my more measured response is that I now recognize that our Church has never claimed the infallibility of its leaders. In fact, God chastised Joseph Smith as he carried out the Herculean task of establishing the restored church. A notable example of Joseph's imperfection is when the Lord chastised him for relenting to Martin Harris and giving him 116 pages of the translated Book of Mormon to show to his wife, who was skeptical about the translation process and did not want her husband to be involved. Finally yielding to Martin Harris, Joseph was rebuked: "For although a man may have many revelations, and have power to do many mighty works, yet if he boasts in his own strength, and sets at naught the counsels of God, and follows after the dictates of his own will and carnal desires, he must fall and incur the vengeance of a just God upon him."[655] As a consequence of his mistake, Joseph lost his gift

---

654 Parkinson, *Roots and Branches*, 133.

655 D&C 3:4

of translation for a season.⁶⁵⁶ Accepting that leaders make mistakes has helped me acknowledge and accept my troubling questions about Church leaders' behavior during the development and cessation of polygamy.

We will never have the answers to some questions concerning polygamy. For example, what course would the Church have taken if the government had not forced the Church to give up The Principle? Would we be a monogamous Church today? Did John Taylor actually receive a revelation in 1886 proclaiming that polygamy should never end? Because I embrace monogamy and enjoy being integrated in mainstream society, I believe the government did the Church a favor. Other questions will have answers in the coming years. Will the Church continue to find avenues to be more open about early Church history and more often acknowledge that our leaders, as part of being human, make mistakes? Will the Church give up the doctrine as well as the practice of plural marriage? In my conversations with active members of the Church concerning the status of the current doctrine, not the practice, of polygamy in the Church, I have been struck by how strongly some feel that the doctrine is in place and will remain so in the next life. This interpretation gives continued credence to the polygamous marriages performed during the fifty years the Church advocated plural marriage and also today to the sealing between a man and his first wife who has died as well as to a second wife who has not been previously sealed.⁶⁵⁷ Others feel strongly that polygamy in any form should be confined to our history and that giving up the doctrine should match giving up the practice. How will the Church deal with these thorny issues and questions?

I had an epiphany when my *Ensign* magazine fell open to "Stand by My Servant Joseph," by Cecil O. Samuelson. The author explores the counsel the Lord gave to Oliver Cowdery when he was acting as a scribe as Joseph Smith translated the Book of Mormon.⁶⁵⁸ The section from which the title of the article was taken reads, "Therefore be diligent; stand by my servant Joseph faithfully, in whatsoever difficult circumstances he may be for the word's sake."⁶⁵⁹ I am sure plural marriage was a very difficult principle for my family members to accept and live. However, once they had accepted it, they gave Joseph their full support. They believed plural marriage was a commandment from God delivered to the earth through Joseph Smith as part of the restored Church and were willing to stake their lives on that belief. As I have grappled with the complexities of polygamy, I have struggled with just what part Joseph Smith played in the

---

656 D&C 3:14

657 This interpretation provides for more women who would otherwise be single to be sealed to a husband. In a second marriage that occurs in a temple, the couple are married for time only if both the man and woman have been sealed previously.

658 Cecil O. Samuelson Jr., "Stand By My Servant Joseph," *Ensign*, February 2013, 34.

659 D&C 6:18. Unfortunately, Oliver Cowdery was unable to do this and subsequently left the Church in 1838. He returned to the Church in 1848.

beginnings of plural marriage. As I read the article I was flooded with certainty that I too stand by Joseph. Although I recognize that he made mistakes, I have come to see that it is a matter of faith for me to stand by Joseph just as it was for my forbears.

Concurrent with continued commitment to my religion, I feel more admiration for the strength of my ancestors, particularly the women, in supporting this difficult commandment. When I was working through the aftermath of Amanda and Sarah being married the same day to Angus, I attended a sealing ceremony in the Chicago Temple. As I listened to the eternal blessings promised to those who live the new and everlasting covenant, I thought of Amanda and Sarah's belief in the covenants they made and was flooded with assurances of how sustaining the promises that we make in the temple were to them as well as to us.

Two vignettes from Leonora's life epitomize the strength and faith of all of these women. In 1857 the Saints were probably in a state of shock with news of the murder of Parley P. Pratt in Arkansas, the Mountain Meadow Massacre, and immediate plans for them to evacuate Salt Lake City because of the impending arrival of Johnston's Army. Amid the uncertainty generated by these events, Leonora and the other sisters of the 14th Ward Relief Society were keeping the fabric of the community together by making an American Album quilt. Leonora's block in capital letters states, "IN GOD IS OUR TRUST," which epitomizes the indomitable spirit that sustained her and her sister Saints.

Another incident that shows Leonora's faith and strength occurred near the end of her journey to the Valley. When the wheels of a wagon rolled over her manly teenage son, George John, crushing his body, a shout went up, "The Taylor boy has been hurt." At the time Leonora was not close to the wagon. That night Leonora wrote in her diary, "*I don't know how I got to him.*"[660] But she did and, with the assistance of Bishop Abraham Hoagland, got her son help. He soon recovered and they finished the journey. Likewise, I don't know how my polygamous forbears met all their challenges, but they did.

Now, as I end this book I see how remarkable are the lasting effects of a practice that lasted about fifty years and ended over a century ago. Plural marriage contributed to the numerical growth of the Church in its crucial beginnings. The first seven presidents of the Church were participants and many other Church leaders down to the present are products of plural marriage. Polygamists were central figures in the settlement of towns in early Utah, Idaho, and Arizona. Accepting the direction to practice polygamy fostered strong allegiance among adherents to the Church under difficult conditions. The question remains of how to regard the polygamy of our past, including how to relate to groups that have different interpretation of its relevance today.

Before I close I need to return to my original question about whether Annie Clark Tanner's heartbreaking story was a minority report. I have learned that my ancestors' lives were more complex and layered than any family reunion skit I recall seeing or participating in. Now I am more aware of polygamy's difficulties and costs; I no longer see plural marriage through

---

660 Leonora Taylor, *Trail Diary*.

rose-colored glasses. Like Annie, my female ancestors showed great resourcefulness and determination to live The Principle well and took the bulk of the parenting responsibilities. Annie gave voice to pain that they likely experienced but did not articulate. Unlike Annie, they had husbands who gave them financial and emotional support and high standing in a community where successful polygamous families earned respect. They lived within the system with integrity and created fulfilling lives. Their belief that The Principle was the celestial way and was a commandment of God remained constant. Their willingness to live it was a testament to their strength, goodness, and faith. I am grateful for my connection with them.

Appendices

Preface to the Appendices

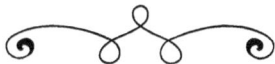

THE APPENDICES that follow include several important primary documents written by my ancestors. These manuscripts offer a unique, personal perspective on the historical events examined in this book. For example, Leonora Cannon Taylor wrote to Governor Ford of Illinois about the people responsible for murdering Joseph and Hyrum Smith and injuring her husband, John Taylor. Her letter reveals the strength of her character, her remarkable courage, and her limited formal education. Winnifred Jardine's engaging account, *Life on the Cannon Farm,* gives us an example of a harmonious polygamous family and a glimpse into the private life and feelings of the patriarch, George Q. Cannon.

Other appendices, such as the 1890 and 1904 Manifestos, are public documents. Though referred to frequently in the book, I do not quote them in full, so I have included both in their entirety here.

The organization of the appendices requires some explanation. Initially this book was going to be a collection of brief histories of my great-grandmothers, my Great Aunt Leonora, and my grandmother Mary Alice (Mamie) Cannon—all of whom were plural wives. The more I read about these women, the clearer it became that their stories were inextricably connected to the story of polygamy. And so, a book about my female ancestors became a history of polygamy told through their personal histories. Because these women were the inspiration for this book, their life sketches appear first in the collection of appendices, preceded only by my book review of Annie Tanner's memoir, *A Mormon Mother*. One great-grandmother, Elizabeth Hoagland Cannon, my father's grandmother, does not have a life sketch because her life story is told in Chapter Two. The order of the appendices after the life sketches is according to the order they are referred to in the book, which is roughly chronological.

As mentioned in the Editor's Preface, we have chosen to retain writers' idiosyncratic spelling and punctuation. If an author makes references that require explanation, we have inserted bracketed information or included explanatory footnotes.

Appendix A

A Book Review of *A Mormon Mother*

by Charlotte Cannon Johnston[661]

A Mormon Mother, which Annie Clark Tanner wrote in long hand in 1941 in her seventy-seventh year, seems especially valuable to me as an honest, perceptive account of the human problems of living polygamy during the peaceful 1870s period as well as the more tumultuous era of the underground and Manifesto. She tells her story with remarkable detail drawn from her own memory, her diary, letters to and from her children and husband, and newspaper accounts. As her son Obert C. Tanner says in the foreword to the second printing in 1969, she "tells it like it was."

Born in 1864 to Ezra Clark, a successful community leader whom she loved dearly, and his second wife, Susan Leggett, a meticulous housekeeper and able homemaker, Annie grew up with a positive attitude toward polygamy. The wives she knew were proud and honored to be chosen to share in the highest exaltation in the Kingdom of God. A common saying was, "I'd rather have his little finger than the whole of a man outside of the Church."

In contrast to her childhood experience, her marriage in 1884 as the second wife to a prominent educator, Joseph Marion Tanner, was extremely difficult. No longer was polygamy the inviolate "capstone of Mormon doctrine." The enforcement of the Edmunds-Tucker Act created unsettled conditions. Homes were broken up and families scattered among friends and relatives. Annie became a wife during the underground, living in borrowed rooms, and hungering to make a home for her children. Her struggles after the Manifesto were no less difficult; her own pain provoked her to re-examine her idealized childhood views.

She began to analyze her own mother's position as a second wife and to remember some negative details. Ezra Clark married his second wife, Susan, a beautiful girl of twenty-four, years after marrying his first wife, Mary, with whom he had lived in Nauvoo, crossed the plains, and raised a large family. Ezra spent most of his time in Mary's more spacious home, the center of activity. There the provisions were kept and frugally distributed. Company and dignitaries were entertained there. The family carriage always loaded there with Aunt Mary, the name Annie Clark Tanner calls the first wife, in the front seat and Annie's mother in the back. When her father and Aunt Mary celebrated their fiftieth wedding anniversary, Annie's mother stood

---

661 Johnston, 127–128. Tanner, 294.

quietly in the background. In recounting a dream she had shortly before her death, Annie's mother said she went to Heaven and met her husband and "Though I looked everywhere, I couldn't find Aunt Mary."

Aloneness is a major theme of the book. Annie was alone on her wedding night. Her husband is never mentioned at the births of any of their ten children. She established her homes alone and largely supported her children even before she and her husband officially separated. She never had the partnership we feel marriage should be today. But she did find some advantages to aloneness. "The wife in polygamy does not feel the security that I imagine monogamous women feel," she writes. Yet, because of her lone position she developed an "independence that women in monogamy never know. . . . The plural wife, in time, becomes conscious of her own power to make decisions."[662]

The results of unquestioningly following her husband's will had been disastrous for her and for the development of her family. She was forced to rely more and more on her own judgment and less on outside authority. As a result, in her middle years, Mrs. Tanner no longer accepted her former belief that it was man's place to create conditions and woman's place to accept them—his right to command and her duty to obey. The reader experiences her evolution from a woman directed and dictated to by forces outside herself to forces within herself.

When the Church changed its position on polygamy in 1890, many of the Saints could not forsake the cornerstone principle of their lives for which they had made such sacrifices. The ambiguous language of the Manifesto left many Saints feeling that polygamy remained a divine commandment. J. M. Tanner was one. Because he married other women after the Manifesto, he lost his standing in the Church and eventually died alone on an unsuccessful farm in Canada. From Annie's account he was a villain, but we never hear his side of the story. In any case, he was a casualty of the transition to monogamy.

A Mormon Mother is an articulate minority report of a difficult era. Mrs. Tanner illuminates dark issues that many of us don't want to see. We prefer to view polygamy as idyllic or at least tolerable, as she did when a child, not as the painful, solitary life she experienced as an adult. For many polygamy was not a nightmare; for Mrs. Tanner it was. *A Mormon Mother* is a unique and important addition to understanding our Mormon heritage.

---

662 Tanner, 269.

Appendix B

Life Sketch of Ann Amanda Mousley Cannon 1836–1905

by Virginia Cannon Nelson[663]

Wife of Angus M. Cannon, talented hostess for her stake president husband, devoted mother of ten[664]

ON THE MORNING of July 18, 1858, Angus M. Cannon, Ann Amanda Mousley, and her sister Sarah Maria Mousley set out on three saddle ponies for the office of President Brigham Young in the Beehive House, where an unusual wedding ceremony would soon take place.

Amanda expected to become the first bride of her handsome young sweetheart; but Brigham Young decided that Sarah, being the older sister, should be married first. Amanda could not suppress a few tears of disappointment; but after a solemn promise by Angus that she would never lose by giving up this privilege, she consented and the ceremony took place.

Amanda had become acquainted with Angus M. Cannon in Wilmington, Delaware, when he labored there as a missionary, acting some of the time as counselor to President George J. Taylor. Many hours had been spent by Elder Cannon and his companions at the pleasant Titus Mousley farm home in Delaware. An Elder Woolley, in company with Angus M. Cannon, baptized Amanda in the Brandywine River, October 23, 1855. Elder Cannon later made arrangements for the Mousley family to emigrate to Utah, and the courtship with Amanda flowered when he returned home to Salt Lake City after his mission.

---

663 Ann Amanda's granddaughter

664 Personal recollection of the author and her father, Eugene M. Cannon. Family records. Diaries of Angus M. Cannon, located in the Church Historian's Office.

There were always the most affectionate and warm feelings between the two sisters. For a few years after their marriages, they shared the same home on West Temple as well as sharing with their husband the Dixie Mission experience.[665] Later, when each had her own home, these sisters and their families lived within walking distance of each other.

Amanda was above average in height and of a stately appearance. Her eyes were blue and her hair was a light brown, becoming darker as she grew older. She wore it always according to the fashion of the times, and the picture taken of her at the time of her marriage shows her hair parted in the middle and becomingly puffed at the sides. Her clothes reflected the current style, and she was particularly fussy about her bonnets.

She was not a woman who cared for public life. She was content to preside in her own home as mother to her ten children and as wife to the president of Salt Lake Stake, acting as gracious hostess for him most of the time to countless visitors he was required to meet and entertain. She was also a tender, devoted mother whose strong sons and daughters were ardently loyal to her and to one another. She loved a good story and, around the table, the conversation was apt to be witty and lively. The tradition of telling good stories to the accompaniment of much laughter is being carried on by her posterity.

Amanda always kept a cook, and the highlight of each day was when her family came home at noon to the hot meal around the big table. She dressed for the occasion in a black silk dress, over which she had tied a white apron trimmed with handmade lace from St. George. After the meal, she would usually go calling—often to see Sarah.

Amanda was a woman who loved peace and never lost either her poise or her composure. In her later years she suffered from asthma and phlebitis and died March 18, 1905, at the age of sixty-eight of what was termed bronchitis. *The Deseret News* carried her obituary on the front page, reporting she had been ailing for three and a half years, "her nervous system having been shattered by a long life of toil and care," but that she had been sufficiently well to enjoy a short drive the previous Tuesday. The article characterized her as "devotedly attached to her husband and children," stating that their welfare and happiness was the greatest desire of her life. It added: "She was of a most kind and charitable disposition" and "her departure from this life will be mourned by a host of friends."

---

665 In 1860 Brigham Young called the Cannon family to move to St. George to help settle the area. My grandfather, Lewis Mousley Cannon, was born in St. George in 1864.

Appendix C

Life Sketch of Charlotte Smart Parkinson 1849–1929

Compiled by her daughter Vivian Parkinson Taylor and granddaughter Deanne Taylor Harrison and rewritten by Vivian's son Lester Parkinson Taylor[666]

"I THOUGHT YOU NEEDED ME, so I've come to help." With these quiet reassuring words, Mother would make her entrance. A few days or weeks later, when the crisis had passed and the equilibrium of the household had been regained, she would suddenly be gone. But the memories of her reassuring presence, her nursing skill, the meals cooked, the house kept and, most of all, her faith—these did not leave.

Charlotte Smart Parkinson was born on November 6, 1849, in St. Louis, Missouri. Her father was Thomas Sharrett Smart, her mother, Ann Hayter Smart. She was christened Charlotte Elisabeth. Though both were English, her mother and father met and were married in France. Her father was a brick maker and had gone to France to supervise a brick factory. Her mother had married a Mr. Henry Fleet, a school teacher, who went to France to teach. It was an unhappy marriage which ended in divorce. Charlotte's mother had three daughters by Mr. Fleet. Charlotte was the first of seven children she bore Mr. Smart.

The Napoleonic wars had ended. During the subsequent reigns of Charles X and Louis Philippe, economic and political turmoil prompted the Smarts to leave France and accept the challenge of life in that raw, young republic, the United States of America. They arrived in the city of St. Louis in 1845. Four years later Charlotte was born.

Mr. Smart rented a farm, at the same time beginning a tannery and a brick business. One of his farm workers belonged to an odd new religion that claimed a modern-day prophet as leader. They called themselves "Mormons." Out of curiosity, Mr. Smart investigated, liked what he heard, and, after Mrs. Smart had reached a similar level of conviction, they were baptized members of The Church of Jesus Christ of Latter-day Saints, which they learned was the proper name of the "Mormons." This was in the summer of 1851. Their new faith was dearly bought when one considers the direction and shape their lives were to take as a result of it.

---

666 Parkinson, 130–33.

Spring of 1852 was awakening the countryside. During the winter the Mormons in St. Louis had talked of little else but joining the main body of "Saints," who, having been driven from their homes in Nauvoo, Illinois, had sought refuge in the Utah Territory, in the vastness of the Rocky Mountains. All who were able to do so were instructed by the leadership of the Church to come. After several family councils and much prayer, Thomas Smart, his wife, Ann, and their five children, ranging in ages from one and a half to ten years, decided to join a small company leaving St. Louis that Spring. They gathered their possessions, converted what monies they had into supplies, a wagon, and oxen and prepared to leave. There were seventeen wagons in all, and twenty families. Charlotte was three and a half years old.

The great trek began April 8, 1852. Day after bone-bruising day the wagons creaked across the vast plains of America's mid-section. The days of heat and dust mixed with those of rain and mud. Each stream to be forded threatened the catastrophic loss of a family's entire possessions. And always there was the fear of sickness, of a wagon breakdown, and [of] Indians.

For five months Charlotte rode in the wagon with her mother and sisters until they could take no more of the jouncing; then they would walk until they were too tired to walk further. The wagon train averaged eleven miles per day. [B]efore making the final descent into the Salt Lake Valley, [they] had traveled slightly more than thirteen hundred miles. Charlotte was too young to fully understand where they were going, or why. But from the conversation of her parents, their family prayers, and the night and morning prayers of the entire wagon train, she sensed it was something very important which required the help of God to successfully accomplish. Thus was laid the foundation of her great faith.

After a few weeks' rest in Salt Lake, during which time Brother and Sister Smart met Brigham Young and other Church leaders, they headed South approximately thirty miles to the recently established village of American Fork. For lack of other accommodations, they endured the Winter in the wagon, a tent pitched alongside. The following year, Brother Smart took his family ten miles further South to the town of Provo, where he was asked to operate a new brick factory. While in Provo, Charlotte reached her eighth birthday and was baptized.

In 1860, when Charlotte was eleven years of age, the Smarts moved again, this time to Cache Valley, on the Utah-Idaho border. Here, Brother Smart, together with Samuel Rose Parkinson and a Brother Sanderson, were set apart as "Presiding Elders" and sent north with fifty families to colonize what was to be known as Franklin, Idaho, the first white community in the state of Idaho.

Charlotte grew up at the wrong time and in the wrong place to gain much of a formal education. But, she had a quick, practical mind. She learned to read. She was accurate with figures, wrote economically, and became an excellent speller. In addition, she learned the many skills of a frontier woman. She was a fine seamstress. She carded wool, spun it, and made good serviceable sweaters and stockings. She could milk a cow, make a bar of soap, make a quilt, and dress a chicken. Her bread was highly regarded by family and neighbors. No count could be made of the number of loaves she sent into the homes of those "needing a hand."

The pattern of Mormon "socials" began to emerge as Branches, then Wards were organized and a favorite pastime was dancing. Charlotte excelled at it! She was of medium height and build, five feet four inches tall and one hundred and thirty pounds. Her hazel eyes responded quickly to her moods. Her smooth complection [sic] was framed by a luxuriant growth of black hair. She was not a beautiful girl, but as she lived life and her face mirrored her honest, straightforward reactions to its trials, she became an arrestingly attractive woman. She carried herself erectly and moved quickly, with much grace. She had a natural sense of style and always dressed in good taste.

She showed a delightful touch of feminine vanity in her refusal to wear anything that might appear as "old lady comforts." She continually urged her daughters to keep up with the times. Her ability to "think young" made her a favorite with her grandchildren.

When Charlotte was one month past her seventeenth birthday, she married Samuel Rose Parkinson. Elder Parkinson, though only thirty-two years of age, was a leading figure in the valley. As previously noted, he came to Franklin as one of the original colonizers, along with Charlotte's father. He became a successful farmer and rancher. He built a dry goods store, which, at the Church's request, he turned into a cooperative venture. He owned and operated a successful woolen mill. He was a school trustee and a "minute man" guarding against Indian uprisings. He bought and operated the first threshing machine in the area. And, he was a member of the first Bishopric of Franklin.

Obviously, as the girls of a later generation would say, Brother Parkinson was, "quite a catch." There was, however, one unsettling element in the picture: Brother Parkinson was already married and had been for ten years and had no intention of forsaking his wife and their eight children!

Both Charlotte and her father were aware of Brother Parkinson's prospering first marriage. However, in faith and conformity with the Church doctrine advocating polygamous marriages for those deemed morally worthy and financially able to support more than one family, Charlotte's father agreed to the marriage and Charlotte accepted Brother Parkinson's proposal. One stipulation was made—that being that a courtship of sorts should be carried forward for the period of one year, in the form of dancing at socials and being together, usually in the company of others, at Church affairs.

Charlotte married Samuel Rose Parkinson on December 8, 1866. By modern standards, their marriage had little to recommend its success. Samuel was fifteen years her senior. He was already married. She still a young girl, was asked to share the attentions and affections of her betrothed with another wife. And, two years later the sacrifice would be further increased when still a third wife would share his provender and companionship—this time her younger sister, Maria. And yet, Charlotte built a happy successful marriage. She proved to be a competent business adviser and maintained a lively interest in her husband's affairs. She bore him ten children who, in order of their birth, were Ann, Lucy, Joseph, Fredrick, Leona, Bertha, Eva, Hazel, Nettie and Vivian. Each of her children were married in the temple.

[Because she had] faced the stresses of a polygamous marriage, Charlotte's counsel to her children carried much weight. She urged them to "do right" by their partners. In this and other attitudes she gained the love and respect of her sons and daughters-in-law.

Charlotte lived polygamy in spirit as well as in deed. She was always solicitous of the other wives' needs. During sickness in one of their homes, she was ever there to nurse and comfort, day or night. For example, during a smallpox epidemic, she left her own family of small children to help out in the homes of the other wives and relatives. When death struck among their children, she stayed to prepare them for burial—with never a question to her own safety.

Charlotte was devoted to the gospel of Jesus Christ. She lived the Word of Wisdom, paid an honest tithe, and reared an honorable family. She supported and sustained her husband in the priesthood. Her church service was mostly devoted to genealogical research and temple work. She labored twenty years in the Logan and Salt Lake Temples, doing vicarious work for over six hundred of her ancestors. Her greatest contribution to her church and her God was in simply and quietly living the first and great commandment. She loved and served her fellow man.

While working in the Temple, she suffered a stroke, which, two years later, resulted in her death. She died on June 14, 1929, in Logan, Utah, at the home of her daughter Ann. Her brother William, speaking at her funeral, said that Charlotte was always forgiving. She found no delight in anything low or unclean. She was a peacemaker in her parents' home, in her own, those of her husband's other wives, and in the homes of her children. Often she deprived herself of her husband's rightful company in order to bring more peace and happiness to a sister wife.[667]

Charlotte Smart Parkinson lived an eventful seventy-nine years. Her life spanned an epoch period both in Church and secular history. It can accurately be said that Charlotte was an active contributor to the times and in the places in which she lived.

---

667 Parkinson, *Roots and Branches*, 133.

Appendix D

A Granddaughter's Memories of Charlotte Smart Parkinson

by Mary Parkinson Cannon[668]

I CAN'T REMEMBER when I first saw my Grandmother Parkinson. From the first, she was a big part of my life. She made such a strong impression on me that she has been one of the big inspirations of my life. She left a single [singular] impression of unselfish helpfulness.

I remember her making and applying onion poultices to bring my brother Seth through a serious illness of bronchitis or pneumonia. I can still see her working tenderly and constantly over this precious grandchild of hers.

Another picture that comes to my mind is of Grandma standing outside the cabin door, skirts blowing about her as she silently prayed to her Heavenly Father that He would send rain to sustain the grain that her boys needed so much to finance their families and farming operations.

She had eight daughters and two sons. She was just as good to my mother, a daughter-in-law, as she was to her own daughters. My mother was threatened with the loss of her eyesight. She made many trips to Salt Lake City to try to get medical help. When Grandma was in her seventies, she came to Rexburg a number of times to care for Father and his eight children while Mother was away.

The doctors had suggested to my mother that she should eat oranges and other fresh fruits, which were harder to get and were more expensive than they are today. While Grandma was taking care of us, she drew my Father aside and said, "Joe, if I were you I'd go on Ida's diet with her."

Alan and I had been married almost a year without hopes of having a baby. I was traveling in Montana with Alan while he was selling woolens. On our way back, we stopped in Logan to see Grandma. She had suffered a stroke and was living with Aunt Hazel [her daughter]. When I telephoned Aunt Hazel, she said, "Mother is worried about you, Mary, because you aren't having a baby. We keep telling her it's because you and Alan are traveling, but she shakes her head and says, 'Not Mary, she wants a baby.' You'd better tell her yourself and try to settle her mind."

---

668 My mother gave me a copy of this manuscript. I don't know when she wrote it or what occasion inspired her to write it.

When we went in to see her, I did my best to ease her—goodness only knows, I had a hard time because I was at least as worried as she was. I had to call out loudly to make her hear. She seemed pacified. I think this was the last time I saw my grandmother. Strangely enough, I was pregnant at this time but didn't know it. When I knew of a certainty in September, my first letter bearing the wonderful news went to Grandma.

So much did I love and admire her that when the time for birth of this first child drew near, I said to my husband, "If it's a girl, I'd like to name her Charlotte." To my delight he answered, "I'd like to name her Charlotte, too." Our first child was a girl, born just three weeks before Grandma died. Those who were caring for Grandma were sure she understood when they told her about her namesake and that she was pleased. And so, Grandma's name is carried in our family. My memories of her are carried in my heart—clear and sweet.

I can never think of a finer example of the womanly virtues that she typified. Her wonderful abilities as a cook and as a homemaker in the finest sense of the word were unexcelled.

Great as these were, I admired her most for her abilities as a loving, unselfish woman who through service gave nourishment and comfort to the soul.

She will always be an ideal to me. How I wish I could be like her!

Appendix E

Life Sketch of Mary Lloyd Maughan 1847–1922

Author Unknown

Mary Lloyd Maughan was born January 1, 1847, in Green Oak, Montgomeryshire, North Wales. Her mother, Ellen Roberts, died when Mary was a baby, and it is believed that her father, David Lloyd, died a short time after. Mary and her twin brother, David, were adopted by Thomas and Catherine Edwards Hughes, who were devout members of the LDS Church. Thomas Hughes was a bishop in Wales. They were well to do and brought considerable money with them when they came to America.

They were on the ocean for thirteen weeks and landed in New Orleans on March 18, 1848. They stayed there for six months before moving on to St. Louis, where Mary's twin brother died at the age of four on April 13, 1851.

Thomas Hughes owned and operated a store in St. Louis and did well financially. In August 1854, he became ill and died. Catherine [his wife] continued the business until 1859, when she married William Fayle.

Thomas Lewis [another pioneer] arrived in St. Louis in 1854 with his three children. His wife, Mary Ann Griffin Lewis, died at sea. Thomas worked in a coal mine until 1856 when he was killed in an accident, leaving his three children orphans.

When Catherine heard of the Lewis children, she went to their home and offered to help. Even though she already had three orphans—Mary Lloyd, John, and Evan Owens[669]—she took Esther Lewis and her little brother Evan with her; their brother went with relatives.

Catherine and William, with their five orphans, moved to Winter Quarters, Nebraska, where they received word that no more emigrants were to come through to Utah, as Johnston's Army was on the way. They bought a place in Columbus, Nebraska, and stayed there for three years. While there, their home and belongings were burned. They decided to move west. They had two teams of horses, eight milk cows, two yoke of oxen, two mules, two work horses, and a riding horse. Mary loved to ride horseback, so she rode most of the way across the plains.

The family arrived in Wellsville on September 8, 1861, coming through Echo Canyon. Mary was fifteen years old.

---

669 It is not clear who John and Evan Owens are.

The Indians were troublesome at times. The family hardly dared move out of the house. One day, Esther, Mary, and Mother Catherine were alone. Six warriors rode up and demanded dinner. The family was very frightened but dared not refuse. Mary hid under the bed. Esther and Mother Catherine prepared dinner. After they had eaten, the Indians told them [the women] to wash and bandage their feet because they were sore and dusty. The Indians wanted Esther as their papoose. Catherine pleaded with them not to take her child. Finally they rode off [without Esther]. In a few days, two of the Indians came back with moccasins decorated with beads for Catherine and Esther. Mary lost out because she had hid under the bed.

Catherine was older than William Fayle and unable to have children. She encouraged William to marry a younger girl and raise a family of his own. After they separated, he remarried and moved to Idaho. Catherine was again known as Catherine Hughes. She never gave birth to a child, but she was a mother to several motherless and homeless children. When Mary was forty-one years old, she and her twin brother David were sealed on July 12, 1888, to Thomas and Catherine Hughes.

On November 23, 1867, Mary Lloyd married Bishop William Harrison Maughan in the Salt Lake Endowment House, becoming his fourth wife. She said she was never sorry or regretted the marriage though they were called upon to go through many trying times. Mary was the mother of nine children, one of whom died at age two. Her children were Catherine, Heber, Fanny, Barbara (who died as a child), Ida, Frank, David, Mildred, and Eva. Mary and her children lived in a red brick home on the farm east of Wellsville. Her youngest child, Eva, recalls their life as very happy. There was always something to look forward to: doing chores, riding horses, hunting for wild flowers, and swimming in their special swimming pool, which was completely surrounded by willows. They loved church activities and Mary saw to it they always attended to their church duties.

Mary was a hard worker and she tried to instill in her children the importance of accomplishment and cleanliness. She was an excellent housekeeper and cook. She did a great deal of sewing and she liked to dress with style and to look respectable. Her children loved and respected her.

Their father, Bishop Maughan, would make early morning visits to the farm to see that everything was being taken care of and to visit the families of two of his wives, Mary and Rachel. Rachel, the fifth wife, had a red brick home next door to Mary. These houses were the first red brick homes in Wellsville. The brick came from the new brickyard.

Mary and Rachel were like sisters. They enjoyed each other's company and children. Eva, Mary's youngest child, remembers when Mary and William traveled to Weston to visit his brother, John. Mary dressed in her very best and was as happy as a new bride as she went with William in his new buggy to stay overnight.

In 1905, after William's death, Mary sold her home on the farm and bought the home [adjoining] that of her son, David Maughan.[670] She and David's family shared the duplex home until her death. On October 24, 1922, Mary broke her hip in an accident. She lived twelve days suffering bravely and intensely. She died Saturday night, November 4, 1922, surrounded by

---

670 Actually, the details of who owned the duplex are unknown.

members of her family. She had lived to see all her children married, making homes and raising their own families. Funeral services were held Wednesday, November 6, 1922, in the Wellsville Tabernacle. The burial was in the Wellsville Cemetery.

Appendix F

Letter from Leonora Cannon Taylor to John Taylor

Montrose[671]
2 January 1840

I wish my John a Happy New Year and many of them. I have just come from meeting in Brother Cathrens. This is the first Prayer Meeting in this place. After this they are to be regular once a week and preaching on [undecipherable]. I must write so as to tell you all the news in a few words. I hope my dear you are well in your body as you seem in yours of the 19th of Nov. to be in your mind. I so pray the Lord to continue to bless and comfort you. I do praise Him for what He has done for you all ready.

I wish you could see George and Mary Ann, as fat and rosy as ever they were. Joseph is better and can run alone again, but teeth are still coming and I have to nurse him a great deal. I feel better able than I was when I last wrote. I have been sick but am better; he is still to be the baby. The Lord knows what is best for us.

I live in Sister [Phoebe] Woodruff's house. Brother Pratt has gone over the river to live. He is well. Sister Woodruff has gone to live to [undecipherable] is well and so is Sarah [Phoebe Woodruff's daughter]. She got two letters and a paper from New York lately. Brother Joseph is likely to get a hearing. I heard a letter read from him—very incouraging indeed. He wants all to pray for him. He sent Brother Manholm over hear some time since with papers relative to the lots on the other side. He came to me and said you had bespoke and I must sign the papers for you. I thought them very dear. He said that he could sell it for you and perhaps get 25 dollars more for it.

He died suddenly soon after poor man. Edward Lawrence is dead. Brother Daniels is also dead; heard the school masters wife and many others also and some families are still sick. Many are well. I have cause to be thankfull. I have suffered little compared with others. I am well supplied with fire wood by Dr. Patten. That has been some trouble to me since you left me. But I hope the worst is past.

Sister Young and family are well and expect to leave this for Kirtland as soon as the boats come along, with Father Granger who is here still. I went across to see him after I got you[r] letter. He was away from home. I told his daughter my business and next day wrote the letter you wished to Brother [Hiram] Kimball and enclosed it open to Bro Granger telling him what you said. (I have seen Bro Granger who says he will do all in his power for you he is going as

---

671 Leonora Cannon Taylor to John Taylor, in Madsen, *In Their Own Words*, 102–06.

soon as the River opens) I asked him to send Bro Humphry his Letter. I have heard nothing from him since but shall go over the River if all is well very soon it is frosen over now very hard. People walk over.

Bro Law and Family are on the other side. I have not seen them yet he sent me four Dollars at Christmas by Brother Ripley—I wish you would write to him as soon as you have anny thing interesting to write and thank him for me   I do want to know how you got Money to pay your way at the Tavern and to travel—if you should go to England or anny where else write as soon as possible and tell me where to direct. we have got a House Boat on the River and a House Mill on each side the River—I have not heard anny thing from your Father's People lately   I wrote to them but have had no answer—there is a conference out in Father Hauley's neibourhood to day where he us'd to live   rather he has removed to Quincy

I spent new Years day in Brother Rosers with some Friends   in the Evining I had three Indian Women a papuce and an Elderly Man all very clean to supper with me the[y] sat around the Fire and talked away quite comfortable   little Joseph kisst the little papuce and was delighted with it   the Children all send there love and a hundred kisses to Father   Joseph gives me one evry day for you and points to your Old Hat   when shall we see dear Father again is my cry and the Childrens, but I do not want to hinder the work of the Lord   my comfort is not to be compard with the worth of one Soul and I do pray that many may hear & believe the truth with whome we shall yet rejoice in the presence of the Lord.

My dear John, Br Law has been to see me   His Brother & Br Snider walked over the River. He is a kind man   askd if I wanted anny thing (I said no) and to remember I had a Friend over the River   whenever I did I got your Letter of the 17th Dec & two papers   I fear you will feel disappointed on receiving this   you know my dear what you have often said to me that every thing is ordered for the best. I fully believe so in this instance. Joseph is the most affectionate little thing   if I look serious he holds up his mouth to kiss   he dont speak anny yet to signify.

George and Mary Anne go to Sunday School to Mrs. Booth   I teach them evry day at home. Geo & M. Ann often dream of father as well as poor Mother.

Sister Young[,] Amelia Rodgers, and I walkd over the River   the way we had to walk was three Miles (there were a great number of our bretherin Lamanites going before us[ )] amongst them was Black Hawks Son and two Sons in law   his Son can speak english   if I had not been alone I should have likd them to have come in   one day the[y] stood outside the Door to have some thing to eat   the[y] were drest very fine, Bells on there legs Feathers on there heads,

we went to take a Letter to J.O. Prat who lives now with Sister Patten that was [when] we saw Sister Vilate Kimball and Sister Frances Turley   the[y] were all well   Brother Snider went with us and returnd to Springfield the next day, he intends to move here in Summer. Br Laws new Store is open—

There has been so many reports about how our bussiness got on at Washington that I have been waiting to have some certainty for you. Brother Joseph, the last acount we have had was in Philadelphia with Br Higby [Higbee] visiting the Church and left Pre'nt Rigdon at

Washington who is to send for them when they are wanted   Br Joseph wrote to new York to say all that had not saild of the twelve were to go to Washington to his assistance   many belive nothing favourable will be done   you had just saild when the Letter went

    I want to hear from you very much   my Health is not good   I pray the Lord to spare me to see you once more   I feel thankfull to the Lord that I am able to do what is needfull for my dear Children   I bought them warm and Wollen frocks and had long wollen stockings knit for myself and them and all had new Shoes on Xmas   I have made my Bed wide   G and M. sleep at one end and Joseph and I at the other, the House is so cold never been plastered   we have had steady cold weather   I have a Screen round the Fire and burn plenty of wood and shall have to pay for it [undecipherable]   D[octor] Patten began to find it at Christmas & he agreed to bring it in from the country   half the time I had to beg it and cary it home   the week before Xmas it stormd and Snowd. I had no wood for 5 days but what I beggd and caryed home in my arms   B Ripley came   I told him I felt discouraged and could not stand it long   he then ingaged my wood of Doctor Patten.

    You must excuse my bad writing, I have a bad pen and no Father to mend it. I hope my dear that you had a good passage; if favorably you were there before I got your letter. Sister Woodruff is well and comfortable. Elder Curtis in New York wrote to Brother Mace that you had sailed and that there are nearly fifty members in Philadelphia, in New York and vicinity nearly five hundred. The work is going on. I hope that you found my friends well and favorable to the truth.[672] Give my love to them all, write soon and often, I don't know how to wait for a letter from you now but hope for the best. The children and I send our love and kisses to a loving Father. Sisters Smith and Thompson are well. Give my best wishes to Brother and Sister Fielding. If you should go to the Isle of Man be sure to stop at Mister Higgins in Peel and try to lead him into the truth. Give my love to all that ask after me in the Isle of Man. May the Lord bless my dear John and bring him safe back is the prayer of your affectionate wife,

    Leonora Taylor

---

[672] Her hopes were realized. Shortly before Leonora wrote this letter, John had indeed introduced her brother George and his wife Ann Quayle to the gospel. They were living in Liverpool.

Appendix G

Letter from Leonora Cannon Taylor to Governor Ford

Nauvoo July 22nd 1844[673]

To His Excellency Thomas Ford[674]
Sir
    The peculearity of my situation will I hope plead my excuse for trubling your Excellency on the present occasion,
    Mr Taylor who was severly wounded in the Jail at Carthage, is still ill and obliged to be lifted in and out of bed; his wounds are slowly healing and we hope he will finally get well if suffered to do so; but Sir, I am sorry to say the Murderers and Mobbers are still at large in our neighborhood—as there has been no steps taken to bring them to Justice they have taken fresh courage and held Meetings to carry out their work of distruction. I have been told they have sent messengers to Missouri, to collect all the force they can to come and extirminate the Mormons after Harvest,
    I have inclosed your Excellency a communication sent Mr Taylor yesterday, which is a sample of meny that are haply coming in, he does not know of my wrighting this letter,— nothing but the urgency of the case could have induced me to remind your Excellency of your promise to bring the Murders to Justice. If a step of that kind is not taken soon I much fear that it cannot benefit us as a People.
    We are without arms in a great measure having delivered them up at your Excellencys request and are forbid to stand even in our own defence, in this peculear position without resources, we can only look to your Excellency for defense, to you sir for protection, and if it is not granted we must be Murdered in Cold Blood.
    My feelings as a Wife and Mother of helpless Children togather with the affections of an injured People, all constrain me to beseech of you to exert the power and authority which the People and God has given you in the cause of the oppressed; you shall have our prayers that wisdom may be given you from on high to act in this case to the Glory of God, your own honour, and that of the state we live in, Your Excellency was warned of our Bretheren's danger who were Murdered, but could not believe that men were so base and degraded; the same men are now plotting our destruction. As an individual who feel myself injur'd and also in behalf

---

673 This letter, which was written one month after the martyrdom of Joseph and Hyrum and the serious injury of John Taylor, gives perspective of the Saints' precarious situation.

674 Leonora Cannon Taylor to Thomas Ford, located in the Church History Library in Salt Lake City, Utah.

of an oppressed injured and persecuted people I again beg your offical interference, your Excellency cannot now be mistaken in the men, nor in their design   I beseech you then for the honor of our bleeding country, for the sake of suffering innocence and the cause of humanity; by the wounds of my husband and the blood of those murdered victims, to use promt measures for our protection and the bringing to Justice those Murderers   sincerly praying that you sir may become a terrour to evil doers and praise of those that do well with great respect I have [the] honor to be

    Your Excellencys
    Humble Servant
    Leonora Taylor

Appendix H

Letter from Mary Alice (Mamie) Cannon to Her Adopted Sister, Rosa

Washington D.C. March 14, 1878[675]

Dear sister Rosa[676]

   I recieved your kind letter dated 2nd and was very glad to get it and to hear that you were all well   tell edna that she is quite welcome to that which I sent her. I am glad that Leroy is growing so much   I think that leroy[677] is a nice name   I would like to see him   when I saw him last he was so small that I could not tell what he looked like.

   you will see A great change in sylvester[678] when he comes home   he is getting so cunning and two such pretty teeth are to be seen.

---

675   In 1878, ten-year-old Mary Alice was in Washington, DC, with her parents when her father was representing the Utah Territory in Congress. While there, she wrote a letter to her married sister, Rosa, who was fifteen years her senior. It was postmarked April 1, 1878, carried a three-cent stamp, and was addressed as follows:
   Mrs. Rosa C. Lambert
   Care of Mr. Geo C. Lambert
   Salt Lake City, Utah
This letter was discovered some years ago by Ken Cannon, Sr., the father of the Ken Cannon, Jr., who has helped me research post-Manifesto Cannon history. My cousin Mary Alice Collins recently gave me a photocopy of it. This letter is particularly important because it is the only piece of writing that we have of Mary Alice other than a letter she wrote to Lewis' brother Eugene on a mission in Tahiti about their experience at the Columbian Exhibition. We know she kept a diary because my father remembered reading it with his siblings in the years after her death. Unfortunately, the diary has been lost.

676   Rosina (Rosa) Matthews Cannon Lambert. Rosina was born in 1852 in Nottingham, England. George Q. Cannon and his wife Elizabeth, who were on a mission in England, met Rosina at church when she was ten years old. She was an orphan and they adopted her in England. While in England, Rosina helped Elizabeth with her two young children, Georgiana and George, both of whom were born in England. When Elizabeth returned to Utah, Rosina went with her. She was married to George C. Lambert on November 4, 1872, in Salt Lake City, Utah, as his second wife. Her husband also has a Cannon connection. His parents were Charles Lambert and Mary Alice Cannon Lambert (both born 1828). They were married in Nauvoo and made a home for Mary Alice's younger siblings, Angus, David, and Leonora.

677   Leroy was born to Rosina and George Lambert on December 24, 1877, so he was just three months old when Mary Alice wrote this letter. The other people Mary Alice mentions—Edna and John—could be other children of Rosina and George, but we have no records to confirm this.

678   Sylvester Quayle Cannon, a younger brother of Mary Alice's, was born June 10, 1877, in Salt Lake City, UT. He served as sixth presiding bishop and as an apostle.

I am learning to play on the piano. my teacher has given me A walz to learn   it is called evergreen waltz.[679] David[680] is trying to learn a little tune on the piano[681]   David often talks about his colt and wishes he had it here   he is as great a tease as ever and is always bothering us blanche and the [about two missing words]   does John tease edna like he used to about her thumb   we are all well   it seems a long time before we shall go home   I hope you are all well.

I wish could see you all and little emily the little pet   I hope she is well.

give my love to cousin george and edna and the same to your self   I am your loving sister

Mary Alice Cannon
Ma pa and David join in love to all
please deliver this note to aunt adelia

---

679 Possibly a simple piece for piano by Isaiah T. Stoddard, published in Baltimore in 1852. See http://webapp1.dlib.indiana.edu/metsnav/inharmony/navigate.do?oid=http://fedora.dlib.indiana.edu/fedora/get/iudl:323202/METADATA&pn=1&size=screen.

680 David Hoagland Cannon was another younger brother of Mary Alice's. He was born April 14, 1871, in Salt Lake City, Utah, and died in Germany in 1892 while serving a mission.

681 This was likely the only time Emily wasn't with Mary Alice on the trips with their parents to Washington, DC.

Appendix I

Letters from Mary Alice and Lewis Cannon to Eugene Cannon

Saltair Beach
June 27, 1893

My Dear Brother;
    I have thought of you many times since you left and have intended to write to you before, but each month I have neglected to do so until too late to catch the mail. I read your letters to your Mother Mary and Lew and am pleased to hear of your good health and contentment in that far off country to one raised as you have been, the customs and ways of the people there must seem very strange indeed yet with the help of the Lord our missionaries can accustom themselves to anything.
    As you see by the heading of this letter we are stationed out to the lake and in little cottage which you, with a party of others, visited last September you know how cosy it is so I need not describe it. We are here for the sole purpose of benefitting LewMar who has never recovered his strength since that severe sick spell he had in the winter, we think, how ever, that he will soon regain his strength here, as the salt air has given him an appitite and he already seems much better by the change.
    The season here is extremely late we had snow and frosts off and on during the greater part of May and we have not had that hot weather as we usually have it at this time of year, tho nights are extremely cool, and it looks as tho we are going to have a cool, pleasant summer.
    John has signified his intention of getting married this summer, either in July or August.[682]
    The young people of your acquaintance seem to be in about the same condition as when you left. My brother Brigham has been notified to prepare for a mission in the Fall and I expect before your return I will have four or five brothers out on missions. There is to be quite a 4th of July celebration down at Abram's this year, which I suppose will be something the same as last year. We are all invited and wish that you absent ones were here to enjoy the festivities.
    The picture you sent Lewmar is very nice and we thank you for your thoughtful kindness. With warmest love in which all join and best wishes for your future welfare.

       I remain
       Your loving sister,
       Mamie

---

682 Probably refers to her brother John Q.

Excerpts from a letter, most of which is too faded to read, that Lewis also wrote from Saltair on June 27, 1893, expressing his concern for Lewmar

My dear Brother,

. . . very many thanks for the picture you sent Lewmar. He thinks it very nice and wishes to send "Gene kiss." He chatters like a parrot and as I write he is lying on the table driving his horse Pete as he calls him. He says Mama-town get papa Pete. . . He can say nearly everything but does not connect his sentences very well. He has been very sick so sick that he could hardly sit up. It is for his sake that we are at Saltair, having come here thinking a change of air would do him good. We have now been here nearly two weeks and he has greatly improved, although he is still very weak. . . I herewith enclose a draft for ten dollars, five as a birthday present from me and five from Mamie. It is not much but perhaps we can send more later one. . . The folks are all pretty well and all join with me in sending love. Ever praying that God may watch over you for good I remain you loving brother.

       Lewis M. Cannon

Sept. 22, 1893

My Dear Brother:

I returned from Chicago on the 19th and found your letter addressed to Mamie and me awaiting us here. It afforded us much pleasure to hear from you. We enjoyed ourselves very much at the Worlds Fair and were gone from home just three weeks to the day. The Chicago Fair is acknowledged to be the greatest fair that the World has ever known. There one can see the whole world, its people, their industries, their mode of living, the worlds products and everything pertaining to mankind that would interest one. On what is called the Midway Plassance one can see the different peoples of the world living as they live at home. Here is to be seen a colony from the Samoan Islands while a little further on can be seen the Esquimaux with their dogs and sledges. The Sandwich Islands are represented by a large panorama painting of their volcano and while one looks at it he is entertained by the chanting and singing of a quarter of native Hawaiians. Germany has her villages shown as natural as life while a little further on one may wander through the "Streets of Cities" and from their surrounding immagine you were really in that city. History, Science, Arts and in fact everything pertaining to man, may be seen and studied in all their branches. I suppose you have read a great deal about the fair and so I will not trouble you with an attempt at describing it, but will say that it came fully up to my expectations.

While we were away we visited Independance, Jackson Co., and saw the old temple lot and other places familiar in the Hist. of our Church. I was much pleased with Jackson County. It is a beautiful place at least would be if the right kind of a people possessed it and the blessings of the Lord were upon it. Independance is about 10 miles to the East of Kansas City and is the home of many of Kansas Cities rich business men. Independance Avenue leading out of Kansas City is lined on each side by many palatial residences whose surroundings are grand in the fullest sence of the word. It is very easy for me to think that Jackson County will be everything that the Saints claim for it.

Trusting that you may be blest in your labors. I remain with much love.

Your Brother
Lewis M. Cannon

The following letters to his brother Eugene reflect Lewis' continued concern for his family, his interest in politics of the time, his business ventures, his efforts to beautify the property where he and Mamie are raising their family, as well as his sense of humor.

Oct. 28, 1893

Dear Brother:

The time of the departure of the mail for your island is near at hand and I take this opportunity of writting you a few lines. We at home are tolerably well in health and spirits. Mamie is looking and feeling better than she has before for months. She and I both enjoyed your words of comfort about Lewmar very much and we feel to acknowledge that what God does is for the best. Our baby although delicate was a great comfort to us and we miss the dear little fellow very much, but still have no desire to complain at what the Lord has seen fit to do. "The Lord giveth and the Lord taketh away blessed be the name of the Lord."

Eugene I am mining a little at present with father in Lewiston but I do not intend to loose my head over it, but intend that the [indecipherable] pay the interest. Goods of all kinds and real estate if sold at a forced sale bring very little   in fact things have reached that condition that unless something is soon done there will be one of the greatest panics man has ever known.

Do you get the newspapers and do you have enough reading matter? Are there any papers, books etc published in the native language? I found reading German news papers helped me very much in the language. I trust you will endeavor to learn the language correctly. Remember it is as easy to learn it correctly as incorrectly. The natives are they who speak properly and if you get the sound from them you will most likely get it right. I suppose you have heard of James Lamberts marriage to Mary Waddel. Ezra Stevenson and Mary Burton, Joe Nelson and of Jos. F. Smith's daughters were also married lately.

Father has received word that a very rich [person] shall pay their way as they go. As you perhaps remember I located some mines there one year ago. We have done nothing with them since then but note that place is having a boom and a substantial one too. Ore in paying quantities is being struck in different parts of that camp and it being gold ore the result is there is considerable demand for ground there. We have, we think, a chance to sell a half interest in all our claims there to same capitalists for several thousand dollars and in case we succeed in doing so we will set aside the money thus obtained to develop our interest in the mines. On Tuesday next (30th) father will take a man out there and we will then know what we will do in the future.

Things are still very dull all over the country   in Salt Lake a citizens ticket has been gotten up to defeat the Liberals which I suppose you have read of in the papers. [Unknown] family are here from Brooklyn, and seem to be very nice people I must close as it is growing late. Excuse brevity. Enclosed you will find $3 to buy you a little something. It isn't much but it will help you a little. Ever praying that God may bless you and assist you in discharging your duties faithfully.

    I remain
    Your loving brother,
    Lew

P.S. Father has just come in and says he is called to the country to see a sick person   he will write you in the morning if possible. He sends his love and $2.

May 28th, 1894

My Dear Brother:
Some time has elapsed since I last wrote you, but I think I wrote one letter that you did not get, or at least if you did I don't recollect your having acknowledged receiving it. It was the last of January and as you had requested I sent you a razor. Did you ever get your razor? If you did not and still desire one let me know and I will send you another. ---- I was much pleased to learn from your last letter that you had been transfered to a new field, that you seemed to like better than Tahiti. I trust you will continue to enjoy your labors and that you will be always blessed with the spirit of the Lord to guide you in your labors. ---- The folks as a rule are well although mother hasn't been feeling well for some time. Mamie is well and sends her love. Our little daughter Elizabeth is healthy and grows very nicely. She favors Lewmar considerable although she is inclined to be darker than he.

I am having our house fixed up as we expect to move to ourselves before a great while. Our place looks nicer at the present than I ever remember seeing it. The trees are growing nicely since I got the City water. I have had last summer a grove of about 100 trees, (lindon, ash and elm) set out just south of the house and they are beginning to show up very nicely. By the time you return they will be large enough for you to eat water melon, with your girl, under their branches. Abram, since you left, has made so many improvements to his place that you would scarcely recognize the neighborhood. He has planted several hundred trees which are all growing and has laid his grounds off beautifully. I suppose, however, that any thing that we can grow in this country will appear to you as very scant and poor, after your having been on those tropical islands. Still Utah is your home and you will undoubtedly always look with loving eyes on the land where you have spent so many happy years.

We have had very plesant weather so far, it still being comfortably cool. Father has been successful in disposing of his coal mine which I trust will help him out until we can dispose of, or get some of our [spelling?]Mining Property in operation. ---We have incorporated all our mines into a company and are now trying to dispose of a half interest therein to some Eastern Capitalists. The prospects at present appear very good, and if we are successful in consumating matters that are now under way it won't be a great while until we will begin paying off fathers obligations. However, as with all mining schemes it may be that nothing will come of it.---

Lewis T. Cannon returned from school this morning. He is looking and feeling well. The people are organizing malitia companies all over the Territory. A company of cavalry was organized in this city last week, and Angus, Geo, John and myself joined. I suppose you have heard of the industrial army craze that is sweeping over the country. They are getting to be quite a nuisance and may be, combined with the strikes, a dangerous element. Times in America are still very bad, and from the riots, strikes etc it almost makes one think that we are on the eve of a revolution. They say that things didn't look so gloomy just preceding the rebellion as they do now. Salt Lake and Davis County are having trouble with Weber co over the industrials. The later have been sending their [unknown] through the former counties, and Salt Lake and Davis County have concluded that it was wrong, and so got permission from the court to stop them. This they did at the boundry between Davis and Weber. There has been a great deal of talk from Weber about using force, dynamite etc but I think it will blow over without bloodshed. Both parties have, however, been camped on the line for several days.

I trust you are well and enjoying the spirit of your mission. All join in sending kindest love. May the Lord preserve you in health and purity is the constant prayer of your loving brother.

    Lewis M. Cannon

Appendix J

Life on the Cannon Farm

by Winnifred Cannon Jardine[683]

One of the most intriguing stories of the Mormon social system and one of the finest examples of the patriarchal order of family life was to be found on the Cannon farm, and no history of George Q. Cannon would be complete without some reference to it. This large farmstead southwest of the heart of Salt Lake City was "home" for Brother Cannon and his wives and children during the last twenty-three years of his life.

George Q. Cannon had housed his family prior to 1878 in a beautiful large gray home that he had built on South Temple and 1st West, but after the death of Brigham Young he felt inclined to sell it to the Church for a rather modest sum of money considering the fine house that it was.

Some years before, he had taken, on a debt, a large tract of land lying along the east bank of the Jordan River about three miles southwest of the temple block and had made some improvements there. He now decided to make this his home and build houses to accommodate his growing family.

"This was about as poor a piece of land for farming as lay in the whole valley," wrote his son Joseph J. Cannon. "It was marshy, subject to flooding in the spring, covered generally with salt grass, and bare in spots which glistened with alkali. On it was an old bed of the river which was filled with water and was called the slough. The lay of the land, low, flat and in some parts traversed by old channels, made irrigation and drainage almost impossible. It was plagued with mosquitoes."

"Moreover," he continued, "George Q. Cannon was not a farmer.... He found no time to tramp across fields to see how crops were growing nor don old clothes and relax with his livestock in corrals or barns. The roads to the city where he traveled every day, including Sunday, were dusty in summer and unbelievably bad in winter, the mud being in spots almost up to the hubs of his buggy.

"But this barren land along the river had one attraction for him—perhaps two. One was isolation. Neighbors were distant and few. It gave him the opportunity to create a special environment for his children. He could arrange for their education according to his own ideas and establish standards of thought and conduct with comparatively small influence from the

---

683 Evans and Cannon, 321–338.

outside. His work in Washington and in the Church took him away from home a great deal and probably no man ever felt the responsibility of rearing children in faith and good works more than he.

"The second attraction may be only imaginary. To this vital man, hard undertakings were congenial. He never sought the easy way of living for himself and did not wish it for his children. He loved to turn hopeless situations into desirable ones. Certainly the 'farm' on the river offered plenty of hardship and a sufficient challenge."[684]

It was one thing for George Q. Cannon to decide to move his family out to this rather desolate spot, and it was another for him to convince his family to go there. Elizabeth and his other wives did not relish the idea. The isolation and difficulties were not to their liking. It is interesting how he met this situation as shown in a letter to Eliza, his third wife, written from Washington under the date of April 18, 1878:

> As I told you, I sold my house in the city. The principal part of which I am to receive for it, is to be applied to my account for what I drew while I worked for the President and the Church. This enables me to stand clear of all obligations, and my services to the Church have been rendered without pay from it. I feel very glad at having been able to make the arrangement. The question now arises where shall we build and in what form?
>
> I want if possible to gratify your wishes as well as the wishes of all my family. I hope we will be united in our views beyond this point. What I would like is to build not far from where the present farm house is, so as to have the family together, and the children where they can associate together and where I can have a school. That is my wish. You know my ideas about the kind of house I would like you to occupy, but upon this point I do not wish to be strenuous.
>
> I would very much like to have Sarah Jane and you and Martha get together and take this matter up, and decide upon what you think is best, seeking the counsel and aid of the Spirit of the Lord. [Elizabeth apparently was to live in the Farmhouse, which was already built, and he had not yet married Carlie.] If you feel unitedly that you would prefer having your houses separate and not too far apart, I will endeavor to comply your wish. If on the other hand you would like them connected and yet separate, all right. If you would like them to be made one building each to have her separate apartments for herself and children, all right. . . .

---

684 Joseph J. Cannon, *The Instructor*, July 1945, 310–11.

You expressed a wish to have a place in the city. Unless there is some stronger reason than I heard you advance for this, I think you will find living near each other advantageous, but I do not wish to bring my pressure to bear upon you, to force a compliance with what I consider best. I will do as I said I would, that if you insisted on having a place in the city I should do my best to procure it for you.

The wives evidently voted each to have her own house on the farm because soon on the low, flat, treeless, salt, grass pasture south of the Farmhouse rose three two-story houses, spaced at a convenience distance apart. They were located together in this lonely spot in harmony with the persuasive husband's desire.[685] A few years later the red brick home called the "Big House" was built at the north end of the row for Carlie and her family.

For nearly a quarter of a century George Q. Cannon presided over the Cannon farm in a remarkable fashion as the patriarch of a large family of five wives and thirty-three children. How he was able to leave such a marked impression upon each child is a testimony to his superiority as a man and as a father. He had strong ideas about what he wanted to give his children and what he wanted of them, and his forcefulness in carrying these objectives to fruition is extraordinary.

Under the tutelage of George Q., that first unwelcoming acreage was nurtured to one of the showplaces of Salt Lake. During its greatest days a tree-lined driveway led through broad green pastures up to the stately homes. Cows, horses, and sometimes sheep grazed in the lush pastures, and high poplars shaded the lane or driveway that passed in front of the dwellings.

"The homes were lined up in a row extending about two city blocks in length," writes Clawson, another son. "Each home was a large two-story affair and it was kept modern as the new gadgets came in. They each had electricity as soon as it could be brought out from the city, bathrooms and central heat, all of which at that early date were not common. Father believed in beautiful things and had the areas around and between the homes all in lawn and flowers. He kept a gardener whose responsibility was to tend the greenhouse in the winter and have the flowers ready for the beds in the spring. We depended on artesian wells to furnish our water supply with a well for each house and extra wells to supply water for lawns and stables."

Starting at the south end of the lane was Eliza's home—a two-story house built of adobes that were plastered over, with a small porch on the front and south side and a long porch on the north. Large oleanders seemed always to bloom at her door.

Sarah Jane's house, with a broader frontage and both downstairs and upstairs porches, came next. Her home had more bedrooms to accommodate a larger family.

Martha's home was larger than either of the other two, more rambling and somewhat similar inside.

The Farmhouse was almost two houses. The frame part was built first and had a porch across the front, reached by a high flight of outside steps. Three steps down under this part of the house was a cool cellar used for storing apples, potatoes, pumpkins and other foods and also containing shelves for bottled fruit. The boys used to sneak down here to "snitch" apples. The adobe part of the Farmhouse was built a little lower to the ground and had a small front porch.

---

685 Joseph J. Cannon, *The Instructor*, August 1945, 348–49.

Carlie's house, a handsome red-brick structure built a few years after the others, was known as the "Big House" and was used in his later years by Brother Cannon for entertaining.

All of the homes were a good deal alike on the inside, although some had more bedrooms than others. As one entered the front door, the staircase was very near, going up to three or four bedrooms. On the main floor there were front and back parlors with double folding doors and a fireplace in each room. Also there were dining room, kitchen, a back hall, pantries, and a summer kitchen where washing, canning fruit, etc., were done. There were usually two back doors, one opening onto a long porch and the other going out the back.

George Q. Cannon's five wives, although spanning an age difference of some fifteen years from the oldest to the youngest, seemed to have had a deep respect for one another, a strong bond of affection tied all the children together.

Espey, George Q.'s son, once wrote: "My mother [Martha] and Aunt Eliza were very good friends. We children were in and out of both houses interchangeably. If my mother was occupied, we would go to Aunt Eliza. The relationships among all Father's family were pleasant and friendly." And another time he wrote that his mother was a very close friend of Eliza and Sarah Jane.

Georgius, the youngest of George Q.'s children and son by his last wife Carlie, recounted the following incident told to him by his older sister Rosannah, who was a daughter of Sarah Jane. He explained first that Carlie, his mother, had been married before, and that she was thirty-three years old and that his father fifty-seven at the time of their marriage. "After Aunt Elizabeth died, Aunt Sarah Jane who was the second wife… should have become the legal wife. Frank J. said to his mother, Sarah Jane, 'Now mother, you're getting along in years. Father is also getting old and he needs someone to take care of him. I think you should tell father to make Aunt Carlie his legal wife. She can take care of him and do his entertaining and travel with him.' Aunt Sarah Jane agreed to this and father made mother his legal wife. This was a real sacrifice, I'm sure. It denoted a great deal of character."

"People have often wondered," he went on, "about relationships in polygamous families. After I was grown and married, the only two wives left were Aunt Sarah Jane, who was bedridden in California where I was living, and Aunt Martha, who was near her last years. Both of them told me in almost identical words, 'Georgius, if your mother had been our own sister, we couldn't have loved her more.' This is the relationship that existed in the Cannon family. I'm not conscious of any difference in my feeling for my own brothers and sisters and my half-brothers and sisters… I can think of nothing that could possibly give me the pleasure and pride I've had in being the youngest of thirty-three such children. I think this is the most wonderful thing that has happened to me in my life."

George Q. strove to show no favoritism towards one wife or another. When he bought something for one, he bought it for all. During a trip to Europe he had five barrels of Haviland china sent home for his wives. Another time he had shipped from the East a carload of silk brocade furniture—five sets. He arranged for a Steinway grand piano to be delivered to each home, a Christmas gift for his daughters. If one wife wanted her home redecorated, they were all redecorated. During the periods when his family was not eating together in the common dining room, George Q. ate dinner one night a week with each family. Espey reports that

Tuesday nights they were always sure of having meat, for that was the night his father came. He added that sometimes they served frogs' legs and, when asked where they got them, answered, "We caught them."

As a member of the First Presidency of the Church, George Q. had a box at the Salt Lake Theatre and the families were rotated regularly in their use of it.

One humorous anecdote related by Collins illustrates again this effort to treat all alike: "Just at this time Utah was entering statehood. There was to be a grand inaugural ball in the Salt Lake Theatre. All of the high fashion of the new state was to be present including, of course, Father and his…. It was proper that George Q.'s wives be appropriately garbed for the grand approaching event. He brought back from the East the necessary dress goods suitable in style and in quality, I'm sure. The family dressmaker was set to work to prepare the gowns. *She* was a conniver with a depraved sense of humor. *She* arranged the selections of patterns and the fittings of each of the wives separately. They didn't know all of the pieces came from the same bolt. The gala night arrived, the high fashion of the state was there. Father was there with his five wives. A fashionable lady from the Eagle Gate District was heard to say, "Wasn't it quaint of Brother George Q. to dress his wives all alike!"

That the education of his children was of utmost importance to George Q. Cannon is attested by the fact that a one-room school house was built around 1879 directly south of the Farmhouse even before he had completed the homes for his other wives. In fact, it was subdivided with temporary partitions into several rooms and used to house Martha and her family until her own home was completed.

George Q. asked this same Martha, his fourth wife, to be the first teacher, since she had been a schoolmistress before their marriage. While her husband was away, much of her correspondence with him seems to have concerned the schooling of children, to which both attached much importance.

George M. Cannon, a nephew of George Q.'s, served as a teacher for a year or two, and Brother Cannon's daughter Rosannah also taught there towards the last years of the school house.

The educational needs of the Cannon children, as well as some of the neighbor children, were taken care of there for more than ten years, until finally the installation of a rail line along the edge of the farm made it possible for the children to attend school in the city.

At this time George Q. "turned the school house into a dining hall," wrote Espey, "where all the family dined together, each wife and her children at her own table…. Each wife had her own housekeeper [who] assisted with serving at meal time. George Q. sat at the head of Elizabeth's family table [Elizabeth had since died], and conducted the family gathering. Each child had to take his turn at leading in family prayer."

He built a kitchen onto the school-house-turned-dining-hall, and the first cook hired by the Cannons was a Chinese named "Sing," who served them for a number of years and became almost a legend among the Cannon children. He was housed in another little room that had been built on, and there he took his favorites for special treats of Chinese candy and fireworks. He had a fiery temper and was known more than once to chase one of the hired help with a meat cleaver, yelling at the top of his lungs.

When Sing left, the dining hall was closed and the families ate in their own homes. But it was re-opened once more after the older girls returned from attending Fannie Farmer's Boston Cooking School, and they took over the planning of menus and the running of the hall—with hired help.

Nor was this useful and historic building limited in its use just for schooling and eating, for the dining hall was also a very gay social place. The comfortable light oak cane-bottomed chairs and other furniture were cleared and wax shaved onto the floor, and parties and dances were held, often following swimming and boating parties in the summer.[686] During the winter months sleighs would bring guests out from town, the group would ice skate on the pond and then they would retire to the dining hall for dancing and refreshments—happy occasions for the eligible Cannon children. Wedding feasts, too, were held there in the old-time grand manner, and at least one family Christmas party was carried on with a beautifully decorated tree.

The joys and delights of life on the Cannon farm were not limited to these social events in the dining hall, nor just to the older set. "Life was easy—I might say idyllic for us youngsters," wrote Collin, one of the younger sons. "There was rafting and boating on the pond, playing on the old abandoned water wheel, swimming in the Jordan River, skating in season, and riding horses. We had parties and dances, for we were becoming old enough to take interest in that. We had a really good tennis court and there were always enough of us to form two teams for rounders or shinny. We had night games—Run Sheep Run and the like—everything, in fact, to delight youngsters. Oh it *was* a happy period in our young lives.

"There was lots of work to be done around a place such as ours," he continued, although he added, "We didn't have to do much of it though. There were hired men for that—sometimes as many as four or five to look after the extensive lawns and flowers, to put up the hay in the summer and the ice in winter—to take care of father's team and elegant closed coach and to drive him to and from his office in the city."

However, George Q. Cannon did recognize the need for his children to work and provided chores for them on his generous acreage. For a time he hired a man to tend his herd of cattle, but as the boys became old enough, he turned the responsibility over to them. Each was assigned a number of cows to milk and tend, according to age and ability. Each separated and cared for his portion of milk, and the last one to finish, cleaned out the separator—i.e., after the family acquired one. The boys were also responsible for keeping the barns clean.

"The feeding of Father's large family created quite a financial problem," wrote Carlie's son Clawson, "which was partially solved by raising much of our food on the land that Father owned. Our home was located near the Jordan River, which over the years had changed its course several times. Just behind our house were several old courses one which had been cut off at both ends so that we had quite a pond, semi-circular in form, in which there was a good

---

686 A double wedding party was held there October 1, 1890. One couple were my grandparents Mary Alice (daughter of George Q. and Elizabeth Cannon) and Lewis Cannon (son of Angus and Amanda Cannon). The other couple were Hugh Cannon (son of George Q. and Sarah Jane Cannon) and May Wilcken. *George Q. Cannon Journal*, October 2, 1890, in Bitton, 312.

supply of fish. Within this semi-circular area Father had our vegetable garden where we were required to work, hoeing and weeding alongside of the men that Father hired." Also growing here were fruit, black walnut, and mulberry trees.

Writing of this same piece of ground, Margaret Cannon Clayton, George Q.'s granddaughter, embellishes: "This piece of ground almost surrounded by water was known as the 'Island.' Here on this pond the children learned to row a boat and to handle a raft. A tight wire was stretched across the water where one, by holding to that and standing on a raft, could safely cross. There was no bridge, so those caring for the garden and carrying produce back used this means of transportation.

"There was never any swimming in this pond, for the family always preferred the running water of the Jordan River and the swimming hole there. Here George Q. Cannon did his swimming and diving right along with his boys and here many of the children and grandchildren were baptized.

"In the wintertime when the water was frozen on the pond, it was wonderful for skating, not only for these children but for all near and far who came to enjoy it. When the ice got heavy and thick enough, it was cut into large blocks and stored between layers of sawdust in an icehouse that had been built just south of the 'Island.' This ice was used in home refrigerators and for freezing ice cream made with real eggs and with lots of real cream."

Incidentally, during hot summer days the boys often gathered in the cool of the ice house for boyish "bull sessions."

Because the Cannon farm was somewhat isolated, the family had to drive several miles into town to do the shopping, and horses and carriages were used for transportation. "The older members of the family will remember," recorded Lewis [Martha's son], "the three-seated carriage or wagon, or bus, or whatever it might be properly called. We ourselves called it the Big Carriage, but it was a well known conveyance wherever we went and was generally known as the "Cannon Hearse." It took us to school after we started to go to school in town. And it took us to Sunday School clear over to Farmer's Ward on State Street below 17th South." Each Sunday the Big Carriage would slowly move down the lane in front of the five family homes, stopping at each place to pick up its load for church. This four-seated coach, driven by four horses, was also used to drive in style the special family whose turn it was to attend the Salt Lake Theatre.

Horses played a big part of life on the Cannon Farm. Between the Farmhouse and Carlie's home was a brick barn or silo where the finest of the Cannon horses were stabled. Here was where the famous family stallion, Corsair, or Peel as he was later named, was kept. He was a beautiful horse, the pride and joy of all the Cannon men and boys and was used for racing at Calder's Park (now Nibley Park) where he frequently was among the winners (although never first, according to Collins). Each son of George Q. Cannon's could speak affectionately of any number of horses by name, those assigned to serve his mother and her family and those who eventually became his own personal property.

There was another mode of transportation that figured prominently in the farm life, and that was the steam-engine street car called the Dinky or the Dummy. The old Dummy line ran out across the Jordan River and skirted the north part of the farm before heading into the city. The car was propelled by a little steam engine which was placed in one end of the coach while the passengers occupied the other part. This Dummy made trips hourly so that it allowed the children to get to school and home without much delay. It was only a few years later that the steam line fell into financial difficulty and was replaced first by a horse-drawn rail car and soon after by an electric line, partly subsidized by Brother Cannon. Finally, transportation was provided by the Rapid Transit Company which had to be caught a number of blocks away, and thus ended the use of the Dummy tracks on the Cannon property.

One may wonder whether a man so fully occupied as George Q. Cannon could exercise a wise rule over thirty-three children, including twenty-four spirited boys. History bears out that he did remarkably well, leaving an indelible impression on each one. Formal family meetings were held from time to time in the dining hall, but it was the front parlor of the Farmhouse where he met every week with his younger boys, dividing them into age groups to assemble at different times. Here he gave counsel and labor assignments, listened to reports of work done, attended to complaints and disagreements, and endeavored to maintain some closeness to each. "By these means," wrote Collins, "Father was able to keep in touch with us. Opportunities to see us individually seldom occurred." At another time Collins wrote:

> Do you recall Father's custom at times in the cool of the evening of sitting just to the north of the front entrance to the Farmhouse cellar? It was pleasant there when the sun was behind the black willow trees with a large scope of his domain in view…. This spot was the setting of many informal conferences between Father and the younger group. Here it was that he received our childish petitions, granting them or denying them as his wisdom dictated. Maybe it was here that he scanned the guest lists of our lawn and dancing parties, deleting from them any names that had a gentile sound. Perhaps it was here that we were reprimanded or punished for our childish pranks.

A particular incident of censure for a number of the boys was reported by Lewis:

> Father invited us in to see him; we were filled with fear and forebodings; we did not know what might happen to us. Father started in very quietly. He said, "I understand that you boys have learned to smoke and that you have entered on a smoking career. You have all been at work pulling weeds under cockle burrs. I probably owe you all some back pay for work down to now, and I imagine that you will be needing this money to buy tobacco, now that you have started to smoke. So I'm prepared to settle with you if you will let me know exactly what I owe.

"Another thing, I shall also want to arrange for you to get rooms and board elsewhere; I imagine you will want to be with others who smoke. You will feel more at home with them than with me because I don't like even the smell of tobacco. So I will be on the lookout for suitable quarters for you elsewhere unless you shall decide to give up smoking."

Well, we all decided there and then to give it up and stay on with him. The decision was our own, arrived at without any compulsion or duress. We were not driven to it and therefore felt no bitterness toward any one.

Collins recalls another occasion:

It included only the group then known as the 'Farm Kids'—Rad, I believe, and down to me in age. This meeting was held in the farm house. it had a *very special purpose*.

It seems that some of us were showing vicious tendencies—symptoms perhaps of turpitude. Our ages ranged from about seven to twelve so we were at about the right age for the development of those tendencies. Father was extremely watchful of and alert for such tendencies. He'd had plenty of experience, doubtless, with our large number of elder brothers.

The subject was opened abruptly. We were instructed to confess and express repentance, each in turn, commencing with the eldest of us. There was no show of bravado—there never was in Father's presence.

The confessions came forth, haltingly in most cases, but thoroughly in all. There was no equivocation. One didn't equivocate with George Q. Cannon. Too soon my dreaded turn came. I was the youngest, I was little, I was but a lamb. I hadn't sinned. I'd nothing to confess. I hardly knew what it was all about. No, there was nothing to confess but there *was* an opportunity to right all the wrongs that had been heaped on me and mine all through the seven or eight years of my life. My jealous fires were burning. I had been neglected; my mother had too. She hadn't fine clothes nor jewels. She didn't go a-traveling to far away places in fine style and take me along. She didn't have a sideboard in her dining room and she wanted one. In short, she and I didn't belong—we were not wanted. *This* was my confession. It all came out of me in soul-tearing sobs.

I can't remember going home. I can't remember how the night passed. I can't remember how the subsequent summons came, as come I was sure it would. It came.

At the appointed time I walked 'the last mile' alone. I mounted the long steps to the Farm House. I was so alone. It was to be unique—the only time I was ever to be with my father alone.

I sat on the edge of a straight chair. Father leaned gracefully at the fireplace with one elbow on the mantle. He was always graceful. No word had been spoken. None had been needed. I knew I was to be dispatched. I knew I wouldn't grow up to be a locomotive engineer or a pirate or a watchmaker. In the spring after the snow had melted, some crocuses and dew drops might grow up and hide the stone on which would be enscribed the awful words: Here Lies the Little Boy Who Sassed George Q. Cannon.

Well sir, it didn't turn out like that at all. Neither of us had broken the silence. Father left the fireplace and put a hand on my shoulder—gently. He spoke—gently—as a gentleman to a gentleman. He didn't descend to my level, but raised me to his.

He recounted patiently—somewhat painfully, too, I seem to remember—some of the things he had lived through down the years. He told me of the cruel Edmunds-Tucker Act, a thing I had never heard of. He told me of the houndings of the U.S. Marshalls, of his being a fugitive with a price on his head like a common criminal. He told me of his capture and incarceration.

He told me of the issuance of a manifesto which he hoped would ameliorate a situation out here in Utah that had become intolerable. He told me of his determination to accept that manifesto to the letter—and then—finally and patiently, oh so patiently, I remember, he told me exactly why he decided to live out the rest of his days in the manner in which he was living it—with one wife only. I was so small to be told these things I could hardly grasp them, but how completely soul-satisfying it all was! I retraced the former 'last mile.' It was short now. I had a song in my heart. I knew now that I wasn't just so much polygamous spawn. I was George Q. Cannon's little boy.

A memorable family custom begun at the farm and persisting long after Brother Cannon's death, was the annual George Q. Cannon birthday party, a celebration for all family members, first held in 1895. John Q., the oldest son, wrote that "somewhat elaborate preparations (were) made, committees appointed, and programs printed and performed." These ornate programs, prepared in rather grand fashion, were issued each year, no doubt because of George Q.'s profession as a printer, and contained the menu, the program of the evening, and such other information as seemed pertinent.

It was at these affairs that the persistent efforts of George Q. Cannon in seeing that his children develop their talents would come to fruition. There were the Mandolin and Guitar Club, the Gibson Girls, the Floradora Octette. There were solos and addresses. Plays were written, original music was composed, special numbers were arranged. And while the older children performed in special groups, the younger children were always included as "flowers" in a birthday bouquet or in some other suitable fashion.

There was the Cannon Chronicle, a detailed account (first written by John Q. and later by his son Theodore) of the yearly happenings within the family. Nothing was too much work for these birthday parties. They have stood out vividly in the minds of all who were involved.

Each family home had the honor of housing at least one of these gala events. One held at Aunt Carlie's included the General Authorities and only the married sons and daughters. The most elaborate was held in 1900 at Aunt Sarah Jane's. And in 1901, the last birthday party during George Q.'s life was held at Aunt Martha's.

Although George Q. Cannon died three months later, the annual family birthday parties continued for three-quarters of a century, and evident at each one are the vigorous spirit and tradition that he fathered. Every one of his more than 1300 descendants has, in some way, felt the influence of this remarkable man who presided with patriarchal dignity over the Cannon farm.

Appendix K

Chart of Polygamous Families Discussed in the Book

KEY
boldfaced — direct ancestor of author
* asterisk — died as infant or young child
# hashtag — children from an earlier marriage

JOHN TAYLOR (1808–1887)
seven wives[687] and thirty-five children

WIVES' NAMES	MARRIED	CHILDREN	
Leonora Cannon (1796–1868)	1833	George John Joseph	Mary Ann *Leonora
Elizabeth Kaighin (1811–1895)	1843	Josephine Arthur	Thomas
Jane Ballantyne (ca. 1813–1900)	1844	Richard David	Annie
Mary Ann Oakley (1826–1911)	1846	Henry Brigham Ezra	*Mary Ida
Sophia Whitaker (1825–1887)	April 1847[688]	Harriet Hyrum Helena Frederick	James John W. Moses Nettie (adopted)
Harriet Whitaker (1816–1882)	Dec. 1847	*John W. Sophia	William

---

687 John Taylor was sealed to other women with whom he had no children. See footnote 132 in Chapter One.

688 In contrast to the Mousley sisters, who were married to Angus Cannon on the same day, the Whitaker sisters were married on different days in the same year.

Margaret Young 1854
(1837–1919)

Ebenezer
Leonora
Margare
Mary
Samuel

Frank
*Robert
Nephi
Abraham

George Q. Cannon (1827–1901)

six wives and forty-two children, including those he adopted

Name	Married	Children	
Elizabeth Hoagland (1835–1882)	1854	*George Q. *Georgiana *Elizabeth *Lillian Emily Rosina (adopted)	John Q. *George H. **Mary Alice** David Sylvester
Sarah Jane Jenne (1839–1928)	1858	Franklin Hugh Joseph	Angus Rosannah Preston
Eliza Tenney (1845–1908)	1865	William Edwin	Read
Martha Telle (1846–1928)	1868	Hester Lewis Willard Radcliffe	Amelia Brigham Grace Collins
Caroline Young Croxall (1851–1903)	1884	#Emily Croxall[689] *#Maude #Mark *#Verna Clawson Anne	*#Charles #Caroline #Tracy #Vera Wilford Georgius
Emily Hoagland Little (1835–1906)	1881	no children by George Q.[690]	

---

689 The children marked with # were Caroline's with her first husband, Mark Croxall, whom Caroline divorced. George Q. Cannon adopted all of these children.

690 Emily married Jesse C. Little in 1856 by whom she had ten children. Jesse and Emily divorced in 1881; later that year, George Q. married Emily. Apparently neither Emily nor her children were integrated into the larger George Q. Cannon family, but she was remembered in his will.

APPENDIX K

ANGUS M. CANNON (1834–1915)
six wives and twenty-nine children

NAME	MARRIED	CHILDREN	
Sarah Maria Mousley (1828–1912)	July 18, 1858	*Maria John M. Leonora	George M. *Henry Ann
Ann Amanda Mousley (1836–1905)	July 18, 1858	Wilhelmina *David Charles Mary Jesse	Angus Jr. **Lewis** Eugene Clarence Quayle
Clarissa Cordelia Moses Mason (1839–1926)	1875	#Camilla[691] #Ambrose *#William *Erastus	*#Carlotta *#Ann *Samuel Alice
Martha Hughes (1857–1932)	1884	Elizabeth Gwendolyn	James
Maria Bennion (1857–1925)	1886	Hattie Eleanor	Ira Glenn
Johanna Cristina Danielson (1850–1922)	1887	One child who died young[692]	

SAMUEL ROSE PARKINSON (1831–1919)
three wives and thirty-two children

NAME	MARRIED	CHILDREN	
Arabella Chandler (1824–1894)	1852	Samuel William Franklin *Albert Caroline	Charlotte George Esther Clara

---

[691] The father of Clarissa's older children is William Henry Mason, who died as a fire fighter. Angus helped raise them.

[692] There is no record of this child's name.

CHART OF POLYGAMOUS FAMILIES DISCUSSED IN THE BOOK

Charlotte Elizabeth 1866 (1849–1929)		Ann **Joseph** Leona Eva Nettie	Lucy Frederick Bertha Hazel Vivian
Maria Hayter Smart 1868 (1851–1915)		Thomas Arabella Olive Clarence Hazen *Chloe Glenn	Luella Sarah Edmond Susanna Henry *Lenora

WILLIAM H. MAUGHAN (1834–1905)
six wives and forty-eight children

NAME	YEAR MARRIED	CHILDREN	
Barbara Morgan 1853 (1834–1888)		Ruth C. Peter M. Sarah Thomas Brigham	Mary Elizabeth William H. Agnes Joseph
Elizabeth Brice Hill 1860 (1834–1908)		#Emerine[693] John Alexander *Francis Elizabeth	Margaret Daniel Robert Archibald Guy
Margaret Wilson Nibley 1863 (1843–1930)		Martha *Charles James Rebecca Elmer	Jane Esther Charles *Maud
Mary Jane Lloyd 1867 (1848–1922)		Catherine Fanny **Ida** David Eva	Heber *Barbara Frank Mildred

---

693 Emerine's father is John Gardner, who froze to death on a mountain pass by Wellsville.

Rachel Barnes Woodward 1871		Hyrum	Henry
(1852–1922)		Willard	*Margaret
		Leona	Christina
		Janet	
Euphemia Nibley 1880		*Wilson	*May
		Elva	George

LEWIS M. CANNON (1866–1924)
three wives and fourteen children

NAME	YEAR MARRIED	CHILDREN	
Mary Alice Cannon 1890		*LewMar	Elizabeth
(1867–1909)		Douglas	**Alan**
		Robert	Marjorie
		Josephine	
Lillian Hamlin[694] . . . . about 1899[695]		#Marba[696]	Matthew
(1870–1920)		Victor	Warren
		Aaron	Moses
		Leah	
Annie Nielsen 1921		Irene	
(1881–1976)	(not polygamous)		

---

[694] Sealed to David Hoagland Cannon, Mary Alice's brother

[695] There is no written record of Lewis and Lillian's marriage.

[696] Marba's father is Abram H. Cannon.

Appendix L

The 1890 Manifesto

Official Declaration 1[697]

To Whom It May Concern:

Press dispatches having been sent for political purposes, from Salt Lake City, which have been widely published, to the effect that the Utah Commission, in their recent report to the Secretary of the Interior, allege that plural marriages are still being solemnized and that forty or more such marriages have been contracted in Utah since last June or during the past year, also that in public discourses the leaders of the Church have taught, encouraged and urged the continuance of the practice of polygamy—

I, therefore, as President of The Church of Jesus Christ of Latter-day Saints, do hereby, in the most solemn manner, declare that these charges are false. We are not teaching polygamy or plural marriage, nor permitting any person to enter into its practice, and I deny that either forty or any other number of plural marriages have during that period been solemnized in our Temples or in any other place in the Territory.

One case has been reported, in which the parties allege that the marriage was performed in the Endowment House, in Salt Lake City, in the Spring of 1889, but I have not been able to learn who performed the ceremony; whatever was done in this matter was without my knowledge. In consequence of this alleged occurrence the Endowment House was, by my instructions, taken down without delay. Inasmuch as laws have been enacted by Congress forbidding plural marriages, which laws have been pronounced constitutional by the court of last resort, I hereby declare my intention to submit to those laws, and to use my influence with the members of the Church over which I preside to have them do likewise.

There is nothing in my teachings to the Church or in those of my associates, during the time specified, which can be reasonably construed to inculcate or encourage polygamy; and when any Elder of the Church has used language which appeared to convey any such teaching, he has been promptly reproved. And I now publicly declare that my advice to the Latter-day Saints is to refrain from contracting any marriage forbidden by the law of the land.

WILFORD WOODRUFF
President of The Church of Jesus Christ of Latter-day Saints.

---

697 D&C OD 1. This document, which follows the end of the Doctrine and Covenants, is referred to as the 1890 Manifesto and the First Manifesto.

President Lorenzo Snow offered the following:

> I move that, recognizing Wilford Woodruff as the President of The Church of Jesus Christ of Latter-day Saints, and the only man on the earth at the present time who holds the keys of the sealing ordinances, we consider him fully authorized by virtue of his position to issue the Manifesto which has been read in our hearing, and which is dated September 24th, 1890, and that as a Church in General Conference assembled, we accept his declaration concerning plural marriages as authoritative and binding.

The vote to sustain the foregoing motion was unanimous.
Salt Lake City, Utah, October 6, 1890.

Appendix M

Excerpts from Three Addresses Regarding the Manifesto

by President Wilford Woodruff[698]

THE LORD WILL NEVER permit me or any other man who stands as President of this Church to lead you astray. It is not in the programme. It is not in the mind of God. If I were to attempt that, the Lord would remove me out of my place, and so He will any other man who attempts to lead the children of men astray from the oracles of God and from their duty.[699]

It matters not who lives or who dies, or who is called to lead this Church, they have got to lead it by the inspiration of Almighty God. If they do not do it that way, they cannot do it at all. . . .

I have had some revelations of late, and very important ones to me, and I will tell you what the Lord has said to me. Let me bring your minds to what is termed the manifesto. . . .

The Lord has told me to ask the Latter-day Saints a question, and He also told me that if they would listen to what I said to them and answer the question put to them, by the Spirit and power of God, they would all answer alike, and they would all believe alike with regard to this matter.

The question is this: Which is the wisest course for the Latter-day Saints to pursue—to continue to attempt to practice plural marriage, with the laws of the nation against it and the opposition of sixty millions of people, and at the cost of the confiscation and loss of all the Temples, and the stopping of all the ordinances therein, both for the living and the dead, and the imprisonment of the First Presidency and Twelve and the heads of families in the Church, and the confiscation of personal property of the people (all of which of themselves would stop

---

698 These excerpts appear in the Doctrine and Covenants directly after the Official Declaration concerning plural marriage.

699 Sixty-first Semiannual General Conference of the Church, Monday, October 6, 1890, Salt Lake City, UT, in *Deseret Evening News,* October 11, 1890, 2.

the practice); or, after doing and suffering what we have through our adherence to this principle to cease the practice and submit to the law, and through doing so leave the Prophets, Apostles and fathers at home, so that they can instruct the people and attend to the duties of the Church, and also leave the Temples in the hands of the Saints, so that they can attend to the ordinances of the gospel, both for the living and the dead?

The Lord showed me by vision and revelation exactly what would take place if we did not stop this practice. If we had not stopped it, you would have had no use for . . . any of the men in this temple at Logan; for all ordinances would be stopped throughout the land of Zion. Confusion would reign throughout Israel, and many men would be made prisoners. This trouble would have come upon the whole Church, and we should have been compelled to stop the practice. Now, the question is, whether it should be stopped in this manner, or in the way the Lord has manifested to us, and leave our Prophets and Apostles and fathers free men, and the temples in the hands of the people, so that the dead may be redeemed. A large number has already been delivered from the prison house in the spirit world by this people, and shall the work go on or stop? This is the question I lay before the Latter-day Saints. You have to judge for yourselves. I want you to answer it for yourselves. I shall not answer it; but I say to you that that is exactly the condition we as a people would have been in had we not taken the course we have.

. . . I saw exactly what would come to pass if there was not something done. I have had this spirit upon me for a long time. But I want to say this: I should have let all the temples go out of our hands; I should have gone to prison myself, and let every other man go there, had not the God of heaven commanded me to do what I did do; and when the hour came that I was commanded to do that, it was all clear to me. I went before the Lord, and I wrote what the Lord told me to write. . . .

I leave this with you, for you to contemplate and consider. The Lord is at work with us.[700]

Now I will tell you what was manifested to me and what the Son of God performed in this thing. . . . All these things would have come to pass, as God Almighty lives, had not that Manifesto been given. Therefore, the Son of God felt disposed to have that thing presented to the Church and to the world for purposes in his own mind. The Lord had decreed the establishment of Zion. He had decreed the finishing of this temple. He had decreed that the salvation of the living and the dead should be given in these valleys of the mountains. And Almighty God decreed that the Devil should not thwart it. If you can understand that, that is a key to it.[701]

---

700 Cache Stake Conference, Logan, Utah, November 1, 1891, in *Deseret Weekly,* November 14, 1891.

701 From a discourse at the sixth session of the dedication of the Salt Lake Temple, April 1893. Typescript of Dedicatory Services, Archives, Church Historical Department, Salt Lake City, Utah.

Appendix N

The 1904 Manifesto

Official Statement by President Joseph F. Smith[702]

INASMUCH AS there are numerous reports in circulation that plural marriages have been entered into, contrary to the official declaration of President Woodruff of September 24, 1890, commonly called the manifesto, which was issued by President Woodruff, and adopted by the Church at its general conference, October 6, 1890, which forbade any marriages violative of the law of the land, I, Joseph F. Smith, President of The Church of Jesus Christ of Latter-day Saints, hereby affirm and declare that no such marriages have been solemnized with the sanction, consent, or knowledge of The Church of Jesus Christ of Latter-day Saints.

And I hereby announce that all such marriages are prohibited, and if any officer or member of the Church shall assume to solemnize or enter into any such marriage, he will be deemed in transgression against the Church, and will be liable to be dealt with according to the rules and regulations thereof and excommunicated therefrom.

  Joseph F. Smith,
  President of The Church of Jesus Christ of Latter-day Saints

RESOLUTION OF ENDORSEMENT

President Francis M. Lyman introduced the following, which carried by unanimous vote:

> Resolved that we, the members of The Church of Jesus Christ of Latter-day Saints, in General Conference assembled, hereby approve and endorse the statement and declaration of President Joseph F. Smith, just made to this Conference concerning plural marriages, and will support the courts of the Church in the enforcement thereof.

---

702 Joseph Fielding Smith. "Official Statement by Joseph F. Smith." *Improvement Era* 7/7 (May 1904): 545–46. This declaration, known as the 1904 Manifesto and as the Second Manifesto, was published in this Church magazine the month after it was presented in general conference.

Appendix O

The Family: A Proclamation to the World

by the First Presidency and Council of the Twelve Apostles of
The Church of Jesus Christ of Latter-day Saints[703]

WE, THE FIRST PRESIDENCY and the Council of the Twelve Apostles of The Church of Jesus Christ of Latter-day Saints, solemnly proclaim that marriage between a man and a woman is ordained of God and that the family is central to the Creator's plan for the eternal destiny of His children.

All human beings—male and female—are created in the image of God. Each is a beloved spirit son or daughter of heavenly parents, and, as such, each has a divine nature and destiny. Gender is an essential characteristic of individual premortal, mortal, and eternal identity and purpose.

In the premortal realm, spirit sons and daughters knew and worshipped God as their Eternal Father and accepted His plan by which His children could obtain a physical body and gain earthly experience to progress toward perfection and ultimately realize their divine destiny as heirs of eternal life. The divine plan of happiness enables family relationships to be perpetuated beyond the grave. Sacred ordinances and covenants available in holy temples make it possible for individuals to return to the presence of God and for families to be united eternally.

The first commandment that God gave to Adam and Eve pertained to their potential for parenthood as husband and wife. We declare that God's commandment for His children to multiply and replenish the earth remains in force. We further declare that God has commanded that the sacred powers of procreation are to be employed only between man and woman, lawfully wedded as husband and wife.

We declare the means by which mortal life is created to be divinely appointed. We affirm the sanctity of life and of its importance in God's eternal plan.

Husband and wife have a solemn responsibility to love and care for each other and for their children. "Children are an heritage of the Lord" (Psalm 127: 3). Parents have a sacred duty to rear their children in love and righteousness, to provide for their physical and spiritual needs,

---

[703] The First Presidency and Council of the Twelve Apostles of The Church of Jesus Christ of Latter-day Saints, "The Family: A Proclamation to the World," (presented at the General Relief Society Meeting, Salt Lake City, UT, September 23, 1995)."

and to teach them to love and serve one another, observe the commandments of God, and be law-abiding citizens wherever they live. Husbands and wives—mothers and fathers—will be held accountable before God for the discharge of these obligations.

The family is ordained of God. Marriage between man and woman is essential to His eternal plan. Children are entitled to birth within the bonds of matrimony, and to be reared by a father and a mother who honor marital vows with complete fidelity. Happiness in family life is most likely to be achieved when founded upon the teachings of the Lord Jesus Christ. Successful marriages and families are established and maintained on principles of faith, prayer, repentance, forgiveness, respect, love, compassion, work, and wholesome recreational activities. By divine design, fathers are to preside over their families in love and righteousness and are responsible to provide the necessities of life and protection for their families. Mothers are primarily responsible for the nurture of their children. In these sacred responsibilities, fathers and mothers are obligated to help one another as equal partners. Disability, death, or other circumstances may necessitate individual adaptation. Extended families should lend support when needed.

We warn that individuals who violate covenants of chastity, who abuse spouse or offspring, or who fail to fulfill family responsibilities will one day stand accountable before God. Further, we warn that the disintegration of the family will bring upon individuals, communities, and nations the calamities foretold by ancient and modern prophets.

We call upon responsible citizens and officers of government everywhere to promote those measures designed to maintain and strengthen the family as the fundamental unit of society.

Illustration Credits

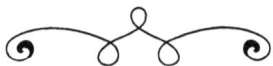

Authors Preface

xiii   Genealogy chart. Designed by Tara Parker and Laura Pierce.

Chapter One

32   **John Taylor.** In John Taylor Portrait Collection, ca. 1870–1887, Church History Library (CHL), The Church of Jesus Christ of Latter-day Saints, Salt Lake City, UT.

32   **Leonora Cannon Taylor.** In Beatrice Cannon Evans and Janath Russell Cannon. *Cannon Family Historical Treasury*. Salt Lake City, UT: George Cannon Family Association, 1967. 310.

34   **Adelaide Street Methodist Church.** Obtained by author in 1983 from a government building in Toronto.

44   **Mormon Trail (map).** In *Church History in the Fulness of Times: Student Manual*, 2nd ed. Salt Lake City, UT: The Church of Jesus Christ of Latter-day Saints, 2003. Copyright © 2003 Intellectual Reserve, Inc. 331.

48   *Winter Quarters* **(painting).** By C. C. A. Christensen. Courtesy of Church History Museum, The Church of Jesus Christ of Latter-day Saints (LDS Church), Salt Lake City, UT.

50–51   **Leonora Cannon Taylor's First Diary.** In George J. Taylor Papers, 1832–1909, CHL.

54   **Mormon Settlements by the Missouri River (map).** In *Church History in the Fulness of Times*. 317.

54   **Winter Quarters (map).** In *Church History in the Fulness of Times*. 320.

63   *John and Leonora's Home* **(sketch).** In *Cannon Family Historical Treasury*. 170.

67 **Leonora Cannon Taylor's quilt block.** By Richard Watkins, Lens Art Photography. In Carol Holindrake Nielson. *The Salt Lake City 14th Ward Album Quilt, 1857: Stories of the Relief Society Women and Their Quilt.* Salt Lake City, UT: University of Utah Press, 2004. 33.

Chapter Two

70 **Elizabeth Hoagland Cannon.** In Davis Bitton. *George Q. Cannon: A Biography.* Salt Lake City, UT: Deseret Book, 1999. 71. Courtesy of Alan M. Cannon and Mary Parkinson Cannon family.

70 **George Q. Cannon.** In *George Q. Cannon: A Biography*. 118. Courtesy of Cannon family.

78–79 **Elizabeth Hoagland Cannon's journal.** Owned by author.

84 **George Q. Cannon's "Big House."** In *Cannon Family Historical Treasury*. 320.

85 **Members of George Q. Cannon's family school.** Courtesy of Cannon family.

85 *The Cannon Farm* **(painting).** By C. Eisele. Courtesy of Cannon family.

86 *Cannon Farm* **(sketch).** By Winnifred C. Jardine. In *Cannon Family Historical Treasury*. 322.

Chapter Three

92 **Angus M. Cannon.** Courtesy of Daughters of Utah Pioneers (DUP) Museum, Salt Lake City, UT.

92 **Ann Amanda Mousley Cannon.** Courtesy of DUP Museum.

94 **Angus M. Cannon.** In *Cannon Family Historical Treasury*. 190.

95 **Angus M. Cannon with his older sons.** In *Cannon Family Historical Treasury*. 202.

Chapter Four

112 **Charlotte Smart Parkinson.** Courtesy of Cannon family.

112 **Samuel Rose Parkinson.** Courtesy of Cannon family.

119 **Sarah Maria Mousley Cannon.** In *Cannon Family Historical Treasury*. 220.

119 **Ann Amanda Mousley Cannon.** In *Cannon Family Historical Treasury*. 224.

ILLUSTRATION CREDITS

122   **Charlotte Smart Parkinson.** In Preston W. Parkinson. *The Family of Samuel Rose Parkinson: Roots and Branches.* Salt Lake City, UT: published by author, 2001. 104.

122   **Maria Smart Parkinson.** In *Family of Samuel Rose Parkinson.* 104. Courtesy of Joanne Austin Linford.

123   **Samuel Rose and Charlotte Smart Parkinson family.** Owned by author.

CHAPTER FIVE

126   **Mary Lloyd Maughan.** Owned by author.

126   **William Harrison Maughan.** Courtesy of Cannon family.

139   **Mary Lloyd Maughan and her children.** Courtesy of Cannon family.

139   **Mary Lloyd Maughan in front of her Wellsville home.** Courtesy of Cannon family.

144   **Prisoners at the Utah Territorial Penitentiary.** Courtesy of Cannon family.

144   **Utah Territorial Penitentiary.** In Orson F. Whitney. *Popular History of Utah.* Salt Lake City, UT: *Deseret News,* 1916. 465.

145   **William H. Maughan and George Q. Cannon's entries in the autograph book of M. B. Wheelwright.** Courtesy of Cannon family.

146   **Bingham County Courthouse.** Courtesy of Cannon family.

CHAPTER SIX

148   **Lewis M. Cannon.** Courtesy of Cannon family.

148   **Mary Alice Cannon.** Courtesy of Cannon family.

156   **Harvesting grain on Rexburg Bench.** Courtesy of Cannon family.

157   **Towns relevant to the Parkinson and Maughan families (map).** Designed by Matt Johnston.

164   **George and Ann Quayle Cannon's children.** In *Cannon Family Historical Treasury.* Title page.

165   **Lewis and Mary Alice's first home first home.** Courtesy of Cannon family.

165   **Lewis and Mary Alice's second home.** Courtesy of Cannon family.

168	**Lewis and Mary Alice Cannon's family.** Courtesy of Cannon family.
174	**Home of Israel and Emily Willey.** Courtesy of Cannon family.
174	**Home of Lewis and Mary Alice's children after Mary Alice's death.** Courtesy of Cannon family.
174	**Home of Lewis and Lillian and their children.** Courtesy of Cannon family.
178	**Five generations of Cannons (chart).** Designed by Arlene Cannon and Laura Pierce.
179	**Charlotte Johnston (author) with friend Irene Salahor.** By Yasemin Miller. Owned by author.
184	**First Presidency and Twelve Apostles, 1898.** By C. R. Savage. Courtesy of CHL.

CHAPTER SEVEN

190	**Mary Parkinson Cannon and Alan M. Cannon.** Owned by author.
194	**Map of Arizona-Utah border.** By Shereth, Wikimedia Commons. Modified by Laura Pierce.

CHAPTER EIGHT

208	**Peter B. Johnston and Charlotte Johnston.** Owned by author.
218	**Charlotte and her grandchildren.** 2006. Owned by author.
218	**Peter B. and Charlotte Johnston and their family.** 1998. Owned by author.

BIBLIOGRAPHY

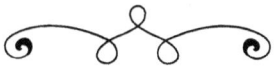

Alexander, Thomas G. *Mormonism in Transition: A History of the Latter-day Saints, 1890–1930*. Urbana, IL: University of Illinois Press, 1996.

Allen, James B., and Glen M. Leonard. *The Story of the Latter-day Saints*. Salt Lake City, Utah: Deseret Book, 1976.

Angus M. Cannon Reunion Materials, ed. Angus M. Cannon Reunion Committee, 1988.

Angus M. Cannon Reunion Materials, ed. Angus M. Cannon Reunion Committee, 1989.

Angus M. Cannon Reunion Materials, ed. Angus M. Cannon Reunion Committee, 1990.

Angus M. Cannon Reunion Materials, ed. Angus M. Cannon Reunion Committee, 1991.

Arrington, Leonard J. *David Eccles: Pioneer Western Industrialist*. Logan, UT: Utah State University, 1988.

Beecher, Maureen Ursenbach, and Lavina Fielding Anderson. *Sisters in Spirit: Mormon Women in Historical and Cultural Perspective*. Chicago: University of Illinois Press, 1987.

Bitton, Davis. *George Q. Cannon: A Biography*. Salt Lake City, UT: Deseret Book, 1999.

Brooks, James. "Utah Struggles with a Renewal of Polygamy." *New York Times* (New York City, NY), Aug. 23, 1998.

Bush, Laura. *Faithful Transgressions in the American West: Six Twentieth-Century Mormon Women's Autobiographical Acts*. Logan, UT: Utah State University Press, 2004.

Bushman, Claudia L., ed. *Mormon Sisters: Women in Early Utah*. Cambridge, MA: Emmeline Press Limited, 1976.

Bushman, Richard Lyman. *Joseph Smith: Rough Stone Rolling*. New York: Vintage Books, 2007.

Cannon, George Q. *The Life of Joseph Smith, the Prophet*. Salt Lake City, UT: Deseret Book, 1972.

Cannon, Kenneth L. II. Review of "Candid Insights of a Mormon Apostle: The Diaries of Abraham H. Cannon, 1889–1895." Significant Mormon Diaries Series, No. 12. *Journal of Mormon History* Vol. 38 No. 1 (Winter 2012), 247–259.

Cannon, Mary Parkinson, ed. *Remember Who You Are: Alan and Mary Cannon Family History*. Privately published, 1981.

Carter, Kate B., ed. *Our Pioneer Heritage*. Salt Lake City, UT: Daughters of Utah Pioneers, 1958.

Christensen, LaRayne B., Wilma J. Hall, and Ruth H. Maughan. *Windows of Wellsville*. Wellsville, UT: Wellsville History Committee, 1985.

Church History in the Fulness of Times: The History of The Church of Jesus Christ of Latter-day Saints. Salt Lake City, Utah: The Church of Jesus Christ of Latter-day Saints, 1993.

Compton, Todd. *In Sacred Loneliness: The Plural Wives of Joseph Smith*. Salt Lake City, Utah: Signature Books, 1997.

Corcoran, Brent, ed. *Multiply and Replenish the Earth: Mormon Essays on Sex and Family*, Book 7. Salt Lake City, UT: Signature Books, 1994.

Daynes, Kathryn M. *More Wives than One: Transformation of the Mormon Marriage System, 1840–1910*. Chicago: University of Illinois Press, 2001.

Derr, Jill Mulvay, Janath Russell Cannon, and Maureen Ursenbach Beecher. *Women of Covenant: The Story of Relief Society*. Salt Lake City, Utah: Deseret Book, 1992.

Embry, Jessie L. *Mormon Polygamous Families: Life in the Principle*. Salt Lake City, Utah: University of Utah Press, 1987.

Evans, Beatrice Cannon, and Janath Russell Cannon, eds., *Cannon Family Historical Treasury*, Salt Lake City, UT: George Cannon Family Association, 1967.

Gibbons, Francis M. *John Taylor: Mormon Philosopher, Prophet of God*. Salt Lake City, Utah: Deseret Book, 1985.

Hardy, B. Carmon. "The Persistence of Mormon Plural Marriage." *Dialogue: A Journal of Mormon Thought* 44, No. 4 (Winter 2011): 43–105.

Hatch, Nelle Spilsbury. *Colonia Juarez: An Intimate Account of a Mormon Village*. Salt Lake City, UT: Deseret Book Company, 1954.

Johnston, Charlotte Cannon. "A Mormon Mother." Review of *A Mormon Mother: An Autobiography*, by Annie Clark Tanner. *Dialogue: A Journal of Mormon Thought* 6, no. 2 (Summer 1971): 127–128.

Jorgensen, Victor W., and B. Carmon Hardy. "Taylor Cowley Affair and the Watershed of Mormon History." *Utah Historical Quarterly* 48 No. 1 (Winter 1980): 4–36.

Kranish, Michael, and Scott Helman. *The Real Romney.* New York City: Harper Collins, 2012.

Madsen, Carol Cornwall. *In Their Own Words: Women and the Story of Nauvoo.* Salt Lake City, Utah: Deseret Book, 1994.

Maughan, Janice Uhl, ed., *William Harrison Maughan Family History.* Providence, UT: Keith W. Watkins and Sons, Inc., 1986.

Nielson, Carol Holindrake. *The Salt Lake 14th Ward Album Quilt, 1857: Stories of the Relief Society Women and Their Quilt.* Salt Lake City, UT: The University of Utah Press, 2004.

Parkinson, Preston Woolley, ed. *The Family of Samuel Rose Parkinson: Roots and Branches*: Salt Lake City, UT, 2001.

Peter Maughan Family Organization. *Peter Maughan Family History.* Logan, UT: Unique Printing Service, 1971.

Pingree, Allison, ed. *Marjorie Cannon Pingree: A Personal History.* Privately published, 1990.

Romney, Joseph Barnard. "'The Lord God of Israel Brought Us Out of Mexico': Junius Romney and the 1912 Mormon Exodus." *Journal of Mormon History* 36, No. 4 (Fall 2010): 208–258.

Smart, William B. *Mormonism's Last Colonizer: The Life and Times of William H. Smart.* Logan, UT: Utah State University Press, 2008.

Tanner, Annie Clark. *A Mormon Mother: An Autobiography.* Salt Lake City, UT: University of Utah Press, 1969.

Taylor, Leonora Cannon. *First Diary, Summary of Her Early Life*. Located in the Church History Library in Salt Lake City, UT.

Taylor, Leonora Cannon, Trail Diary: *February 1846–October 1847*. Located in the Church History Library in Salt Lake City, UT.

Taylor, Lester Parkinson. *Samuel Rose Parkinson: Portrait of a Pioneer.* Provo, UT: The Claymont Co., 1977.

Taylor, Samuel W. *The Last Pioneer: John Taylor, a Mormon Prophet.* Salt Lake City, UT: Signature Books, 1999.

Taysom, Stephen C. "A Uniform and Common Recollection: Joseph Smith's Legacy, Polygamy, and the Creation of Mormon Public Memory 1852–2002," *Dialogue: A Journal of Mormon Thought* 35 No. 3 (2009): 113–44.

Ulrich, Laurel Thatcher. "An American Album, 1857." *The American Historical Review.* 115, no. 1 (February 2010): 1–25.

Van Wagoner, Richard S. *Mormon Polygamy: A History.* Salt Lake City, UT: Signature Books, 1989.

White, O. Kendall, and Daryl White, "Polygamy and Mormon Identity," *Journal of American Culture* 28, Issue 2 (June 2005): 165–77.

Whitney, Orson F. *Popular History of Utah.* Salt Lake City, UT: The Deseret News, 1916.

Wood, V. A. *The Alberta Temple: Centre and Symbol of Faith.* Calgary, AB: Detselig Enterprises, 1989.

INDEX

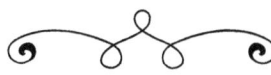

NOTE:
Images are indicated in boldface.
The contents of the timeline and genealogy charts are not indexed.

A

Ames, Eva Maughan   128, 137, **139**, 235
Anti-polygamist legislation
    Cullom Bill   8
    Edmunds–Tucker Act   12, 65, 107, 134, 149–150, 159, 185, 197, 202, 210, 224, 258
    Edmunds Anti-polygamy Act   11, 12, 88, 130, 132, 134, 198, 202
    Morrill Anti-Bigamy Act   8–10, 75–76, 78, 154
Austin, Joanne (See Linford, Joanne Austin)

B

Ballantyne, Jane (See Taylor, Jane Ballantyne)
Bennion, Maria (See Cannon, Maria Bennion)
Bluffdale, Utah   140–141, 196
Brooks, Joanna   203
Brown, Bishop Francis   10, 16
Budge, Ann Hyer (wife of William Budge)   118–119
Budge, Elizabeth Pritchard (wife of William Budge)   118
Budge, Julia Stratford (wife of William Budge)   118–119
Budge, William   118
Bush, Laura   7, 203

C

Canada   16, 34–37, 68, 133, 172, 180, 182–183, 185–187, 225
Cannon, Abram (Abraham) Hoagland   5, 13, 47, 61, 65, 75, 77, 89, 100, 150, 163–164, 166, 169–170, 173, 174, 175, 221, 244, 248
Cannon, Alan M.   99, 142, 160–162, 166, **168**, 172, 175–176, 179, **190**, 214, 232–233
Cannon, Angus M.   5, 33, 39, 41, 45, 68, 71–72, 82, 89, **92**, 93, **94**, **95**, 96–100, 107–108, 115–117, 119–121, 130–131, 135, 140–144, 146, 158, 160, 163, **164**, 166, 168, 171, 177, 179, 188, 192, 204, 212–213, 221, 226, 242, 248, 254
Cannon, Ann Amanda Mousley (wife of Angus M. Cannon)   5, **92**–95, 97–98, 100, 115–116, **119**–121, 140–141, 143, 158, 160, 212–213, 217, 221, 254
    Life sketch of (Appendix B)   226–227
Cannon, Ann (See Woodbury, Ann Cannon)
Cannon, Ann Quayle   39–40, 65, 161, 163, 164, 239
Cannon, Annie Nielsen (monogamous wife of Lewis Cannon)   177, 179, 210
Cannon, Caroline (Carlie) Young Croxall (wife of George Q. Cannon)   9, 85, 90, 98, 100, 106, 158, 142, 146, 250–252, 254–255, 259
Cannon, Clarissa Cordelia Moses Mason (wife of Angus M. Cannon)   97–100, 120, 141
Cannon, Collins   124, 142, 158–159, 253, 255–258
Cannon, David H.   82, 87–89, 163–164, 166, 169–170, 175, 179, 210, 243
Cannon, David M.   5, 41, 72–74, 94, 163–**164**, 242
Cannon, Eliza Tenney (wife of George Q. Cannon)   82, 84–85, 105, 114, 117, 121, 123–124, 130, 142, 158, 163, 197, 250–252
Cannon, Elizabeth. (See Sauls, Elizabeth Cannon)

Cannon, Elizabeth Hoagland (wife of George Q. Cannon) 4, 8, 44, 61, 65, **70**–90, 93, 98, 100, 103, 114, 116–117, 121–122, 127–128, 141, 159–160, 163, 170, 197, 213, 223, 242, 250, 252–254
    Journal 76–77, **78–79**, 80, 82–83
Cannon, Emily (See Willey, Emily Cannon)
Cannon, Emily Hoagland Little (wife of George Q. Cannon) 4, 88, 100, 116, 122
Cannon, Eugene **95**, 161–162, 167, 242
Letters from Mary Alice and Lewis Cannon to Eugene Cannon (Appendix I) 244–248
Cannon Farm 84, **85, 86**, 105–106, 114, 117, 130, 140, 142, 162, 197, 223
    Life on the Cannon Farm (Appendix J) 249–259
Cannon, Frank Jenne 75, 82, 150–151, 187, 252
Cannon, George (the immigrant) 33, 39, 40–41, 46, 63, 65, 68, 163–164
Cannon, George M. **95**, 158, 171–172, 188, 253
Cannon, George Q. 4, 7–9, 12, 15, 33, 35, 39, 40–41, 43, 47, 49, 58, 61, 63, 65, 68, **70**–90, 95, 98–100, 104–106, 113–114 116–117, 121, 123–124, 127–130, 132, 134–135, 140–142, **144**, 145–146, 149–152, 154, 158–161, 163, **164**, 165, 170, 175, **184**, 187, 192, 197, 212–213, 223, 242, 244, 249–259
Cannon, Georgiana 75–77, 81–82, 114, 159, 242
Cannon, Irene (See Salahor, Irene Cannon)
Cannon, Johanna Cristina Danielson (wife of Angus M. Cannon) 143
Cannon, John M. **95**, 171–172, 204
Cannon, Leonora (See Taylor, Leonora Cannon)
Cannon, Leonora (See Gardner, Leonora Cannon)

Cannon, Lewis 5, 16, 68, **95**, 99, **148**, 153, 160–162, 165–180, **168**, 189, 210, 212, 214–215, 227, 254
    Letters to Eugene Cannon (Appendix I) 244–248
Cannon, Lillian Hamlin (wife of Lewis Cannon) 16, 163–164, 166–167, 169–170, 172–179, 189, 212, 215
Cannon, Margaret. (See Clayton, Margaret Cannon)
Cannon, Maria Bennion (wife of Angus M. Cannon) 120, 140–141, 143, 146
Cannon, Marjorie. (See Pingree, Marjorie Cannon)
Cannon, Martha Hughes (wife of Angus M. Cannon) 115, 120, 130–131, 141
Cannon, Martha Telle (wife of George Q. Cannon) 83–87, 105–106, 114, 117, 121, 124, 142, 158–159, 162, 165, 172, 197, 250–253, 259
Cannon, Mary Alice. (See Lambert, Mary Alice Cannon)
Cannon, Mary Alice (wife of Lewis Cannon) 5, 16, 68, 81–82, **85**, 87–90, 99, **148**, 153, 159–163, 165–170, **168**, 172, 174, 175–177, 178–180, 212, 223, 254
    Letter to adopted sister, Rosa (Appendix H) 242–243
    Letter to Eugene Cannon (Appendix I) 244–248
Cannon, Mary Parkinson 128, 161, 181, 188, **190**, 232–233
Cannon, Rosa 77, 167, 242–243
Cannon, Sarah Jane Jenne (wife of George Q. Cannon) 74–77, 82–85, 98, 105, 113, 121, 123, 128, 150, 158, 161, 187, 250–252, 254, 259
Cannon, Sarah Maria Mousley (wife of Angus M. Cannon) 5, 71, 93–98, 115–116, **119**–121, 140–141, 158, 166, 171, 188, 204, 212–213, 221, 226–227

Cannon, Sylvester 82, 87–89, 163, 167, 169–170, 180, 243
Cannon, Wilhemina Hoagland (wife of Abram Cannon) 5, 94
Cannon, Wilhemina Mousley (wife of David Cannon) 5, 166
Cannon, Winnifred (See Jardine, Winnifred Cannon)
Carthage Jail 45, 52, 127 135, 195, 240
Casterline, Gail 115
Chandler, Arabella (See Parkinson, Arabella Chandler)
Chart illustrating author's relationship to the people discussed in the book xiii
Chart of five generations of Cannons 178
Chart of polygamous families discussed in the book (Appendix K) 12/5/16 260–264
Clark, Annie (See Tanner, Annie Clark)
Clark, J. Reuben 180, 193
Clayton, Margaret Cannon 82, 117, 124, 163, 167, 255
Cleveland, Grover 15
Columbian Exposition (1993 World's Fair) 105, 153, 162, 242, 245
Congress 8–9, 11, 15, 87–88, 90, 127, 132, 135, 151–152, 154, 158, 160, 182, 213, 242, 265
Cowdery, Oliver 220
Cowley, Luella Parkinson (wife of Matthias Cowley) 108–110, 118, 121, 137–138, 155, 185, 188, 214–215
Cowley, Matthias F. 17, 109–110, 181, 183, **184**, 185, 188, 205, 214–215
Croxall, Caroline Young (See Cannon, Caroline Young Croxall)
Cullom Bill 8

D

Danielson, Johanna Cristina (See Cannon, Johanna Cristina Danielson)

Diary
    Elizabeth Hoagland Cannon's Journal 76–77, **78–79**, 80, 82–83
    Leonora Taylor Cannon's First Diary 33, 35, 38, 40–43, **50–51**, 210–211
    Leonora Taylor Cannon's Trail Diary 46–49, 52, 53, 55–63, 210–211, 221

E

Edmunds Anti–Polygamy Act of 1882 (Edmunds Act) 12, 65, 107, 134, 149–150, 159, 185, 197, 202, 210, 224, 258
Edmunds–Tucker Act 11, 12, 88, 130, 132, 134, 198, 202
Excommunication 16, 182, 185, 187, 195, 199–200, 204, 205, 269

F

Family: A Proclamation to the World, The (Appendix O) 193, 270–271
Ford, Governor Thomas 46, 223
    "Letter from Leonora Cannon Taylor to Governor Ford (Appendix G)" 240–241
Fourteenth (14th) Ward Album Quilt 38, 66–**67**, 116–117, 221

G

Gardner, Leonora Cannon (wife of Robert Gardner) 41, 72, 163, **164**
Grant, Heber J. 4, 96, 133, **184**, 188, 191–193, 201
Gravestone (See Headstone)

H

Hale, Emma (See Smith, Emma Hale)
Hamlin, Lillian (See Cannon, Lillian Hamlin)
Harrison, Benjamin 15, 137
Headstone 68, 71–72, 114
Hill, Elizabeth Brice (See Maughan, Elizabeth Brice Hill)
Hinckley, Gordon B. 199–200
Hoagland, Abraham 47, 61, 65, 100, 221

Hoagland, Elizabeth (See Cannon, Elizabeth Hoagland)
Hoagland, Emily Little (See Cannon, Emily Hoagland Little)
Hoagland, Wilhemina (See Cannon, Wilhemina Hoagland)
Hughes, Martha (See Cannon, Martha Hughes)
Hyer, Ann (See Budge, Ann Hyer)

I

Indians 39–40, 46, 49, 53, 59, 60–61, 66, 229–230, 235, 238
Isle of Man 34–35, 39, 42, 46, 239

J

Jardine, Winnifed Cannon 86, 106, 223, 249–259
Jenne, Sarah Jane (See Cannon, Sarah Jane Jenne)
Johnston, David Alan 217
Johnston, Peter B. 33, 118, **208**, 215, **218**
Johnston's Army 66–67, 73–74, 221, 234
Journal (See Diary)

K

Kaighin, Elizabeth (See Taylor, Elizabeth Kaighin)
Kimball, Heber C. 3, 36, 75, 129
Kimball, Spencer W. 103, 180
King, Larry 199
Kirtland, Ohio 1, 36–37, 67, 205, 237

L

Lambert, Mary Alice Cannon (wife of Charles Lambert) 41, 47, 72, 81, 163, **164**
Lambert, Rosa Cannon (See Cannon, Rosa)
Lincoln, Abraham 8, 76
Linford, Joanne Austin 109, 185, 214–215, 219
Lloyd, Mary Jane (See Maughan, Mary Jane Lloyd)
Lund, Anthon H. **184**

Lyman, Francis M. 182, 184–185, 269

M

Manifesto
    First Manifesto (also referred to as the Manifesto and the 1890 Manifesto) (Appendix L) 12–17, 96–97, 110, 124, 140, 146, 149–155, 158–159, 161, 164, 170–172, 180–183, 185–188, 193, 196–197, 202, 204–205, 212–215, 223–225, 258, 265–266
        Excerpts by Wilford Woodruff about the First Manifesto (Appendix M) 267–268
    Second Manifesto (1904 Manifesto) (Appendix N) 16, 17, 182, 185, 196, 214–215, 223, 269
Mason, Clarissa Cordelia Moses (See Cannon, Clarissa Cordelia Moses Mason)
Maughan, Barbara Morgan (wife of William H. Maughan) 137, 142, 155
Maughan, Clarke 138
Maughan, Dave **139**, 154, 235
Maughan, Elizabeth Brice Hill (wife of William H. Maughan) 99, 138
Maughan, Euphemia Nibley (wife of William H. Maughan) 116, 146
Maughan, Eva (See Ames, Eva Maughan)
Maughan, Frank 138, **139**
Maughan, Margaret Wilson Nibley (wife of William H. Maughan) 116
Maughan, Mary Ann Weston (wife of Peter Maughan) 4, 128
Maughan, Mary Jane Lloyd (wife of William H. Maughan) 4, 5, 100, 108, 116, 124, **126**, 128, 137–**139**, 154–155, 210, 213
    Life sketch of (Appendix E) 234–236
Maughan, Peter 4, 107, 128
Maughan, Rachel Barnes Woodward (wife of William H. Maughan) 116, 235

Maughan, William H. 5, 71–72, 98–101, 106, 113, 116–117, 124, **126**, 136–138, 140, 142, **144**–146, 154–155, 210, 235

McKay, David O. 183

Merrill, Marriner W. 183, **184**

Mexico 16, 120, 132–133, 136–137, 150, 171–172, 182, 185–187, 193, 204

Morgan, Barbara (See Maughan, Barbara Morgan)

Mormon Battalion 55, 63

Mormon Mother, A 3, 83, 108, 191, 223
    Charlotte Johnston's review of (Appendix A) 224–225

Mormon Tabernacle Choir 15, 153

Morrill Anti-Bigamy Act 8–10, 75–76, 78, 154

Mousley, Ann Amanda (See Cannon, Ann Amanda Mousley)

Mousley, Sarah Maria. (See Cannon, Sarah Maria Mousley)

Mousley, Wilhemina. (See Cannon, Wilhemina Mousley)

Mountain Meadow Massacre 66, 221

N

Nauvoo, Illinois 1, 4, 33, 37–38, 40–41, 43, 45–47, 49, 56, 58–59, 61, 67, 72, 98, 100, 102, 116–117, 127, 195, 205, 210, 224, 229, 240, 242

New and everlasting covenant 2, 100, 221

Nibley, Euphemia (See Maughan, Euphemia Nibley)

Nibley, Margaret Wilson (See Maughan, Margaret Wilson Nibley)

Nielsen, Annie (See Cannon, Annie Nielsen)

O

Oakley, Mary Ann (See Taylor, Mary Ann Oakley)

P

Parkinson, Arabella Chandler (wife of Samuel Rose Parkinson) 108, 117–118, 121, 124–125, 142, 155, 157, 180–181, 212–214, 219

Parkinson, Charlotte Smart (wife of Samuel Rose Parkinson) 5, 100, 109, **112**, 116, 118, 121, **122**, **123**–125, 137–138, 142, 146, 155–158, 181, 212–213, 217, 219
    Life sketch of (Appendix C) 228–231
    Granddaughter's memories of (Appendix D) 232–233

Parkinson, Fannie Woolley (wife of George C. Parkinson) 180

Parkinson, George C. 180

Parkinson, Joseph S. 124, 139, 156, 212

Parkinson, Luella (See Cowley, Luella Parkinson)

Parkinson, Maria Hayter Smart (wife of Samuel Rose Parkinson) 5, 109, 116–118, 121, **122**, 124, 137–138, 142, 146, 155, 157–158, 181, 213–214, 219, 230

Parkinson, Mary (See Cannon, Mary Parkinson)

Parkinson, Preston 180–181, 212

Parkinson, Samuel Rose 5, 71, 98–101, 107–109, **112**, 115–118, 121–124, **123**, 127–128, 137–138, 142–143, 146, 155–158, **156**, 180–181, 212–213, 219, 229–230

Pingree, John 169, 177

Pingree, Marjorie Cannon (Aunt Marge) 68, 162, 166–170, **168**, 172–173, 175–179

Post-Manifesto marriages 16, 140, 164, 169–183, 204–205, 212, 214

Pratt, Parley P. 36–37, 42, 47, 53, 66, 75, 221

Pritchard, Elizabeth (See Budge, Elizabeth Pritchard)

Proposition 8 197–198

Q

Quayle, Ann (See Cannon, Ann Quayle)

R

Redfield, Mary Ann Taylor 37–38, 47, 49, 52–53, 58, 60–61, 64, 237–238
Relief Society 33, 66, 68, 101–102, 105, 116, 130, 187, 201, 221
Revelation 1, 3, 10, 12, 14–15, 96, 100, 127, 151–152, 171, 186, 192, 199, 202, 214–215, 220, 268
Reynolds, George 9–10
Reynolds v. United States 11, 87–88, 132
Richards, Franklin D. 64, 114, **184**
Roberts, B. H. 16, 35, 41–43, 135, 182
Romney, Junius 187

S

Salahor, Irene Cannon 166, 177–**179**, 210
Sauls, Elizabeth Cannon (Aunt Ips) 81, 83, **168**, 175
Senate 8, 16, 182
Short Creek, siege of 194–196
Sister wives 2, 5, 46, 53, 56, 64, 66, 68, 71, 75, 82, 93, 95–97, 100, 113–116, 121–125, 130, 155, 198
    Dynamics among 42, 47, 57–58, 83, 108, 116–120, 155, 219
Smart, Charlotte Elizabeth (See Parkinson, Charlotte Smart)
Smart, Maria Hayter (See Parkinson, Maria Hayter Smart)
Smith, Emma Hale 1, 6, 101–102, 202, 205
Smith, Hyrum 45–46, 52, 135, 223, 240
Smith, John Henry **184**
Smith, Joseph F. 16, 132, 135, 149, 151, 166, 182, **184**, 201, 204, 269
Smith, Joseph Jr. 1–3, 6, 13, 17, 38, 40–42, 45, 96, 101–102, 130, 146, 152, 195, 202, 205, 215, 219–221, 237–239
    Martyrdom 4, 46, 52, 127, 135, 195, 223, 240
Smart, William H. 100, 125, 181, 231
Smoot, Reed 16, 182–183, 186
Snow, Lorenzo 16, 64, **184**, 202, 266

Stratford, Julia (See Budge, Julia Stratford)
Supreme Court 9–10, 87, 132, 154–155, 216

T

Talmage, James E. 103, 192
Tanner, Annie Clark (wife of Joseph Marion Tanner) 3, 83, 108–110, 122, 131, 142, 180, 191, 203–204, 209, 221–225
Taylor, Elizabeth Kaighin (wife of John Taylor) 42, 47, 56–58, 62, 114, 117, 121, 141
Taylor, Harriet Whitaker (wife of John Taylor) 42, 47, 59, 62, 64, 68, 114, 116
Taylor, George John 37–38, 47, 49, 55–56, 61, 64–65, 68, 117, 221
Taylor, Jane Ballantyne (wife of John Taylor) 42, 47–49, 52, 56–58, 114
Taylor, John 4–6, 10–11, 13, 16, **32**–43, 45–49, 52–53, 55–66, 68, 72, 93, 96, 99, 102, 114, 116, 127, 132–135, 141, 146, 149–150, 185–187, 196, 201, 202, 211, 216, 220, 223, 237–240
    1886 revelation 186, 220
Taylor, John W. 17, 136, 183, **184**–187, 205, 214
    1886 revelation 186, 220
    Excommunication 185, 187
Taylor, Joseph 37–39, 41, 47–49, 53, 58, 60, 238
Taylor, Leonora Agnes 40, 42, 68
Taylor, Leonora Cannon (wife of John Taylor) 4, 6, 11, **32**–53, 55–68, 71–72, 76, 99, 113–114, 116–118, 121, 127–128, 132, 135, 141, 146, 210–213, 221, 223
    Leonora Taylor Cannon's First Diary 33, 35, 40–43, **50–51**, 210–211
    Leonora Taylor Cannon's Trail Diary 46–49, 52, 53, 55–63, 210–211, 213, 221
    Letter to John Taylor (Appendix F) 237–239

Letter to Governor Ford (Appendix G) 240–241
Taylor, Margaret Young (wife of John Taylor) 42, 65–66, 68, 114, 135
Taylor, Mary Anne Oakley (wife of John Taylor) 42, 47–49, 52, 56–58, 60, 64, 68, 114, 135
Taylor, Mary Ann (See Redfield, Mary Ann Taylor)
Taylor Row 63–66, 117
Taylor, Sophia Whitaker (wife of John Taylor) 42, 47, 59–60, 63–64, 68, 114, 116, 185
Teasdale, George 183, **184**
Telle, Martha (See Cannon, Martha Telle)
Tenney, Eliza (See Cannon, Eliza Tenney)
Trail diary (See Diaries, Leonora Cannon Taylor's Trail Diary)

U

Uchtdorf, Dieter F. 205–206
Underground, The 11, 41, 68, 97, 110, 123–124, 127, 132–134, 136–138, 140, 142, 185, 189, 196, 201, 212, 224
Utah Historical Quarterly 13, 104–105, 130, 149, 183, 204–205
Utah Territory 5, 7–9, 11–12, 15, 66, 74–76, 84, 87, 130, 132, 134, 150, 172, 198, 213–214, 242, 248, 265

W

Washington, DC 38, 65, 76–78, 81, 83, 87–89, 117, 149, 159, 167, 185, 197, 213, 238–239, 242–243, 250
Wellsville, Utah 5, 99–100, 108, 116–117, 124, 128, 131, 136, 138–140, 154, 210, 235–236
Western Standard 73
Weston, Mary Ann (See Maughan, Mary Ann Weston)
Whitaker, Harriet (See Taylor, Harriet Whitaker)
Whitaker, Sophia (See Taylor, Sophia Whitaker)
Willey, Emily Cannon (Aunt Emily) 88–89, 122, 163, 167, 172–174, 177, 243
Willey, Israel (Uncle Ike) 172–173, 174, 177
Winter Quarters 44, 46–48, 49, 52–54, 55, 58–62, 117, 210–211, 234
Whitney, Orson F. 12, 180, 183
Woman's Exponent 102, 105
Women's suffrage 8–9, 12, 103–105, 134
Woodbury, Ann Cannon (wife of Orin Nelson Woodbury) 63, 140, 163, **164**
Woodruff, Abraham O. 183, **184**
Woodruff, Phoebe (wife of Wilford Woodruff) 37–38, 64, 66, 116–117, 237
Woodruff, Wilford 3, 12–15, 37, 96, 149–153, 183, **184**, 192, 197, 200, 201, 202, 216
  Published documents about the First Manifesto (Appendix M) 265, 267–268
Woodward, Rachel Barnes (See Maughan, Rachel Barnes Woodward)
Woolley, Fannie (See Parkinson, Fannie Wooley)

Y

Young, Brigham 3–4, 6–8, 13, 15, 61, 64–65, 67, 73–76, 83, 94, 96–99, 103–105, 119, 124, 128–130, 171, 195–196, 201, 226–227, 229, 249
Young, Brigham Jr. **184**
Young, Margaret (See Taylor, Margaret Young)

www.ingramcontent.com/pod-product-compliance
Lightning Source LLC
Chambersburg PA
CBHW050457110426
42742CB00018B/3286